O Maidens in your Savage Season

1

Story by **Mari Okada**
Art by **Nao Emoto**

【 *Contents* 】

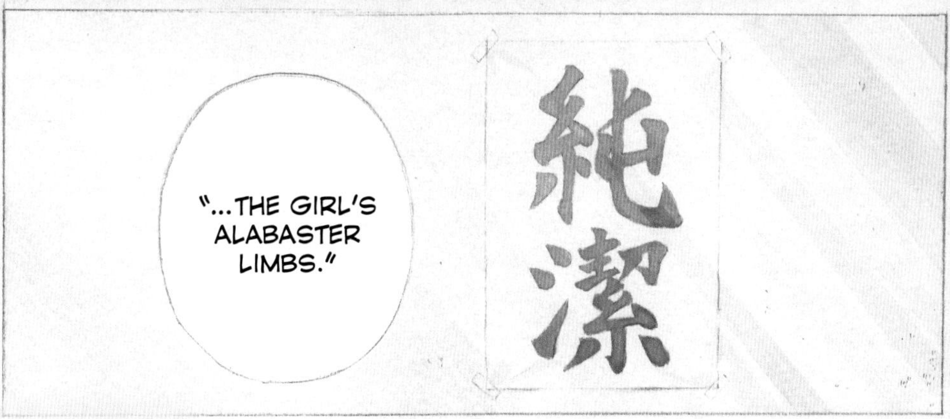
純潔
"...THE GIRL'S ALABASTER LIMBS."
SIGN: Chastity

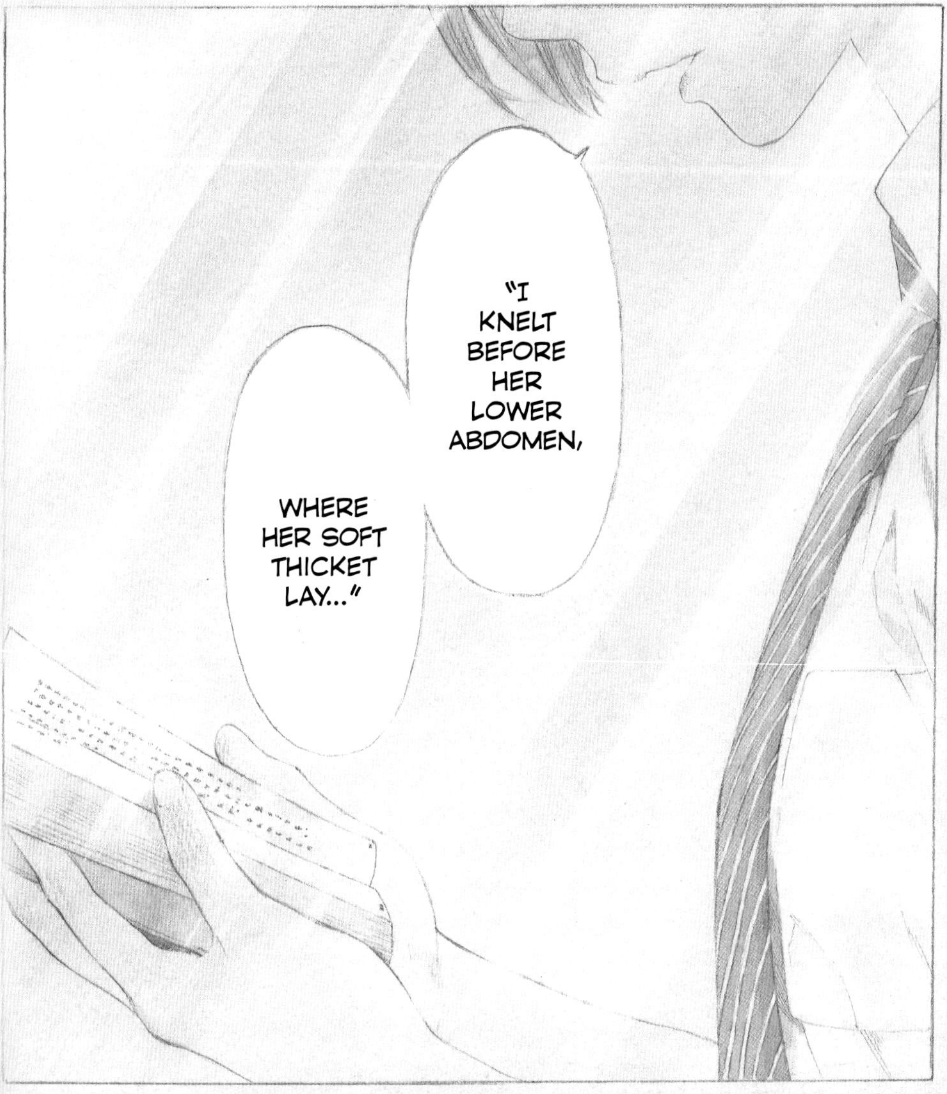
"I KNELT BEFORE HER LOWER ABDOMEN,
WHERE HER SOFT THICKET LAY..."

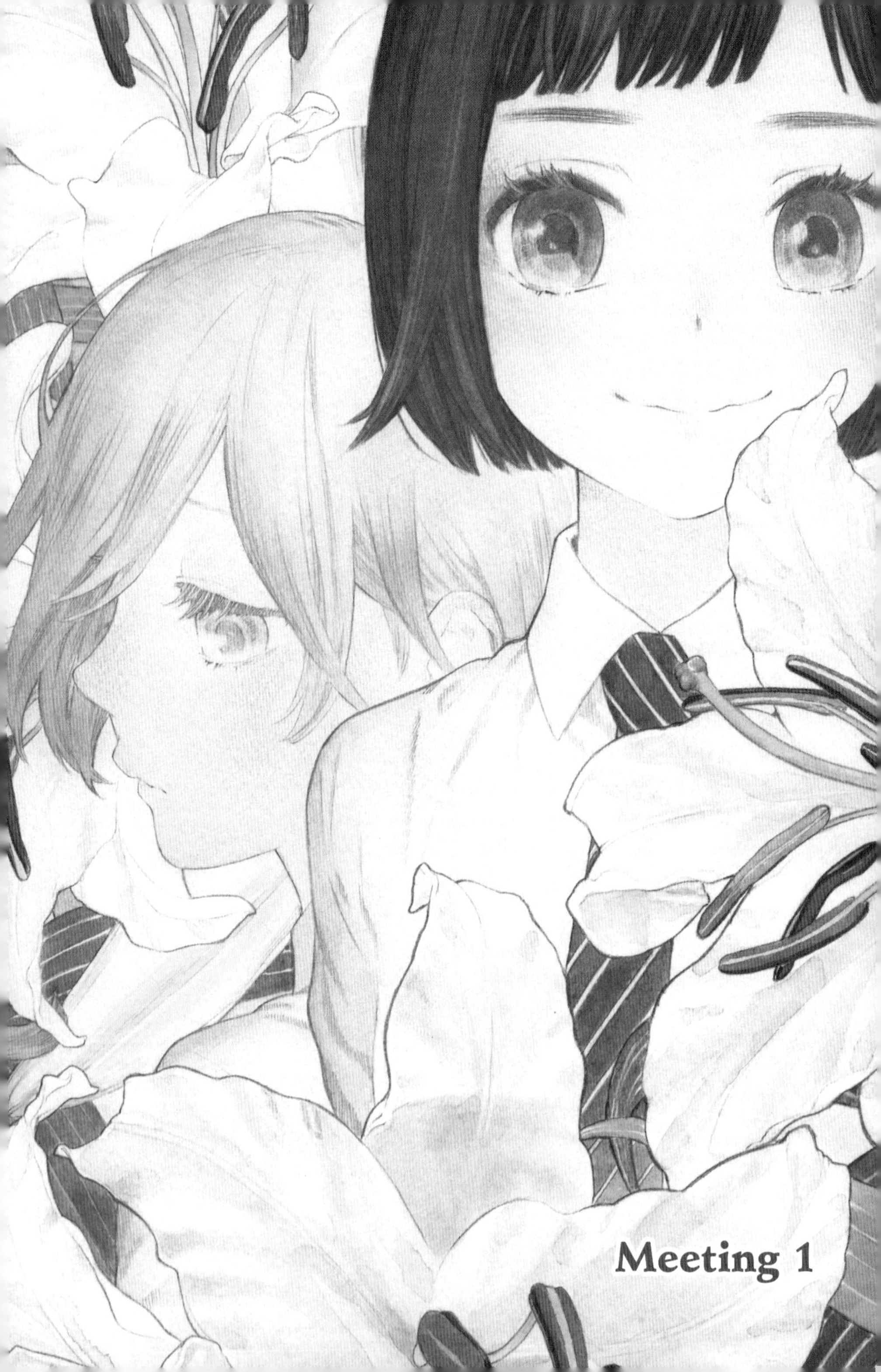

Meeting 1

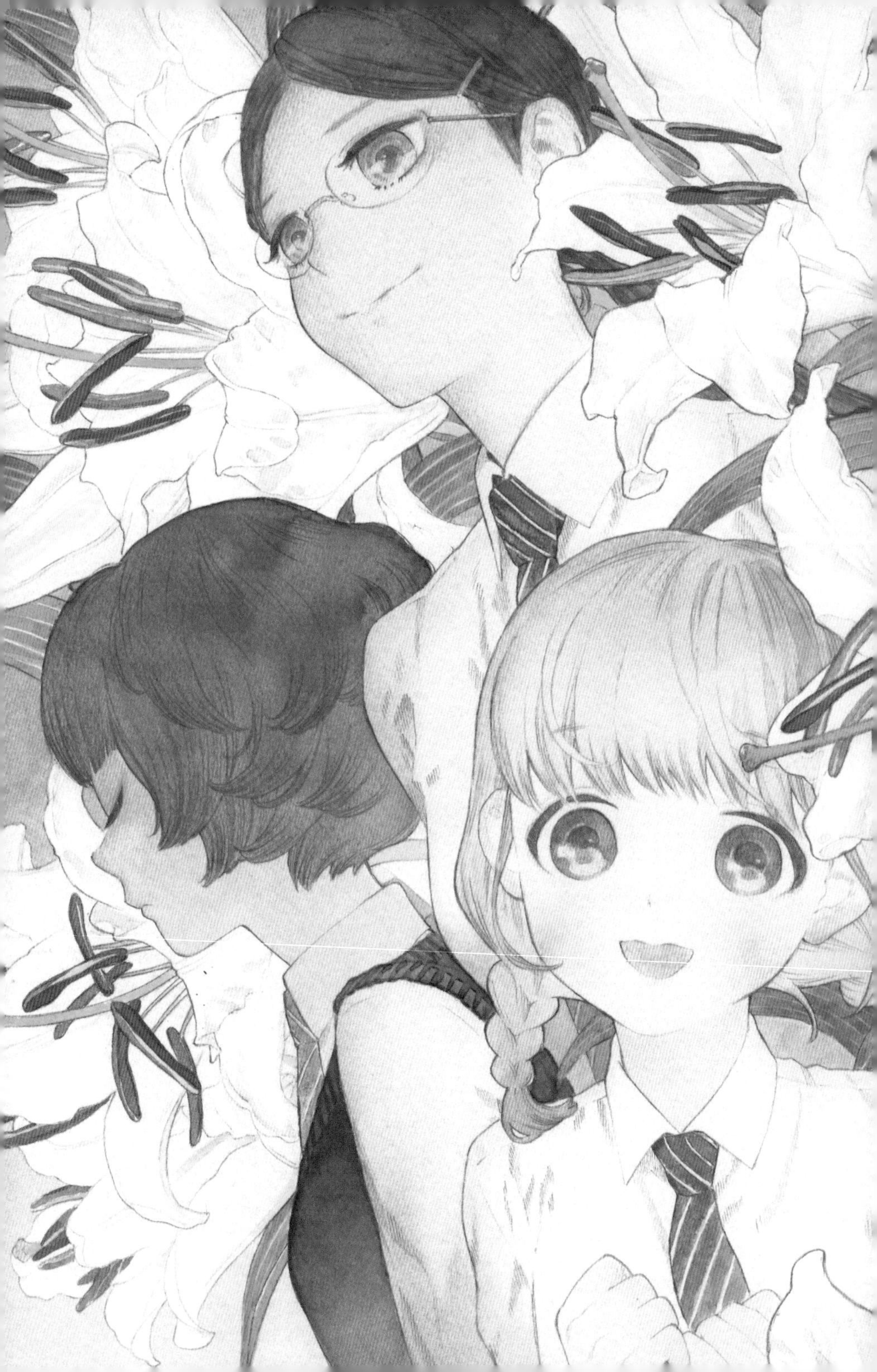

O Maidens in Your Savage Season

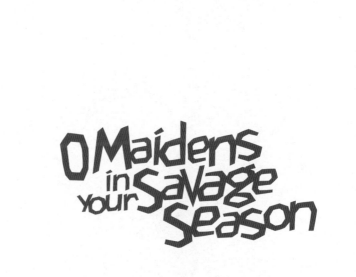

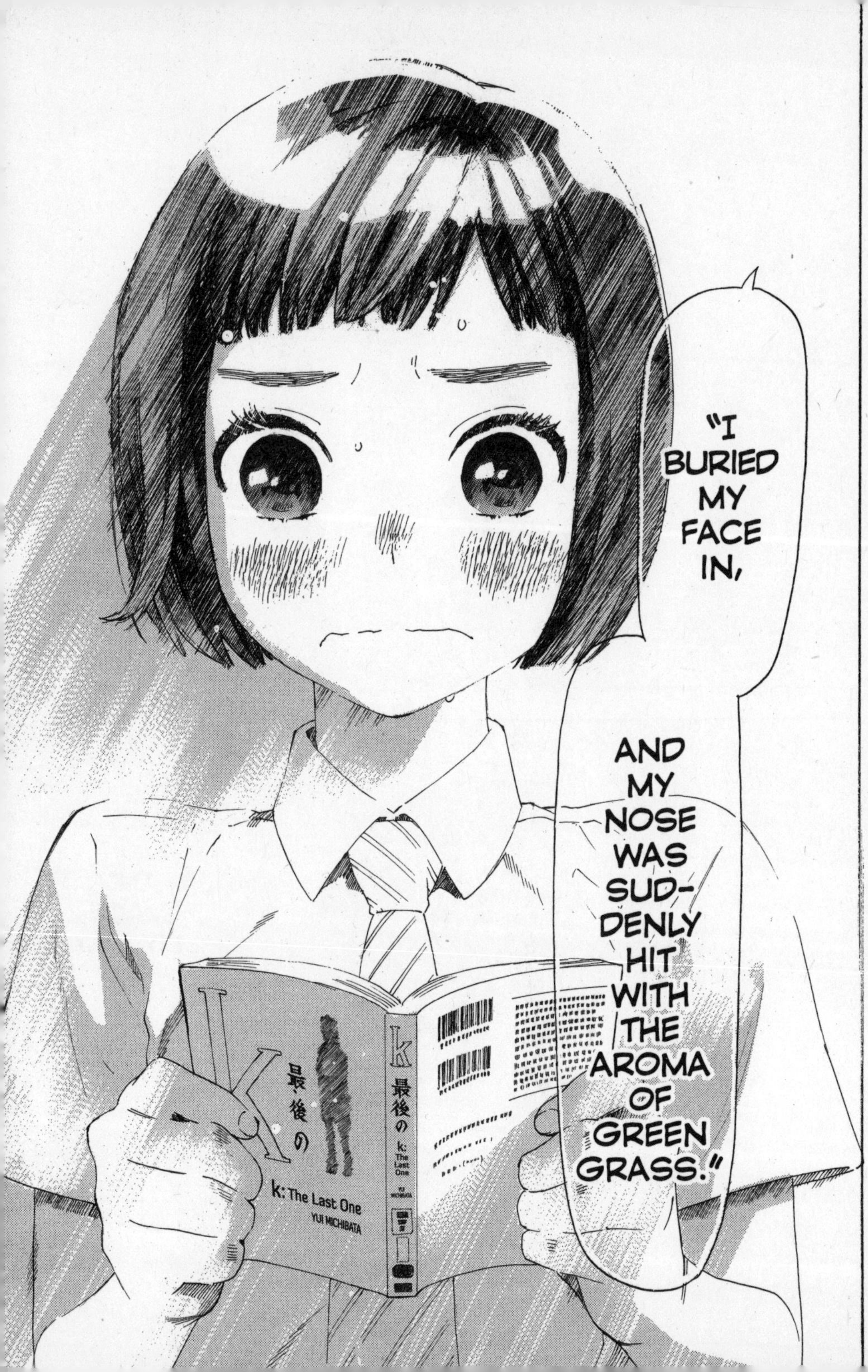
"I BURIED MY FACE IN,
AND MY NOSE WAS SUD-DENLY HIT WITH THE AROMA OF GREEN GRASS."
k
最後の
k: The Last One
YUI MICHIBATA
最後の k: The Last One

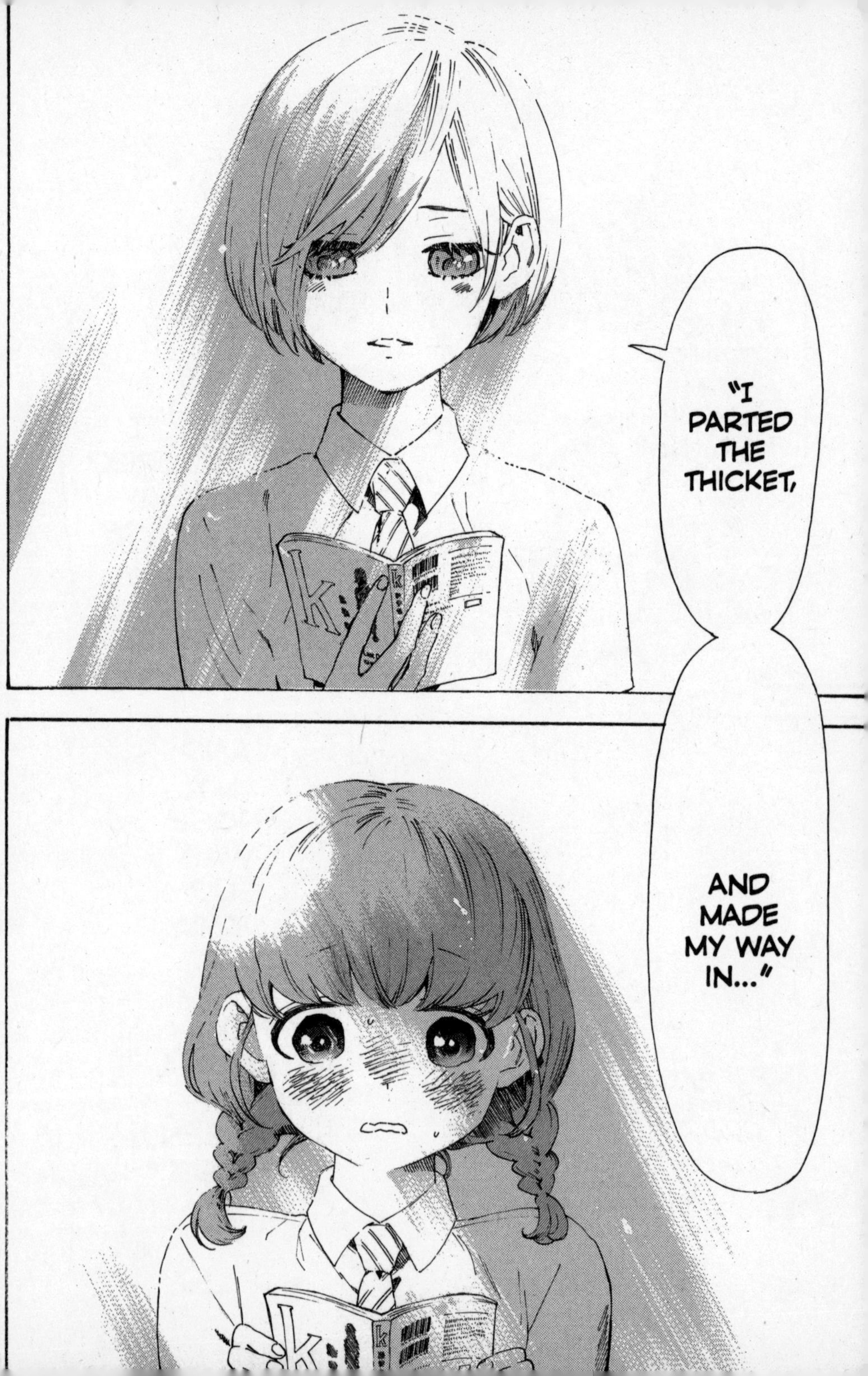
"I PARTED THE THICKET,
AND MADE MY WAY IN..."

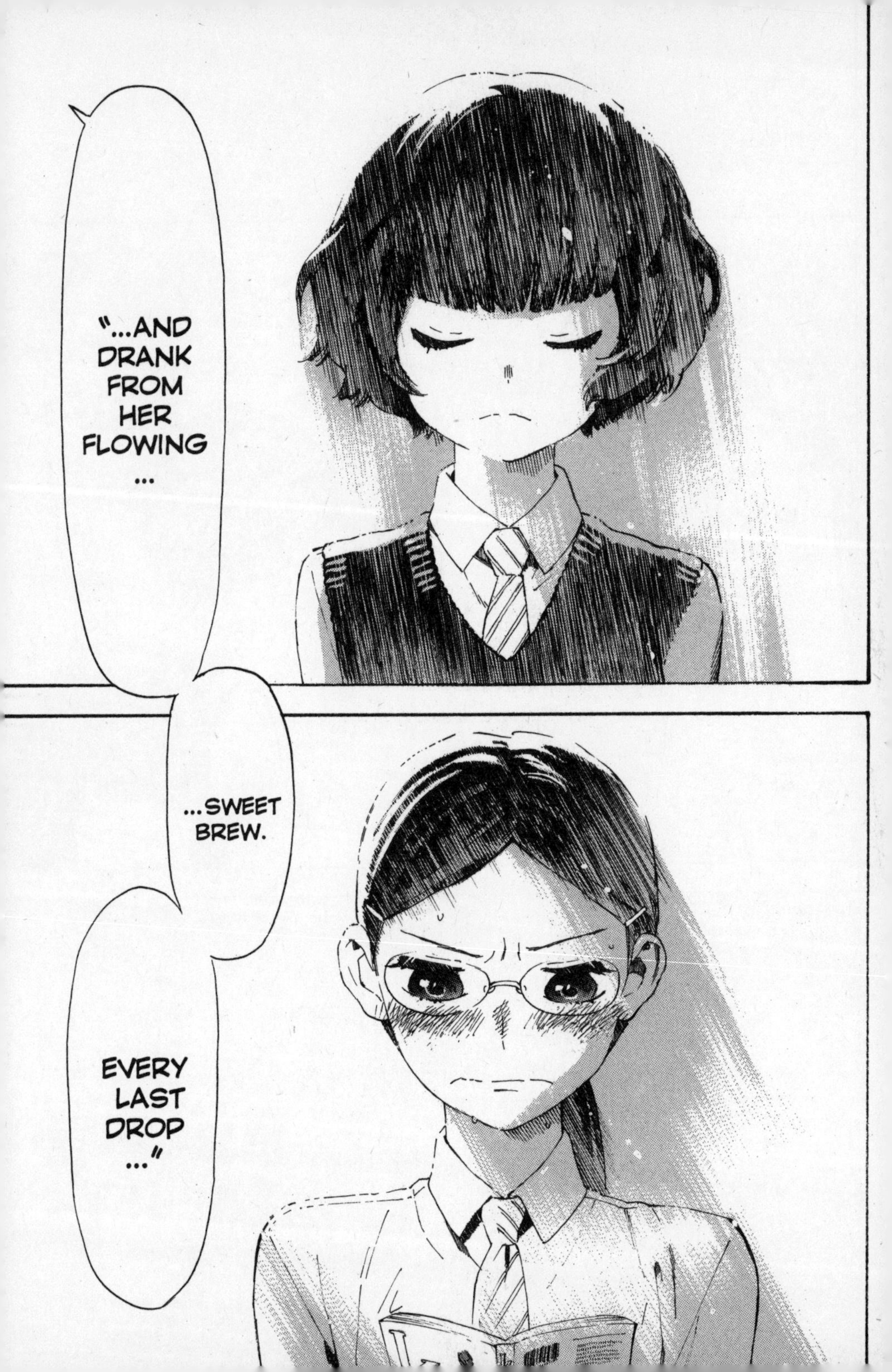
"...AND DRANK FROM HER FLOWING ...
...SWEET BREW.
EVERY LAST DROP ..."

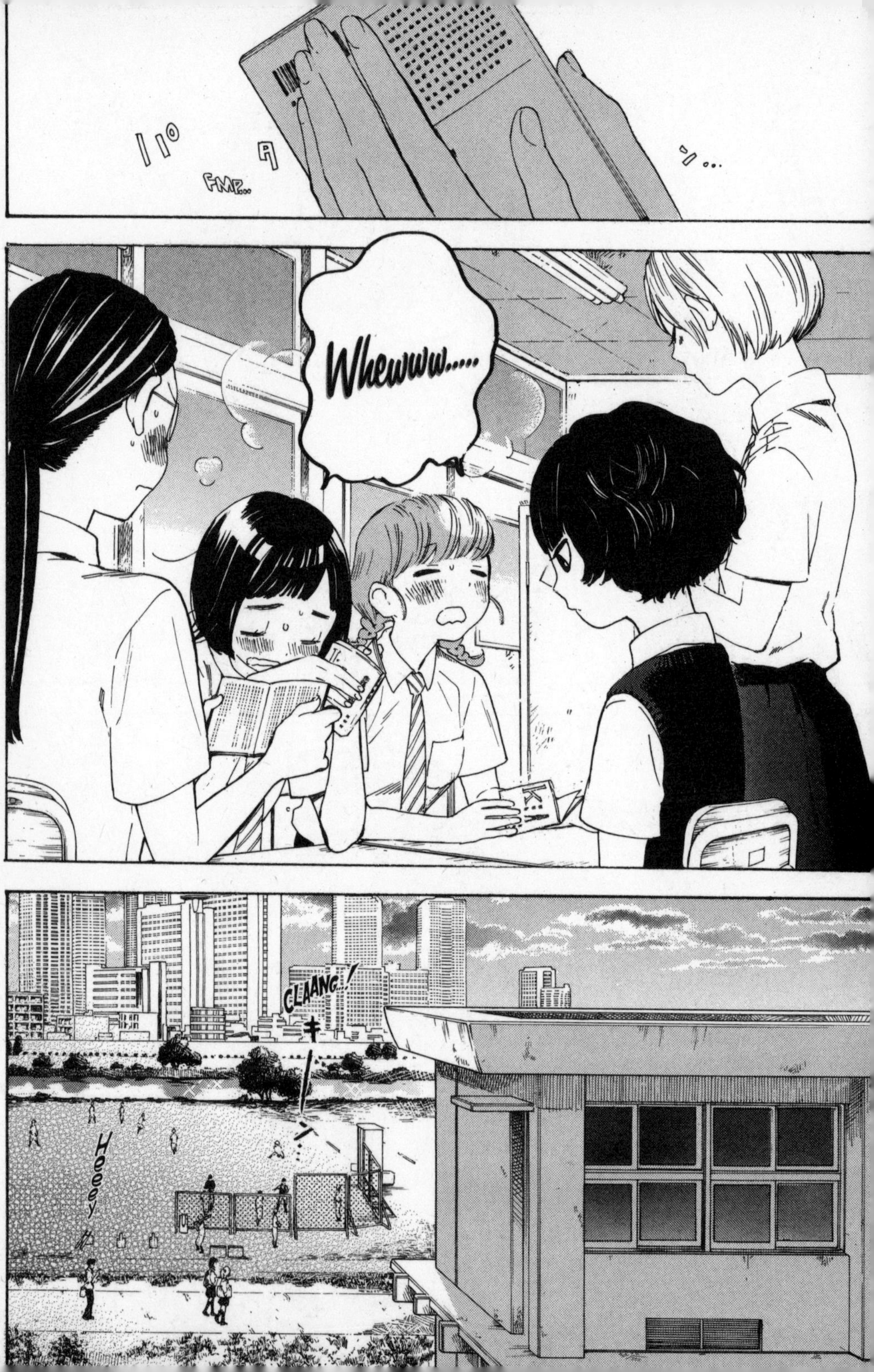
FMP...
Wheww.....
CLAANG..!
Heeey

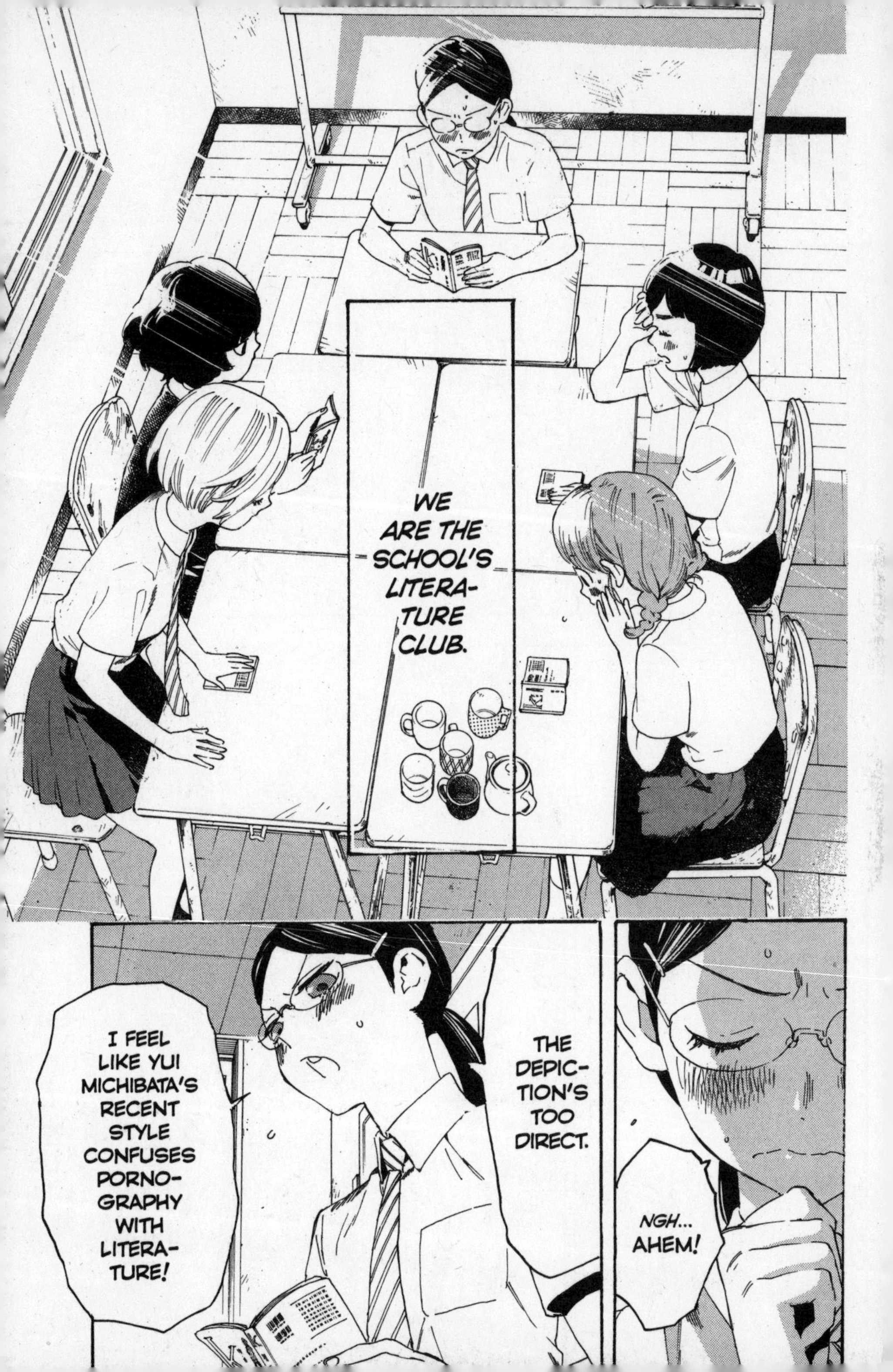
WE ARE THE SCHOOL'S LITERATURE CLUB.
NGH... AHEM!
THE DEPICTION'S TOO DIRECT.
I FEEL LIKE YUI MICHIBATA'S RECENT STYLE CONFUSES PORNOGRAPHY WITH LITERATURE!

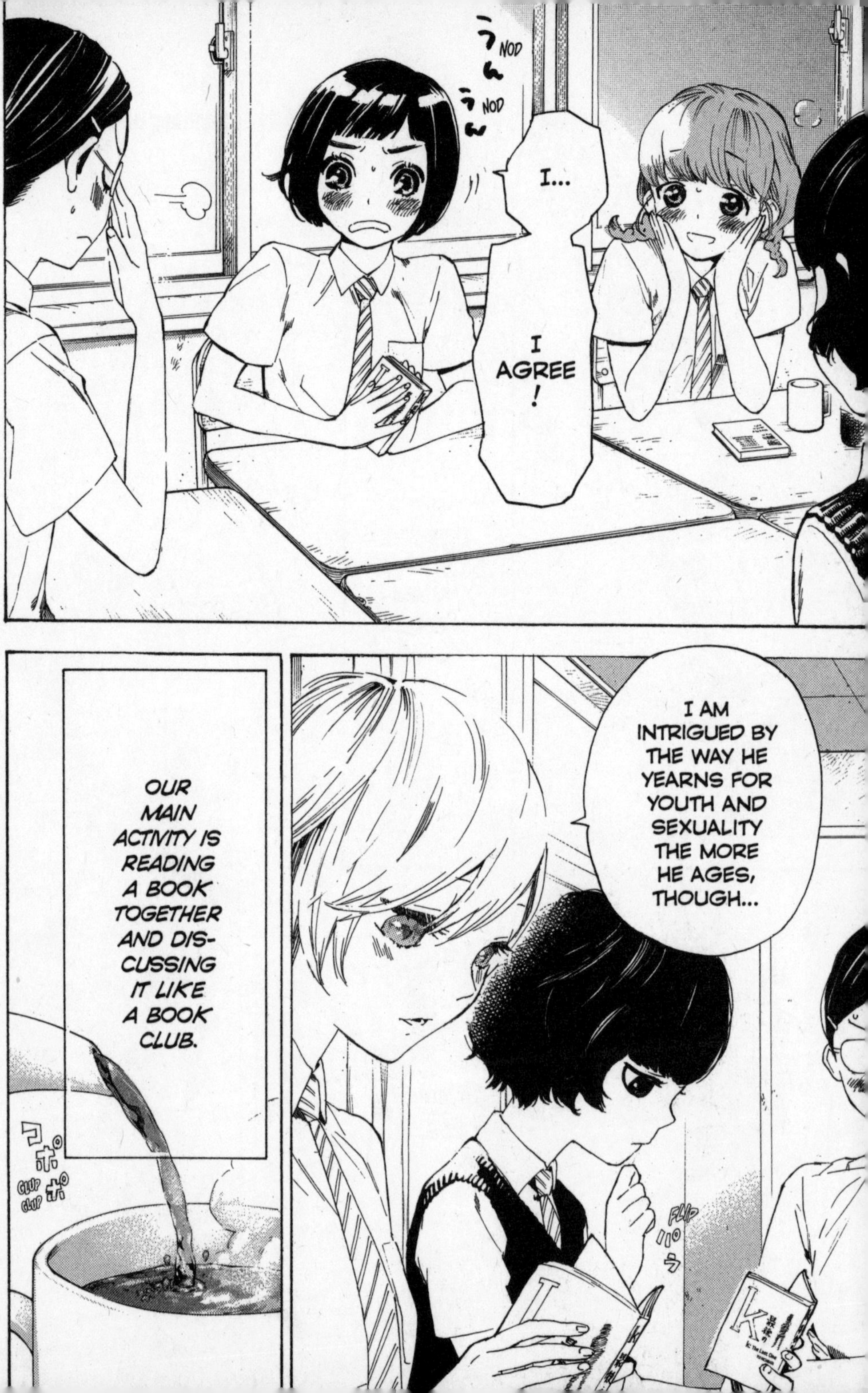 うん NOD
うん NOD
I...
I AGREE!
I AM INTRIGUED BY THE WAY HE YEARNS FOR YOUTH AND SEXUALITY THE MORE HE AGES, THOUGH...
パラ FLIP
OUR MAIN ACTIVITY IS READING A BOOK TOGETHER AND DIS-CUSSING IT LIKE A BOOK CLUB.
コポポ GLUP GLUP

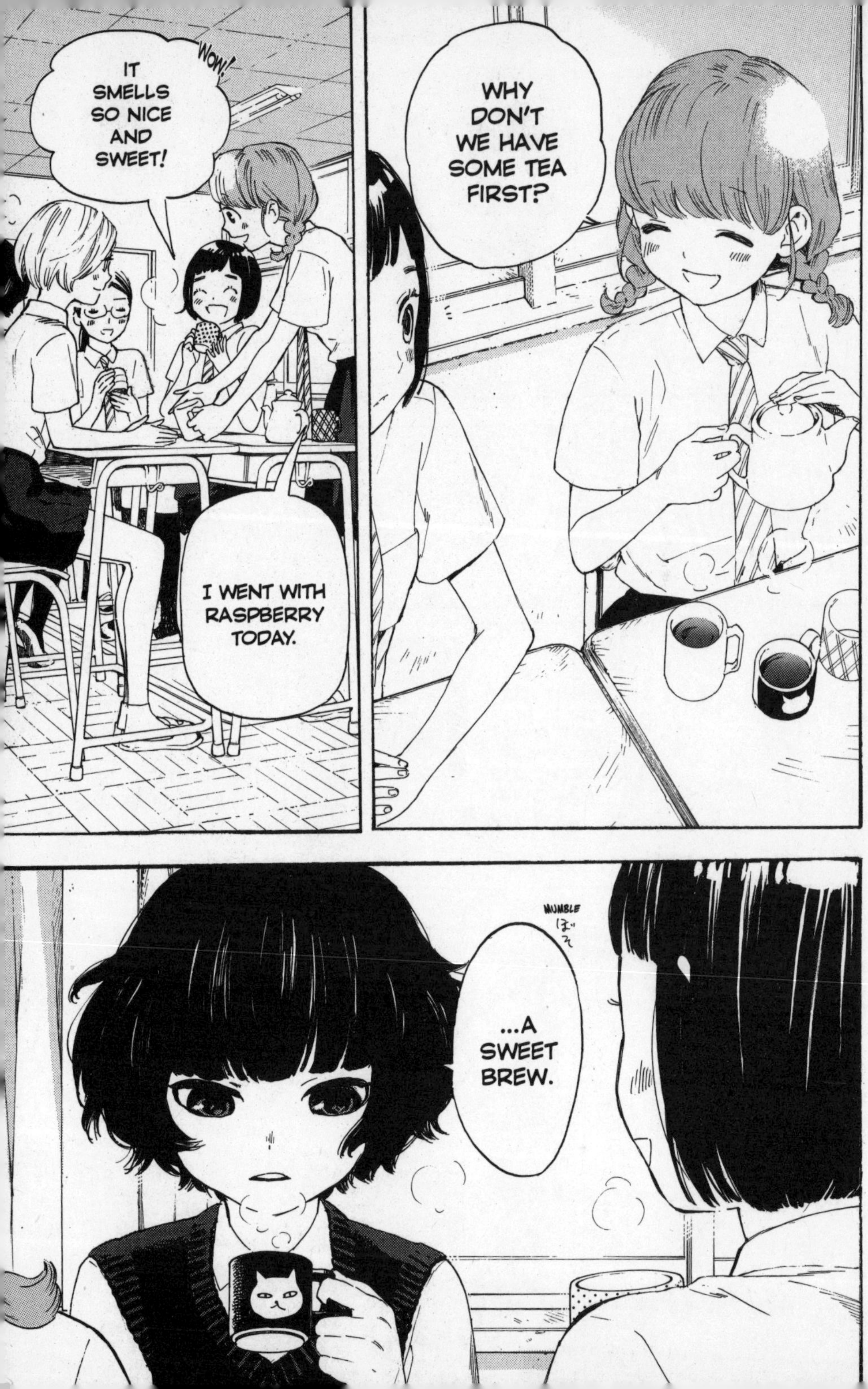
WHY DON'T WE HAVE SOME TEA FIRST?
WOW!
IT SMELLS SO NICE AND SWEET!
I WENT WITH RASPBERRY TODAY.
MUMBLE
ぼそ
...A SWEET BREW.

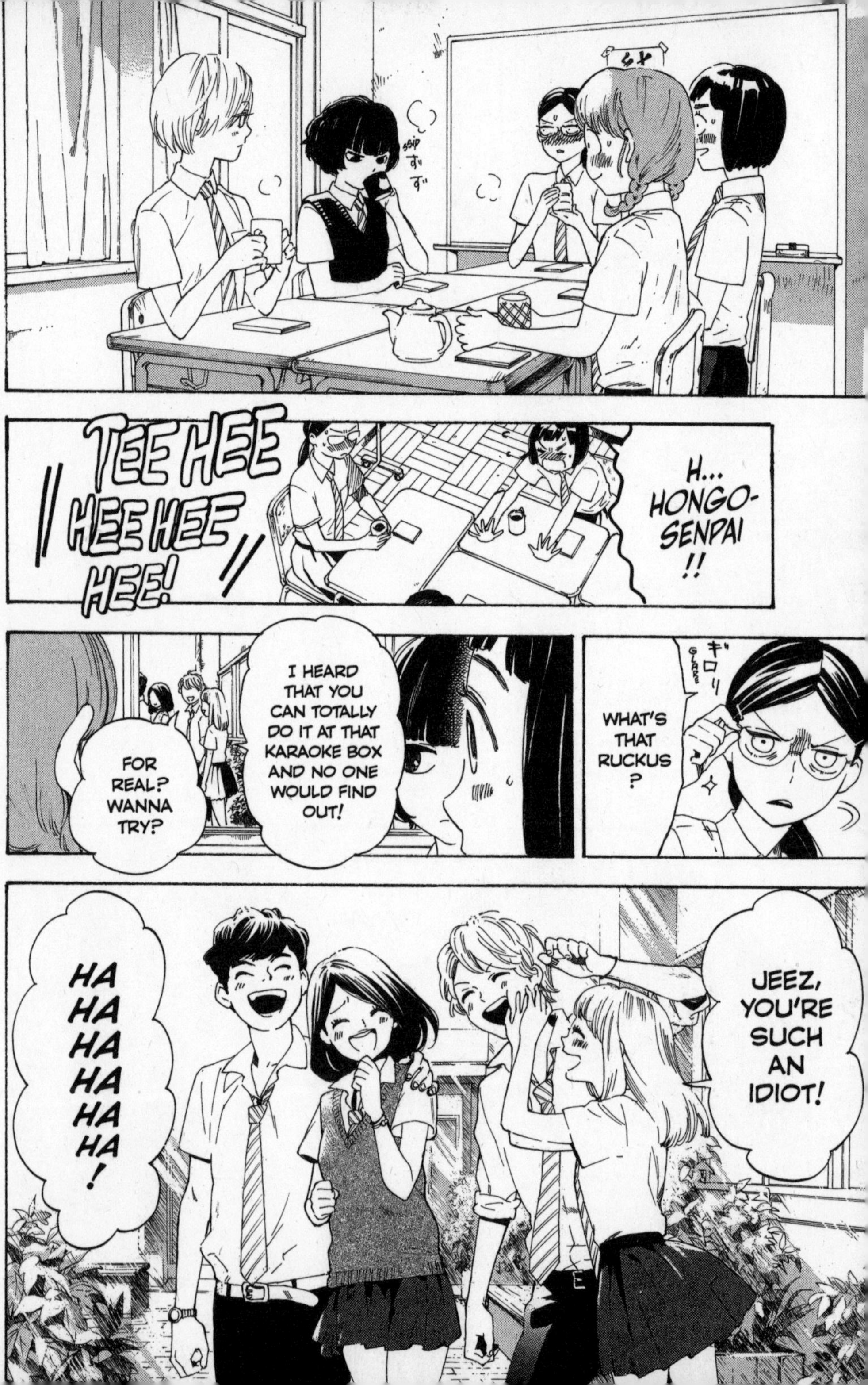
SSIP
すず
H... HONGO-SENPAI!!
TEE HEE HEE HEE HEE!
GLARE
ギロリ
WHAT'S THAT RUCKUS?
I HEARD THAT YOU CAN TOTALLY DO IT AT THAT KARAOKE BOX AND NO ONE WOULD FIND OUT!
FOR REAL? WANNA TRY?
JEEZ, YOU'RE SUCH AN IDIOT!
HA HA HA HA HA HA HA!

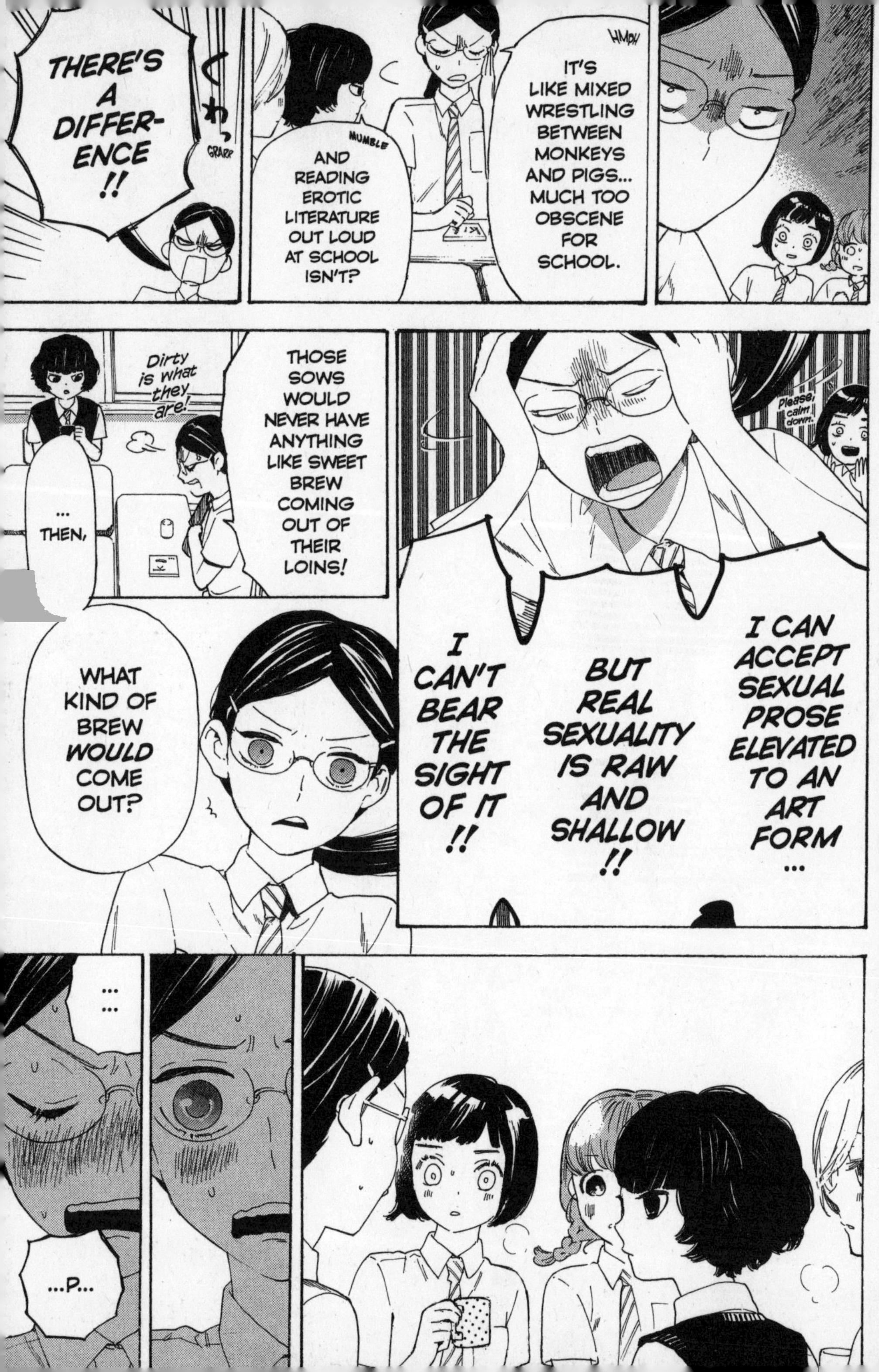
HMPH
IT'S LIKE MIXED WRESTLING BETWEEN MONKEYS AND PIGS... MUCH TOO OBSCENE FOR SCHOOL.
MUMBLE
AND READING EROTIC LITERATURE OUT LOUD AT SCHOOL ISN'T?
くわっ
GRARR
THERE'S A DIFFERENCE!!
Please, calm down.
I CAN ACCEPT SEXUAL PROSE ELEVATED TO AN ART FORM...
BUT REAL SEXUALITY IS RAW AND SHALLOW!!
I CAN'T BEAR THE SIGHT OF IT!!
THOSE SOWS WOULD NEVER HAVE ANYTHING LIKE SWEET BREW COMING OUT OF THEIR LOINS!
Dirty is what they are!
...THEN,
WHAT KIND OF BREW WOULD COME OUT?
......
...P...

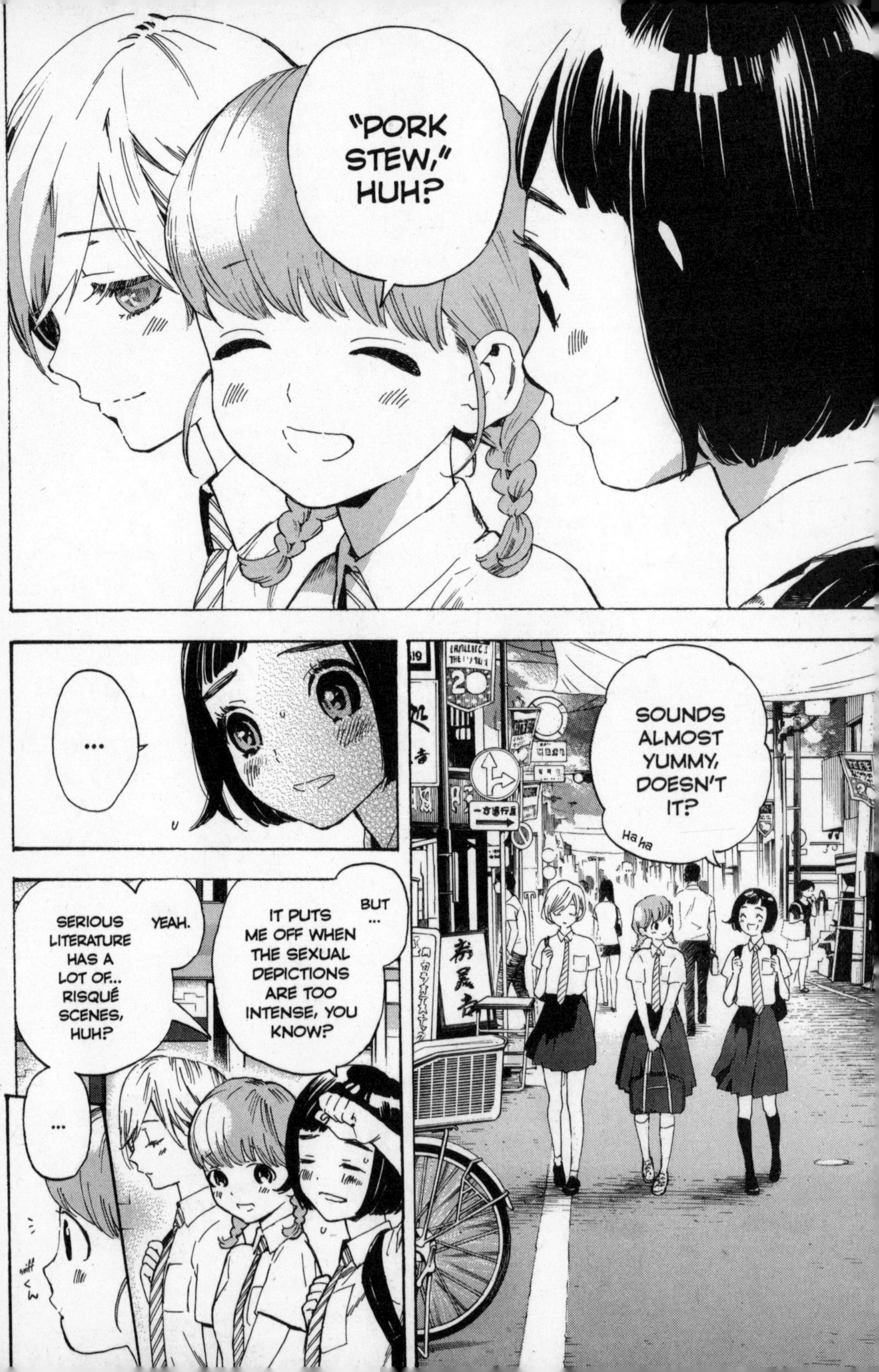
"PORK STEW," HUH?
SOUNDS ALMOST YUMMY, DOESN'T IT?
Ha ha
...
BUT ...
IT PUTS ME OFF WHEN THE SEXUAL DEPICTIONS ARE TOO INTENSE, YOU KNOW?
YEAH.
SERIOUS LITERATURE HAS A LOT OF... RISQUÉ SCENES, HUH?
...
sniff

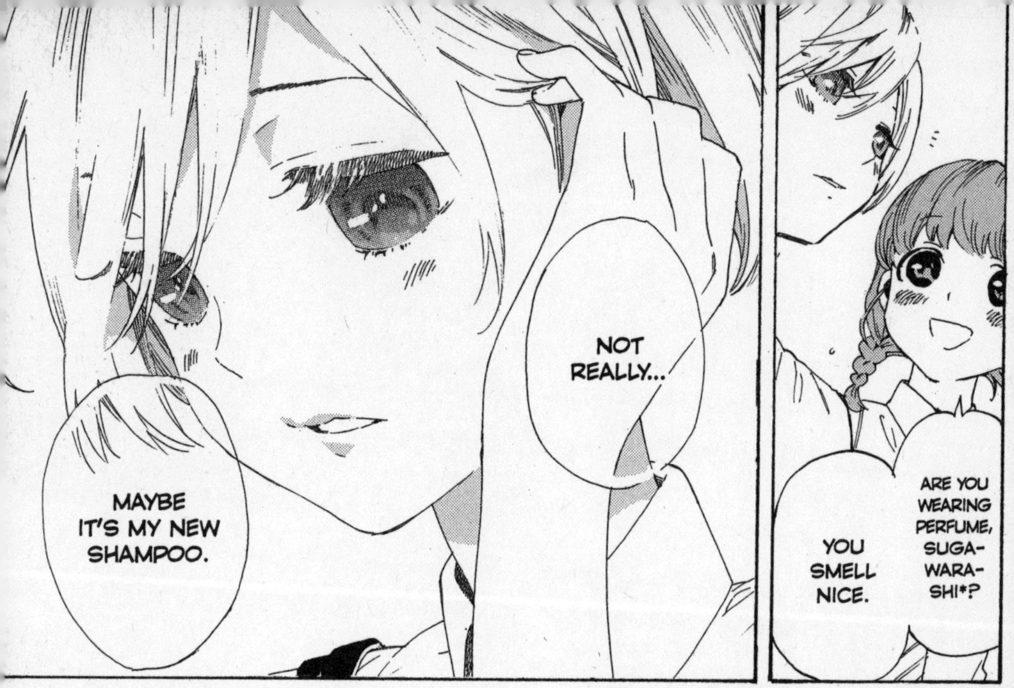
ARE YOU WEARING PERFUME, SUGAWARA-SHI*?
YOU SMELL NICE.
NOT REALLY...
MAYBE IT'S MY NEW SHAMPOO.

*"-Shi" is a formal honorific, often only used in writing.

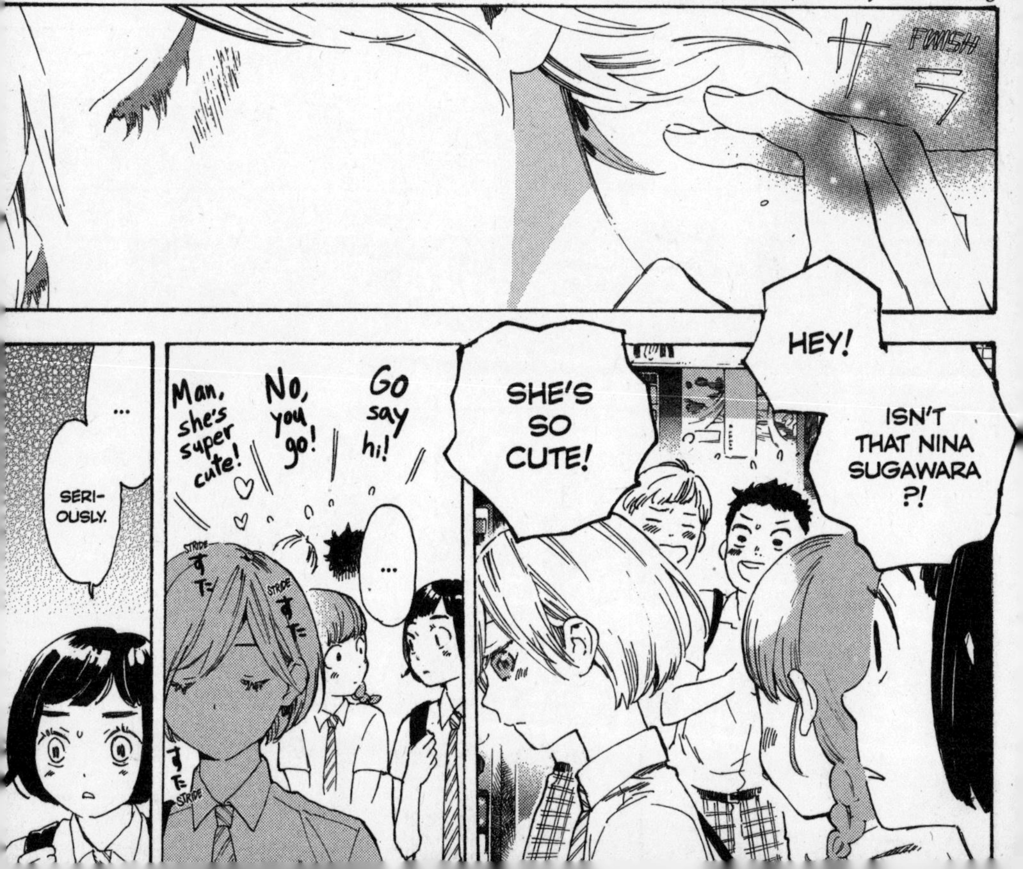
FWISH
HEY!
ISN'T THAT NINA SUGAWARA?!
SHE'S SO CUTE!
Go say hi!
No, you go!
Man, she's super cute!
...
STRIDE
STRIDE
STRIDE
...
SERIOUSLY.

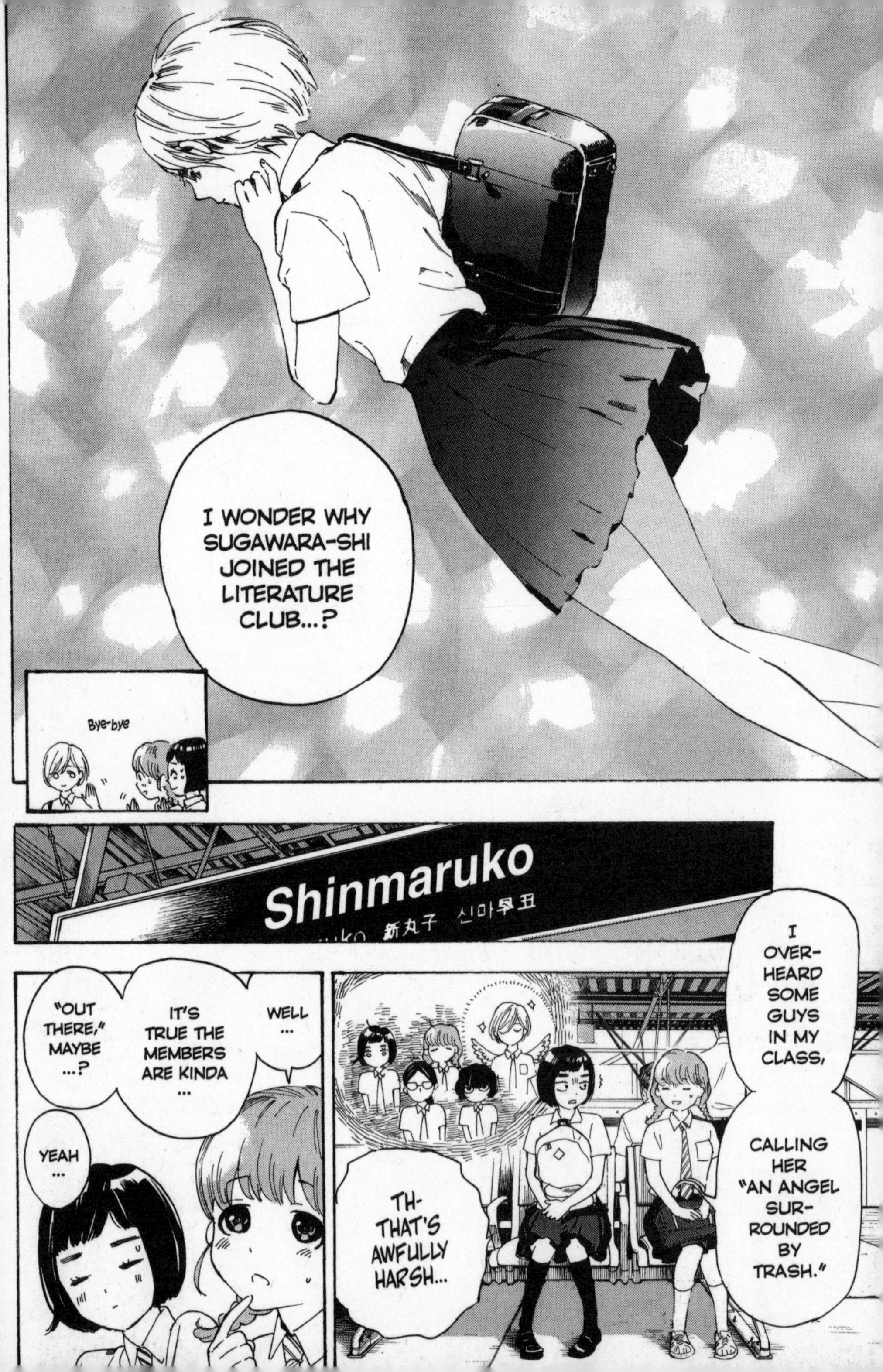
I WONDER WHY SUGAWARA-SHI JOINED THE LITERATURE CLUB...?
Bye-bye
Shinmaruko
新丸子 신마루코
I OVER-HEARD SOME GUYS IN MY CLASS,
CALLING HER "AN ANGEL SUR-ROUNDED BY TRASH."
TH-THAT'S AWFULLY HARSH...
WELL ...
IT'S TRUE THE MEMBERS ARE KINDA ...
"OUT THERE," MAYBE ...?
YEAH ...

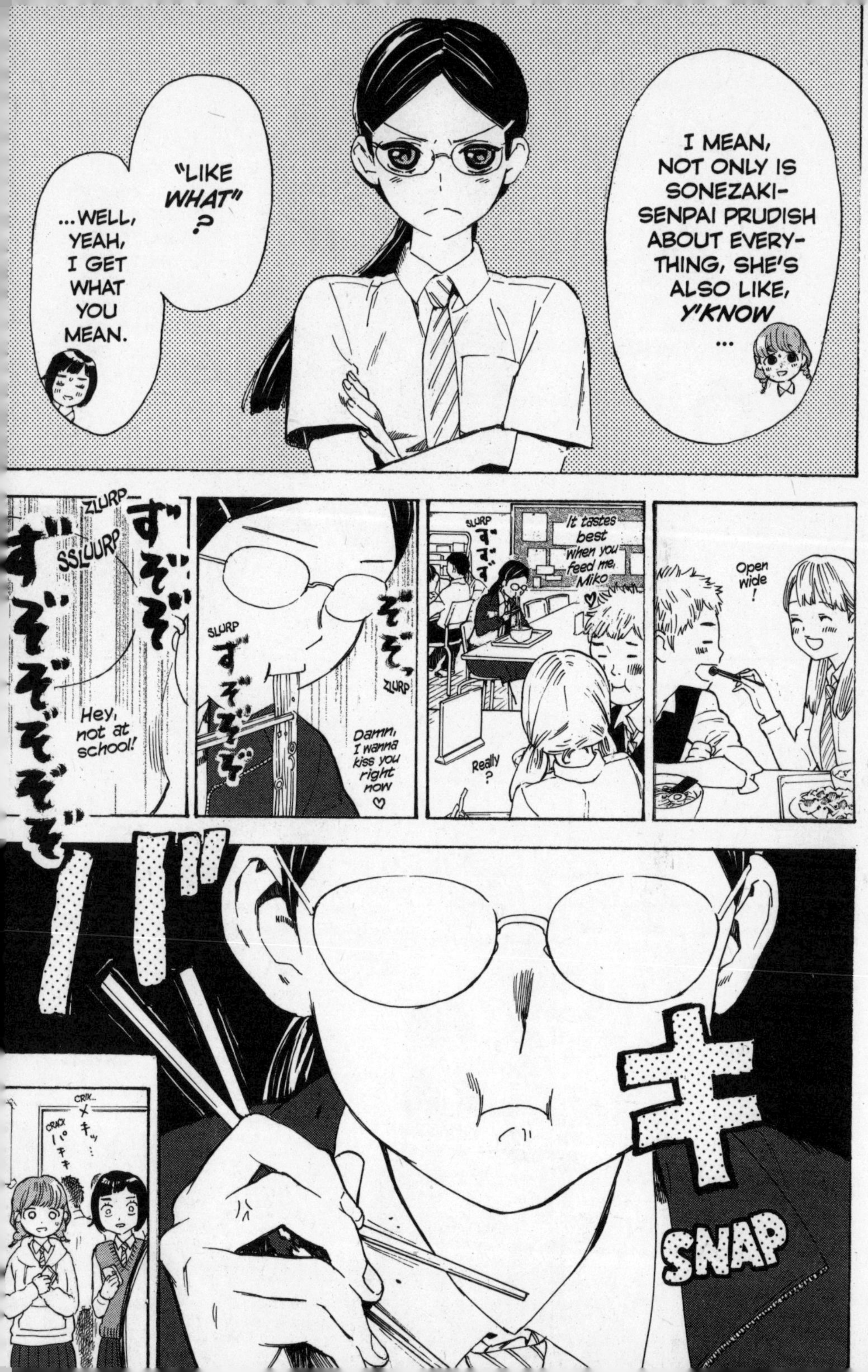
I MEAN, NOT ONLY IS SONEZAKI-SENPAI PRUDISH ABOUT EVERY-THING, SHE'S ALSO LIKE, *Y'KNOW* ...
"LIKE *WHAT*"?
...WELL, YEAH, I GET WHAT YOU MEAN.
Open wide!
It tastes best when you feed me, Miko ♡
Really?
SLURP
ずずず
SLURP
ずぞぞぞ
ぞぞ
ZLURP
Damn, I wanna kiss you right now ♡
ZLURP
ずぞぞ
SSLUURP
ずぞぞぞぞぞぞ
Hey, not at school!
ギ
SNAP
CRIK...
メキッ...
CRACK
パキキ

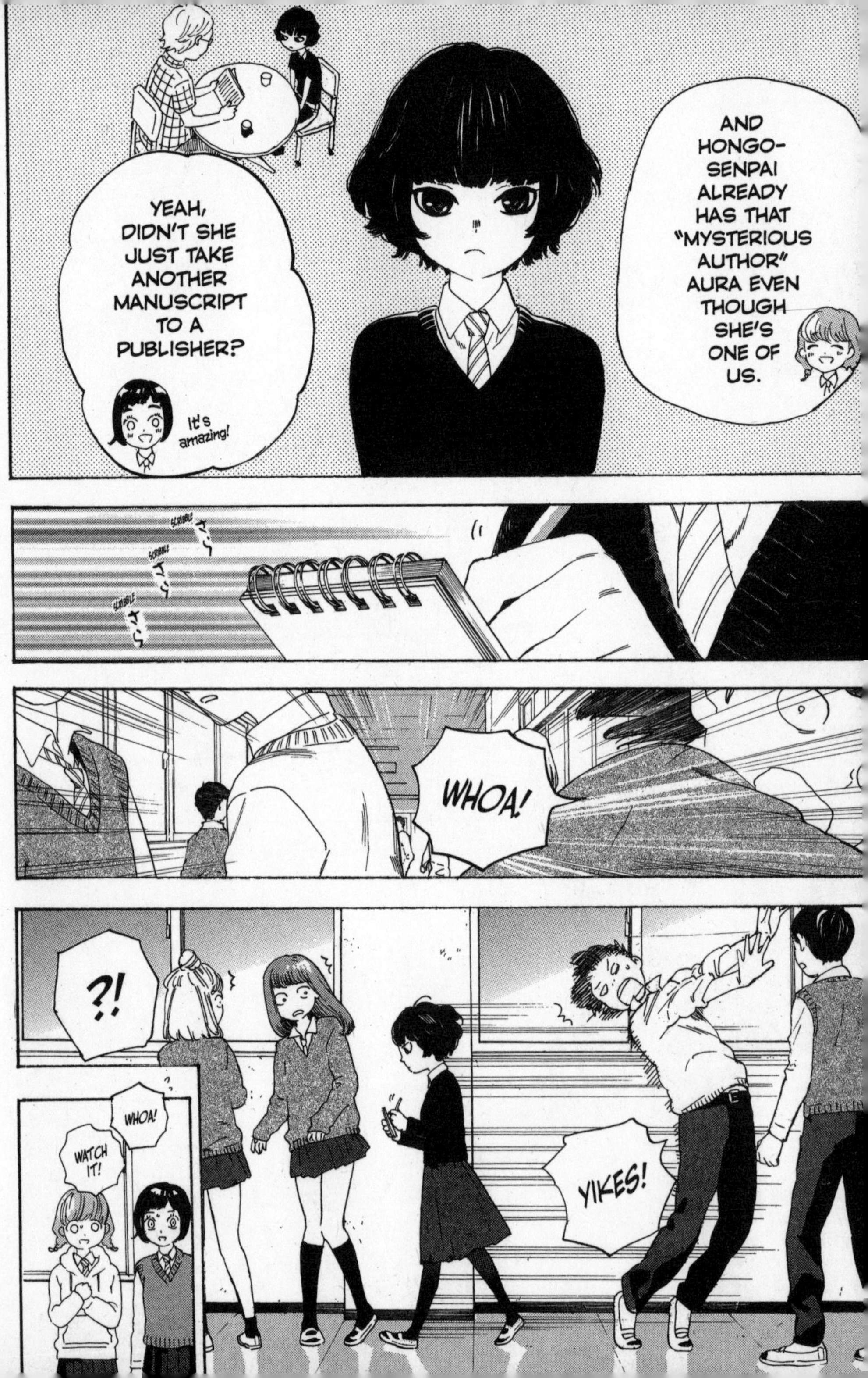
AND HONGO-SENPAI ALREADY HAS THAT "MYSTERIOUS AUTHOR" AURA EVEN THOUGH SHE'S ONE OF US.
YEAH, DIDN'T SHE JUST TAKE ANOTHER MANUSCRIPT TO A PUBLISHER?
It's amazing!
SCRIBBLE
SCRIBBLE
SCRIBBLE
WHOA!
?!
YIKES!
WHOA!
WATCH IT!

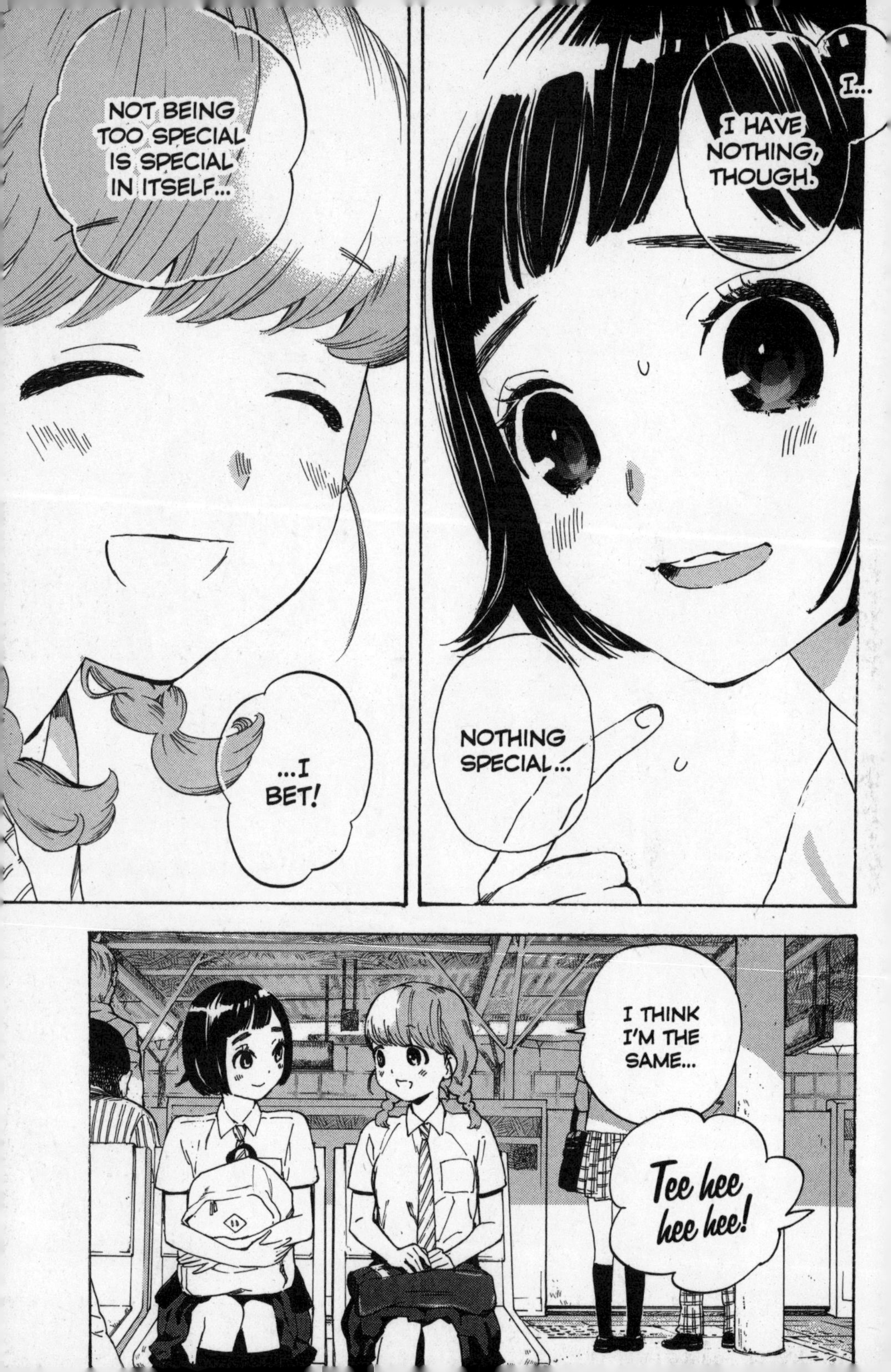
I...
I HAVE NOTHING, THOUGH.
NOTHING SPECIAL...
NOT BEING TOO SPECIAL IS SPECIAL IN ITSELF...
...I BET!
I THINK I'M THE SAME...
Tee hee hee hee!

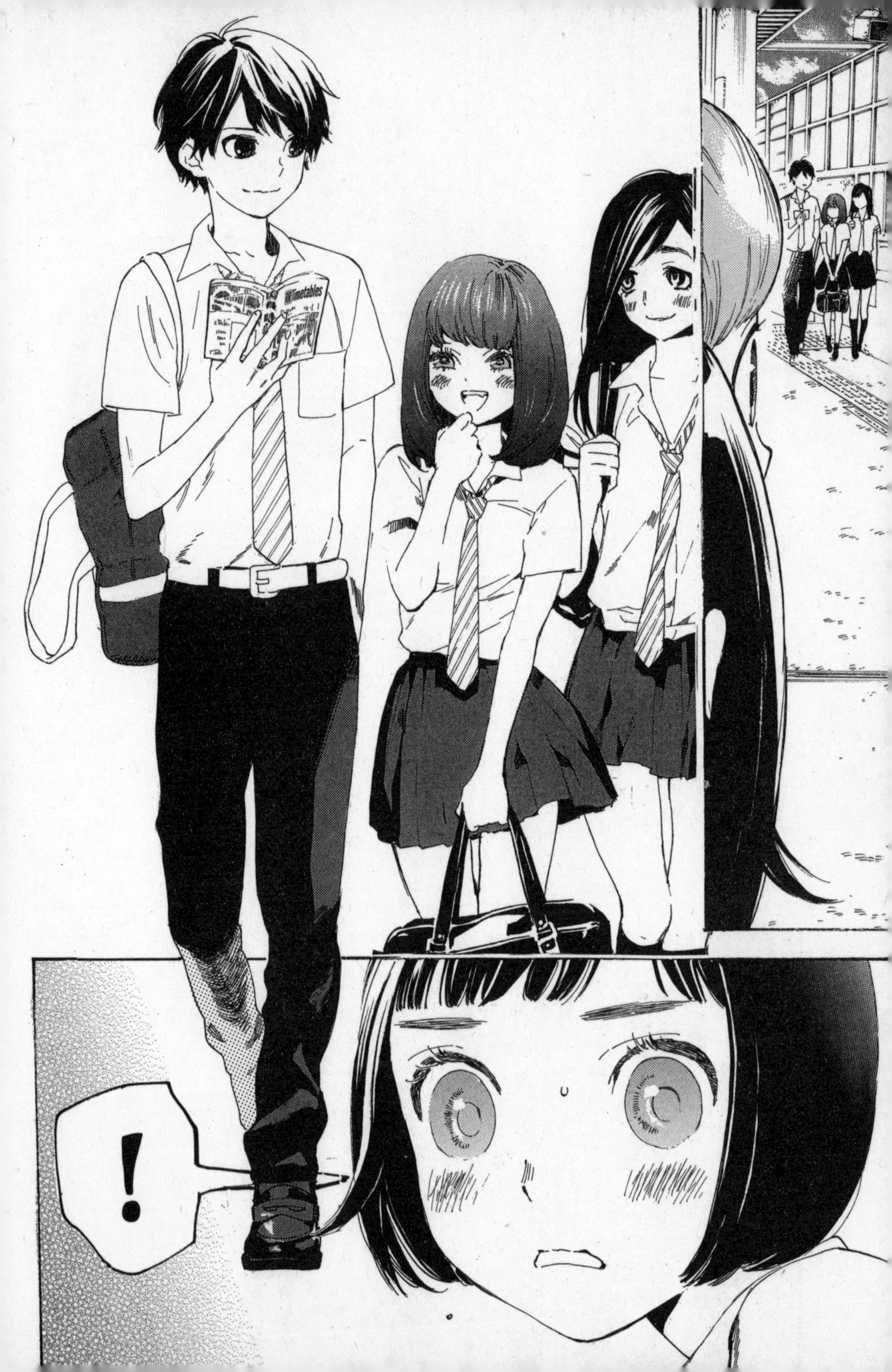
Timetables
!

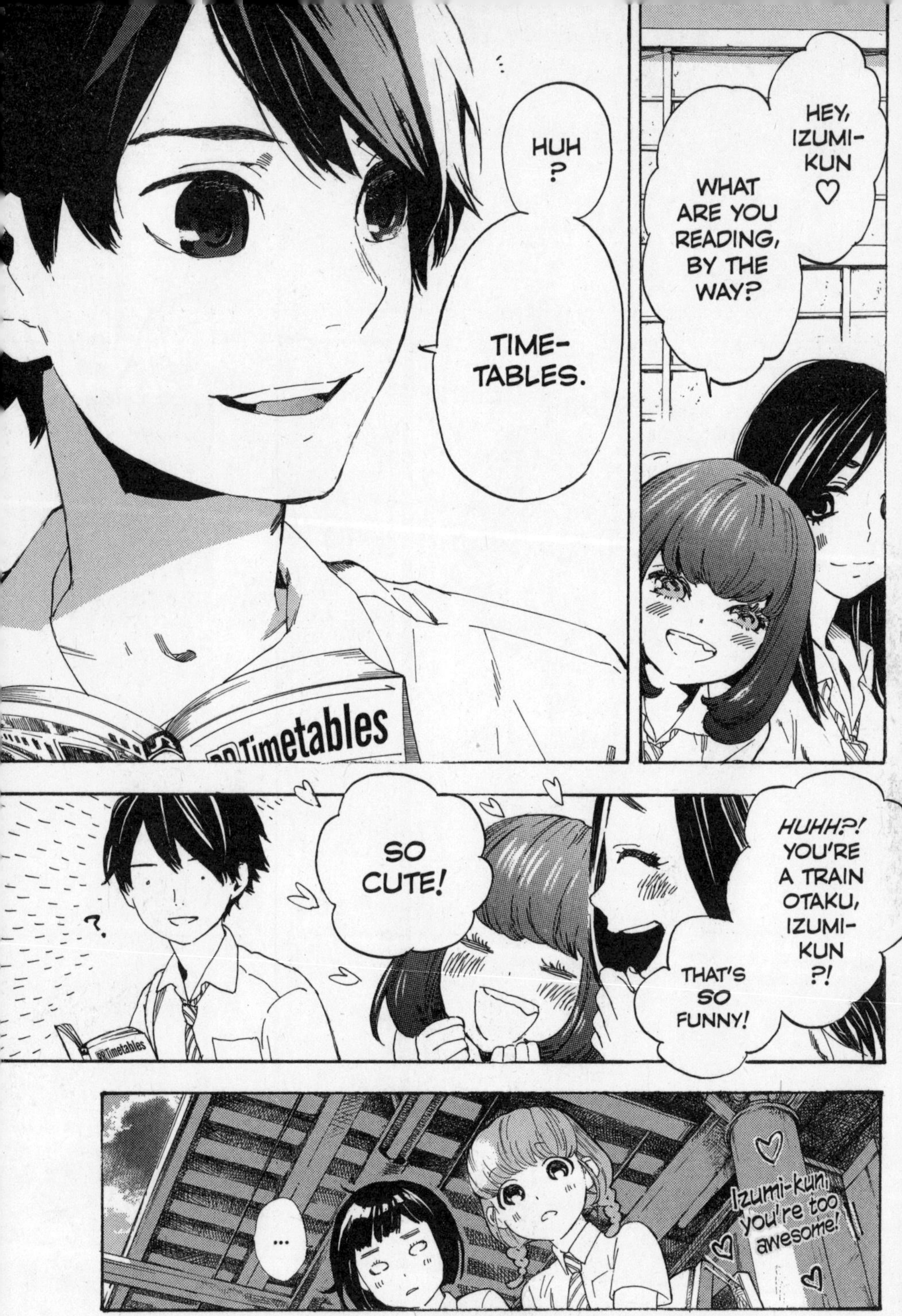
HEY, IZUMI-KUN ♡
WHAT ARE YOU READING, BY THE WAY?
HUH?
TIME-TABLES.
Timetables
HUHH?! YOU'RE A TRAIN OTAKU, IZUMI-KUN?!
THAT'S SO FUNNY!
SO CUTE!
?
Timetables
Izumi-kun, you're too awesome!
...

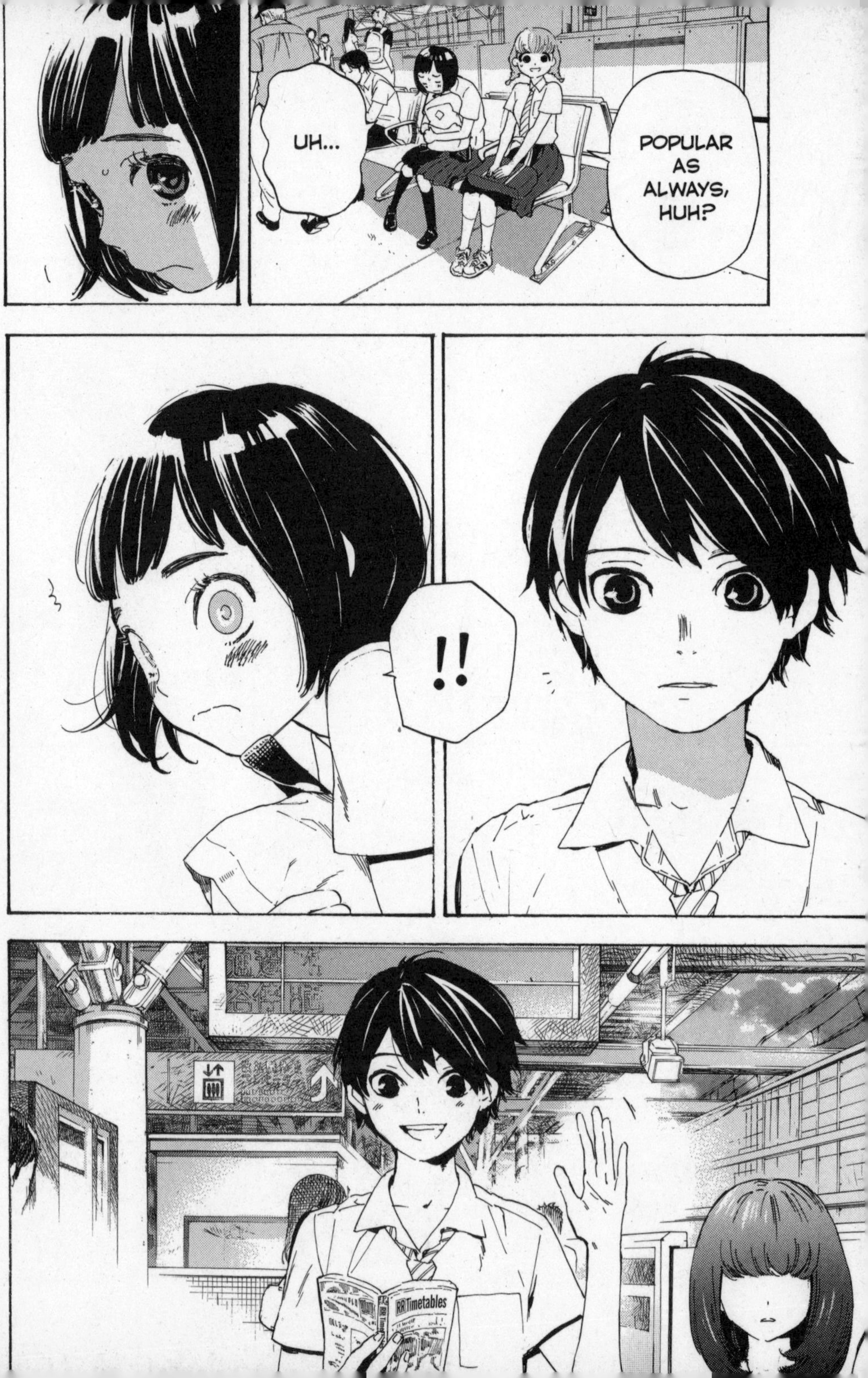
POPULAR AS ALWAYS, HUH?
UH...
!!
RR Timetables

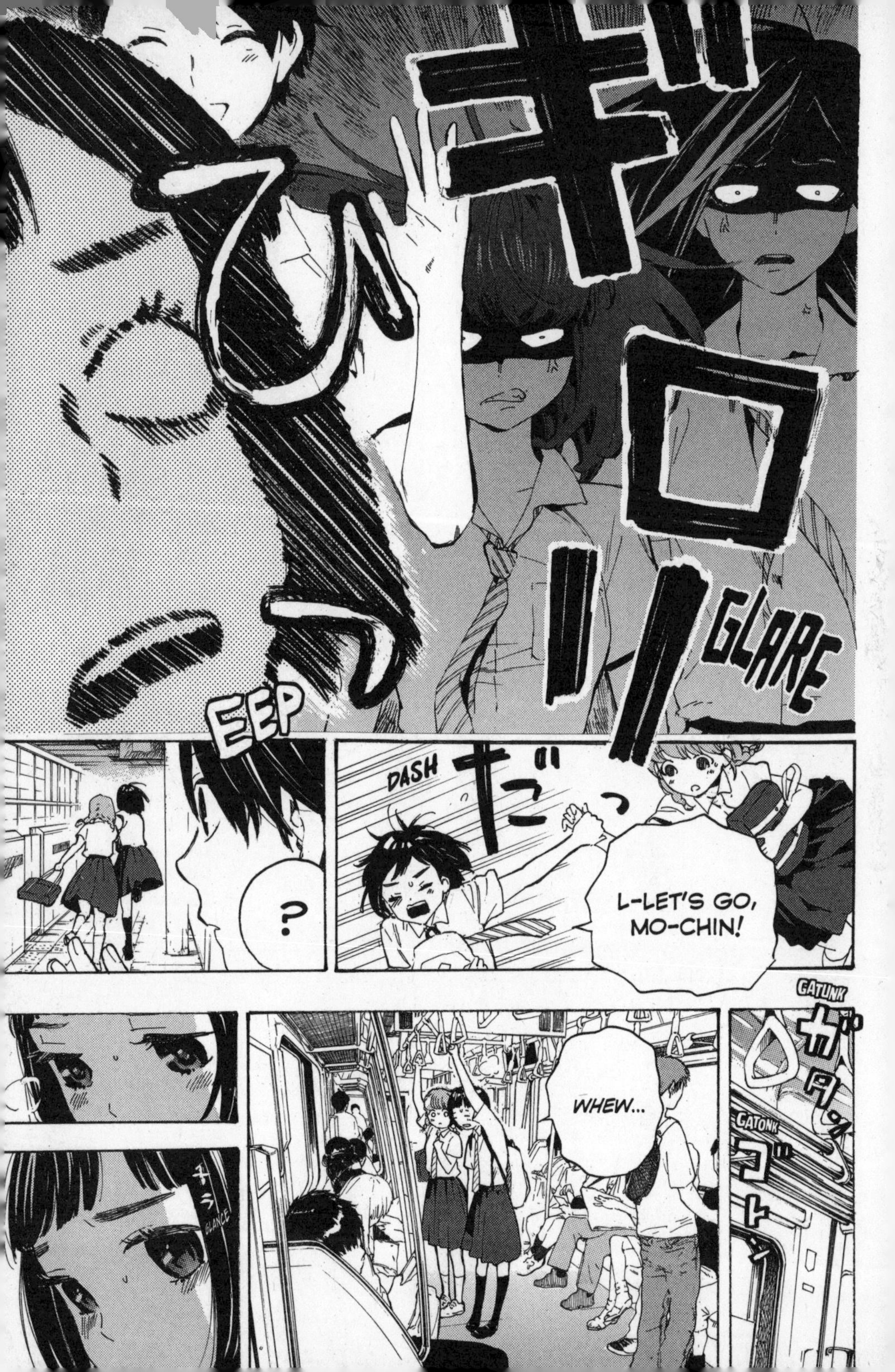

ギロッ
GLARE
EEP
DASH
L-LET'S GO, MO-CHIN!
?
GATUNK
GATONK
WHEW...
チラ
GLANCE

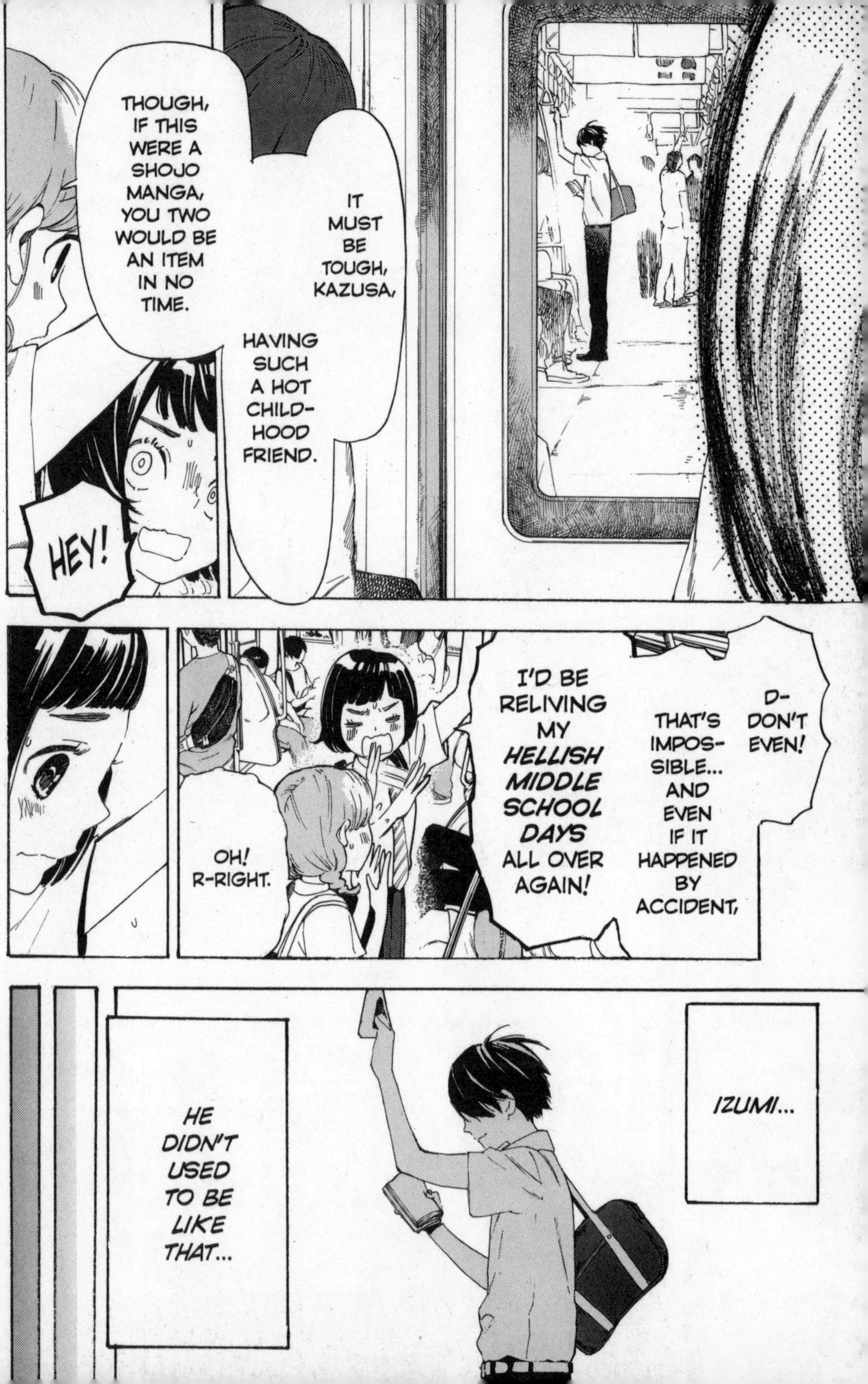
IT MUST BE TOUGH, KAZUSA, HAVING SUCH A HOT CHILDHOOD FRIEND.
THOUGH, IF THIS WERE A SHOJO MANGA, YOU TWO WOULD BE AN ITEM IN NO TIME.
HEY!
D-DON'T EVEN!
THAT'S IMPOSSIBLE... AND EVEN IF IT HAPPENED BY ACCIDENT,
I'D BE RELIVING MY *HELLISH MIDDLE SCHOOL DAYS* ALL OVER AGAIN!
OH! R-RIGHT.
IZUMI...
HE DIDN'T USED TO BE LIKE THAT...

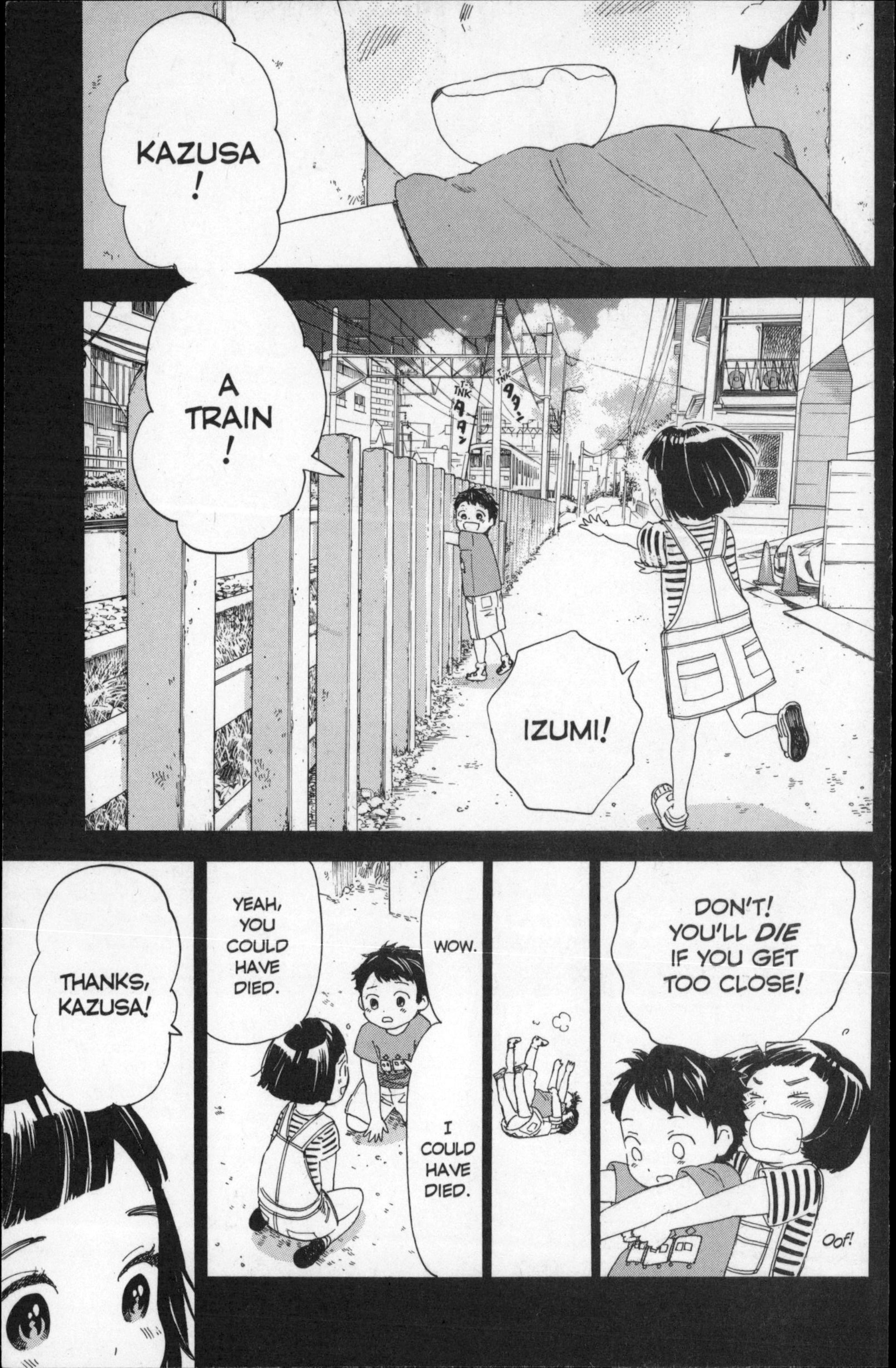
KAZUSA!
A TRAIN!
T-TNK タタン
T-TNK タタン
IZUMI!
DON'T! YOU'LL *DIE* IF YOU GET TOO CLOSE!
Oof!
WOW.
I COULD HAVE DIED.
YEAH, YOU COULD HAVE DIED.
THANKS, KAZUSA!

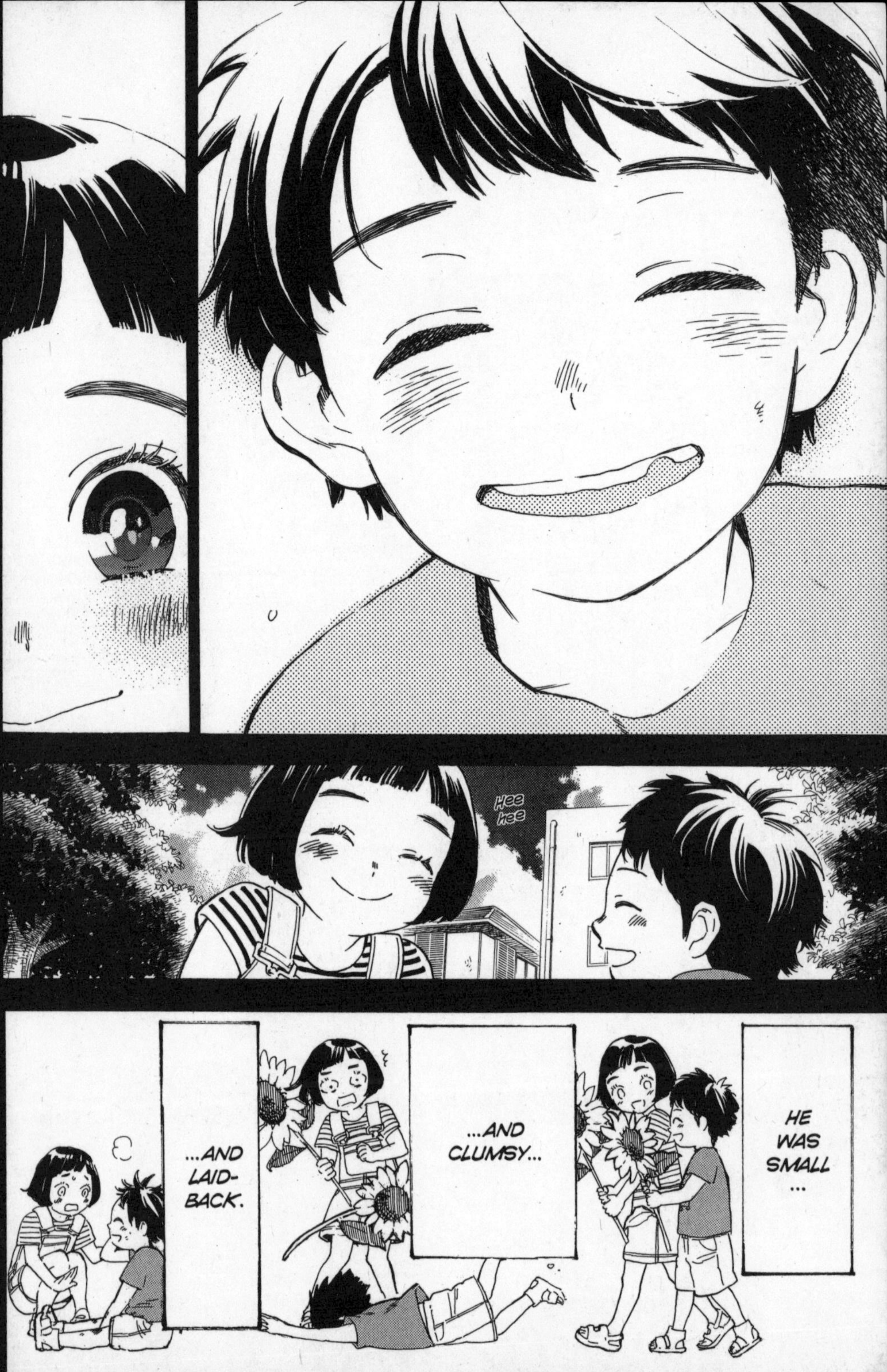
Hee hee
HE WAS SMALL ...
...AND CLUMSY...
...AND LAID-BACK.

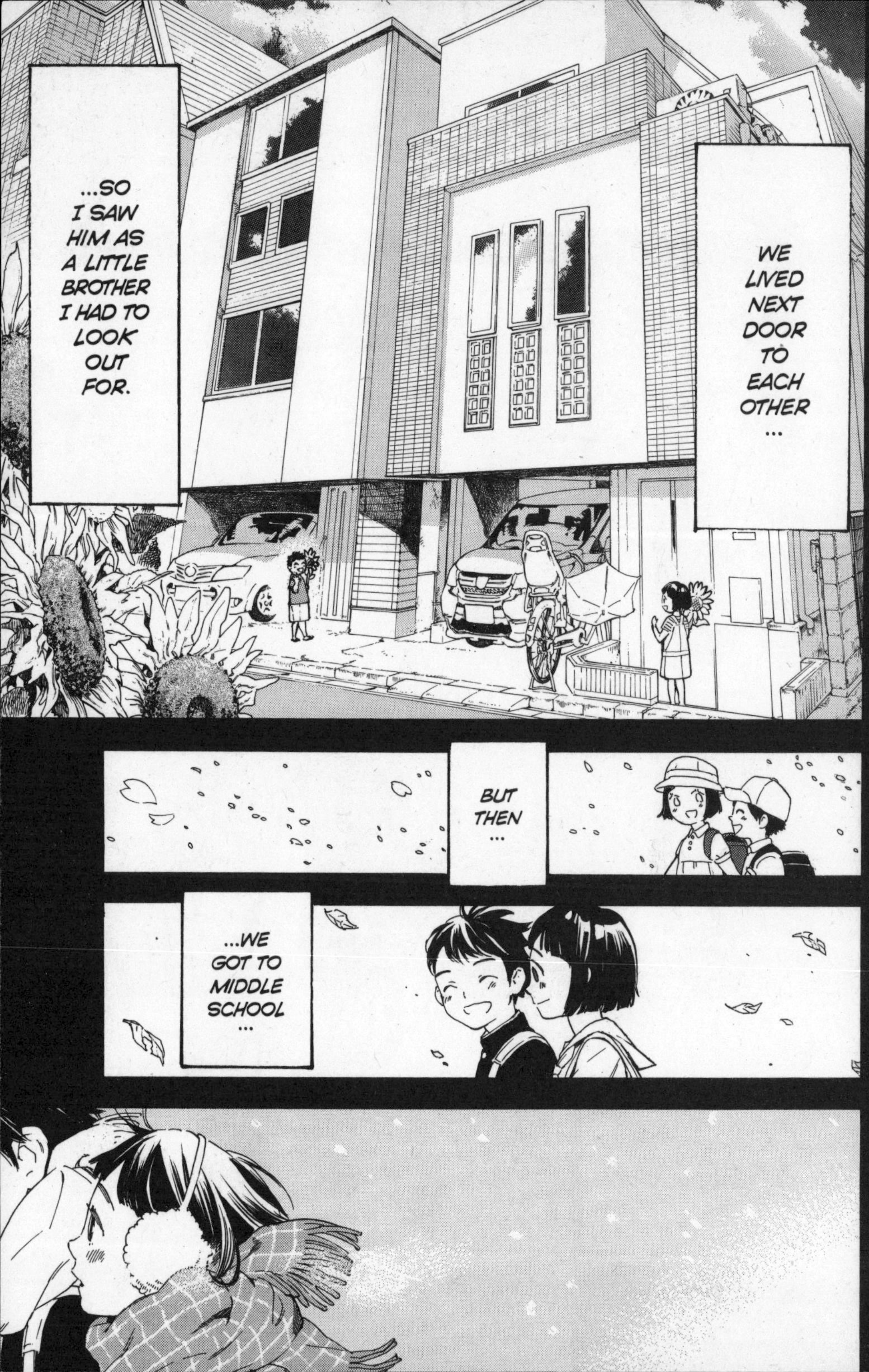
WE LIVED NEXT DOOR TO EACH OTHER...
...SO I SAW HIM AS A LITTLE BROTHER I HAD TO LOOK OUT FOR.
BUT THEN...
...WE GOT TO MIDDLE SCHOOL...

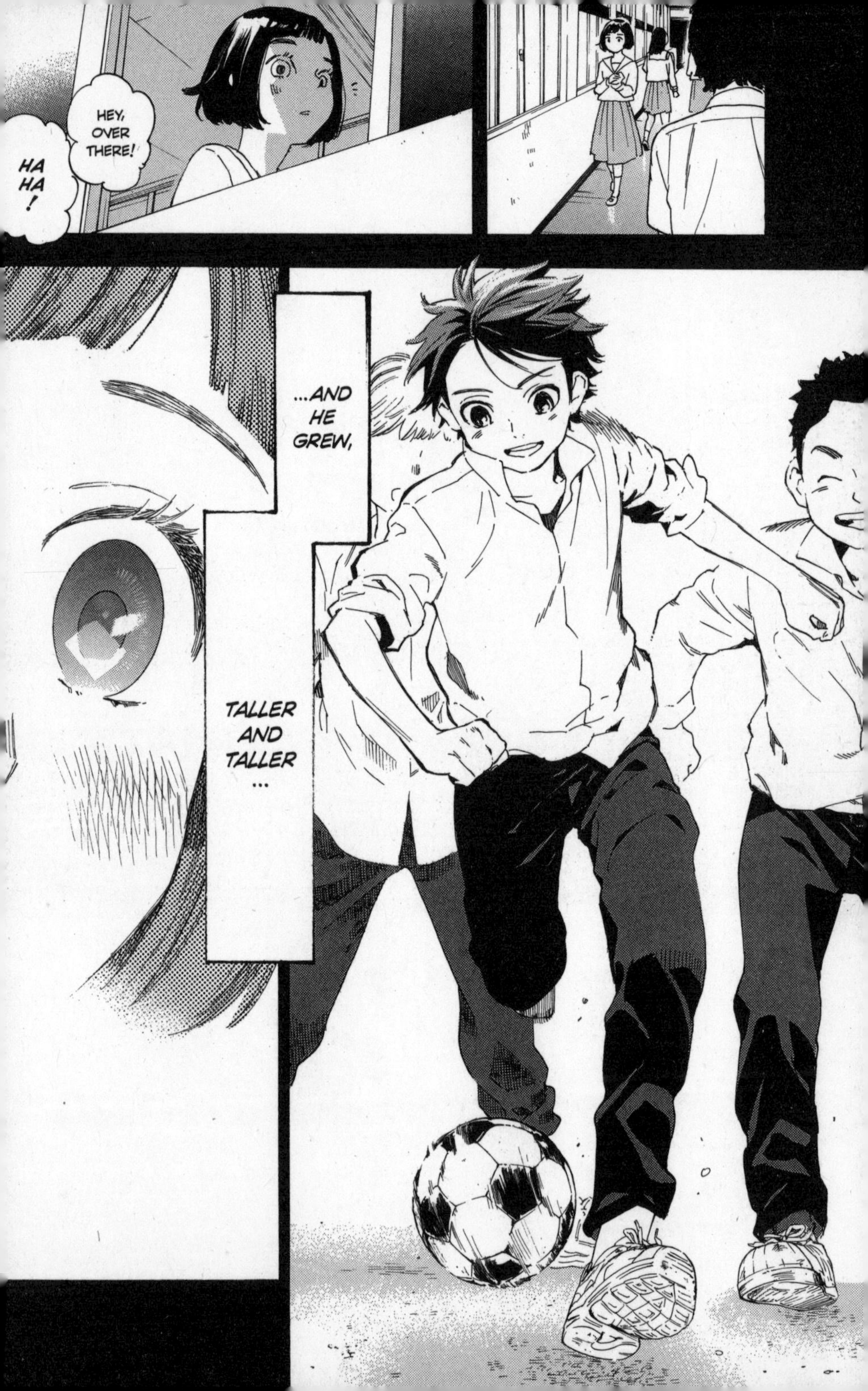
HEY, OVER THERE!
HA HA!
...AND HE GREW,
TALLER AND TALLER ...

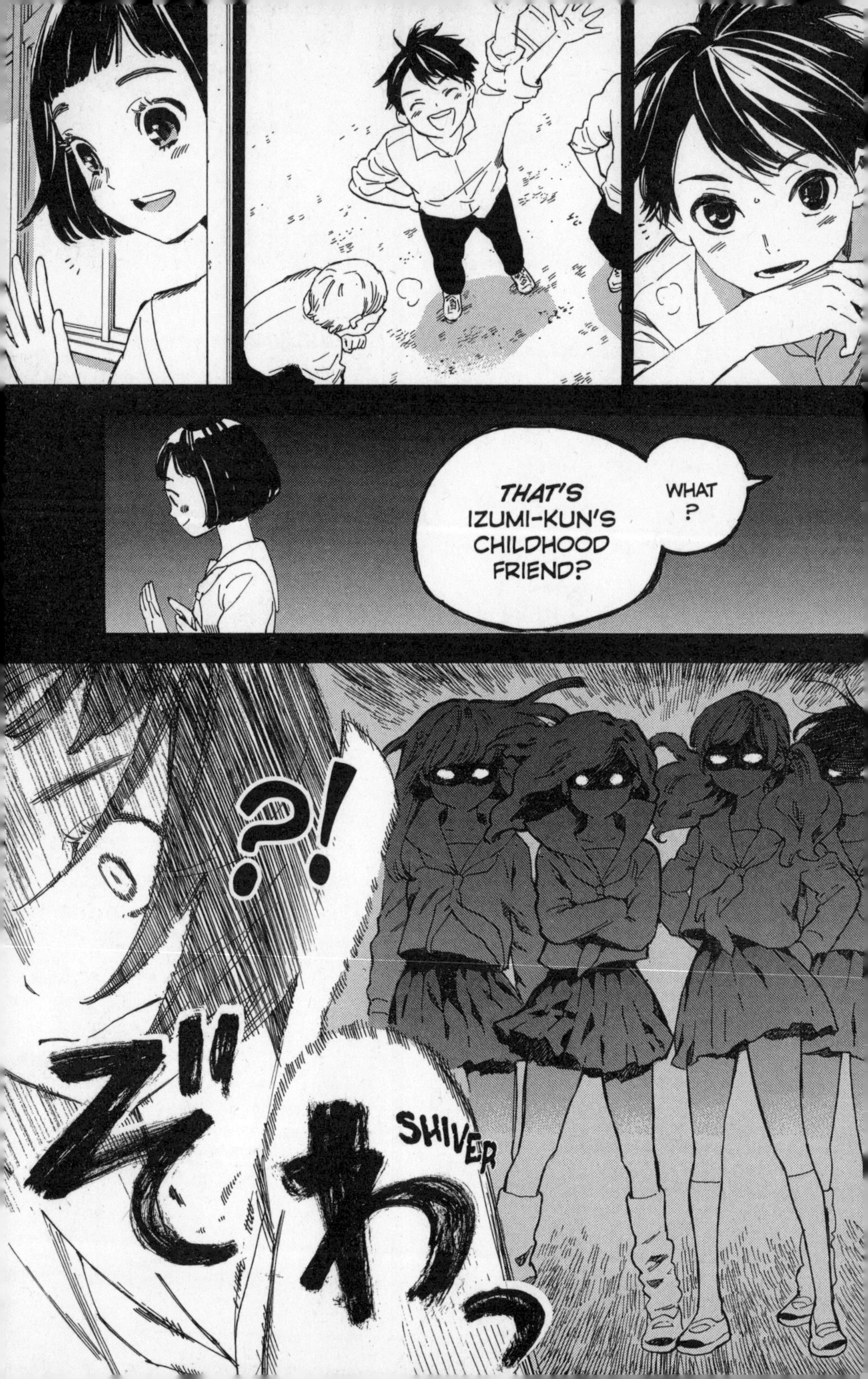
WHAT?
THAT'S IZUMI-KUN'S CHILDHOOD FRIEND?
?!
SHIVER
ぞわっ

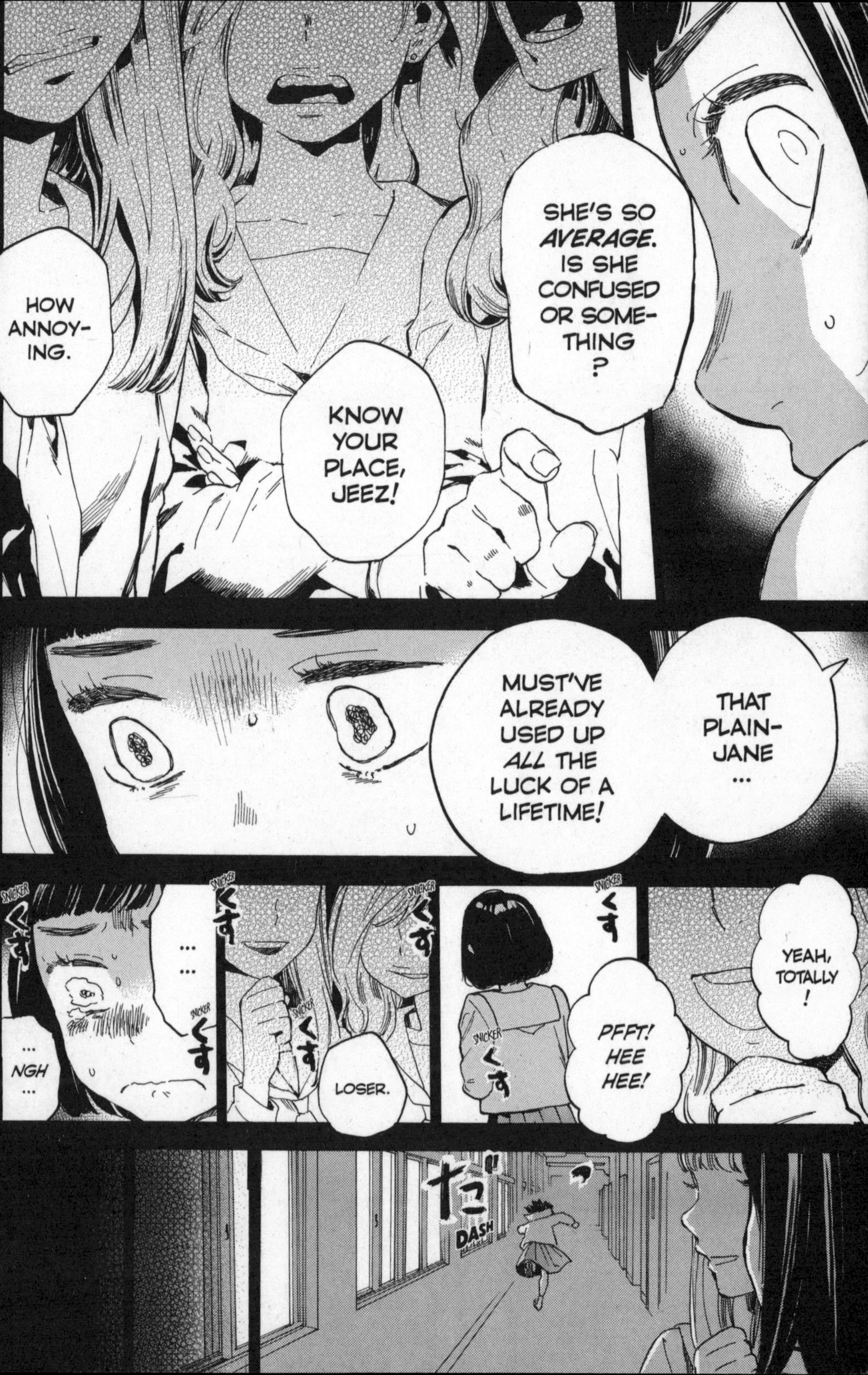
SHE'S SO *AVERAGE*. IS SHE CONFUSED OR SOME-THING?
KNOW YOUR PLACE, JEEZ!
HOW ANNOY-ING.
THAT PLAIN-JANE...
MUST'VE ALREADY USED UP *ALL* THE LUCK OF A LIFETIME!
YEAH, TOTALLY!
SNICKER くす
PFFT! HEE HEE!
SNICKER くす
SNICKER くす
SNICKER くす
LOSER.
......
SNICKER くす
SNICKER くす
...NGH...
すっ DASH

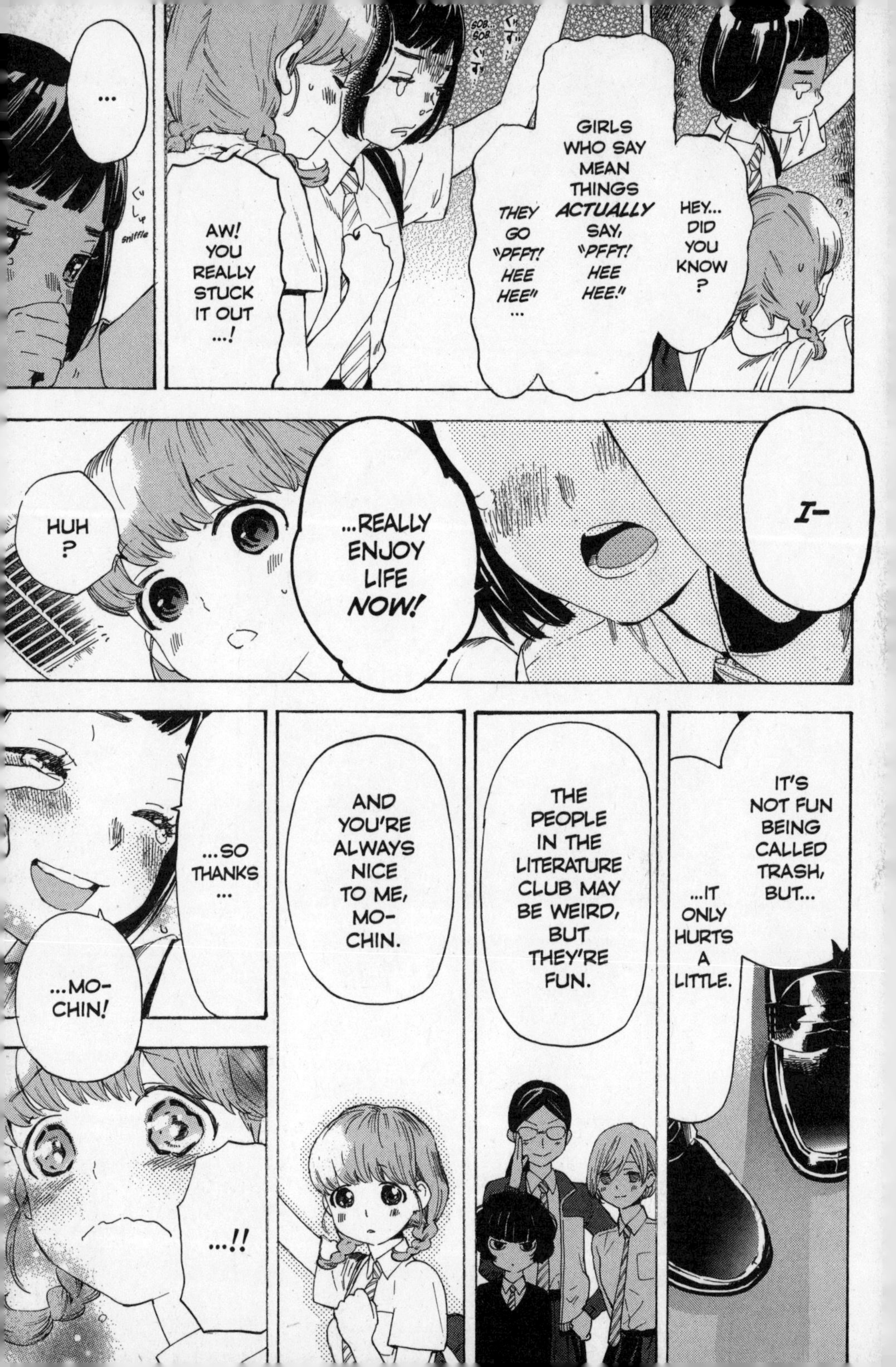
SOB... SOB...
HEY... DID YOU KNOW?
GIRLS WHO SAY MEAN THINGS ACTUALLY SAY, "PFFT! HEE HEE."
THEY GO "PFFT! HEE HEE"...
AW! YOU REALLY STUCK IT OUT...!
...
sniffle
I–
...REALLY ENJOY LIFE NOW!
HUH?
IT'S NOT FUN BEING CALLED TRASH, BUT...
...IT ONLY HURTS A LITTLE.
THE PEOPLE IN THE LITERATURE CLUB MAY BE WEIRD, BUT THEY'RE FUN.
AND YOU'RE ALWAYS NICE TO ME, MO-CHIN.
...SO THANKS...
...MO-CHIN!
...!!

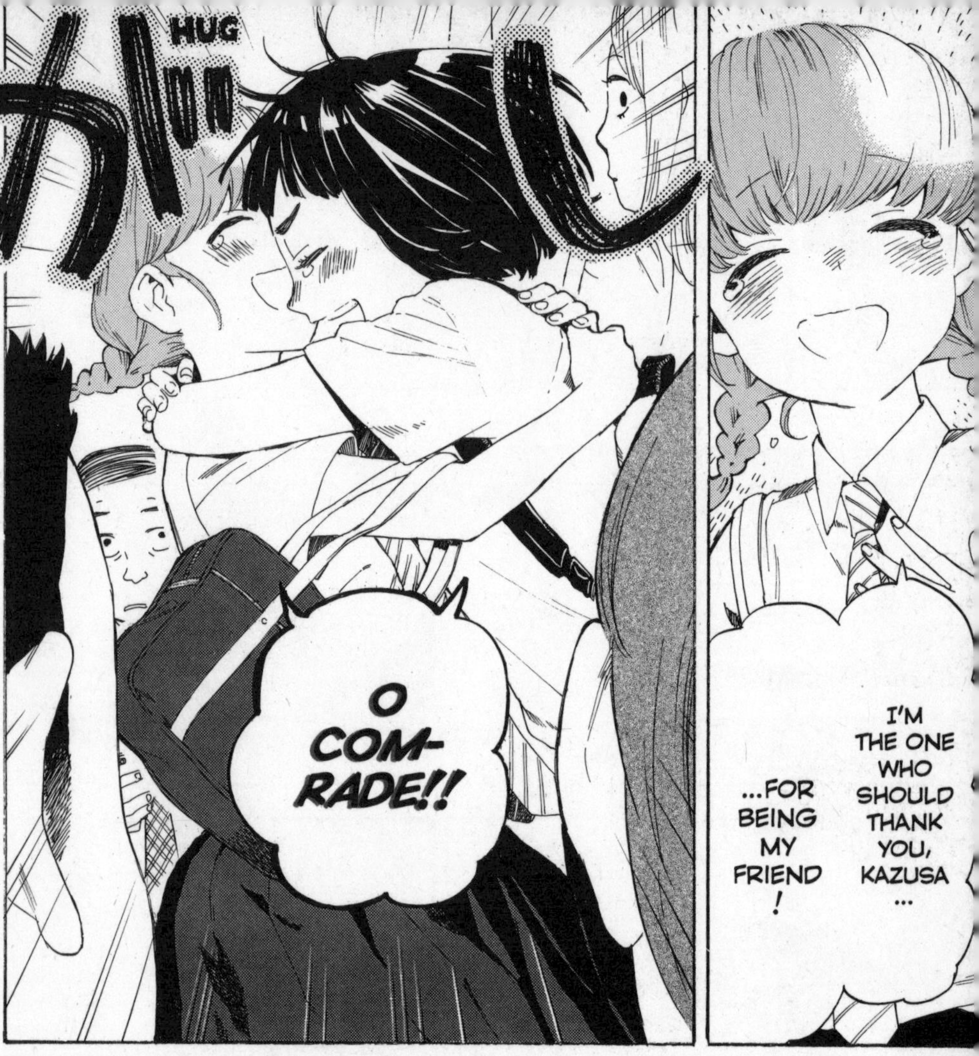
I'M THE ONE WHO SHOULD THANK YOU, KAZUSA...
...FOR BEING MY FRIEND!
HUG
O COM-RADE!!

*Osamu Dazai is a famous 20th-century author. *Goodbye* is his last unfinished work.

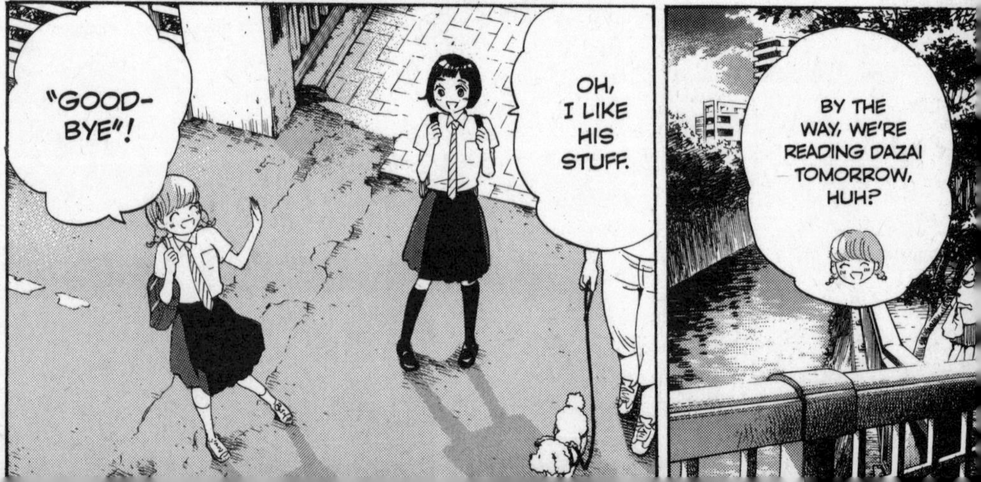
BY THE WAY, WE'RE READING DAZAI TOMORROW, HUH?
OH, I LIKE HIS STUFF.
"GOOD-BYE"!

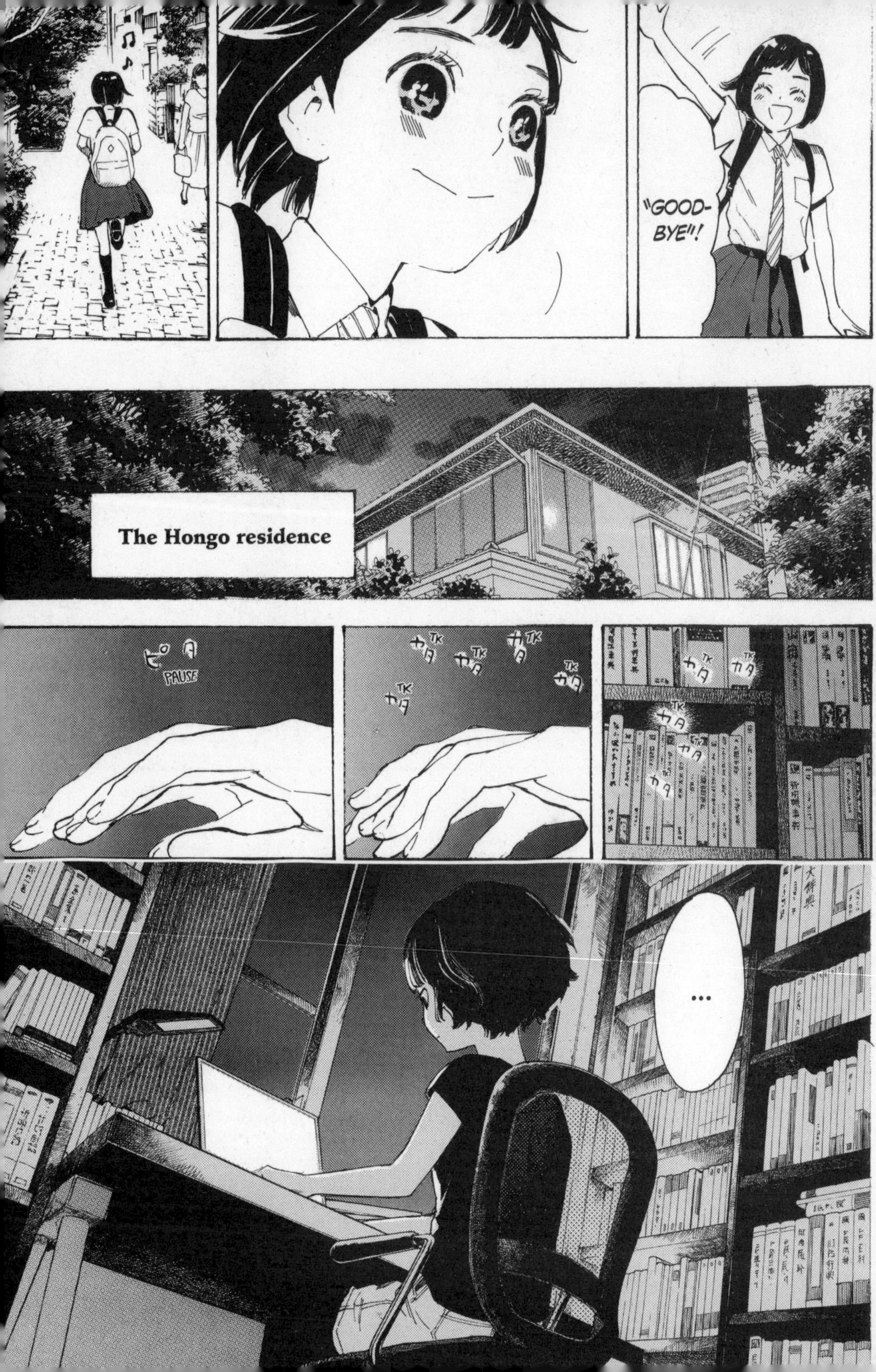

"GOOD-BYE"!
The Hongo residence
カタ TK
カタ TK
カタ TK
カタ TK
カタ TK
カタ TK
カタ TK
カタ TK
カタ TK
カタ TK
カタ TK
ピタ PAUSE
...

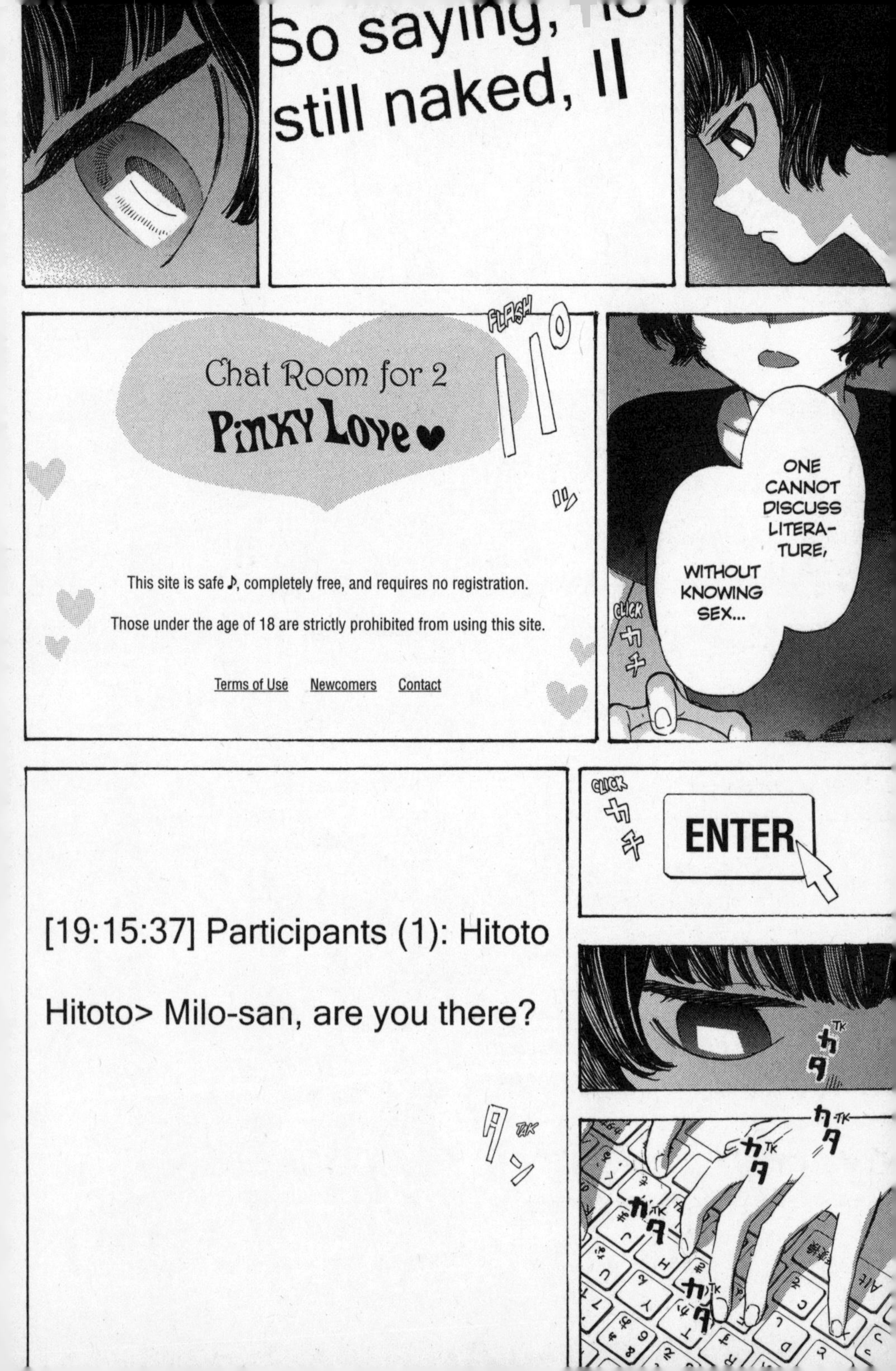

So saying,
still naked,
ONE CANNOT DISCUSS LITERATURE,
WITHOUT KNOWING SEX...
CLICK
FLASH
Chat Room for 2
Pinky Love
This site is safe ♪, completely free, and requires no registration.
Those under the age of 18 are strictly prohibited from using this site.
Terms of Use Newcomers Contact
CLICK
ENTER
TK
TK
TK
TK
TK
[19:15:37] Participants (1): Hitoto
Hitoto> Milo-san, are you there?
TAK

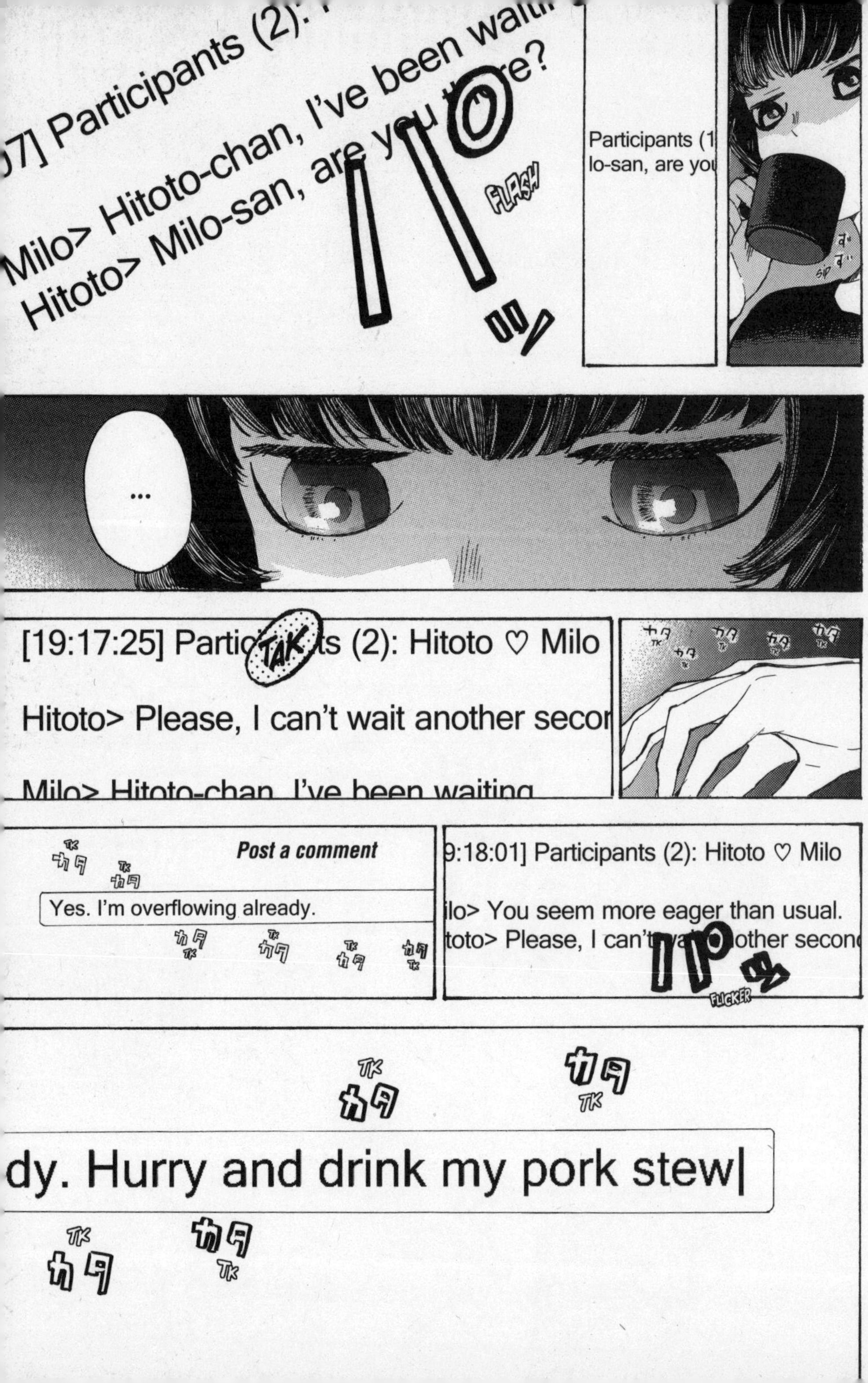

SIP
Participants (1
lo-san, are you
07] Participants (2):
Milo> Hitoto-chan, I've been waiti
Hitoto> Milo-san, are you there?
FLASH
...
TK
[19:17:25] Partic TAK ts (2): Hitoto ♡ Milo
Hitoto> Please, I can't wait another secon
Milo> Hitoto-chan, I've been waiting
9:18:01] Participants (2): Hitoto ♡ Milo
ilo> You seem more eager than usual.
toto> Please, I can't wait another secon
FLICKER
Post a comment
Yes. I'm overflowing already.
TK
dy. Hurry and drink my pork stew|
TK

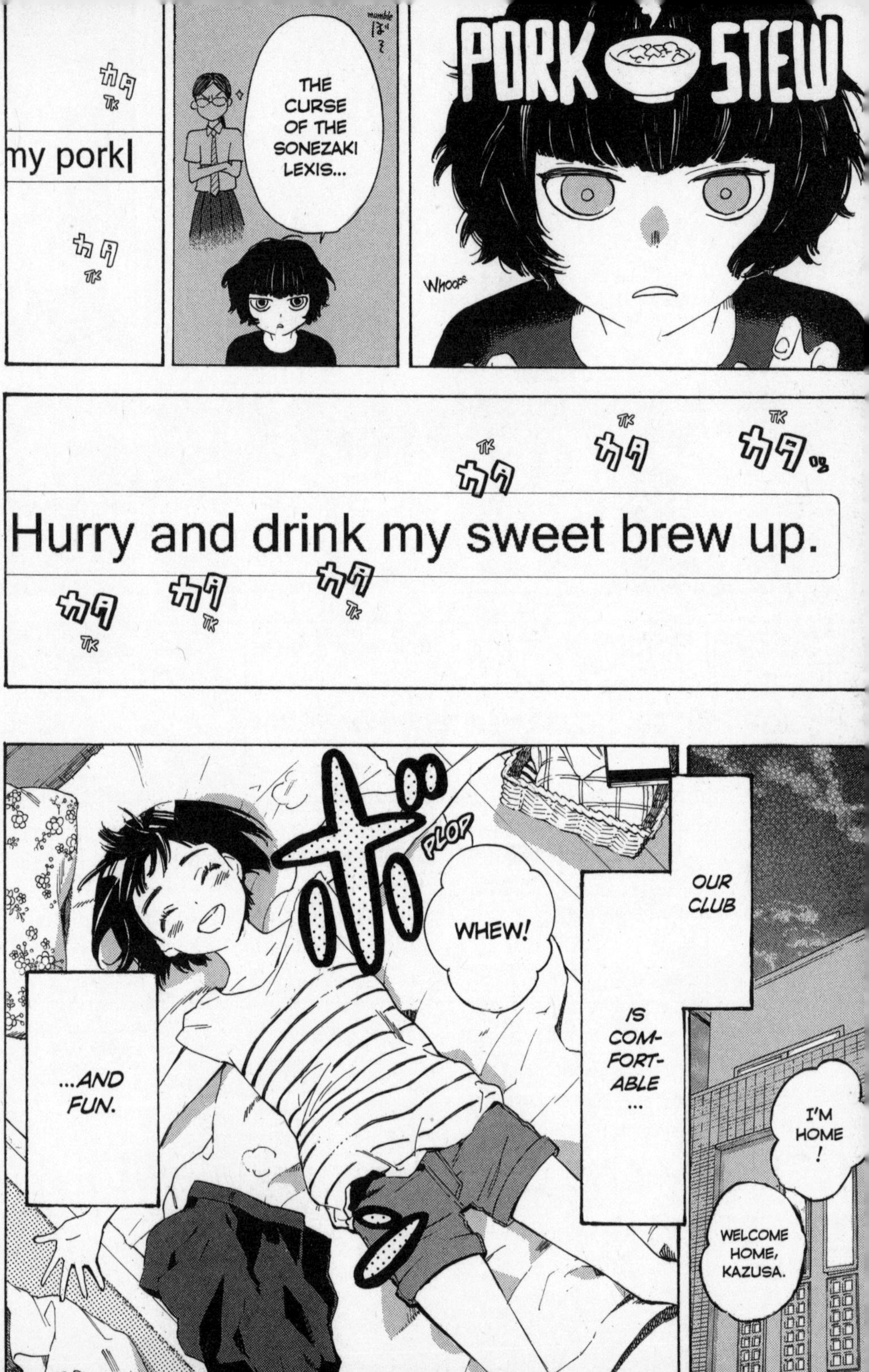
PORK STEW
Whoops.
mumble
THE CURSE OF THE SONEZAKI LEXIS...
カタ TK
my pork|
カタ TK
カタ TK
Hurry and drink my sweet brew up.
I'M HOME!
WELCOME HOME, KAZUSA.
OUR CLUB IS COMFORTABLE...
PLOP
WHEW!
...AND FUN.

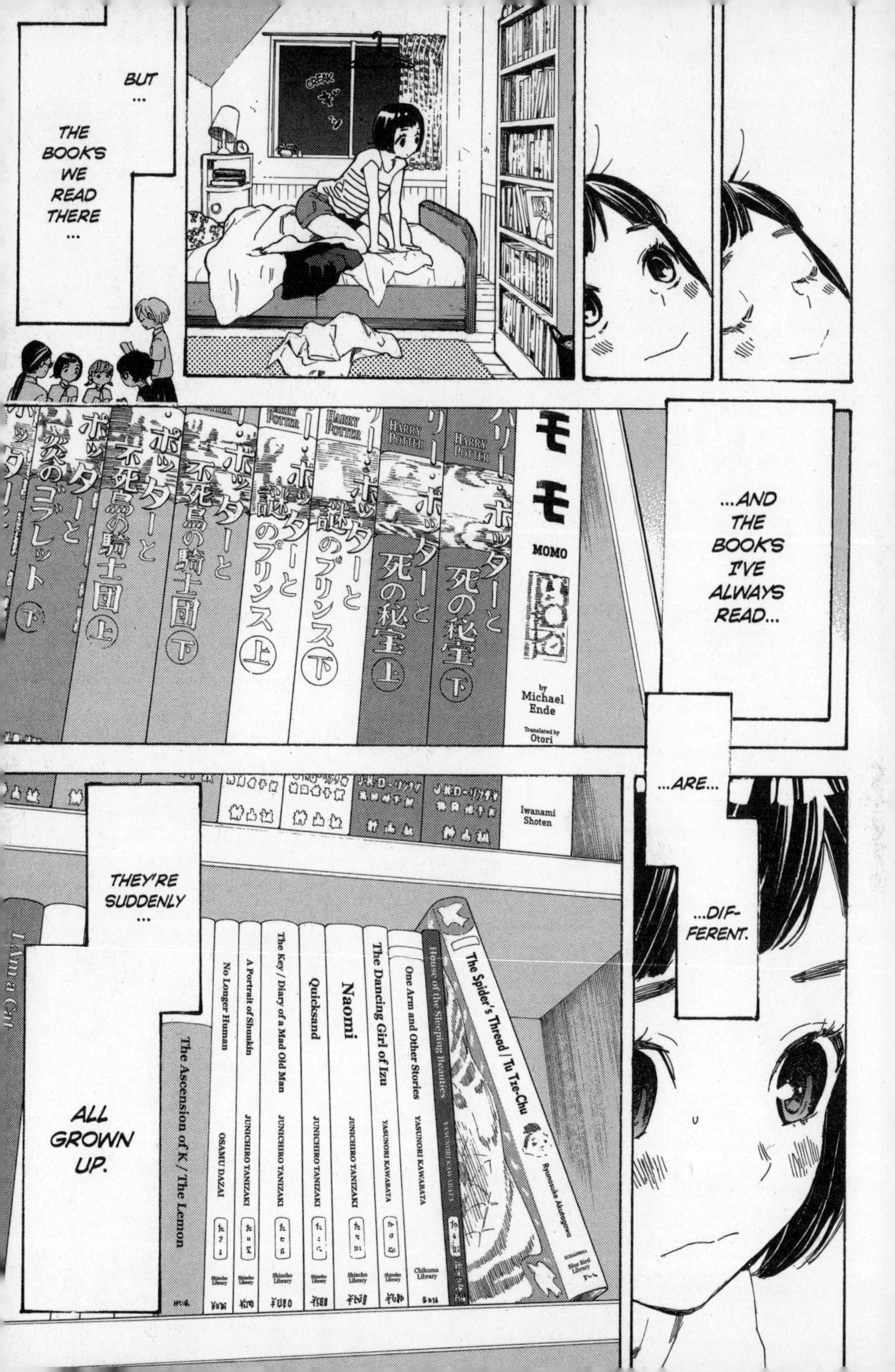
CREAK
BUT ...
THE BOOKS WE READ THERE ...
HARRY POTTER
ハリー・ポッターと死の秘宝(下)
HARRY POTTER
ハリー・ポッターと死の秘宝(上)
HARRY POTTER
ハリー・ポッターと謎のプリンス(下)
HARRY POTTER
ハリー・ポッターと謎のプリンス(上)
ハリー・ポッターと不死鳥の騎士団(下)
ポッターと不死鳥の騎士団(上)
ポッターと炎のゴブレット(下)
モモ
MOMO
by Michael Ende
Translated by Otori
Iwanami Shoten
...AND THE BOOKS I'VE ALWAYS READ...
...ARE...
...DIF- FERENT.
THEY'RE SUDDENLY ...
ALL GROWN UP.
The Spider's Thread / Tu Tze-Chu
Ryunosuke Akutagawa
KODANSHA Blue Bird Library
House of the Sleeping Beauties
One Arm and Other Stories
YASUNORI KAWABATA
Chikuma Library
The Dancing Girl of Izu
YASUNORI KAWABATA
Shincho Library
Naomi
JUNICHIRO TANIZAKI
Shincho Library
Quicksand
JUNICHIRO TANIZAKI
Shincho Library
The Key / Diary of a Mad Old Man
JUNICHIRO TANIZAKI
Shincho Library
A Portrait of Shunkin
JUNICHIRO TANIZAKI
Shincho Library
No Longer Human
OSAMU DAZAI
Shincho Library
The Ascension of K / The Lemon
I Am a Cat

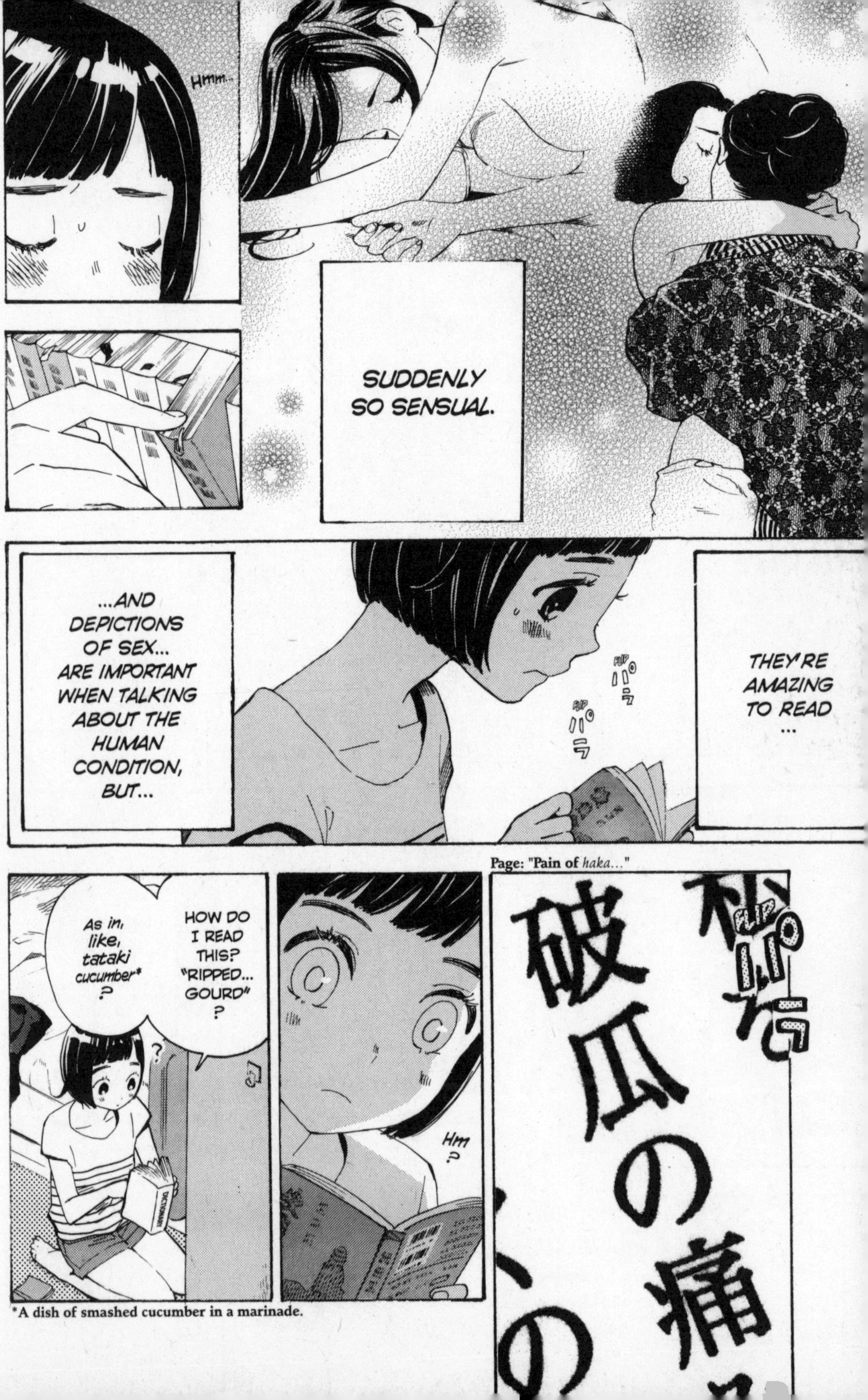
SUDDENLY SO SENSUAL.
Hmm..
THEY'RE AMAZING TO READ ...
FLIP パラ
FLIP パラ
...AND DEPICTIONS OF SEX... ARE IMPORTANT WHEN TALKING ABOUT THE HUMAN CONDITION, BUT...
Page: "Pain of haka..."
FLIP パ
FLIP パ
破瓜の痛
の
Hm?
HOW DO I READ THIS? "RIPPED... GOURD"?
As in, like, tataki cucumber*?
?
DICTIONARY

*A dish of smashed cucumber in a marinade.

はか【破瓜】

Haka

The breaking of the hymen when a woman experiences sexual intercourse for the first time, or a literary euphemism for losing one's virginity.

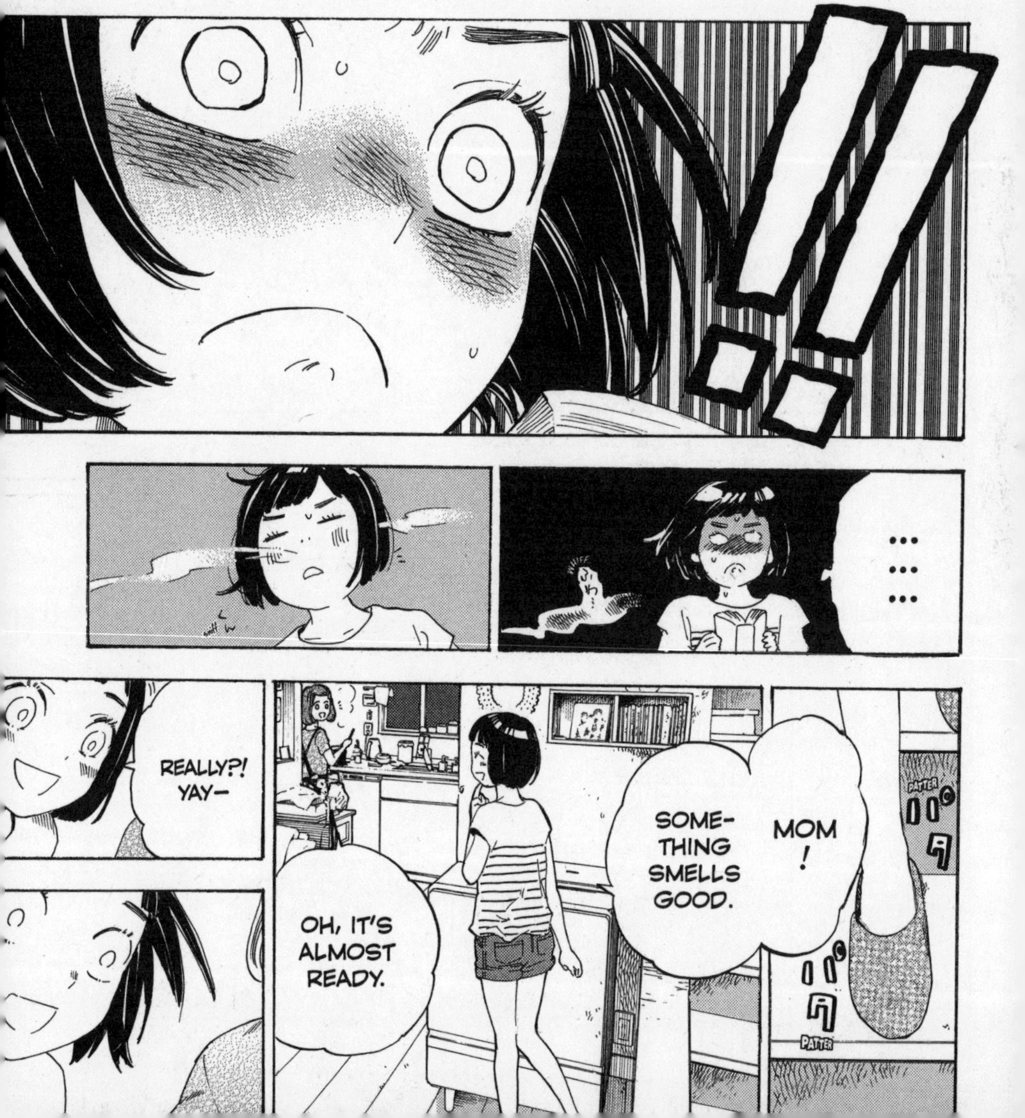

!!
……
……
……
PATTER
PATTER
MOM!
SOMETHING SMELLS GOOD.
OH, IT'S ALMOST READY.
REALLY?! YAY—

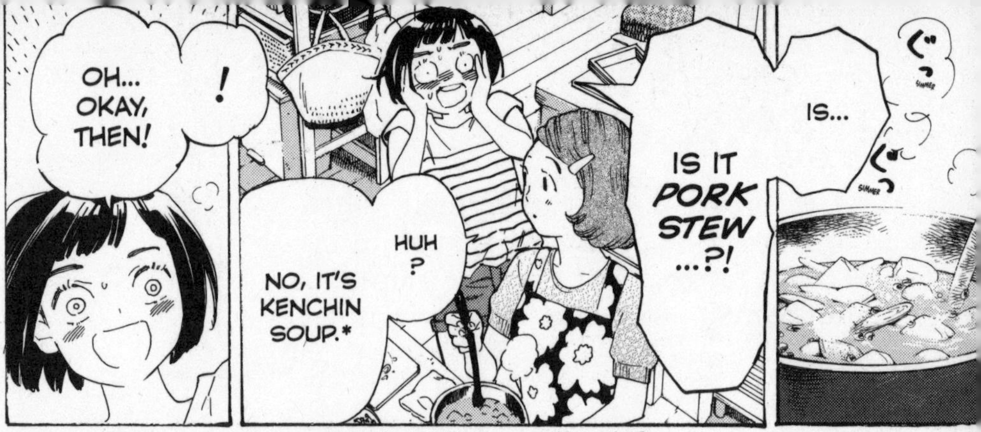
IS...
IS IT PORK STEW ...?!
SIMMER
SIMMER
HUH ?
NO, IT'S KENCHIN SOUP.*
!
OH... OKAY, THEN!

*A soy sauce-based soup with root vegetables and tofu.

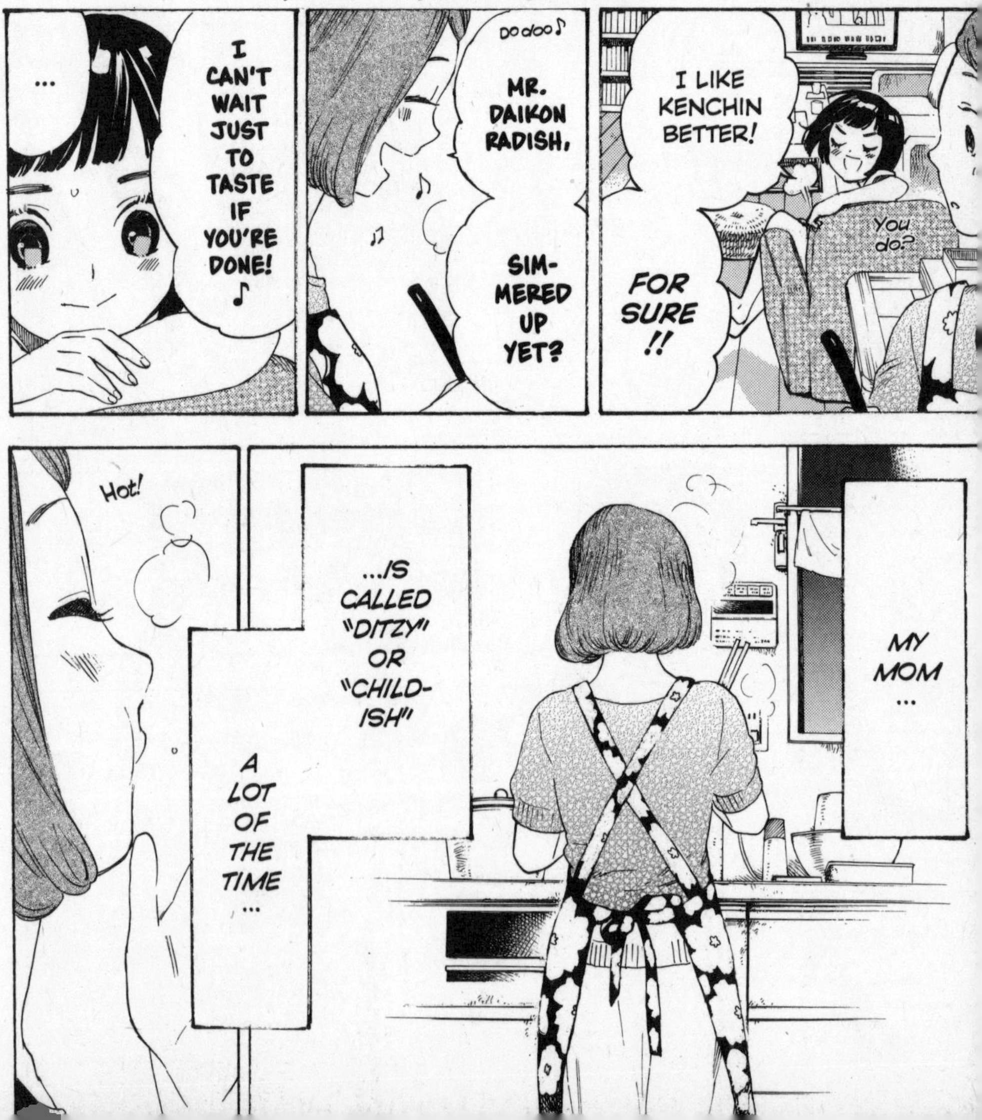
I LIKE KENCHIN BETTER!
You do?
FOR SURE !!
Do doo ♪
MR. DAIKON RADISH,
SIM-MERED UP YET?
I CAN'T WAIT JUST TO TASTE IF YOU'RE DONE! ♪
...
MY MOM ...
...IS CALLED "DITZY" OR "CHILD-ISH"
A LOT OF THE TIME ...
Hot!

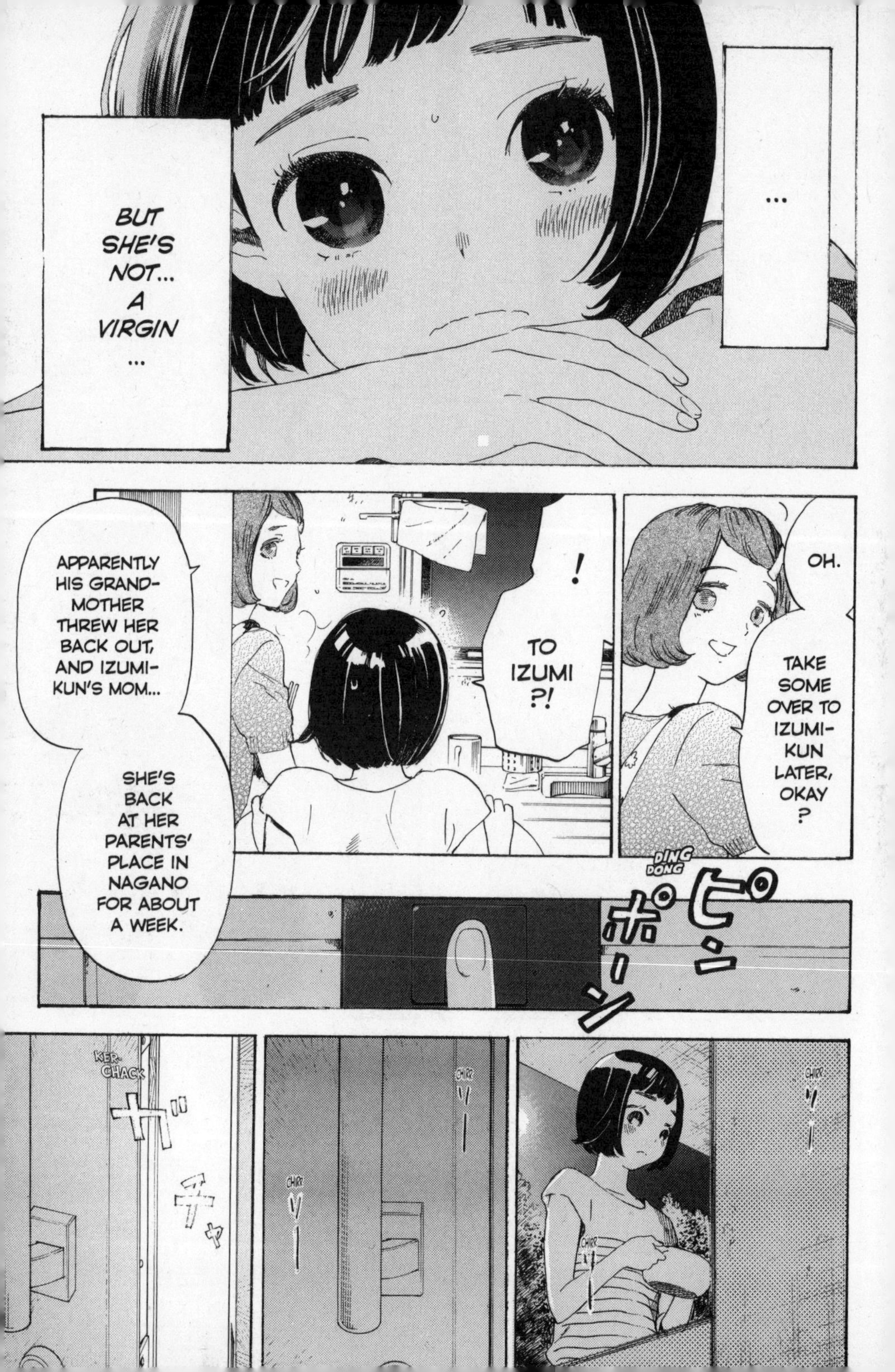
...
BUT SHE'S NOT... A VIRGIN ...
OH.
TAKE SOME OVER TO IZUMI-KUN LATER, OKAY?
!
TO IZUMI?!
APPARENTLY HIS GRANDMOTHER THREW HER BACK OUT, AND IZUMI-KUN'S MOM...
SHE'S BACK AT HER PARENTS' PLACE IN NAGANO FOR ABOUT A WEEK.
DING DONG
CHIRR
CHIRR
CHIRR
CHIRR
KER-CHACK

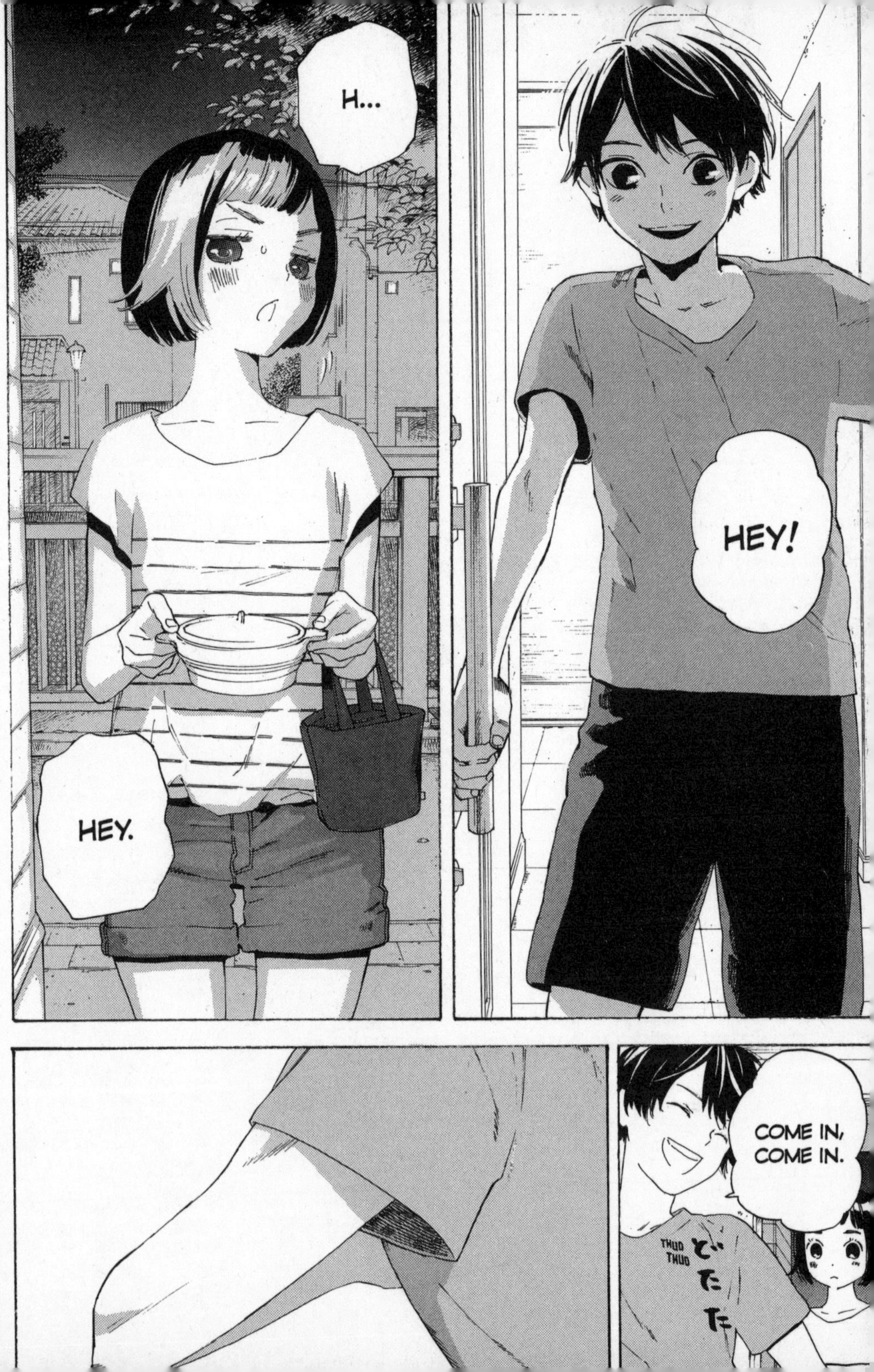
HEY!
H...
HEY.
COME IN, COME IN.
THUD THUD
どたた

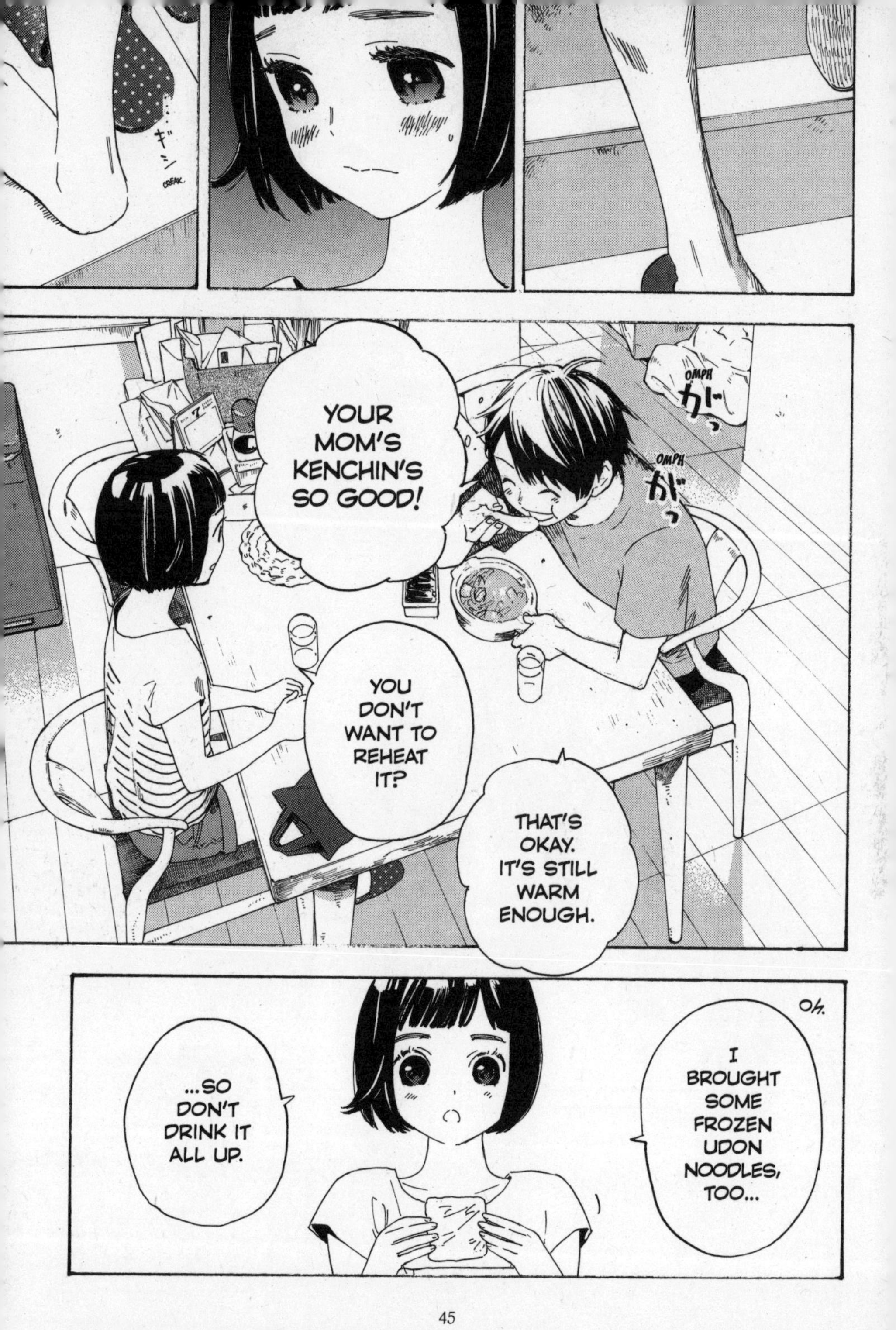
ギシ
CREAK
OMPH
がっ
OMPH
がっ
YOUR MOM'S KENCHIN'S SO GOOD!
YOU DON'T WANT TO REHEAT IT?
THAT'S OKAY. IT'S STILL WARM ENOUGH.
Oh.
I BROUGHT SOME FROZEN UDON NOODLES, TOO...
...SO DON'T DRINK IT ALL UP.

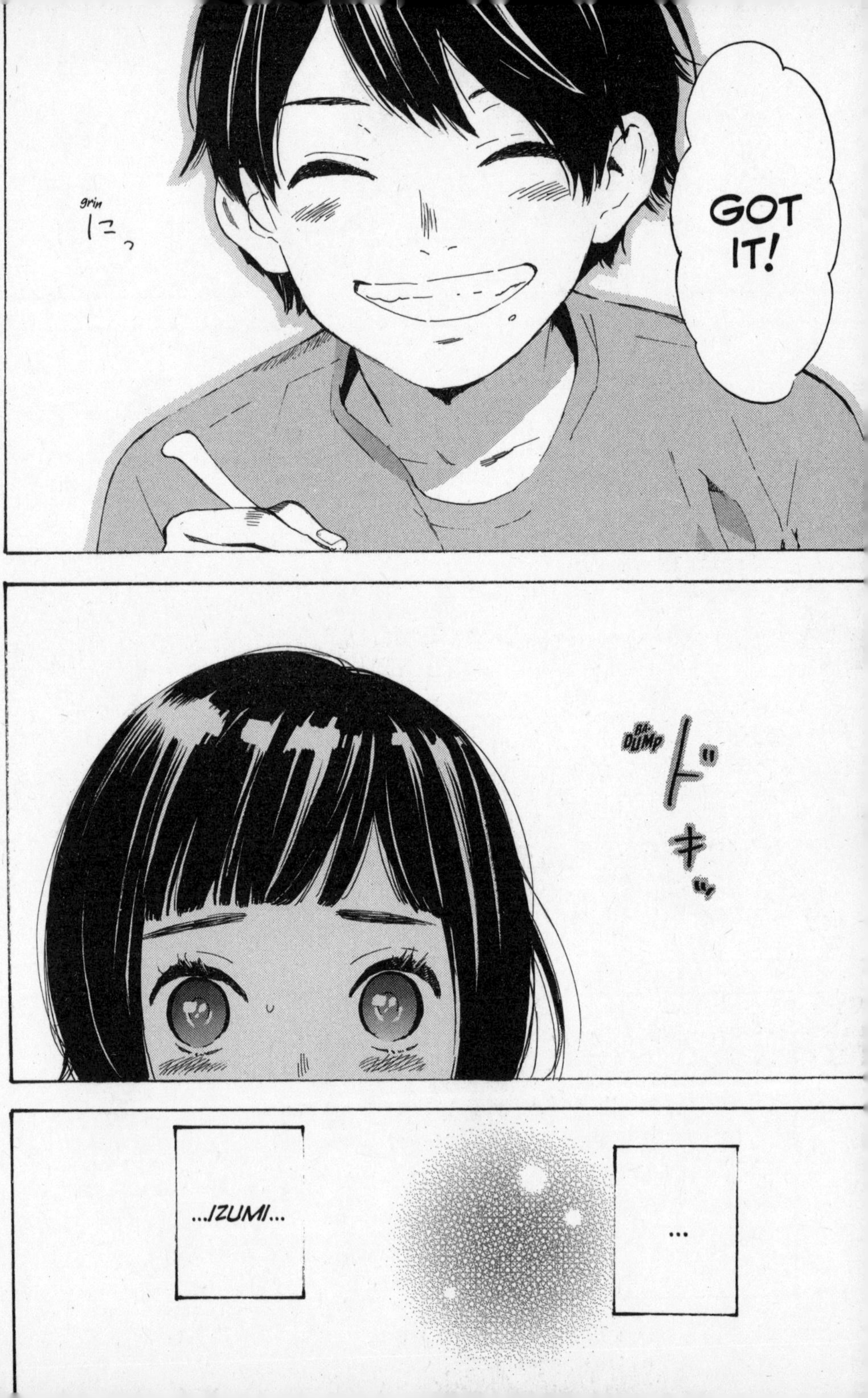
GOT IT!
grin
にっ
BA-DUMP
ドキッ
...
...IZUMI...

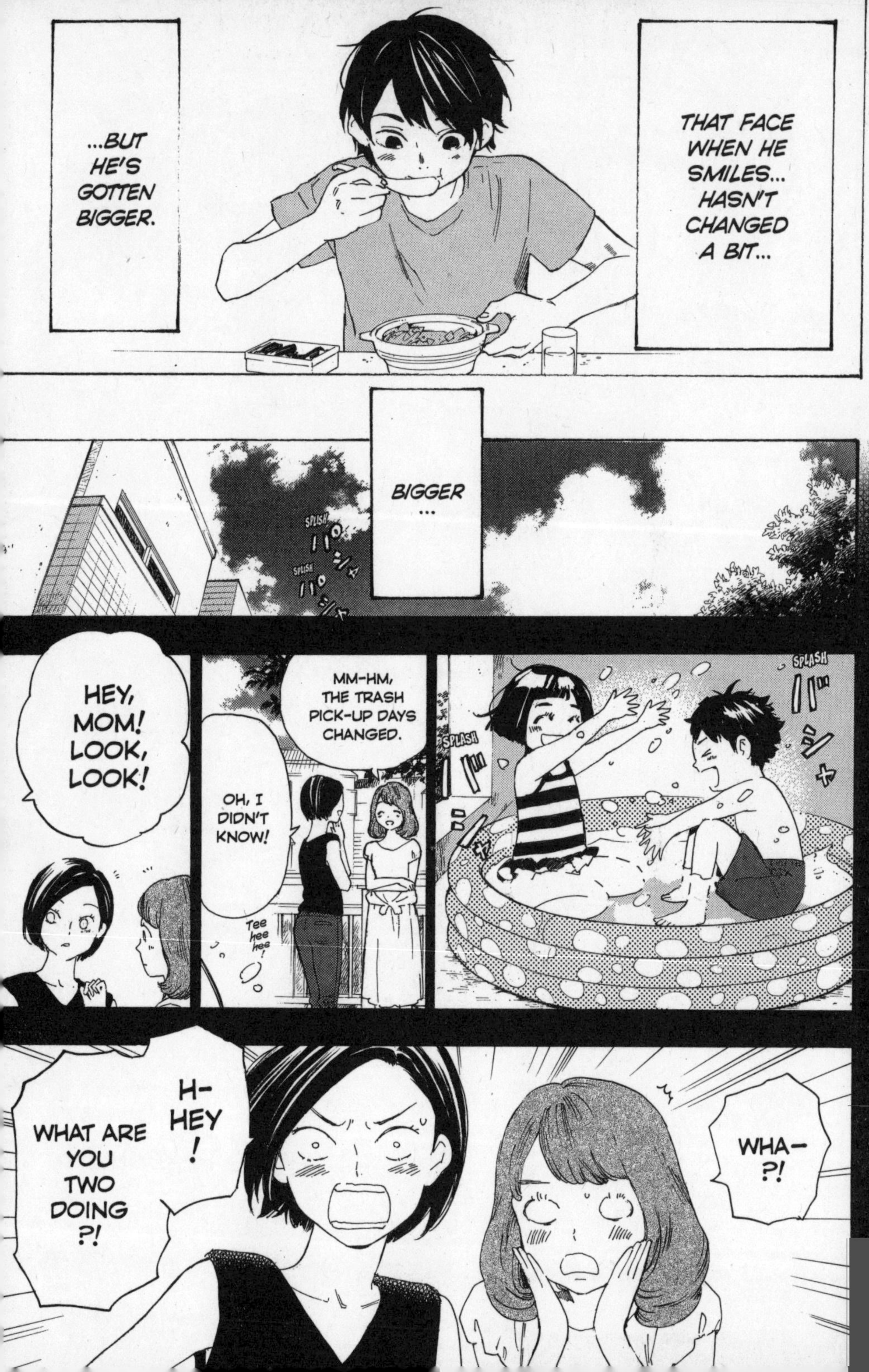
THAT FACE WHEN HE SMILES... HASN'T CHANGED A BIT...
...BUT HE'S GOTTEN BIGGER.
BIGGER ...
SPLISH
SPLISH
SPLASH
SPLASH
MM-HM, THE TRASH PICK-UP DAYS CHANGED.
OH, I DIDN'T KNOW!
Tee hee hee!
HEY, MOM! LOOK, LOOK!
WHA-?!
H-HEY!
WHAT ARE YOU TWO DOING?!

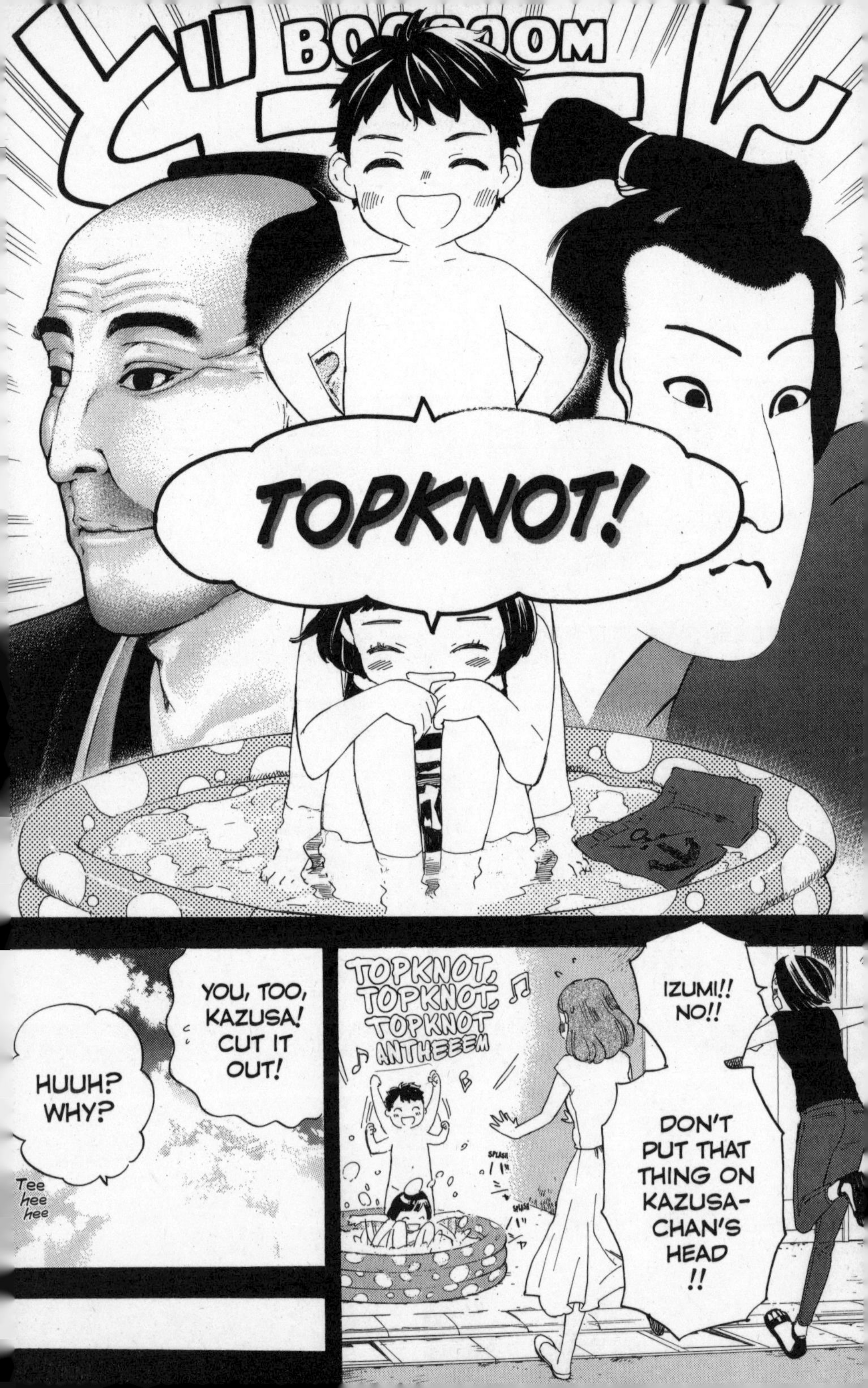
BOOOOM
TOPKNOT!
IZUMI!! NO!!
DON'T PUT THAT THING ON KAZUSA-CHAN'S HEAD!!
TOPKNOT, TOPKNOT, TOPKNOT ANTHEEEM
SPLASH
SPLASH
YOU, TOO, KAZUSA! CUT IT OUT!
HUUH? WHY?
Tee hee hee

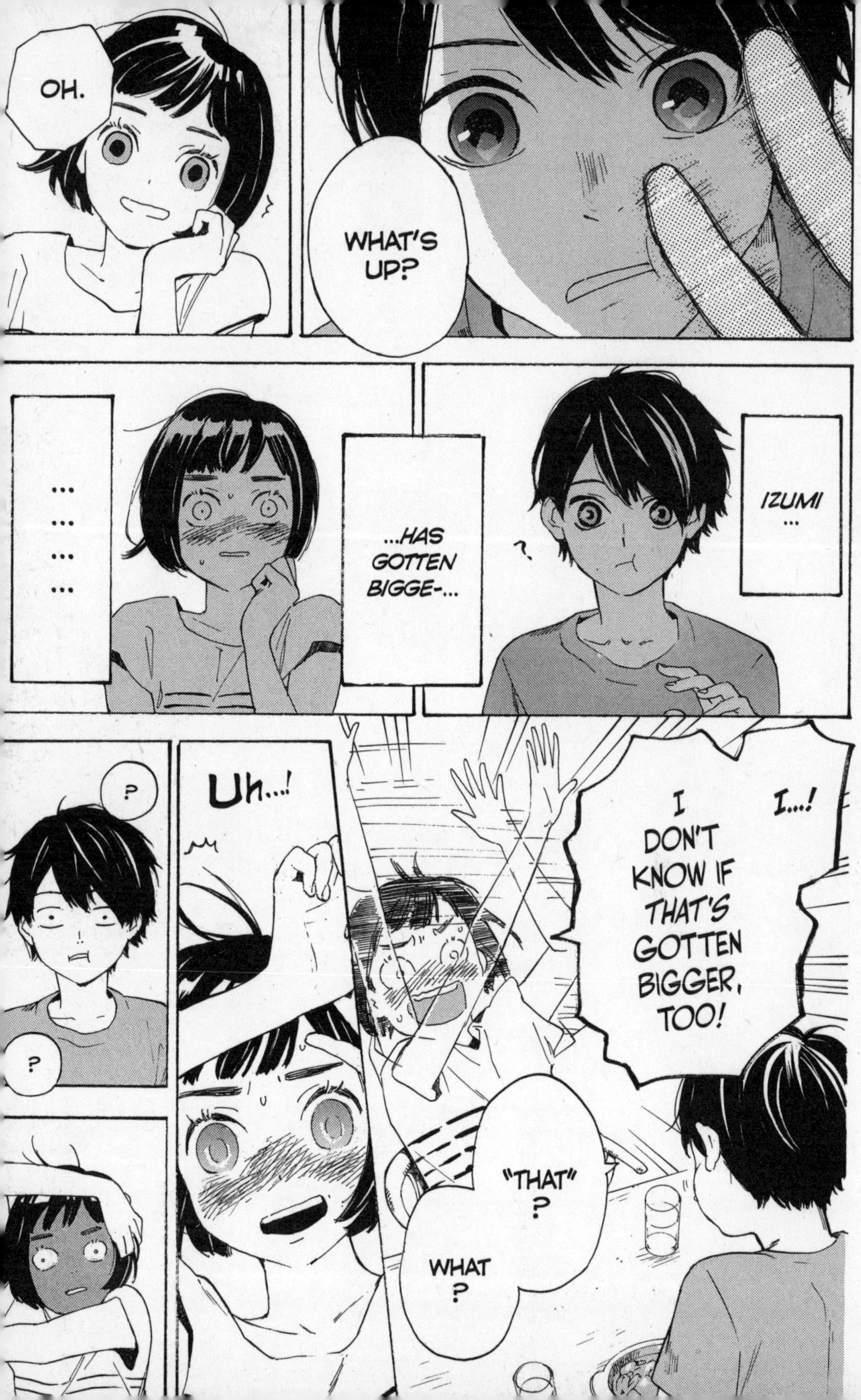
WHAT'S UP?
OH.
IZUMI ...
...HAS GOTTEN BIGGE-...
...
...
...
...
I...! I DON'T KNOW IF THAT'S GOTTEN BIGGER, TOO!
"THAT"?
WHAT?
Uh...!
?
?

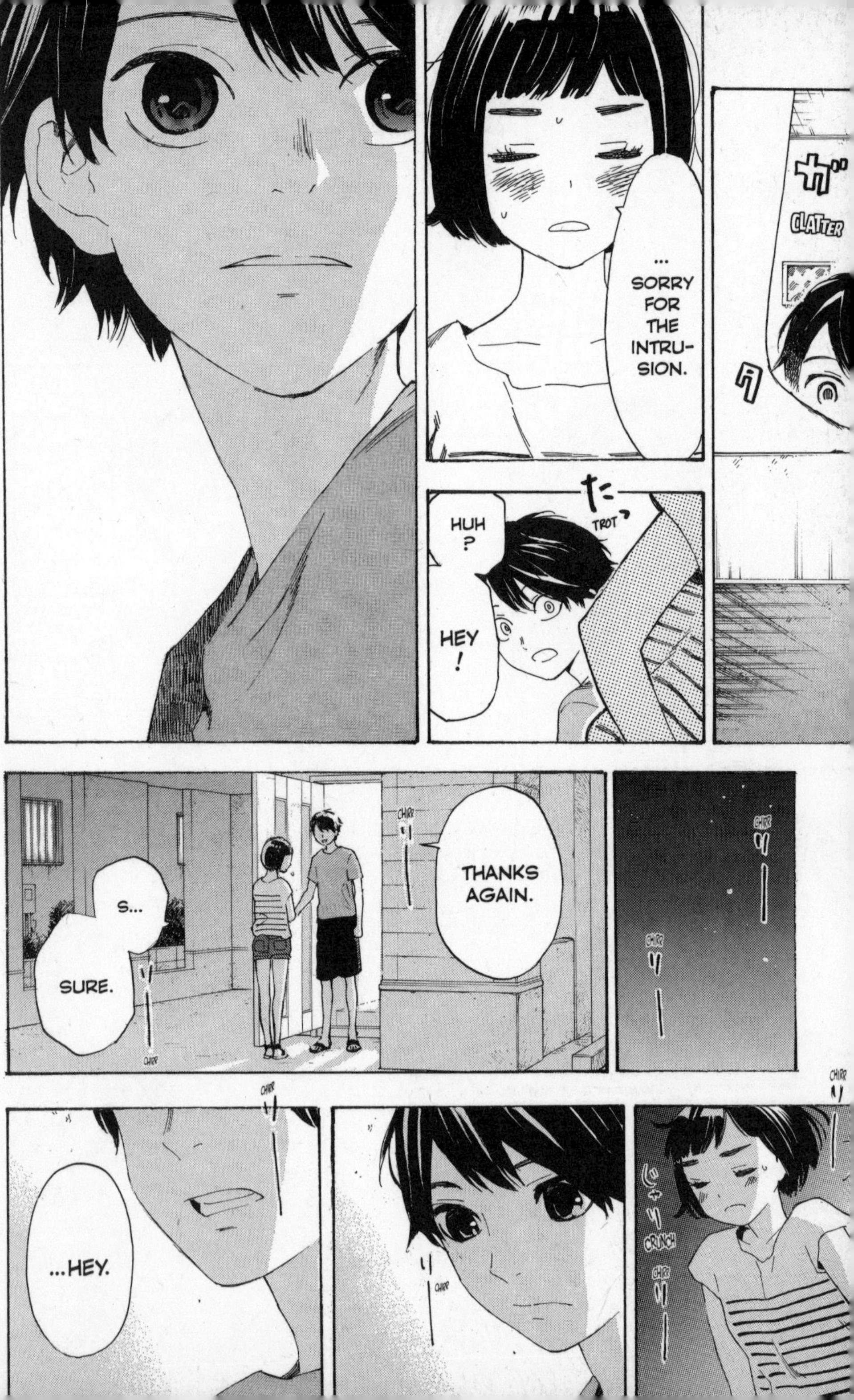
ガ
CLATTER
...SORRY FOR THE INTRUSION.
た
TROT
HUH?
HEY!
CHIRR
CHIRR
THANKS AGAIN.
CHIRR
S...
SURE.
CHIRR
CHIRR
CRUNCH
CHIRR
CHIRR
CHIRR
...HEY.

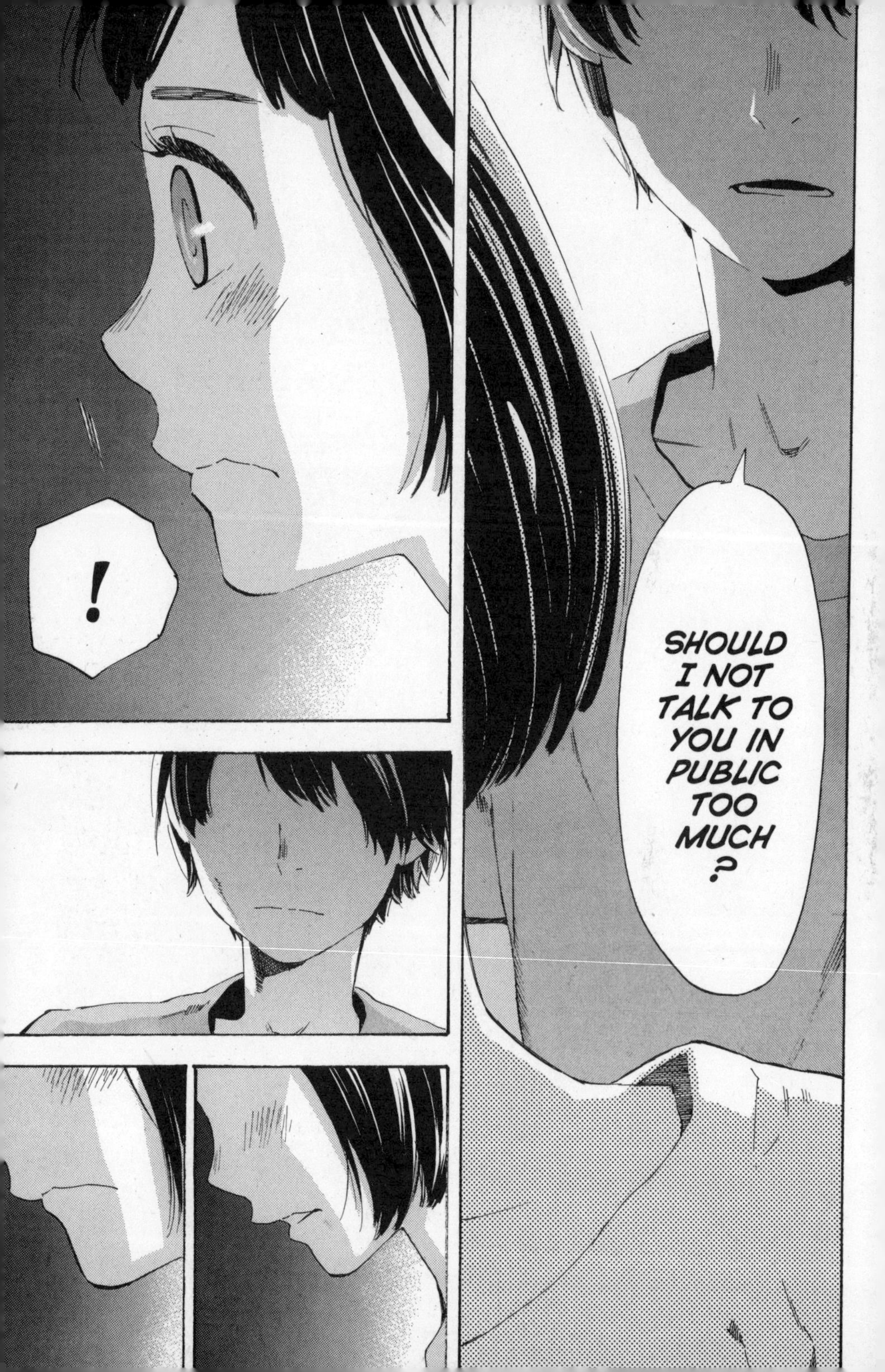
SHOULD I NOT TALK TO YOU IN PUBLIC TOO MUCH?
!

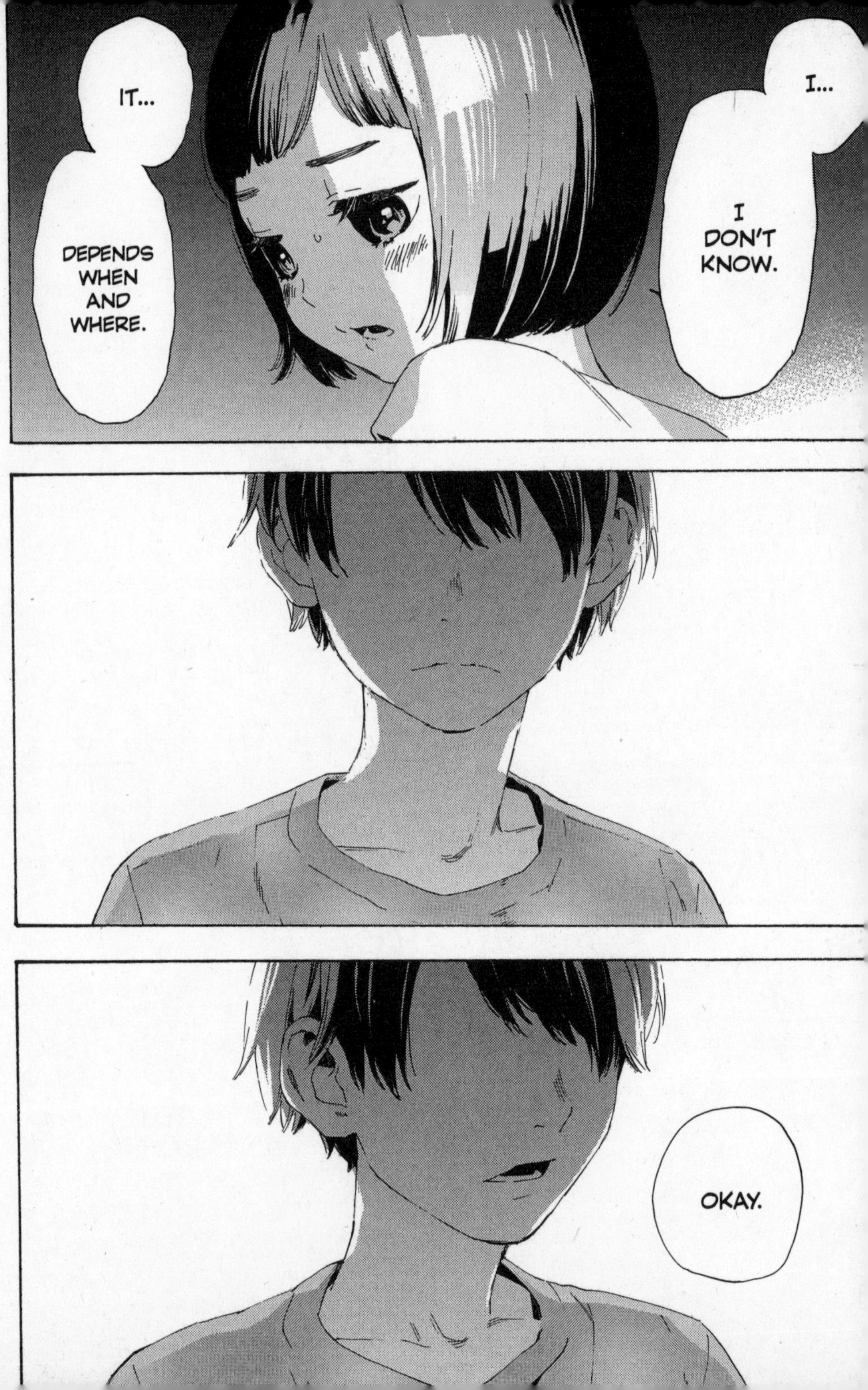
I...
I DON'T KNOW.
IT...
DEPENDS WHEN AND WHERE.
OKAY.

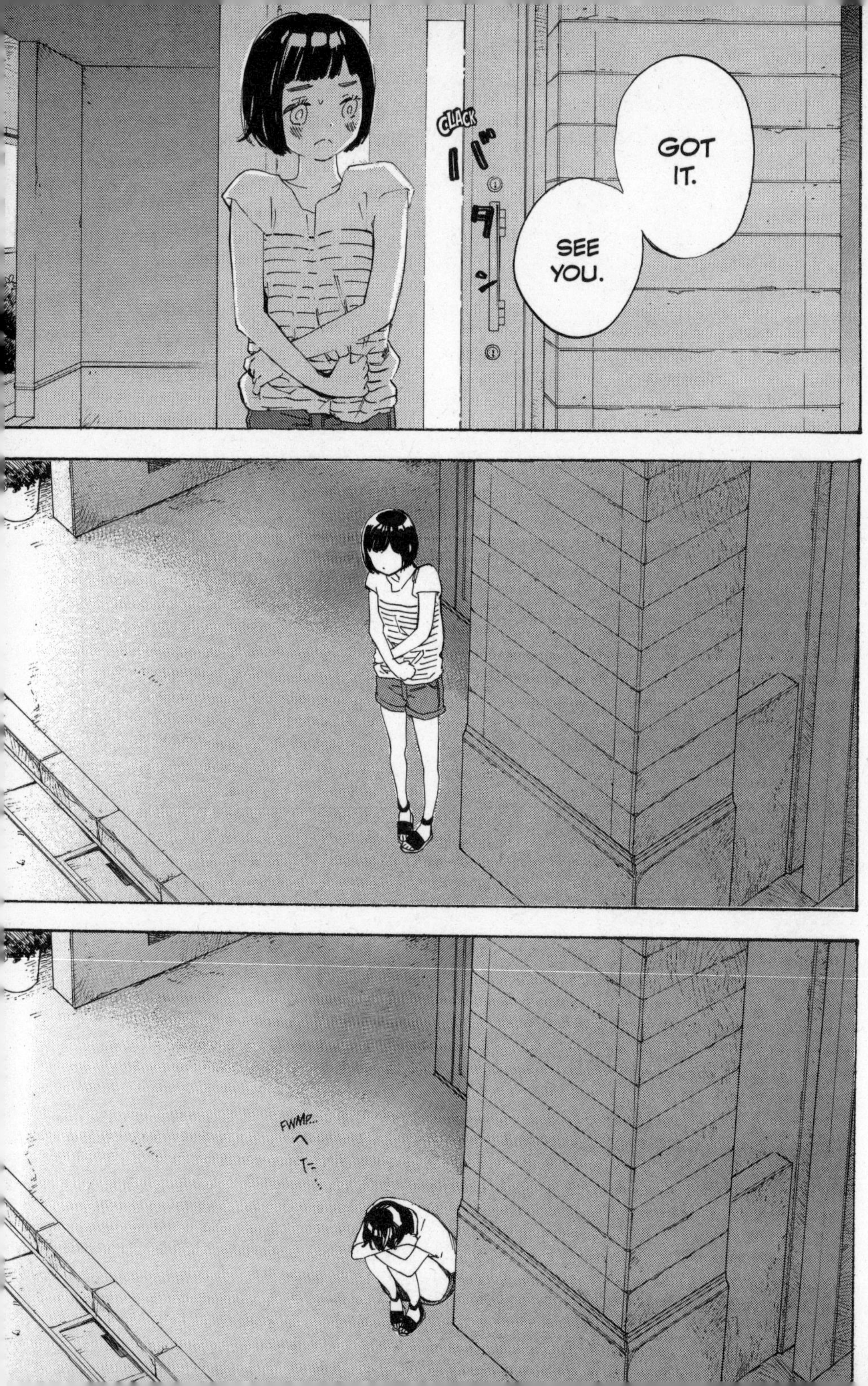
GOT IT.
SEE YOU.
CLACK
FWMP...

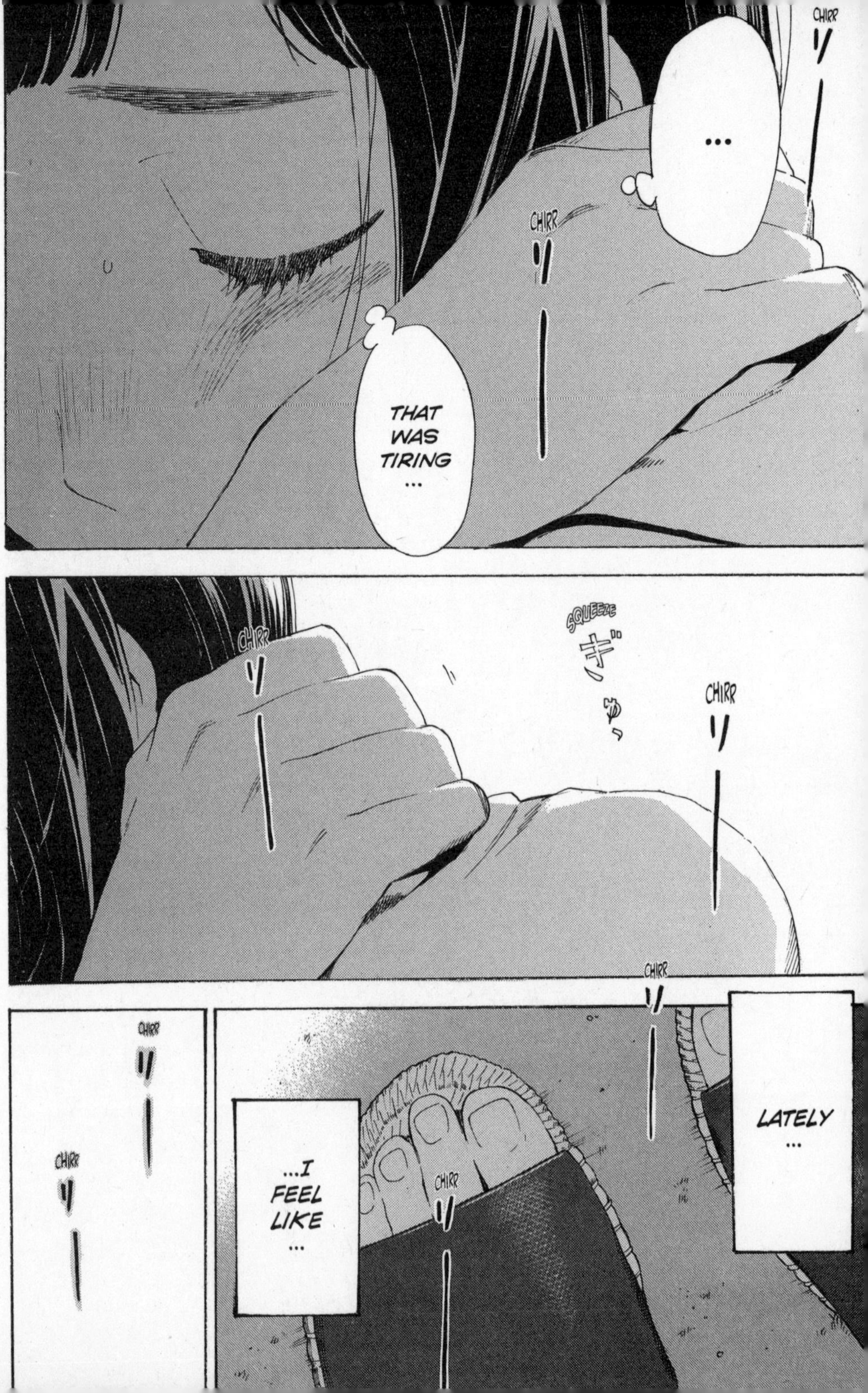
CHIRR
リー
...
CHIRR
リー
THAT WAS TIRING ...
CHIRR
リー
SQUEEZE
ぎゅっ
CHIRR
リー
CHIRR
リー
LATELY ...
CHIRR
リー
...I FEEL LIKE ...
CHIRR
リー
CHIRR
リー

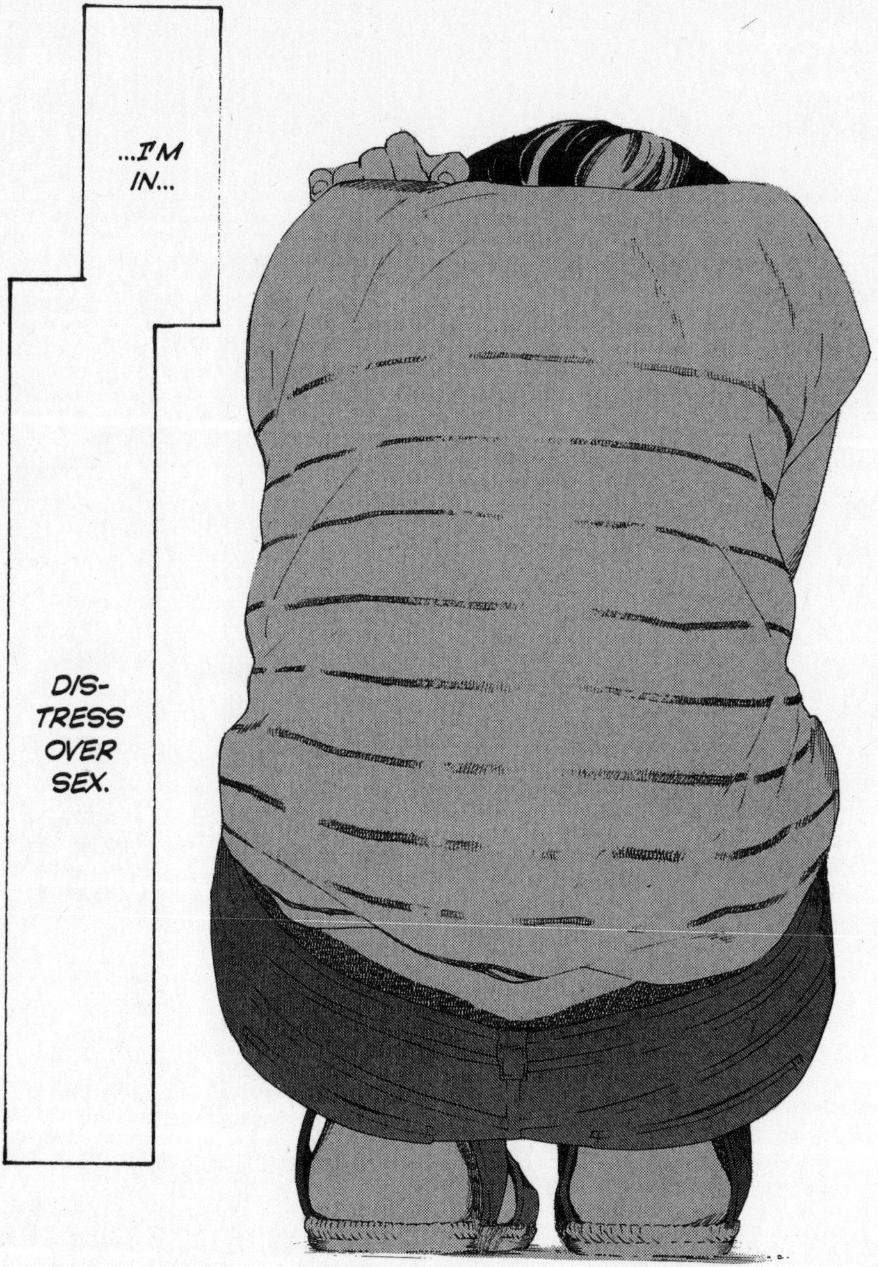
...I'M IN...
DIS-
TRESS
OVER
SEX.

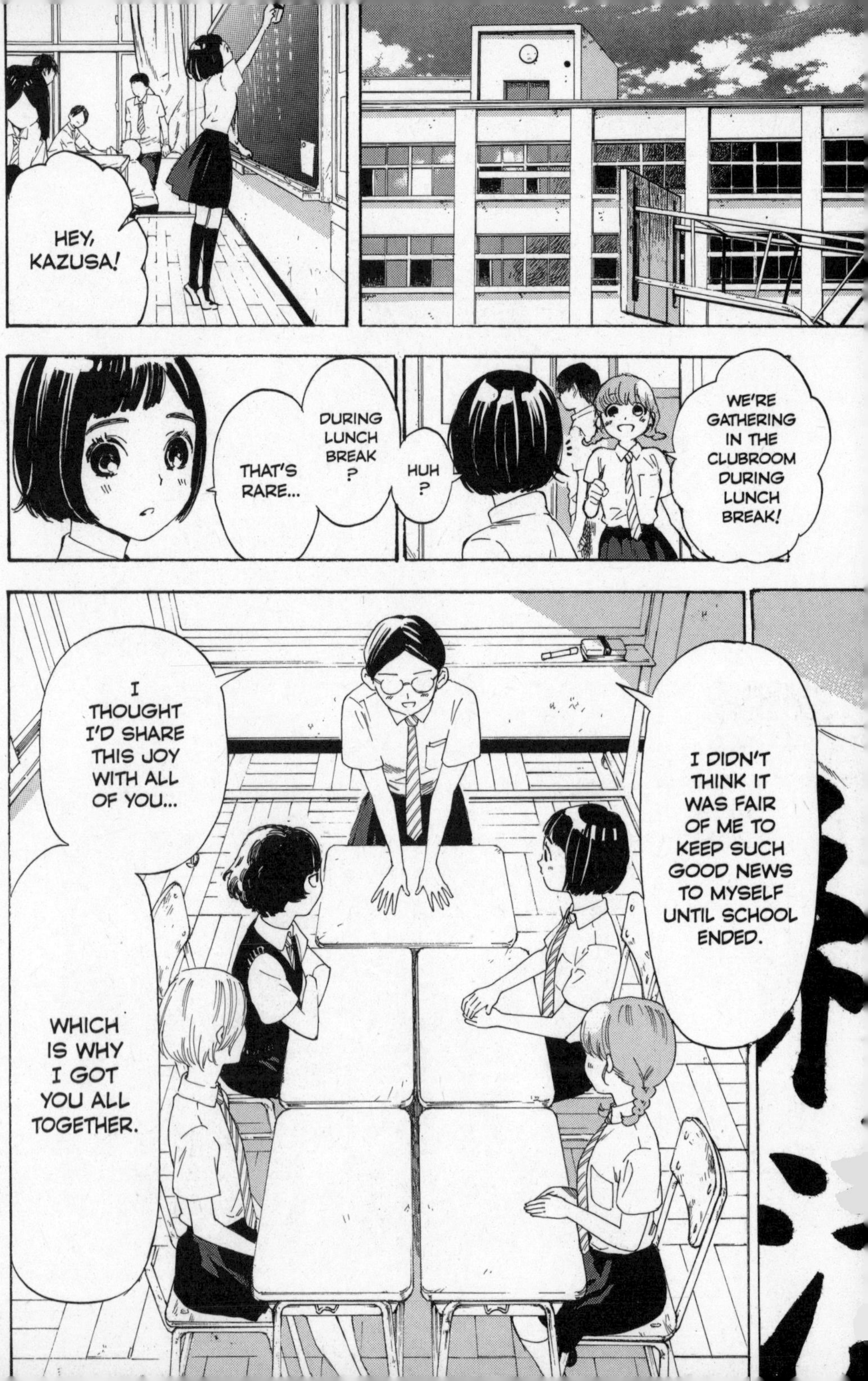
HEY, KAZUSA!
WE'RE GATHERING IN THE CLUBROOM DURING LUNCH BREAK!
HUH?
DURING LUNCH BREAK?
THAT'S RARE...
I DIDN'T THINK IT WAS FAIR OF ME TO KEEP SUCH GOOD NEWS TO MYSELF UNTIL SCHOOL ENDED.
I THOUGHT I'D SHARE THIS JOY WITH ALL OF YOU...
WHICH IS WHY I GOT YOU ALL TOGETHER.

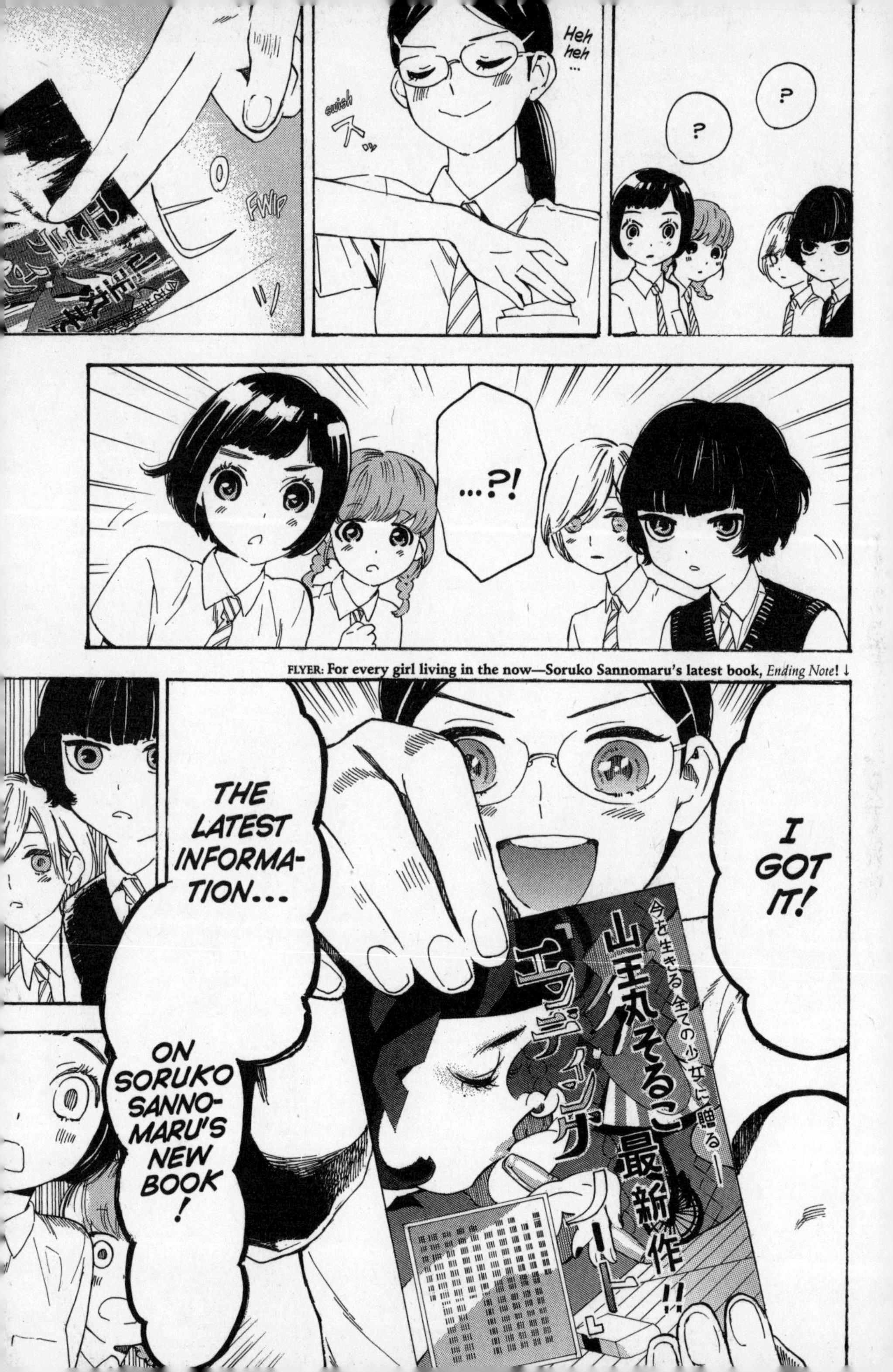
?
?
Heh heh ...
swish
ス
FWIP
...?!
FLYER: For every girl living in the now—Soruko Sannomaru's latest book, *Ending Note*! ↓
I GOT IT!
THE LATEST INFORMATION...
ON SORUKO SANNOMARU'S NEW BOOK!
今を生きる全ての少女に贈るー
山王丸そるこ最新作!!

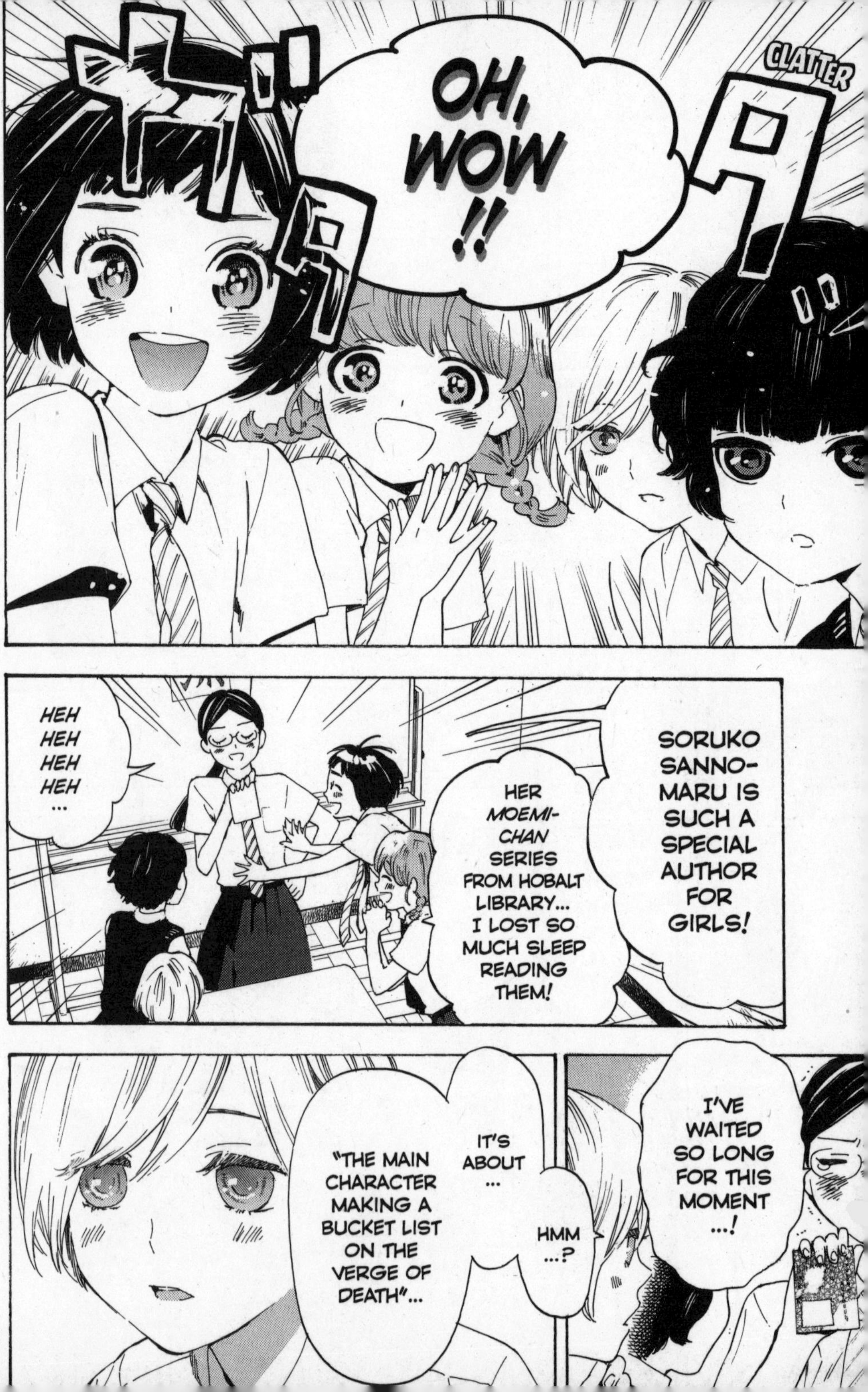
CLATTER
OH, WOW!!
SORUKO SANNO-MARU IS SUCH A SPECIAL AUTHOR FOR GIRLS!
HER *MOEMI-CHAN* SERIES FROM HOBALT LIBRARY... I LOST SO MUCH SLEEP READING THEM!
HEH HEH HEH HEH...
I'VE WAITED SO LONG FOR THIS MOMENT...!
IT'S ABOUT...
HMM...?
"THE MAIN CHARACTER MAKING A BUCKET LIST ON THE VERGE OF DEATH"...

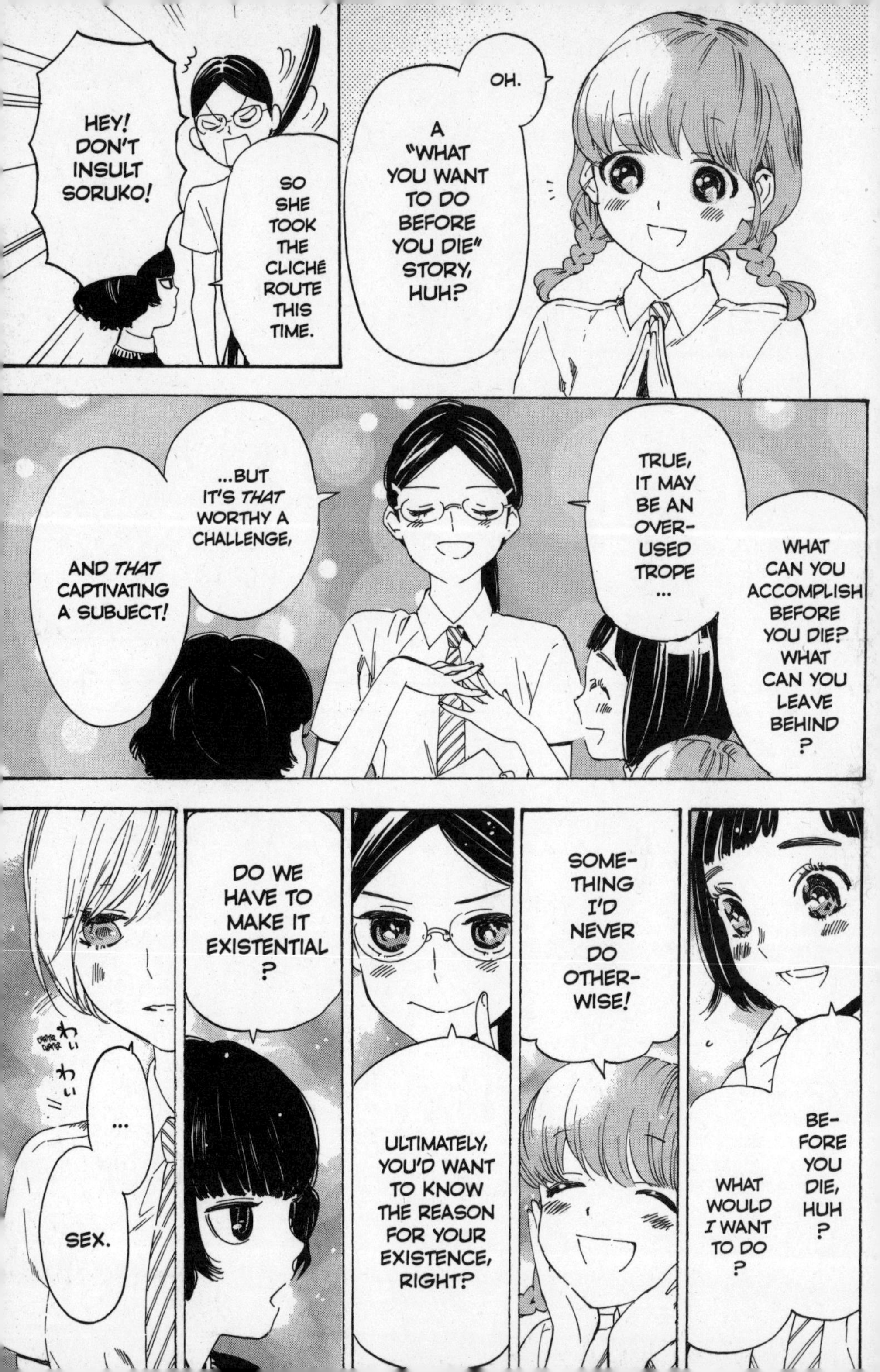
OH.
A "WHAT YOU WANT TO DO BEFORE YOU DIE" STORY, HUH?
SO SHE TOOK THE CLICHÉ ROUTE THIS TIME.
HEY! DON'T INSULT SORUKO!
TRUE, IT MAY BE AN OVER-USED TROPE...
WHAT CAN YOU ACCOMPLISH BEFORE YOU DIE? WHAT CAN YOU LEAVE BEHIND?
...BUT IT'S *THAT* WORTHY A CHALLENGE,
AND *THAT* CAPTIVATING A SUBJECT!
BE-FORE YOU DIE, HUH?
WHAT WOULD *I* WANT TO DO?
SOME-THING I'D NEVER DO OTHER-WISE!
ULTIMATELY, YOU'D WANT TO KNOW THE REASON FOR YOUR EXISTENCE, RIGHT?
DO WE HAVE TO MAKE IT EXISTENTIAL?
わい わい
CHATTER CHATTER
...
SEX.

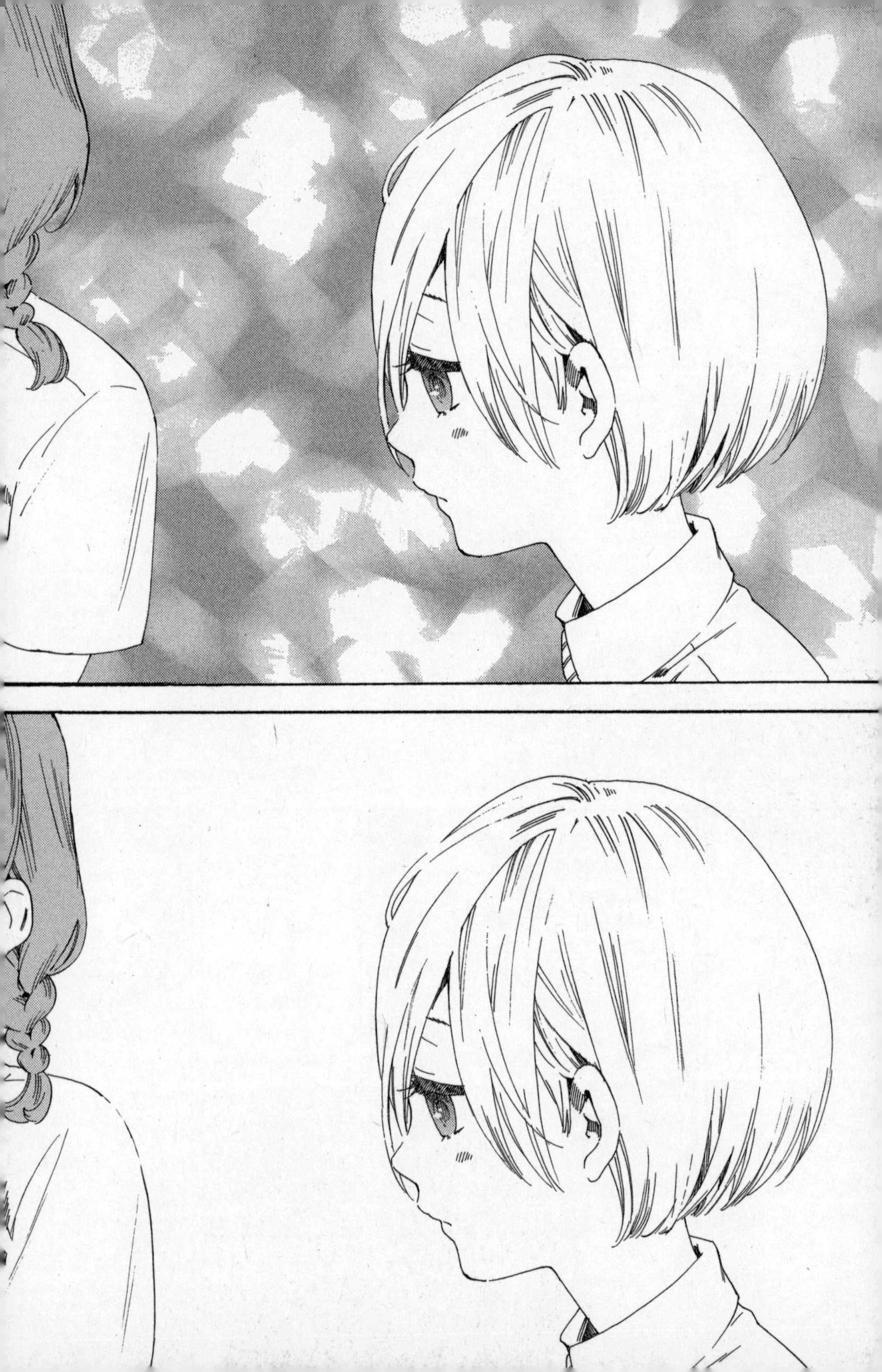

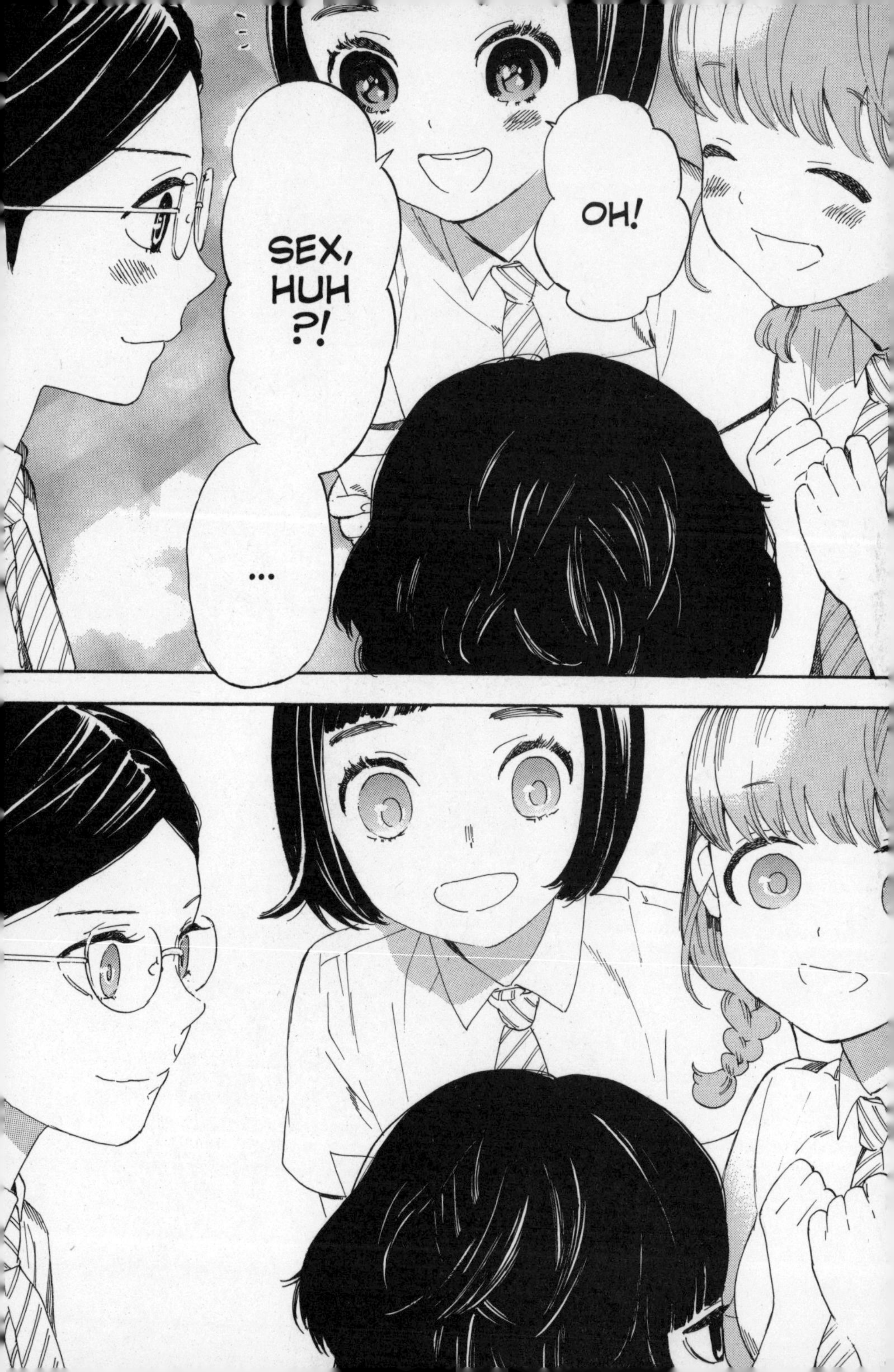
OH!
SEX, HUH?!
...

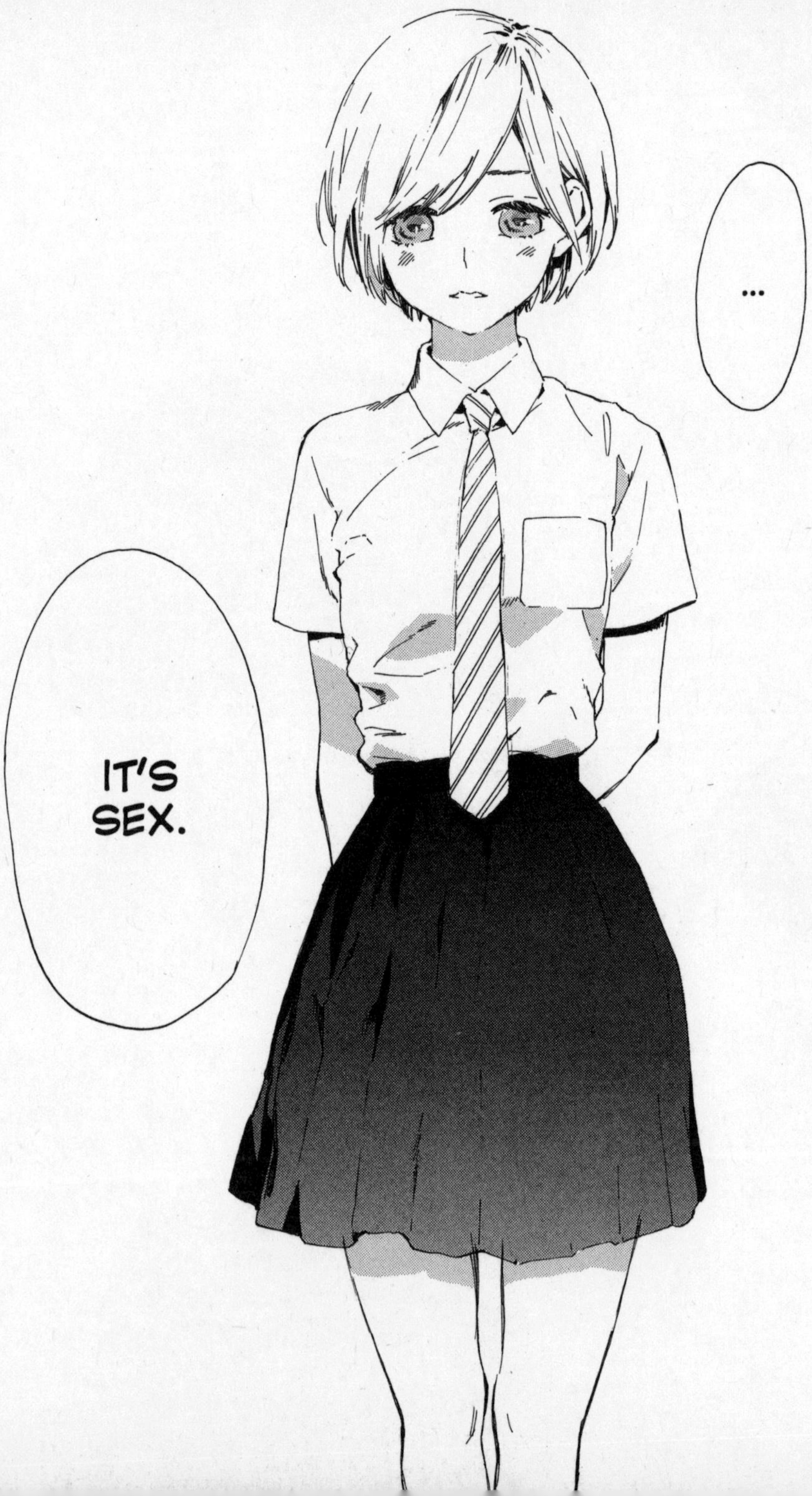
...
IT'S SEX.

Meeting 2

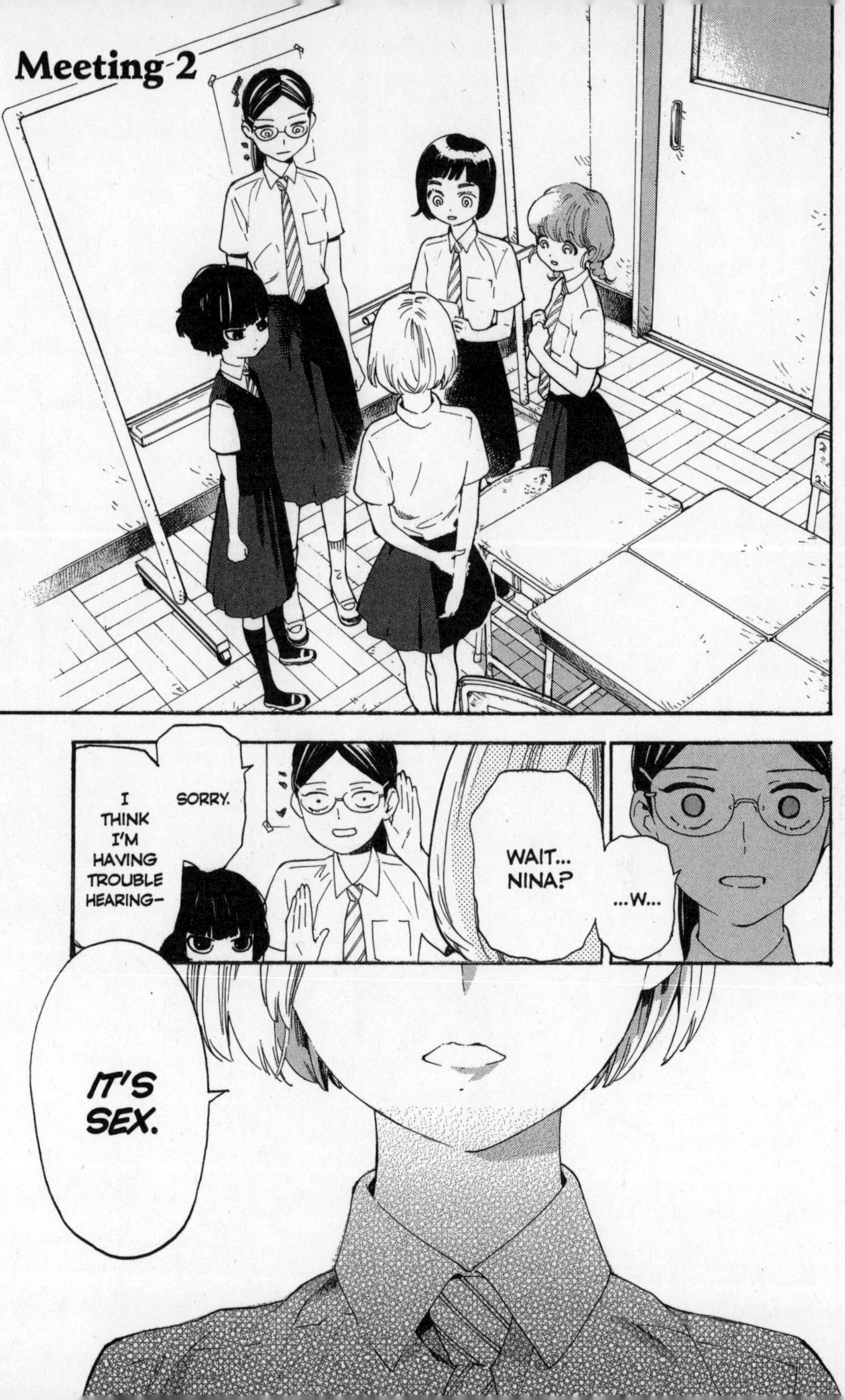

...W...
WAIT... NINA?
SORRY.
I THINK I'M HAVING TROUBLE HEARING–
IT'S SEX.

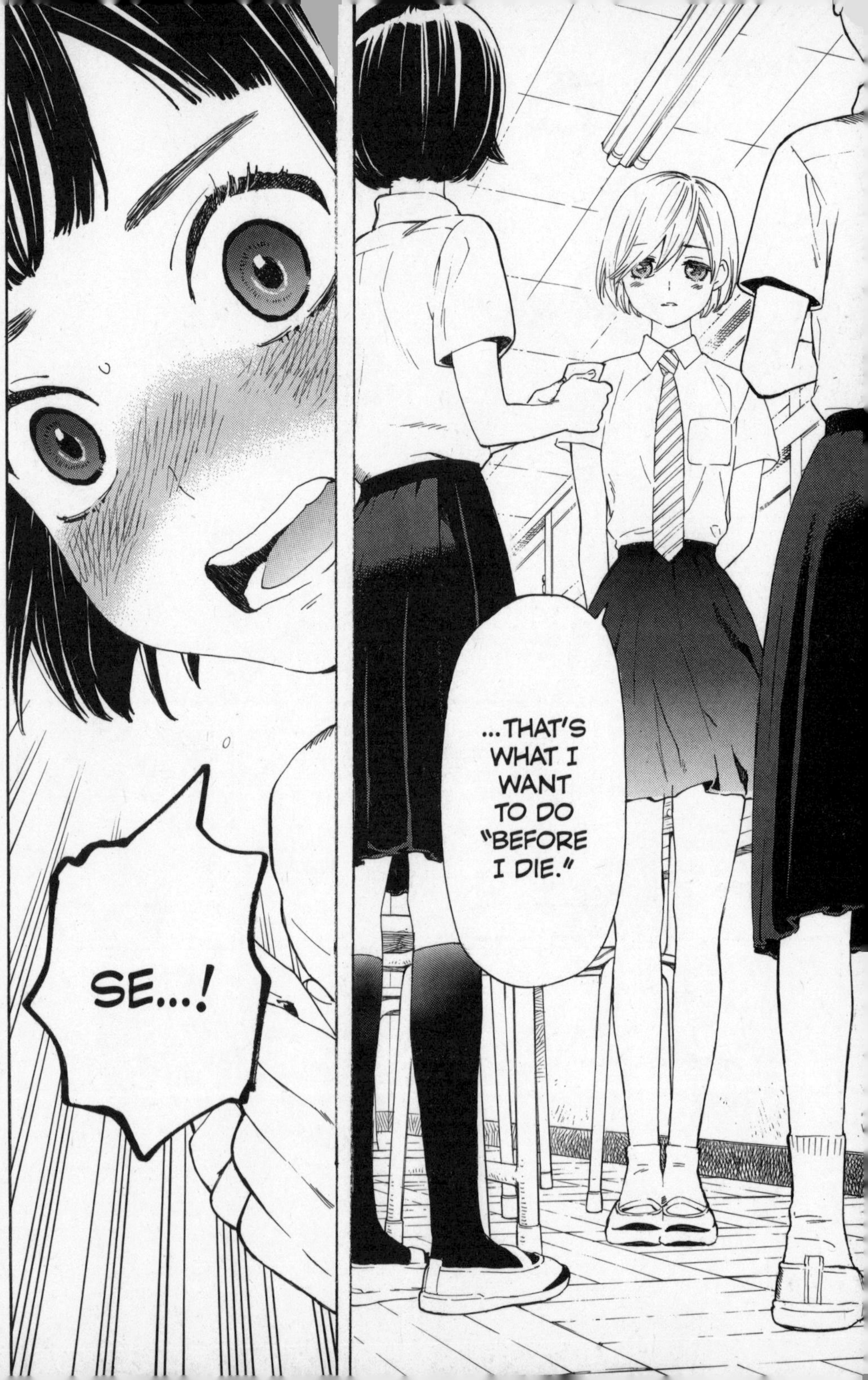
...THAT'S WHAT I WANT TO DO "BEFORE I DIE."
SE...!

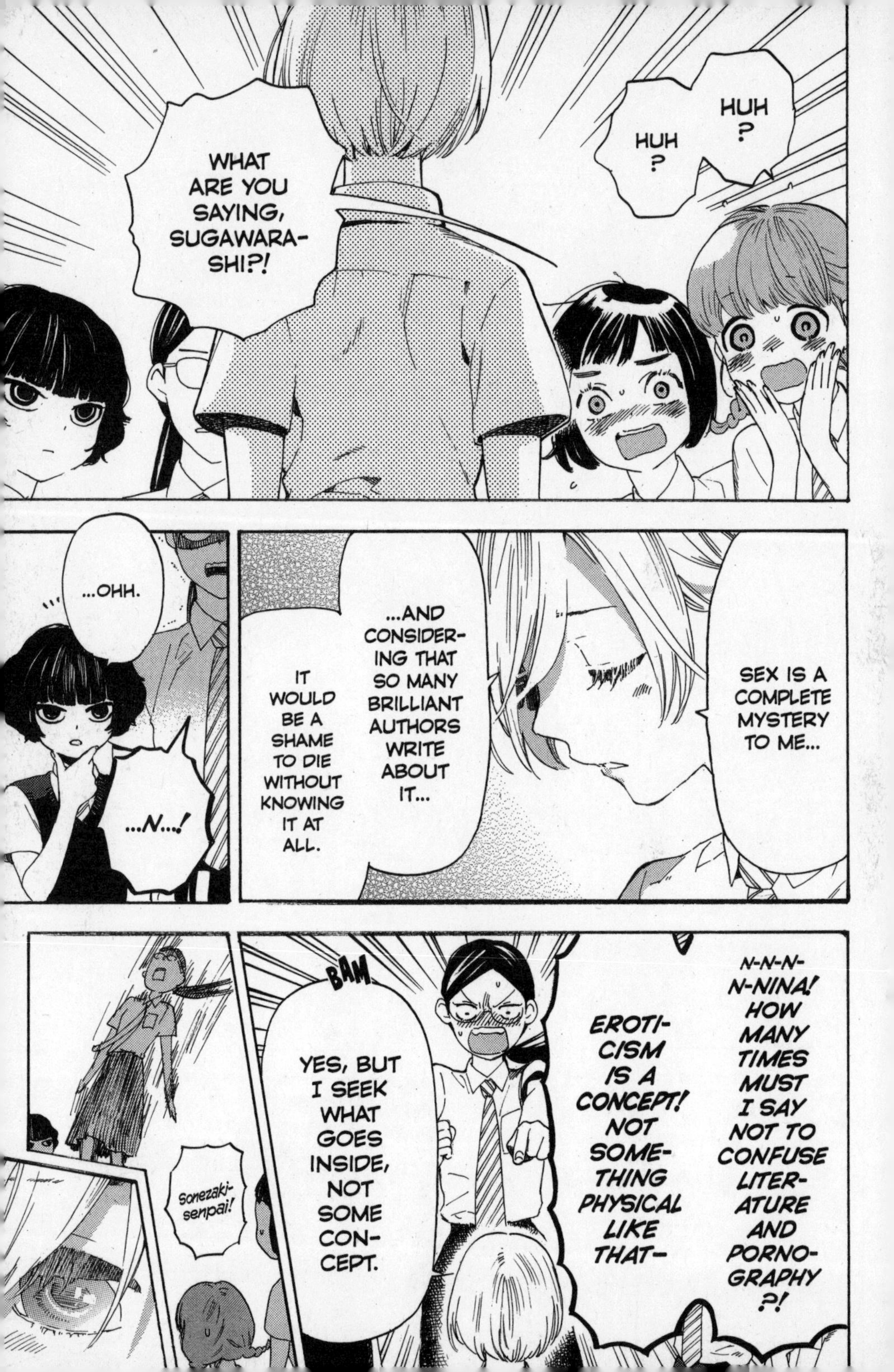
HUH?
HUH?
WHAT ARE YOU SAYING, SUGAWARA-SHI?!
SEX IS A COMPLETE MYSTERY TO ME...
...AND CONSIDERING THAT SO MANY BRILLIANT AUTHORS WRITE ABOUT IT...
IT WOULD BE A SHAME TO DIE WITHOUT KNOWING IT AT ALL.
...OHH.
...N...!
N-N-N-N-NINA! HOW MANY TIMES MUST I SAY NOT TO CONFUSE LITERATURE AND PORNOGRAPHY?!
EROTICISM IS A CONCEPT! NOT SOMETHING PHYSICAL LIKE THAT-
BAM
YES, BUT I SEEK WHAT GOES INSIDE, NOT SOME CONCEPT.
Sonezaki-senpai!

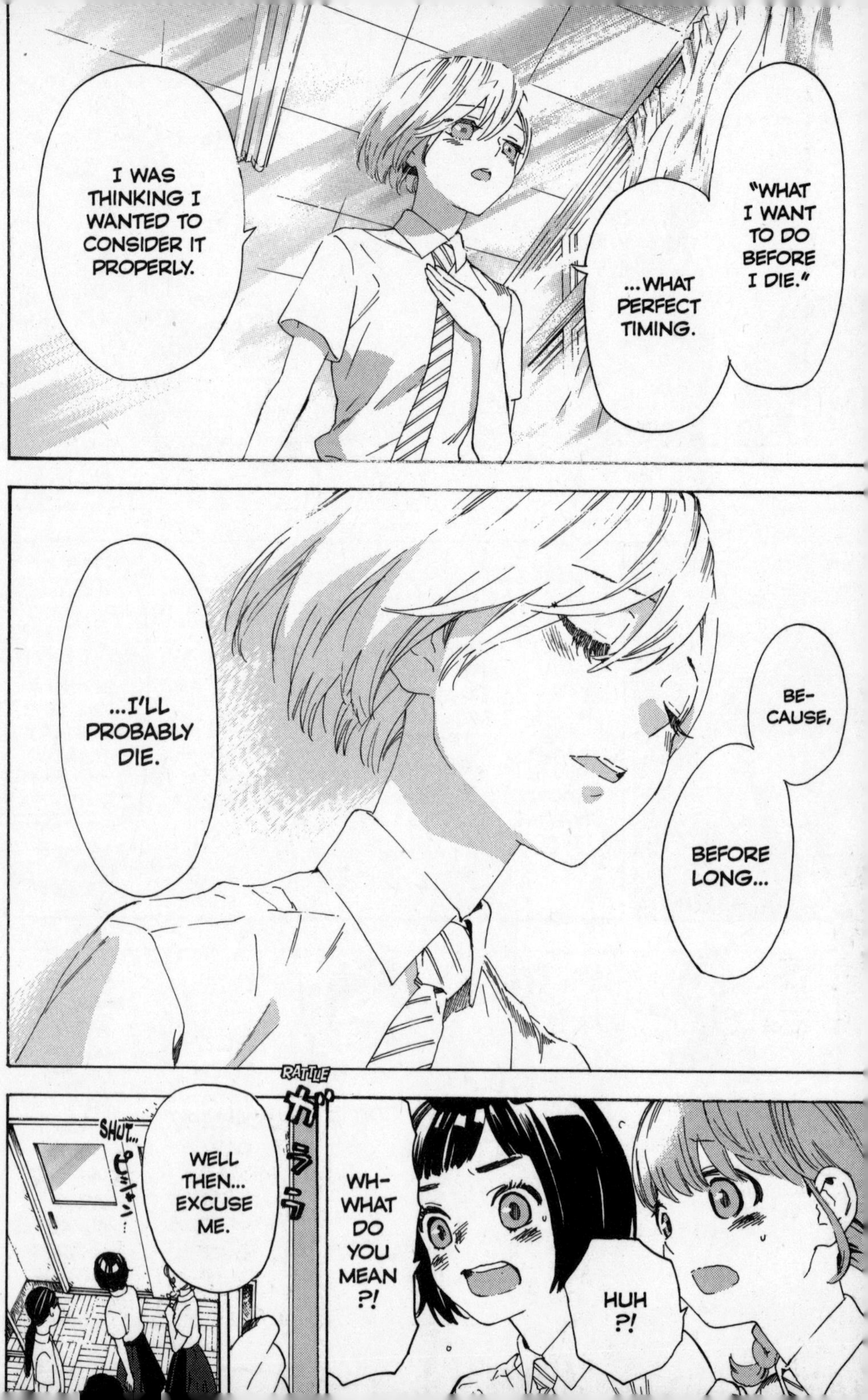
"WHAT I WANT TO DO BEFORE I DIE."
...WHAT PERFECT TIMING.
I WAS THINKING I WANTED TO CONSIDER IT PROPERLY.
BE-CAUSE,
BEFORE LONG...
...I'LL PROBABLY DIE.
WH-WHAT DO YOU MEAN?!
HUH?!
RATTLE
WELL THEN... EXCUSE ME.
SHUT...

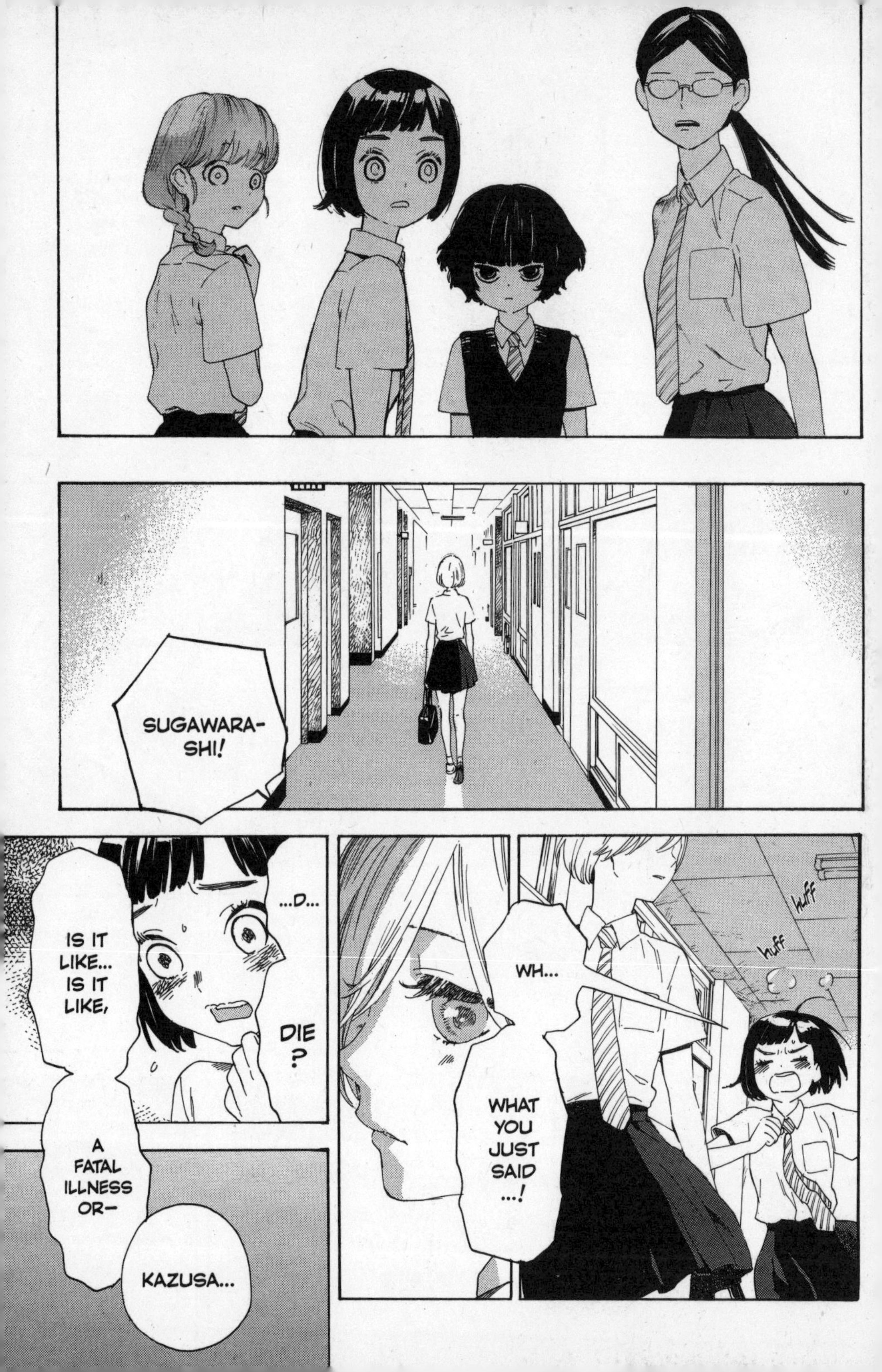
SUGAWARA-SHI!
huff
huff
WH...
WHAT YOU JUST SAID ...!
...D...
IS IT LIKE... IS IT LIKE,
DIE?
A FATAL ILLNESS OR—
KAZUSA...

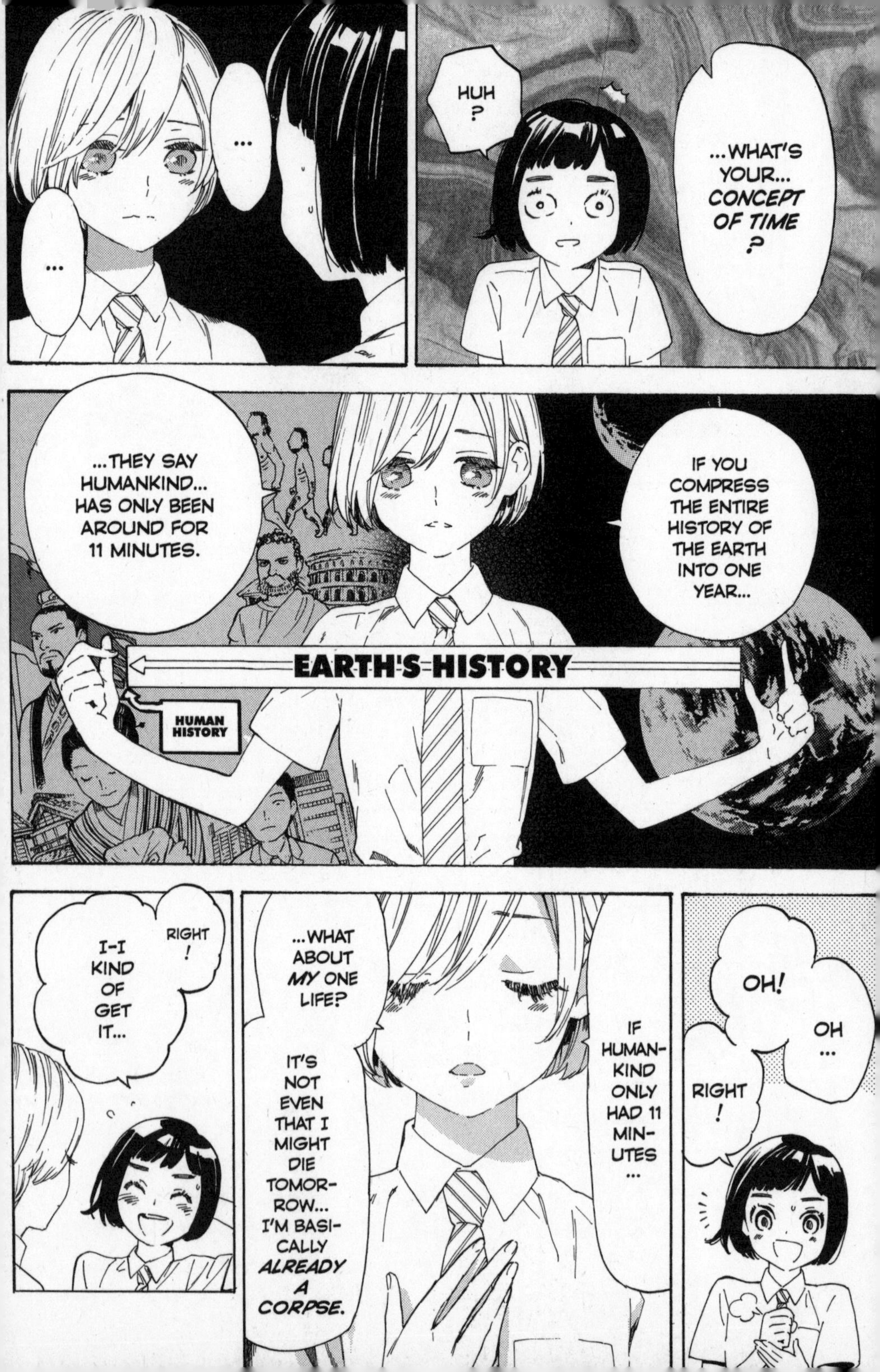
...WHAT'S YOUR... CONCEPT OF TIME?
HUH?
...
...
IF YOU COMPRESS THE ENTIRE HISTORY OF THE EARTH INTO ONE YEAR...
...THEY SAY HUMANKIND... HAS ONLY BEEN AROUND FOR 11 MINUTES.
EARTH'S HISTORY
HUMAN HISTORY
OH!
OH...
RIGHT!
IF HUMAN-KIND ONLY HAD 11 MIN-UTES...
...WHAT ABOUT MY ONE LIFE?
IT'S NOT EVEN THAT I MIGHT DIE TOMOR-ROW... I'M BASI-CALLY ALREADY A CORPSE.
RIGHT!
I-I KIND OF GET IT...

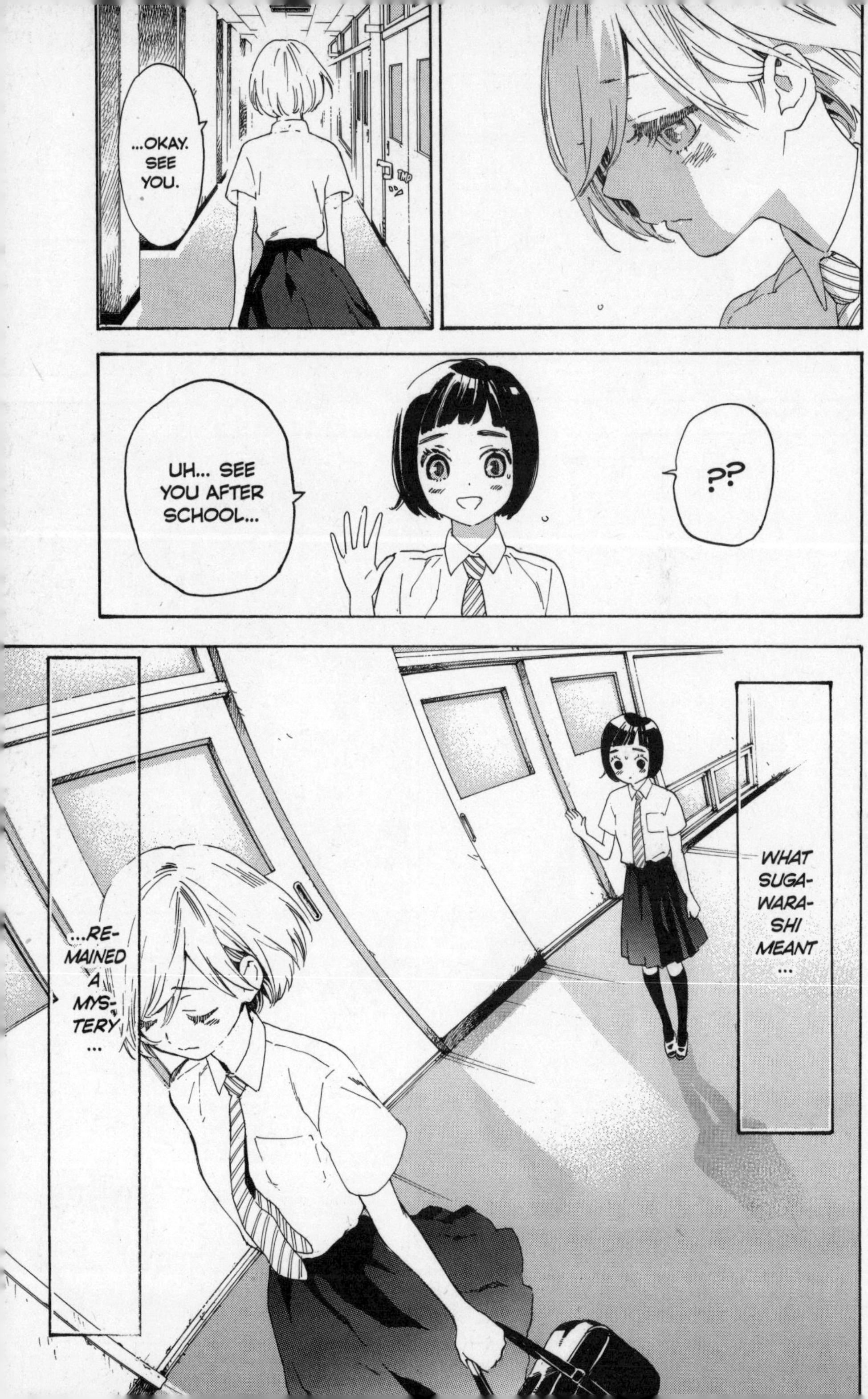
...OKAY. SEE YOU.
TMP
??
UH... SEE YOU AFTER SCHOOL...
WHAT SUGA-WARA-SHI MEANT ...
...RE-MAINED A MYS-TERY ...

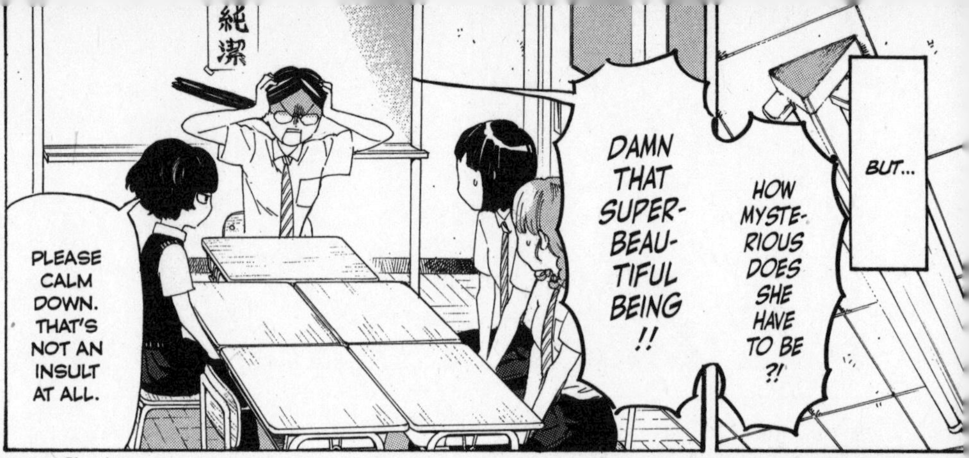
BUT...
DAMN THAT SUPER-BEAUTIFUL BEING!!
HOW MYSTERIOUS DOES SHE HAVE TO BE?!
PLEASE CALM DOWN. THAT'S NOT AN INSULT AT ALL.

POSTER: Chastity

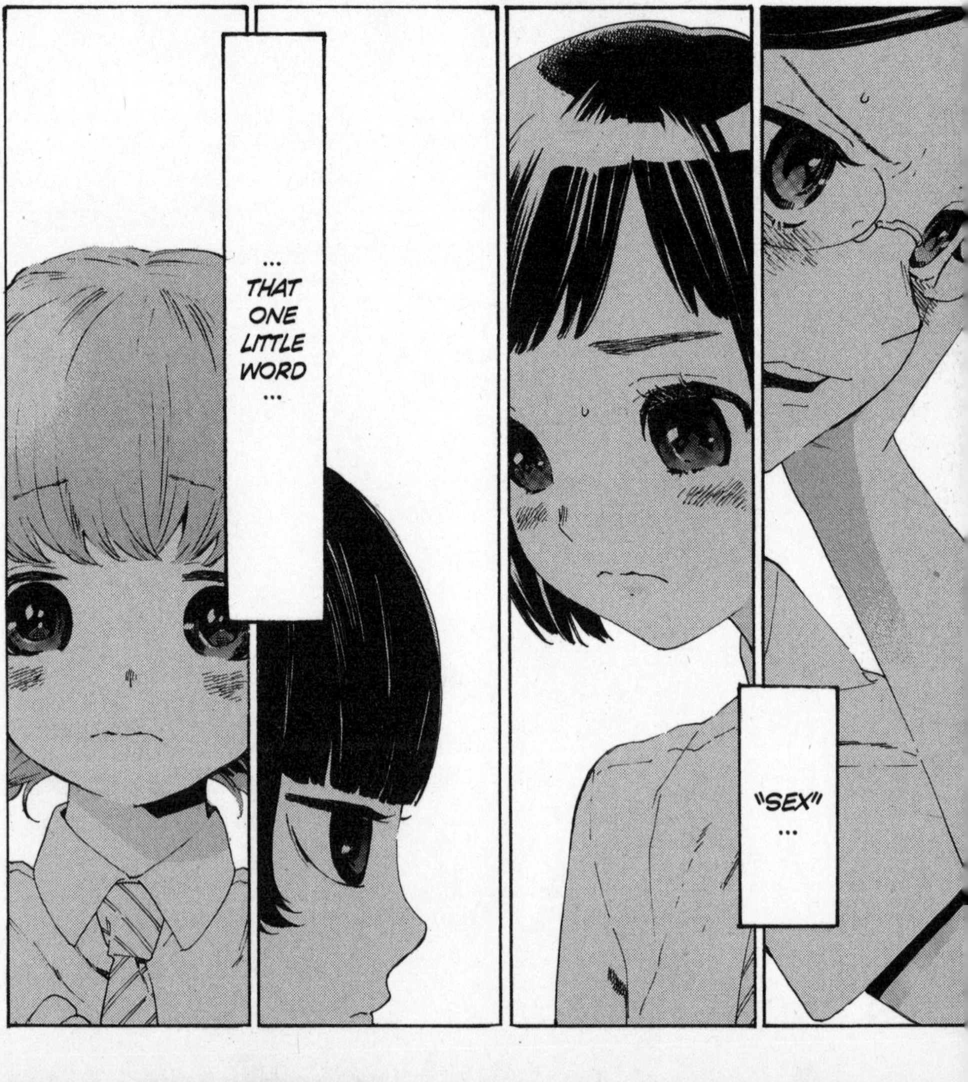
"SEX"...
... THAT ONE LITTLE WORD ...

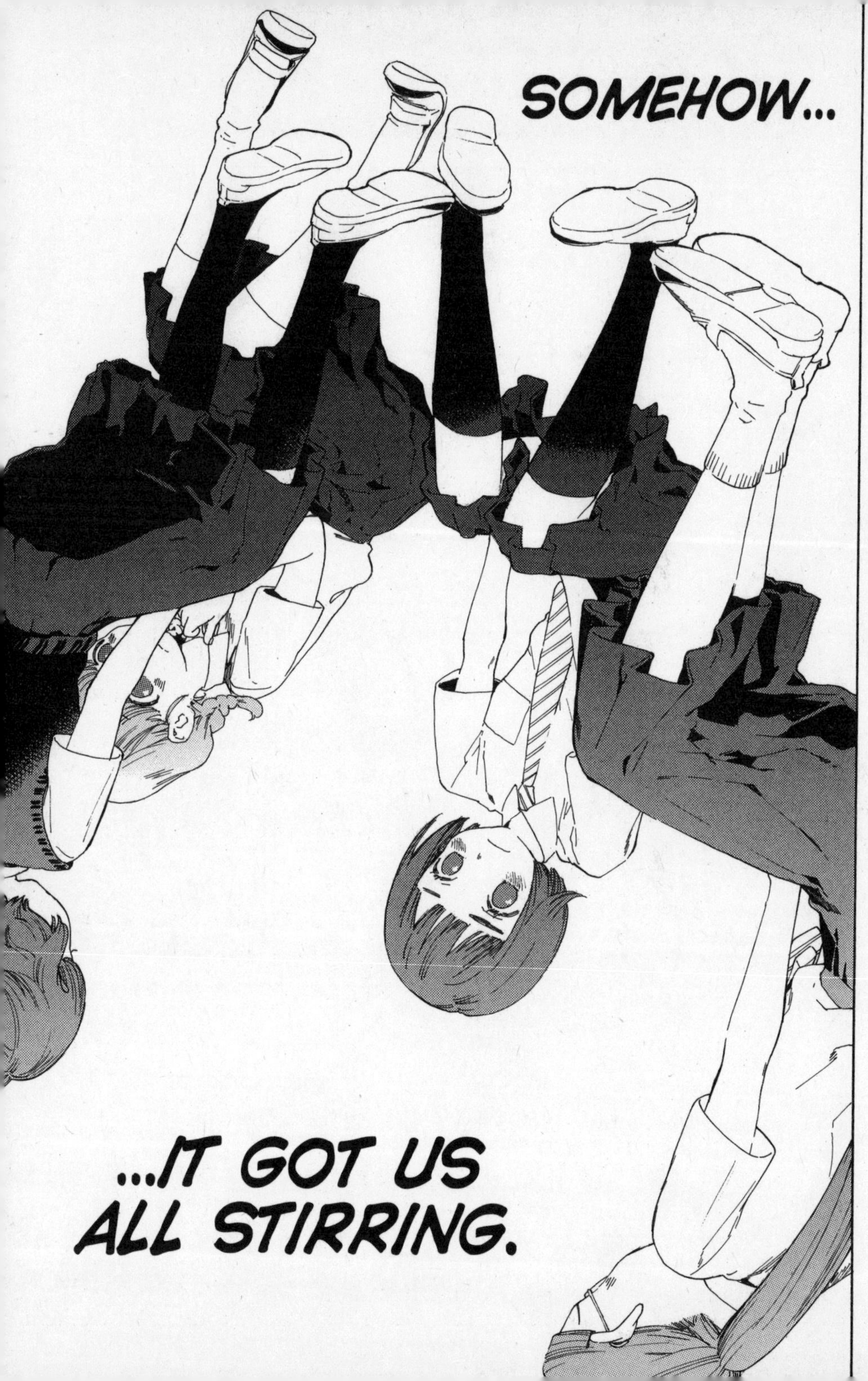
SOMEHOW...
...IT GOT US ALL STIRRING.

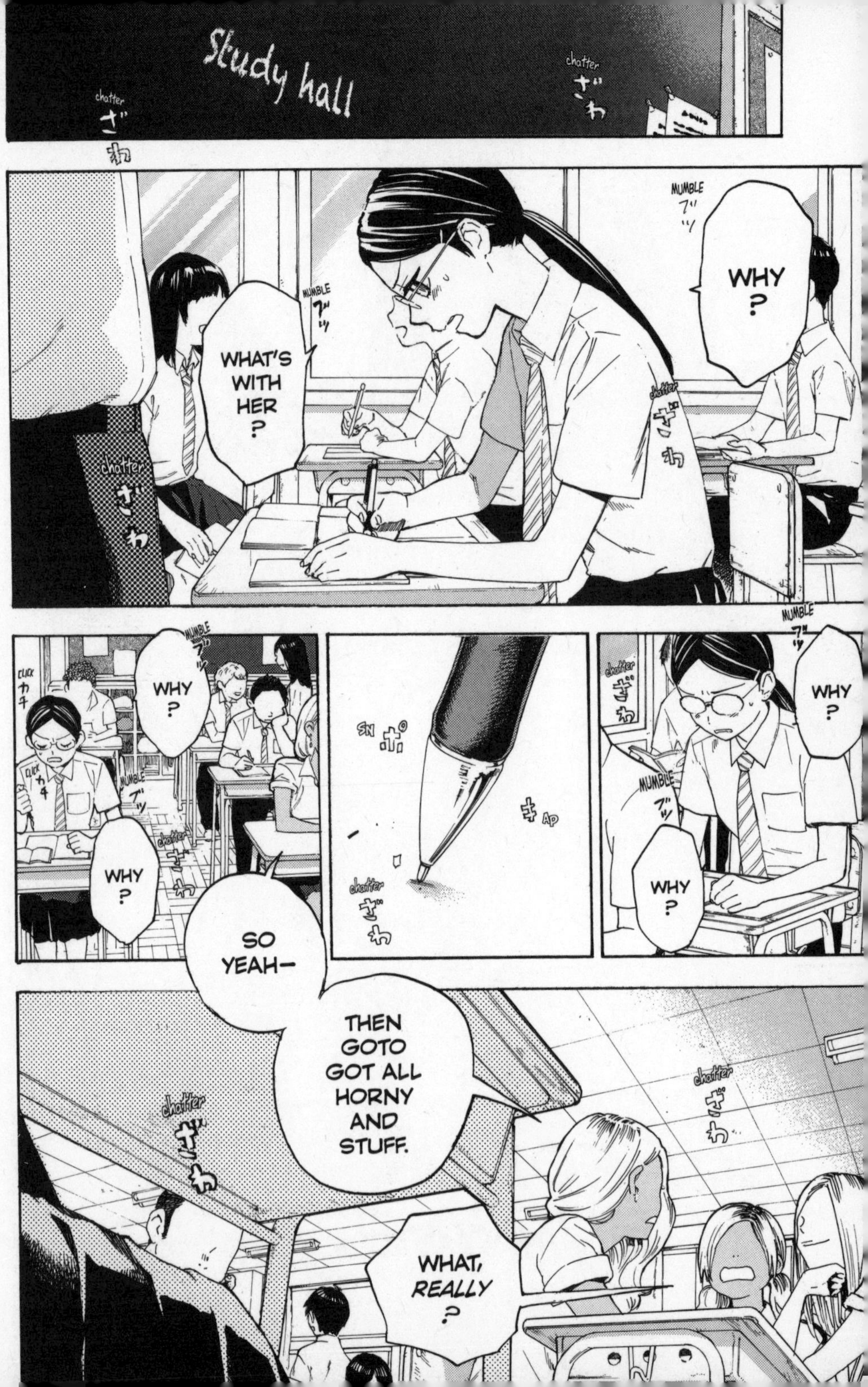
Study hall
chatter ざわ
chatter ざわ
MUMBLE ブツ
WHY?
MUMBLE ブツ
WHAT'S WITH HER?
chatter ざわ
chatter ざわ
MUMBLE ブツ
chatter ざわ
WHY?
MUMBLE ブツ
WHY?
SN ポ
キ AP
chatter ざわ
CLICK カチ
MUMBLE ブツ
WHY?
CLICK カチ
MUMBLE ブツ
WHY?
chatter ざわ
SO YEAH—
THEN GOTO GOT ALL HORNY AND STUFF.
chatter ざわ
chatter ざわ
WHAT, *REALLY*?

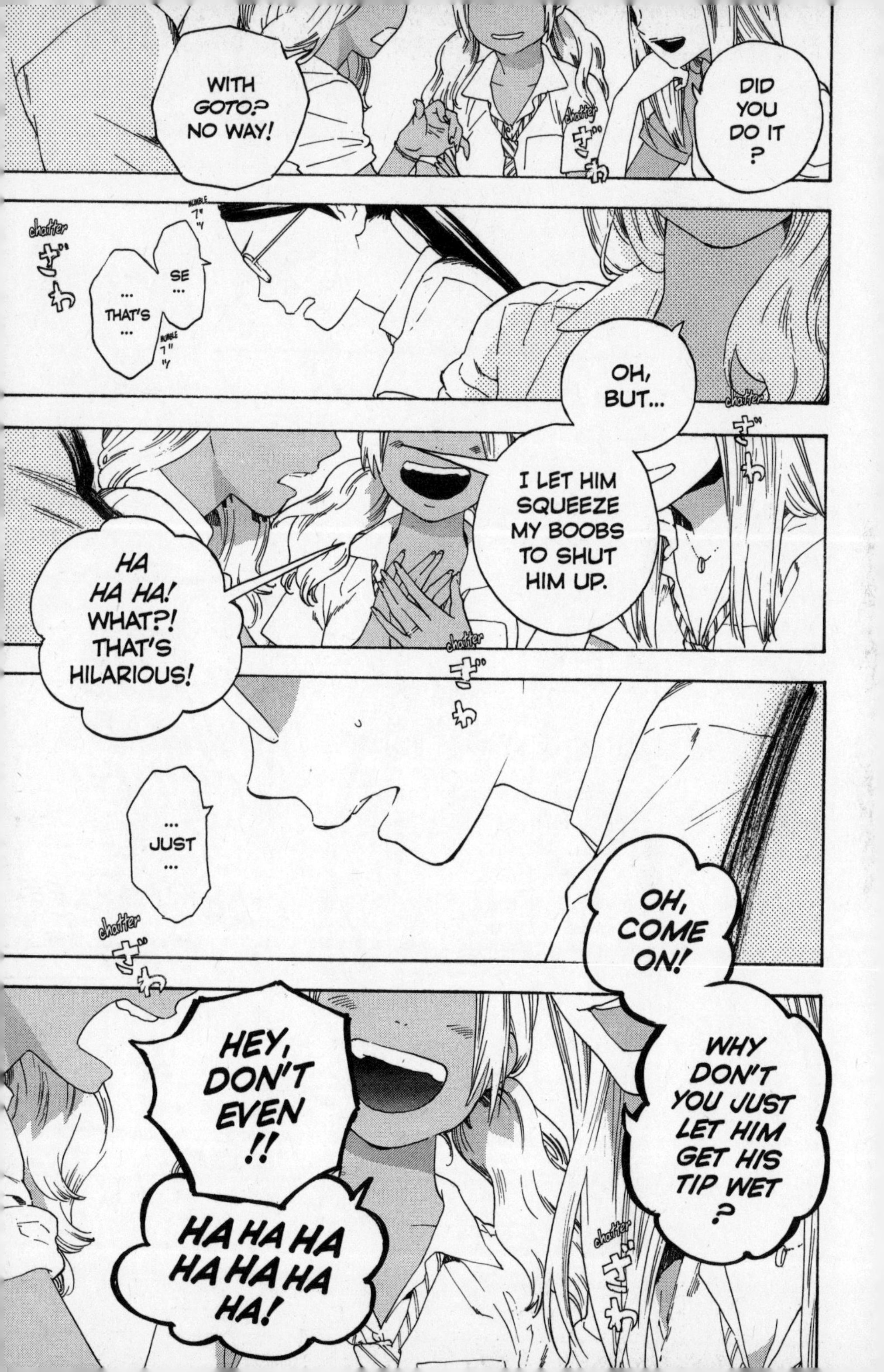
DID YOU DO IT?
chatter
WITH GOTO? NO WAY!
chatter
mumble
SE... ...THAT'S...
mumble
OH, BUT...
I LET HIM SQUEEZE MY BOOBS TO SHUT HIM UP.
chatter
HA HA HA! WHAT?! THAT'S HILARIOUS!
chatter
OH, COME ON!
...JUST...
chatter
WHY DON'T YOU JUST LET HIM GET HIS TIP WET?
chatter
HEY, DON'T EVEN!!
HA HA HA HA HA HA HA HA HA!

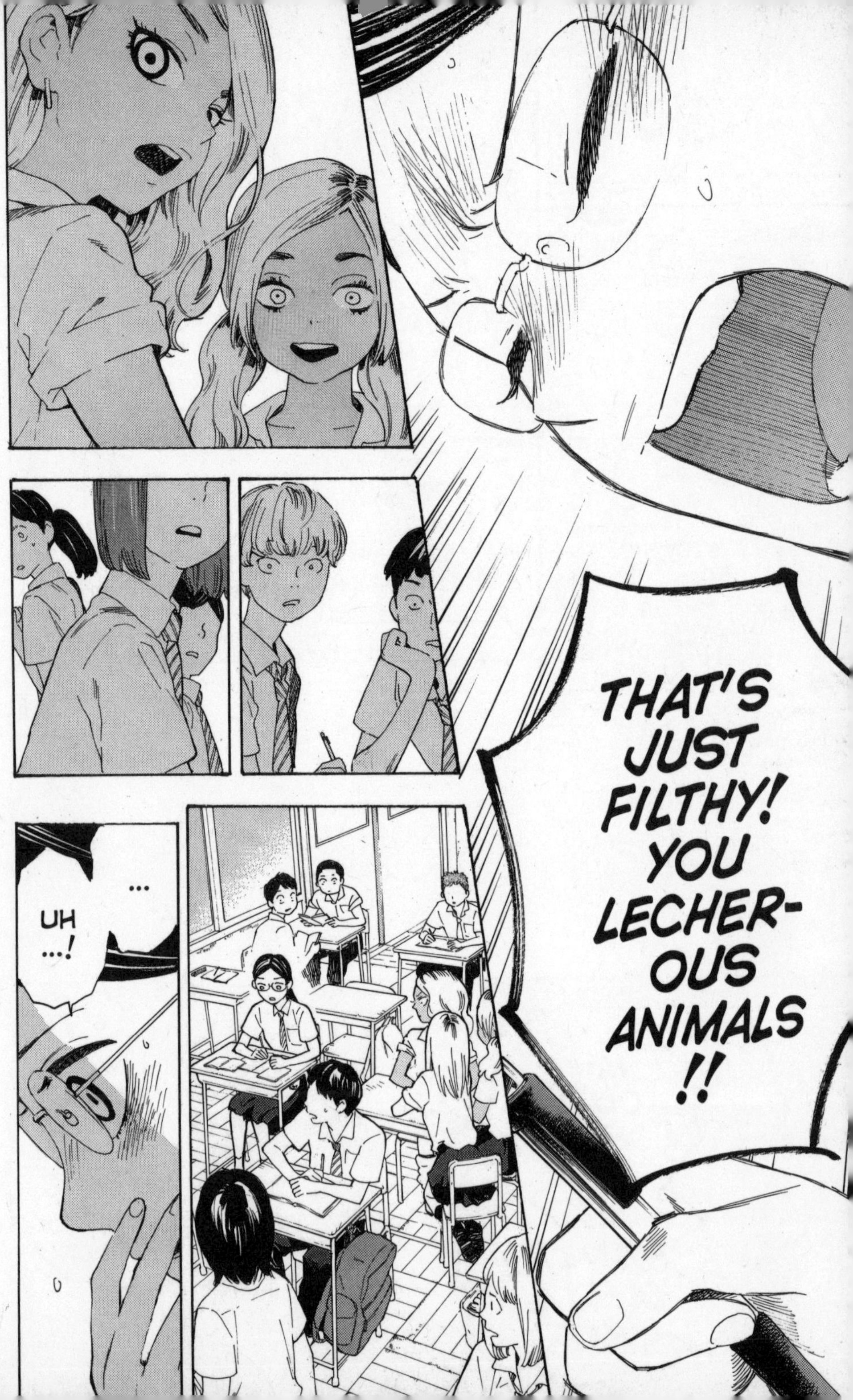
THAT'S JUST FILTHY! YOU LECHER-OUS ANIMALS!!
... UH ...!

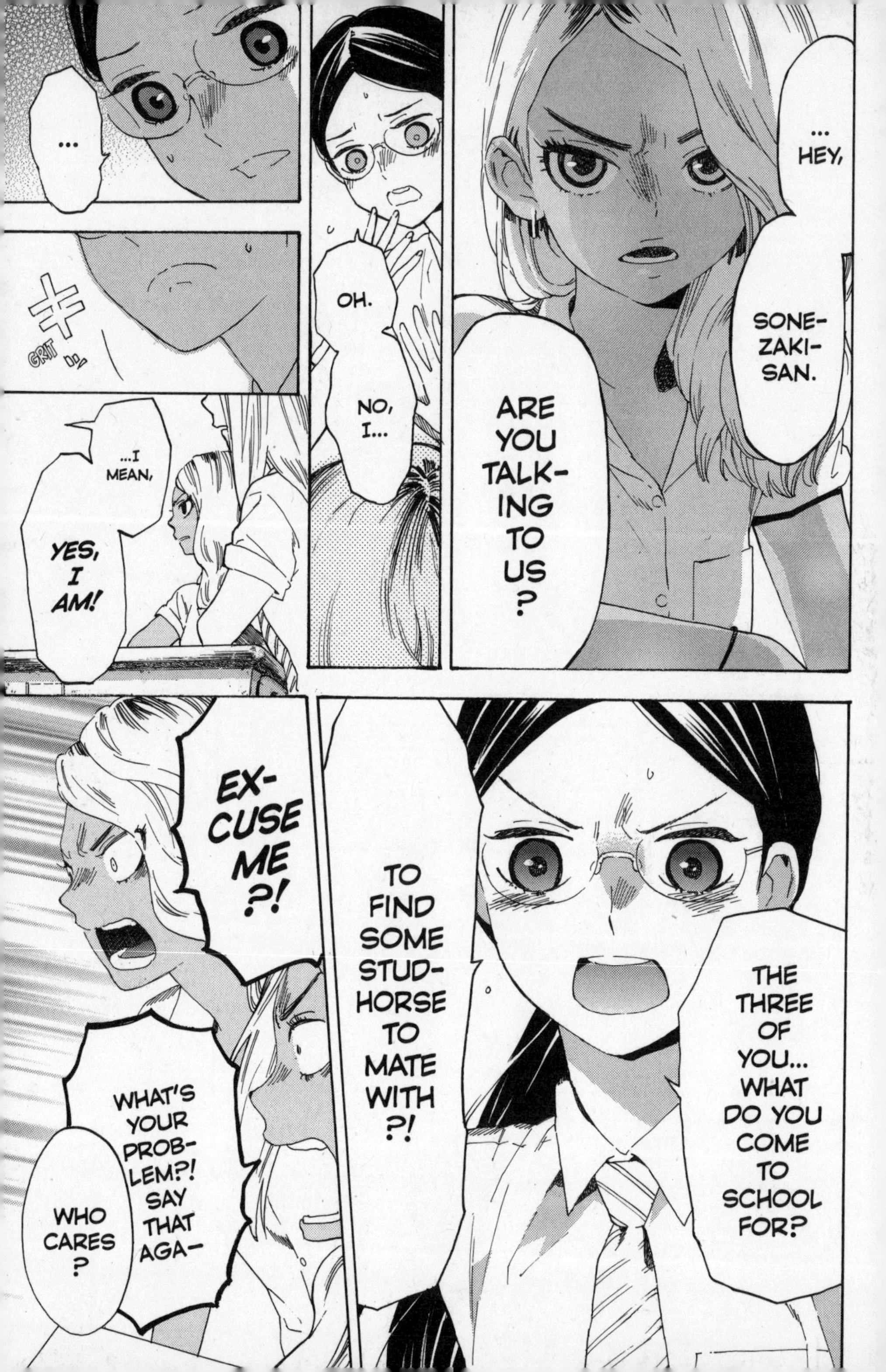
... HEY,
SONE-ZAKI-SAN.
ARE YOU TALKING TO US?
OH.
NO, I...
...
GRIT
...I MEAN,
YES, I AM!
THE THREE OF YOU... WHAT DO YOU COME TO SCHOOL FOR?
TO FIND SOME STUD-HORSE TO MATE WITH?!
EX-CUSE ME?!
WHAT'S YOUR PROB-LEM?! SAY THAT AGA-
WHO CARES?

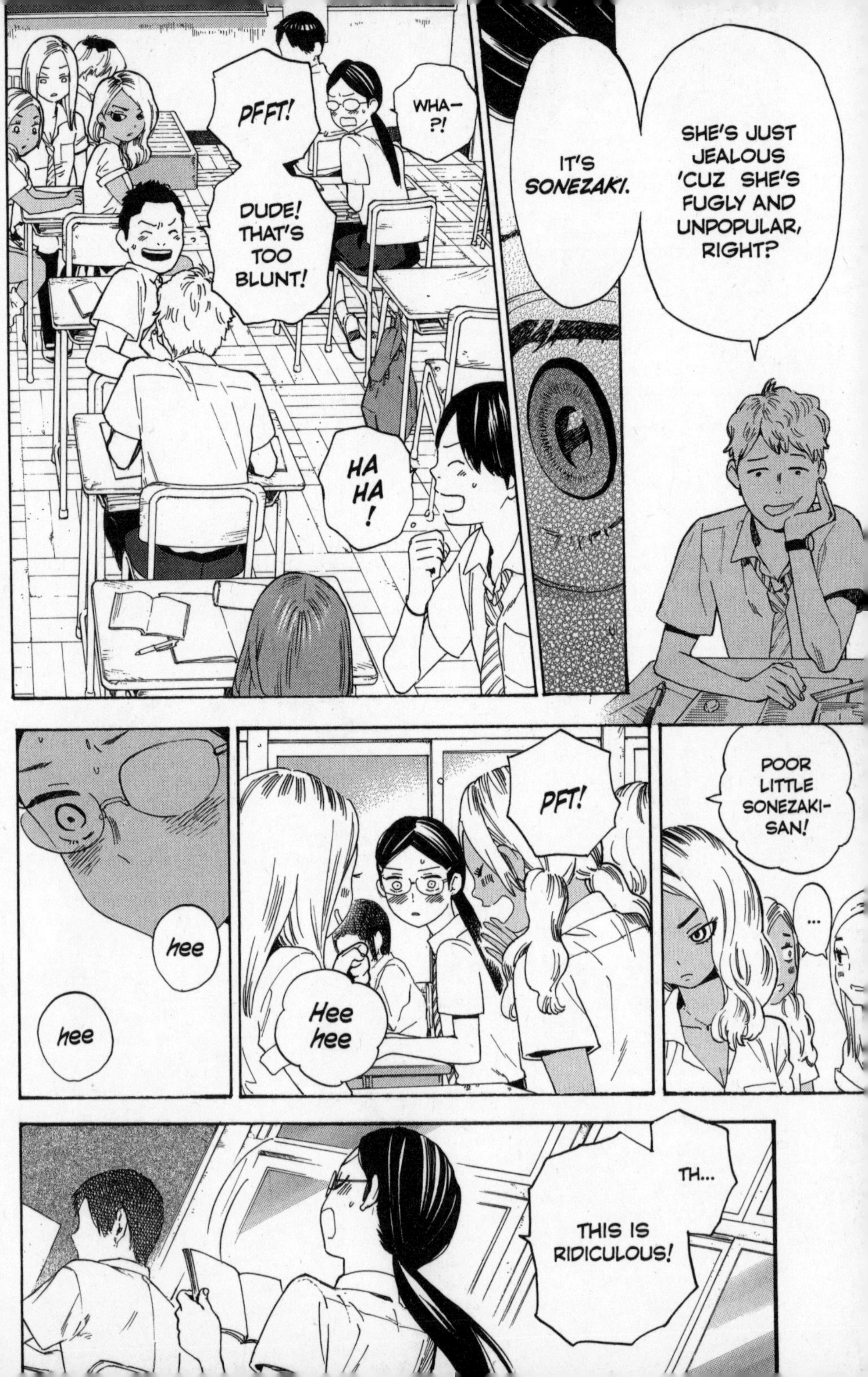
SHE'S JUST JEALOUS 'CUZ SHE'S FUGLY AND UNPOPULAR, RIGHT?
IT'S SONEZAKI.
WHA--?!
PFFT!
DUDE! THAT'S TOO BLUNT!
HA HA!
POOR LITTLE SONEZAKI-SAN!
...
PFT!
Hee hee
hee
hee
TH...
THIS IS RIDICULOUS!

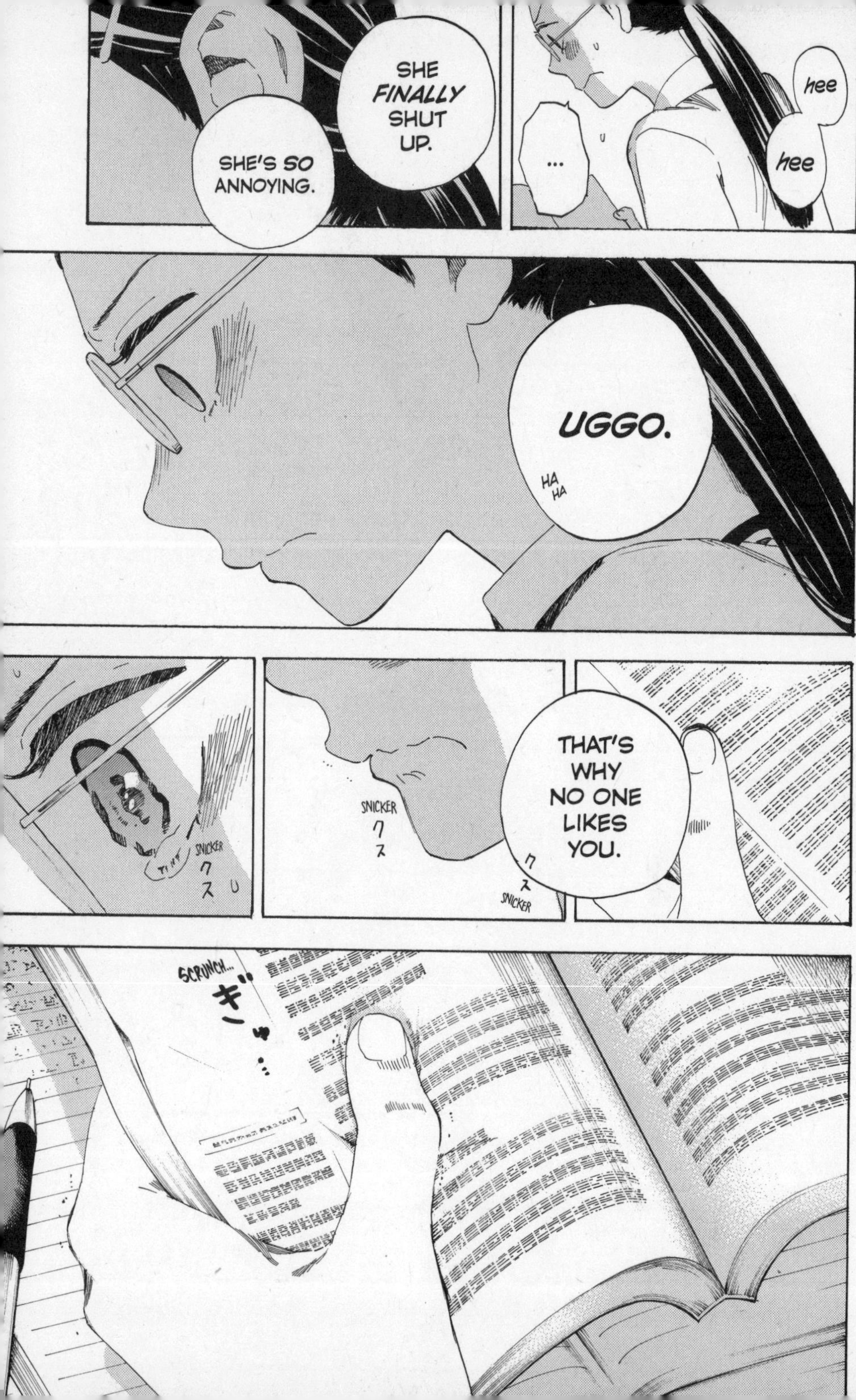
hee
hee
...
SHE FINALLY SHUT UP.
SHE'S SO ANNOYING.
UGGO.
HA HA
THAT'S WHY NO ONE LIKES YOU.
クス SNICKER
SNICKER クス
SNICKER クス
SCRUNCH...
ぎゅ...

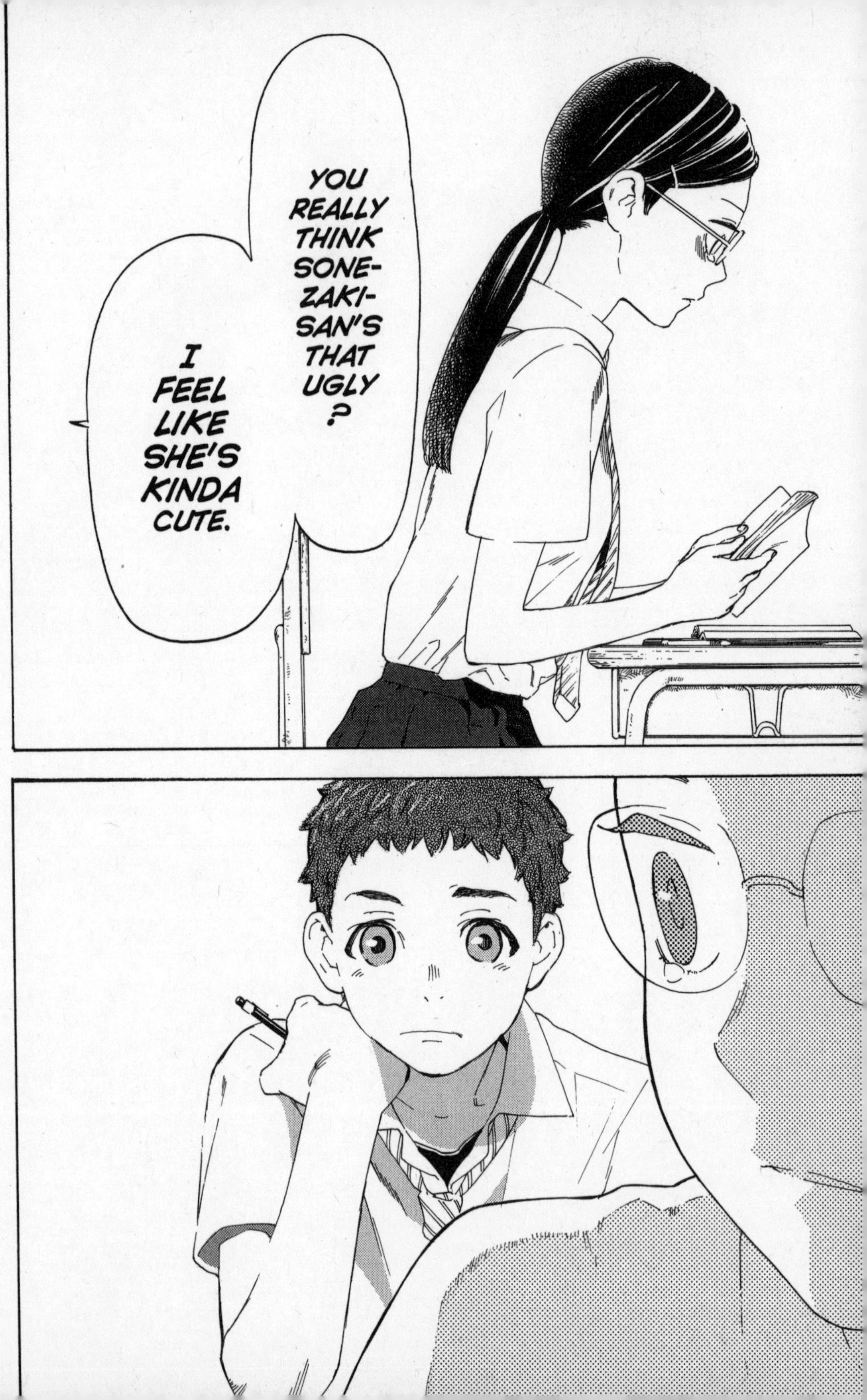
YOU REALLY THINK SONE-ZAKI-SAN'S THAT UGLY?
I FEEL LIKE SHE'S KINDA CUTE.

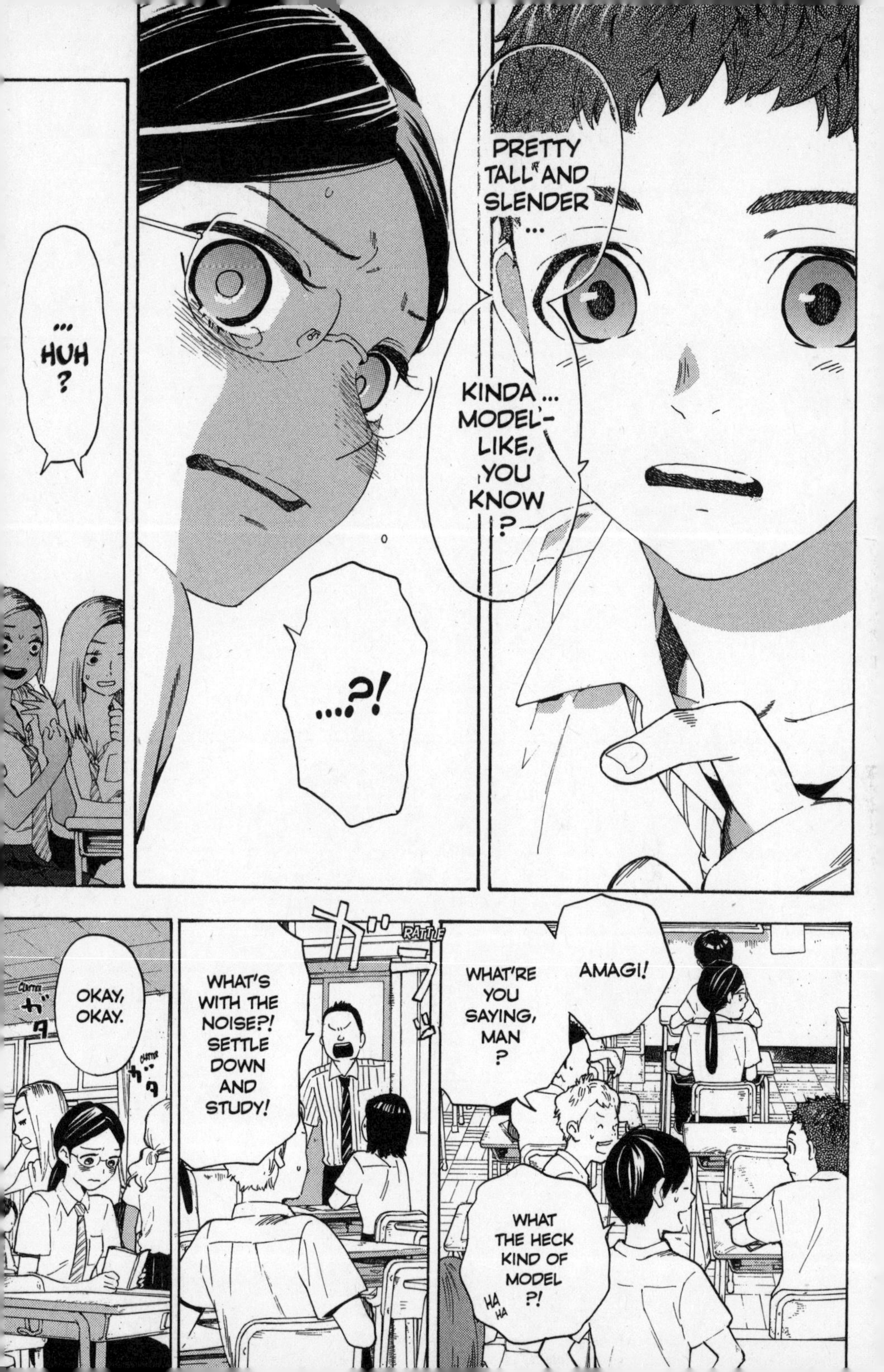
PRETTY TALL AND SLENDER...
KINDA... MODEL-LIKE, YOU KNOW?
...?!
...HUH?
AMAGI!
WHAT'RE YOU SAYING, MAN?
WHAT THE HECK KIND OF MODEL?!
HA HA
RATTLE
WHAT'S WITH THE NOISE?! SETTLE DOWN AND STUDY!
OKAY, OKAY.
CLATTER
CLATTER

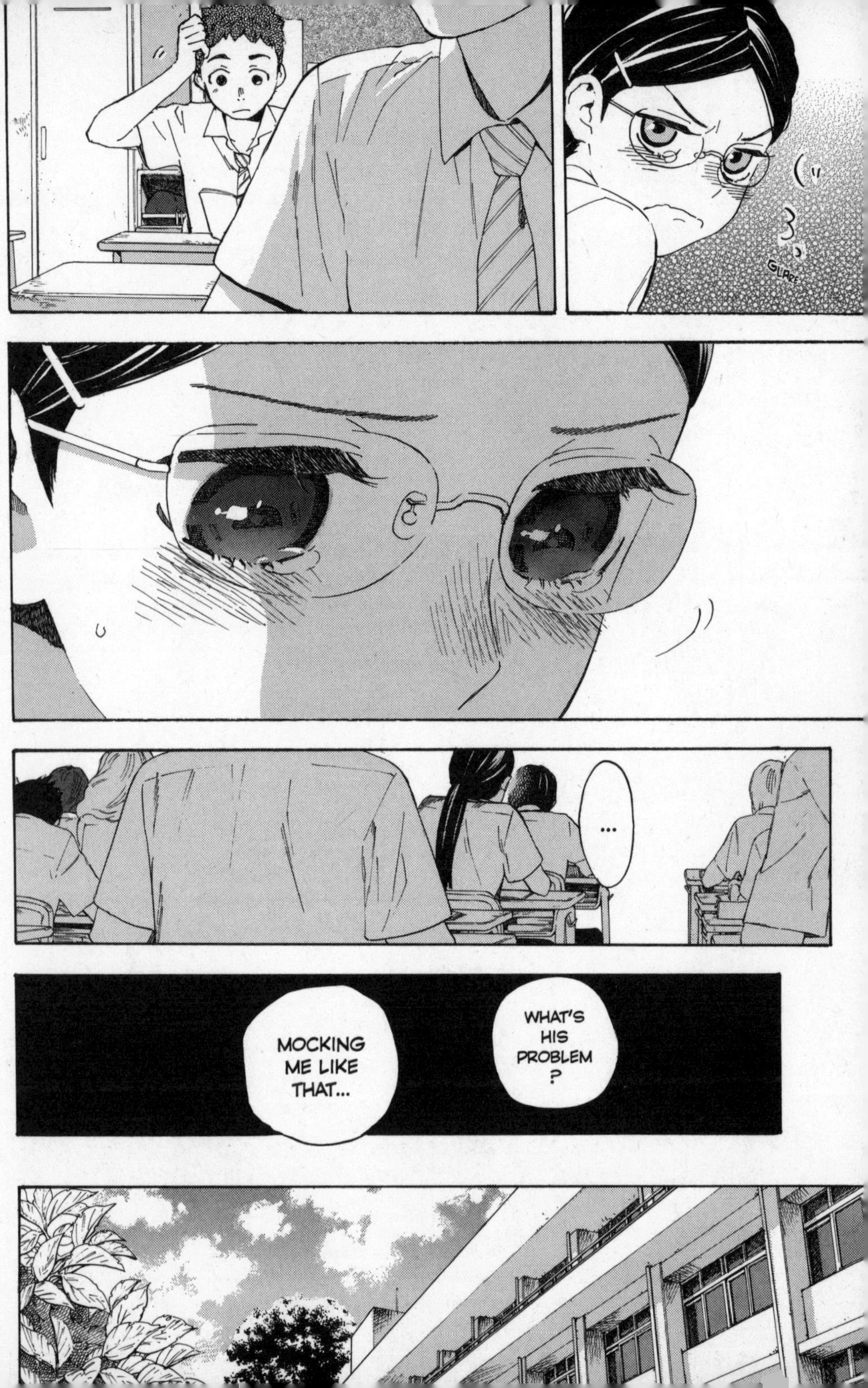
GLARE
...
WHAT'S HIS PROBLEM?
MOCKING ME LIKE THAT...

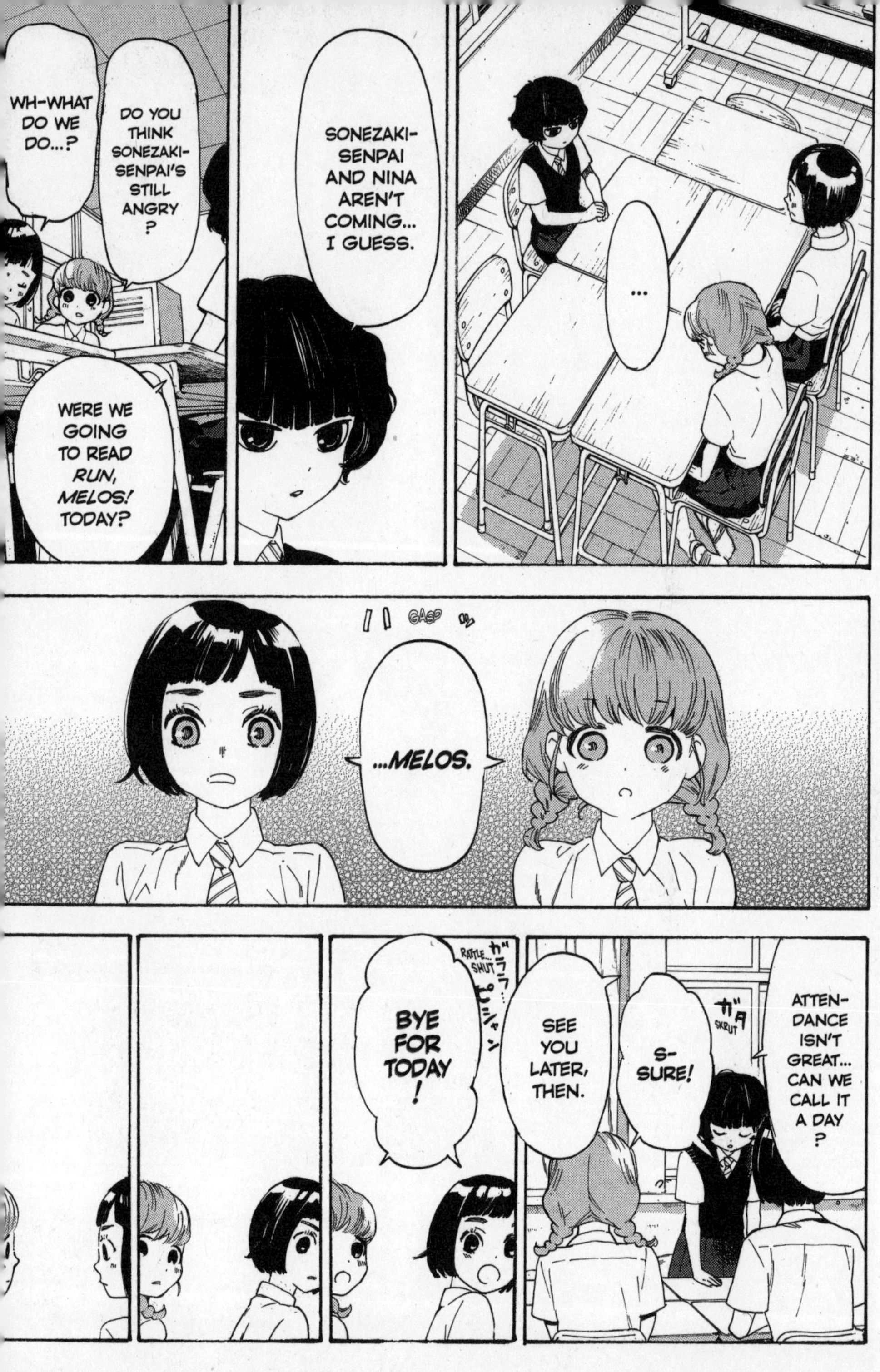
...
SONEZAKI-SENPAI AND NINA AREN'T COMING... I GUESS.
DO YOU THINK SONEZAKI-SENPAI'S STILL ANGRY?
WH-WHAT DO WE DO...?
WERE WE GOING TO READ *RUN, MELOS!* TODAY?
GASP
...MELOS.
ATTEN-DANCE ISN'T GREAT... CAN WE CALL IT A DAY?
SKRUT
S-SURE!
SEE YOU LATER, THEN.
RATTLE... SHUT
BYE FOR TODAY!

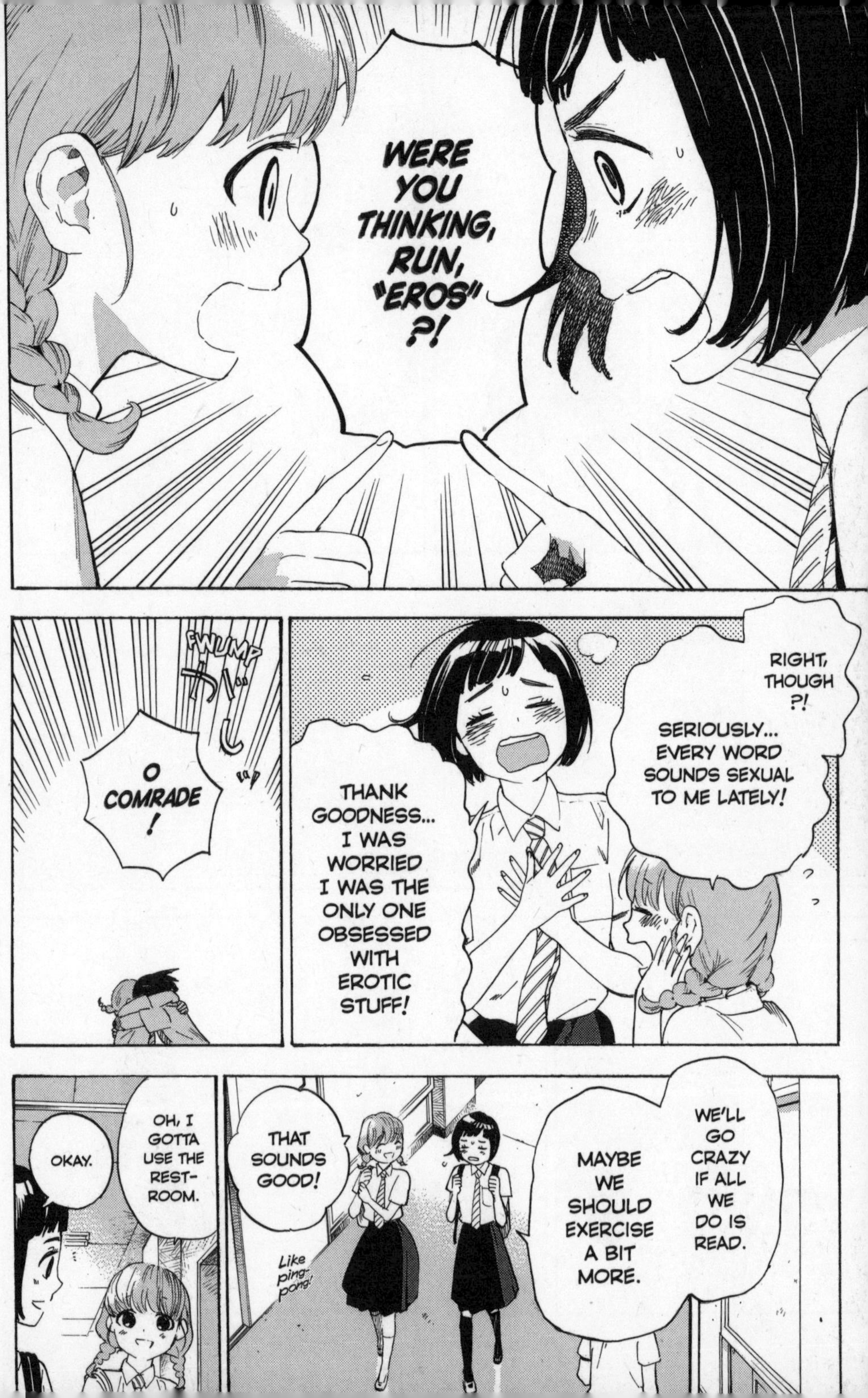
WERE YOU THINKING, RUN, "EROS"?!
RIGHT, THOUGH?!
SERIOUSLY... EVERY WORD SOUNDS SEXUAL TO ME LATELY!
THANK GOODNESS... I WAS WORRIED I WAS THE ONLY ONE OBSESSED WITH EROTIC STUFF!
FWUMP
O COMRADE!
WE'LL GO CRAZY IF ALL WE DO IS READ.
MAYBE WE SHOULD EXERCISE A BIT MORE.
THAT SOUNDS GOOD!
Like ping-pong!
OH, I GOTTA USE THE REST-ROOM.
OKAY.

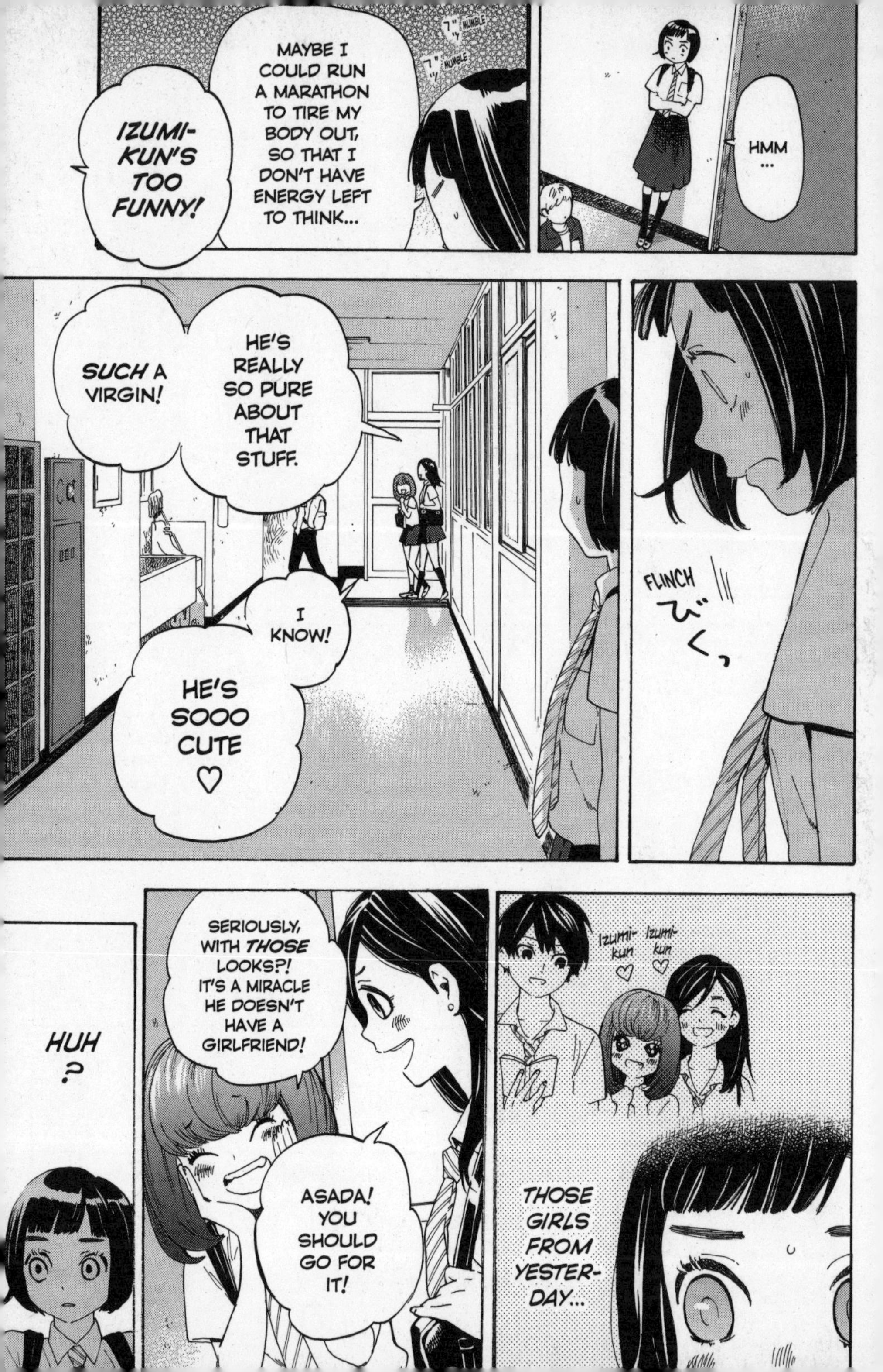
HMM ...
MUMBLE
MUMBLE
MAYBE I COULD RUN A MARATHON TO TIRE MY BODY OUT, SO THAT I DON'T HAVE ENERGY LEFT TO THINK...
IZUMI-KUN'S TOO FUNNY!
FLINCH
びくっ
HE'S REALLY SO PURE ABOUT THAT STUFF.
SUCH A VIRGIN!
I KNOW!
HE'S SOOO CUTE ♡
Izumi-kun ♡
Izumi-kun ♡
THOSE GIRLS FROM YESTER-DAY...
SERIOUSLY, WITH THOSE LOOKS?! IT'S A MIRACLE HE DOESN'T HAVE A GIRLFRIEND!
ASADA! YOU SHOULD GO FOR IT!
HUH ?

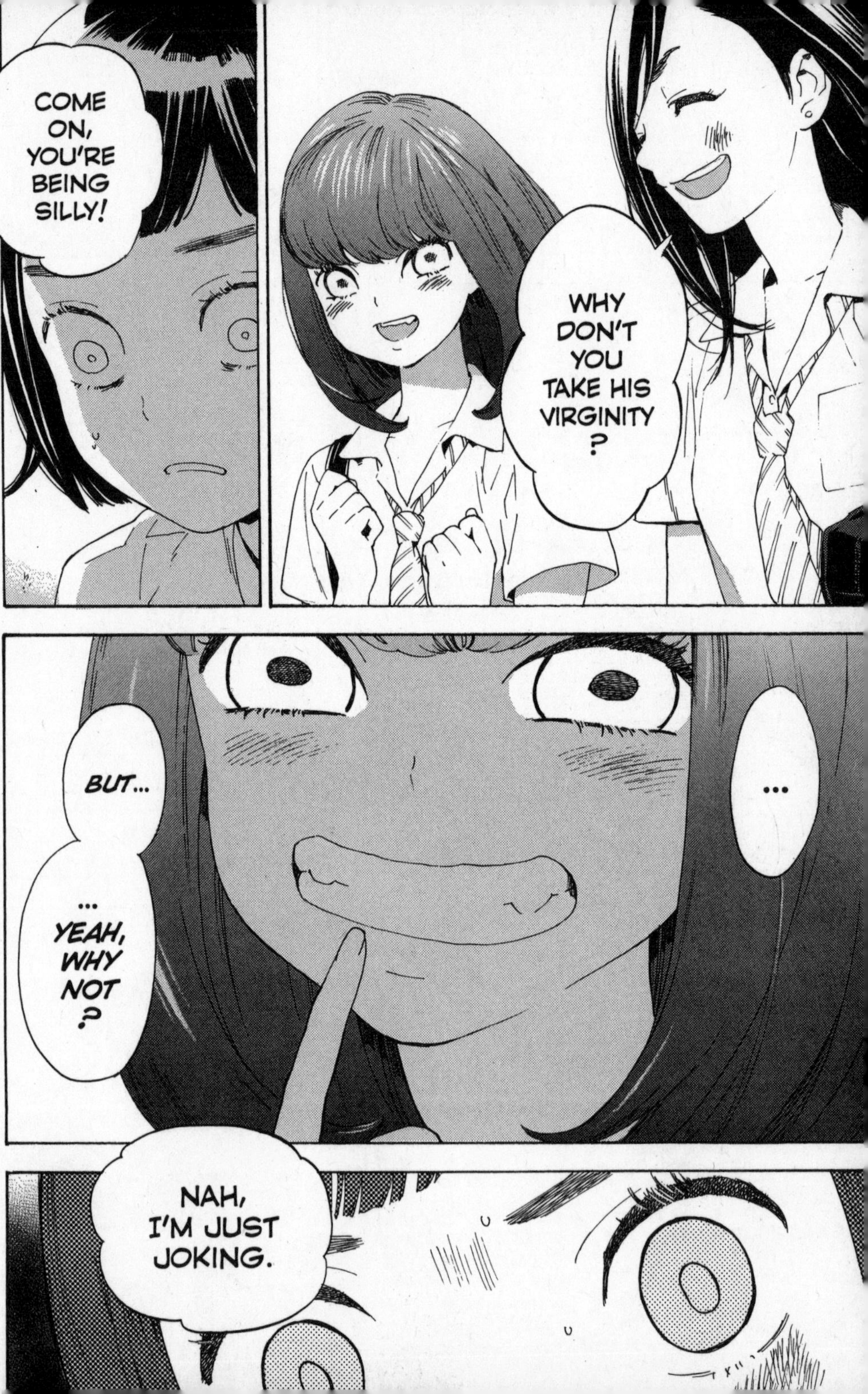
WHY DON'T YOU TAKE HIS VIRGINITY?
COME ON, YOU'RE BEING SILLY!
...
BUT...
... YEAH, WHY NOT?
NAH, I'M JUST JOKING.

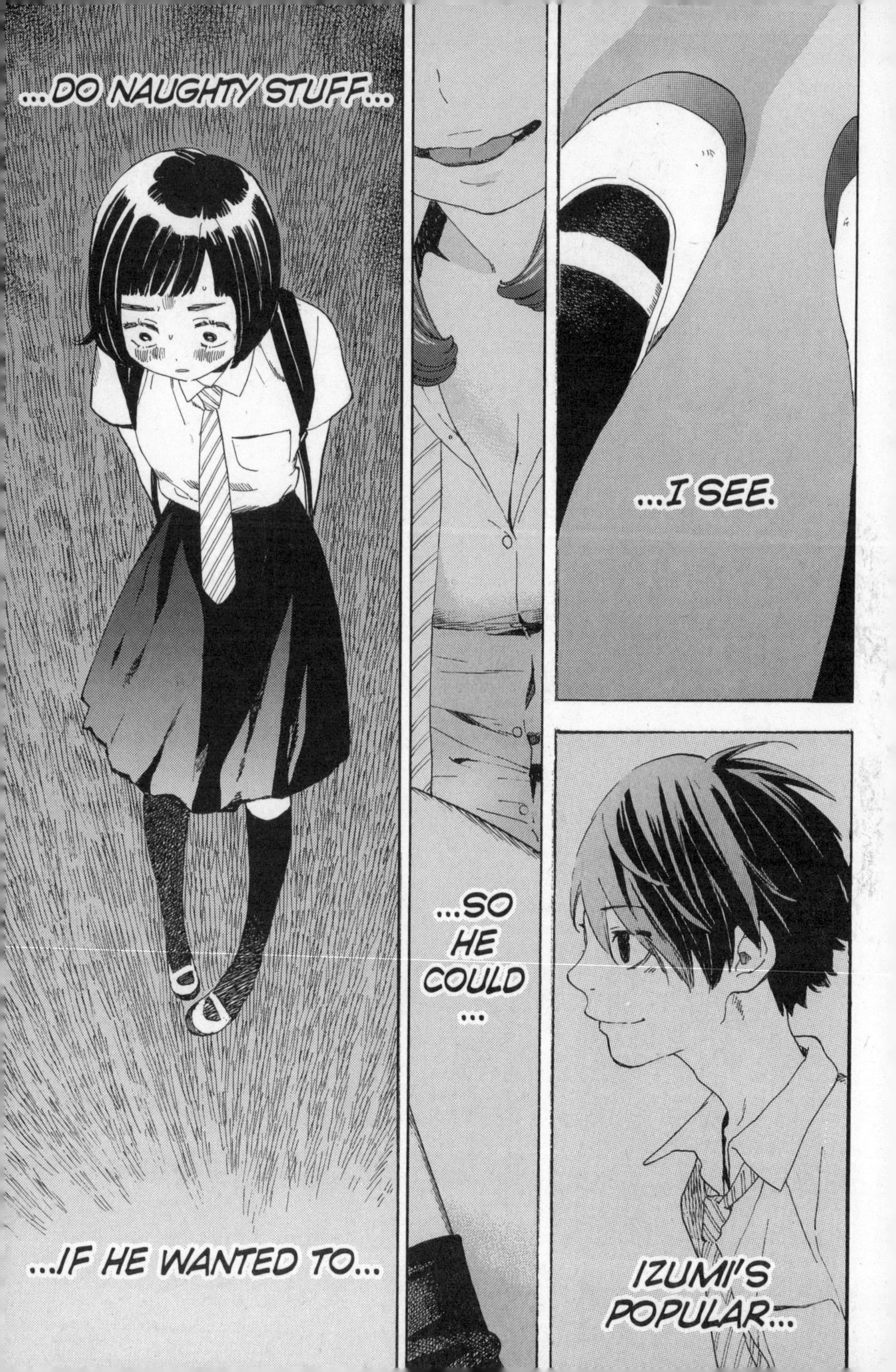
...I SEE.
IZUMI'S POPULAR...
...SO HE COULD ...
...DO NAUGHTY STUFF...
...IF HE WANTED TO...

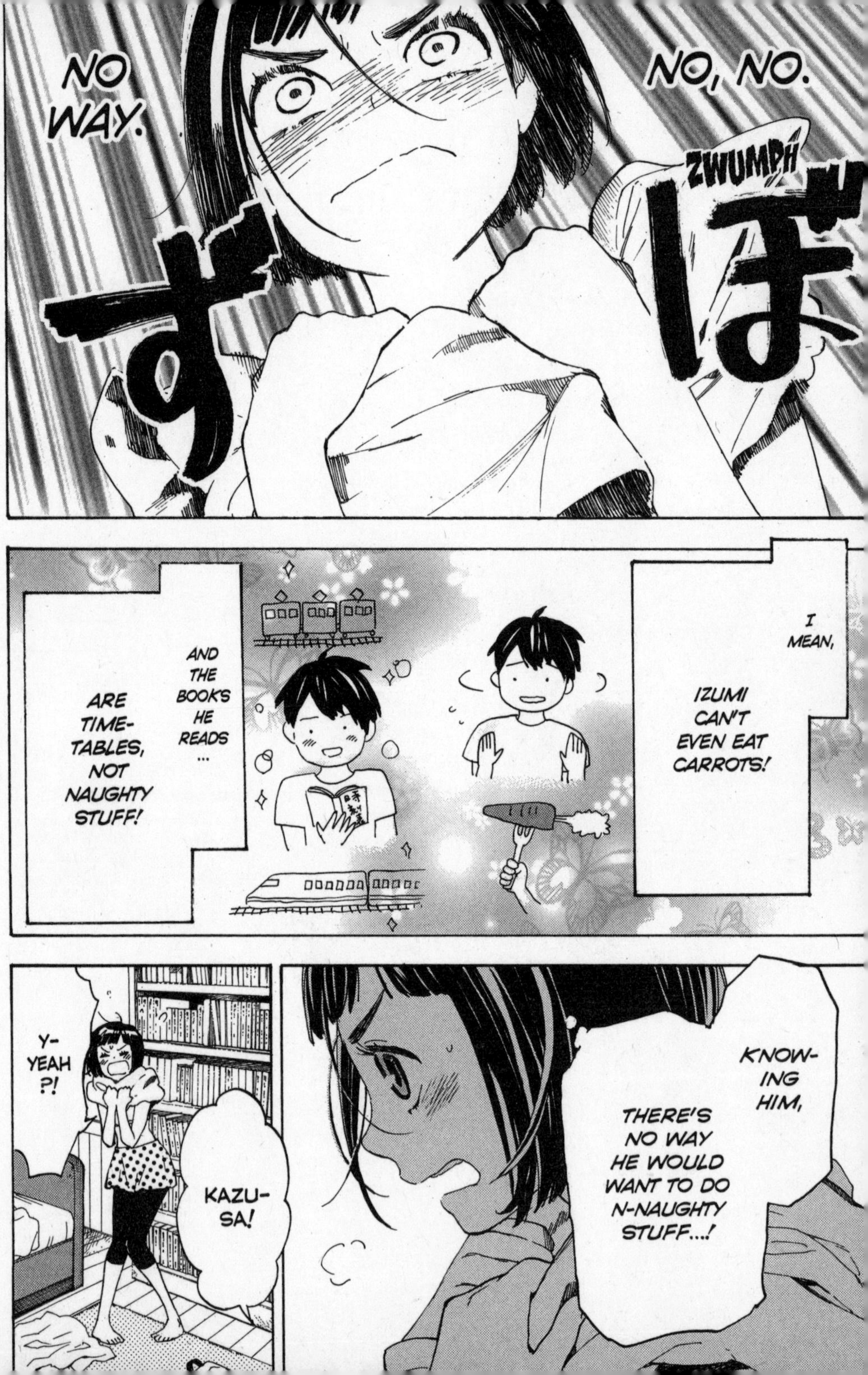
NO, NO.
NO WAY.
ZWUMPH
ずぼ
I MEAN,
IZUMI CAN'T EVEN EAT CARROTS!
AND THE BOOKS HE READS ...
ARE TIME-TABLES, NOT NAUGHTY STUFF!
KNOWING HIM,
THERE'S NO WAY HE WOULD WANT TO DO N-NAUGHTY STUFF...!
KAZUSA!
Y-YEAH?!

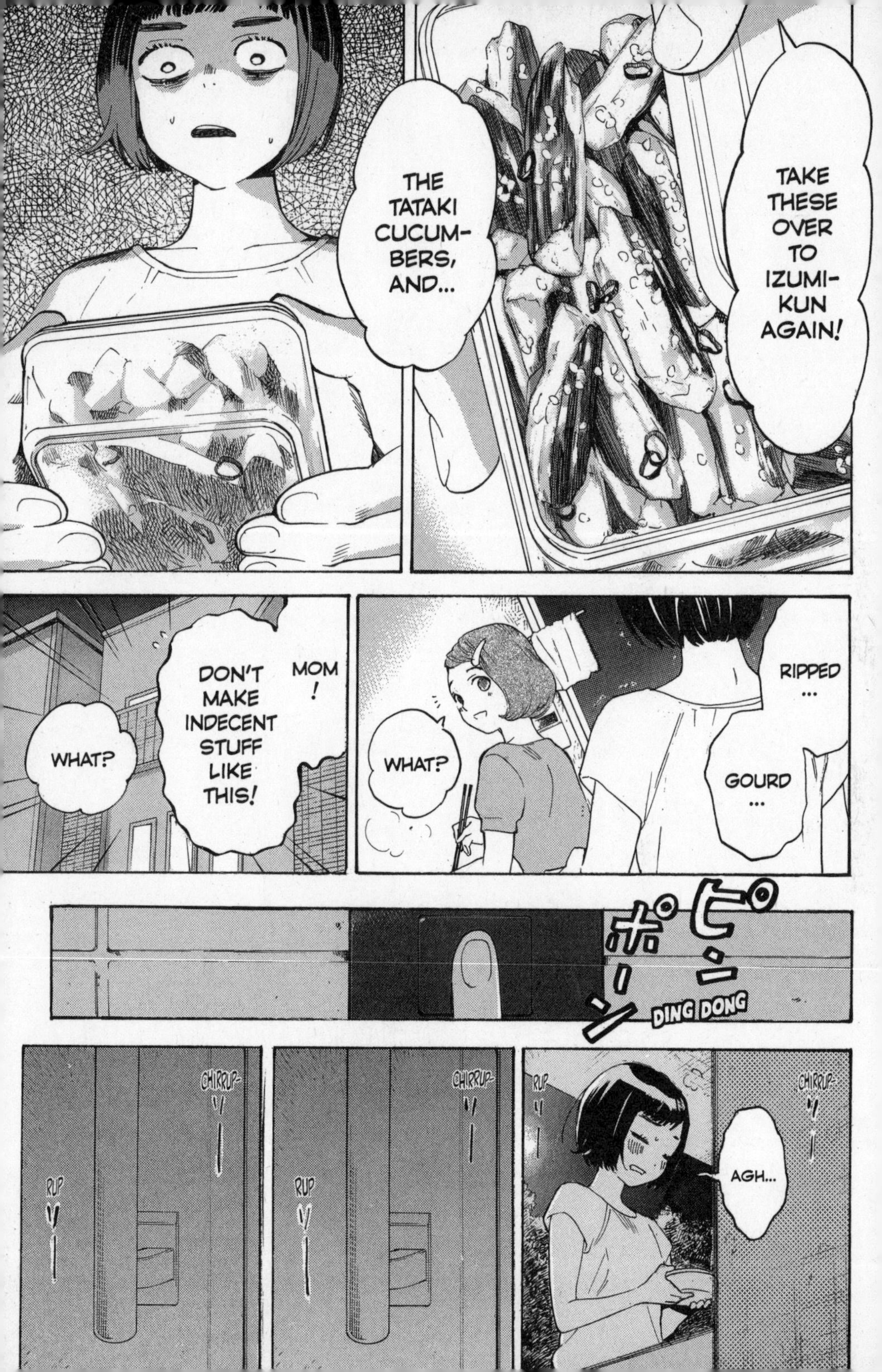
TAKE THESE OVER TO IZUMI-KUN AGAIN!
THE TATAKI CUCUMBERS, AND...
RIPPED...
GOURD...
WHAT?
MOM!
DON'T MAKE INDECENT STUFF LIKE THIS!
WHAT?
ピンポーン
DING DONG
CHIRRUP-
RUP
AGH...
CHIRRUP-
RUP
CHIRRUP-
RUP

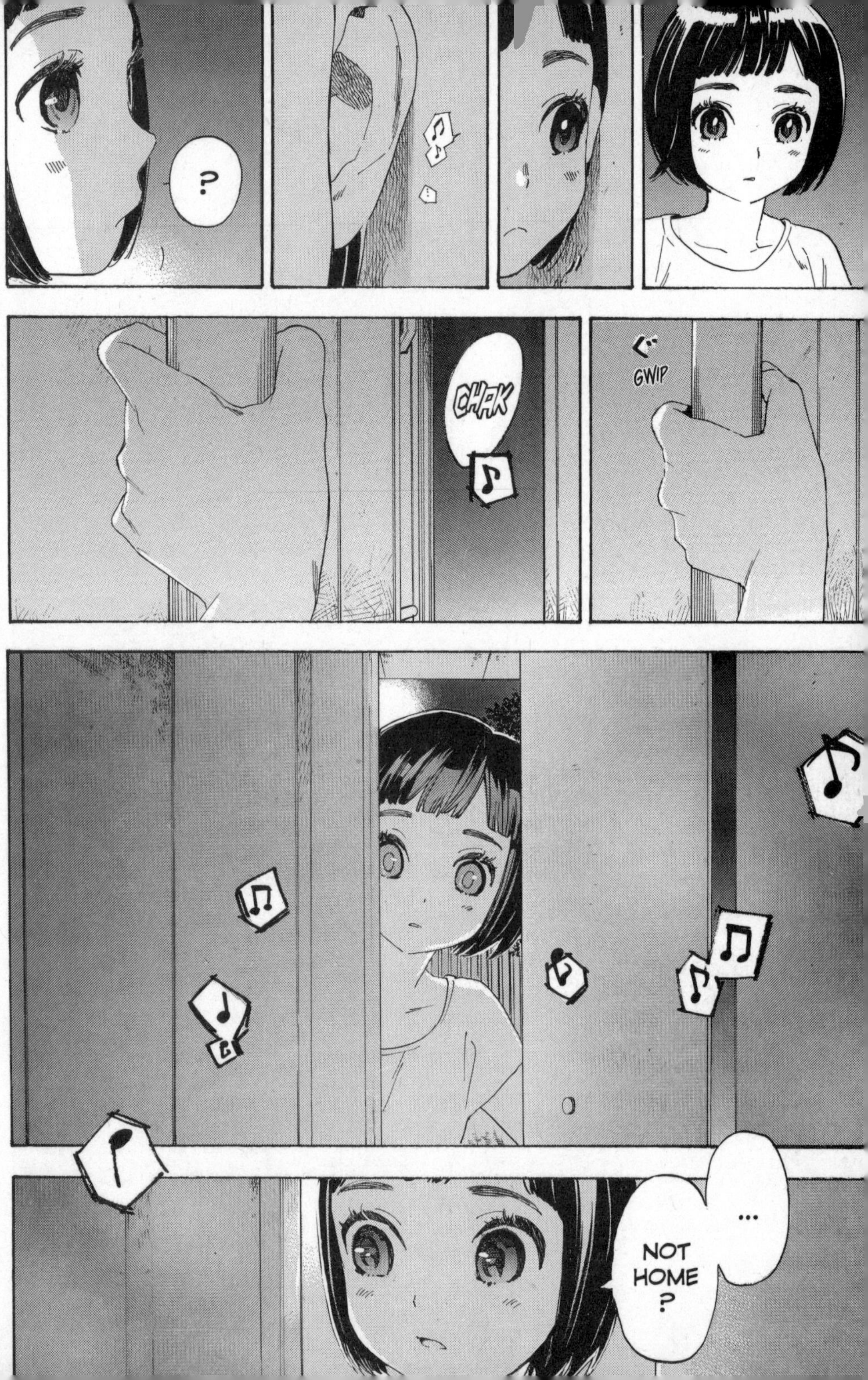
?
GWIP
CHAK
...
NOT HOME ?

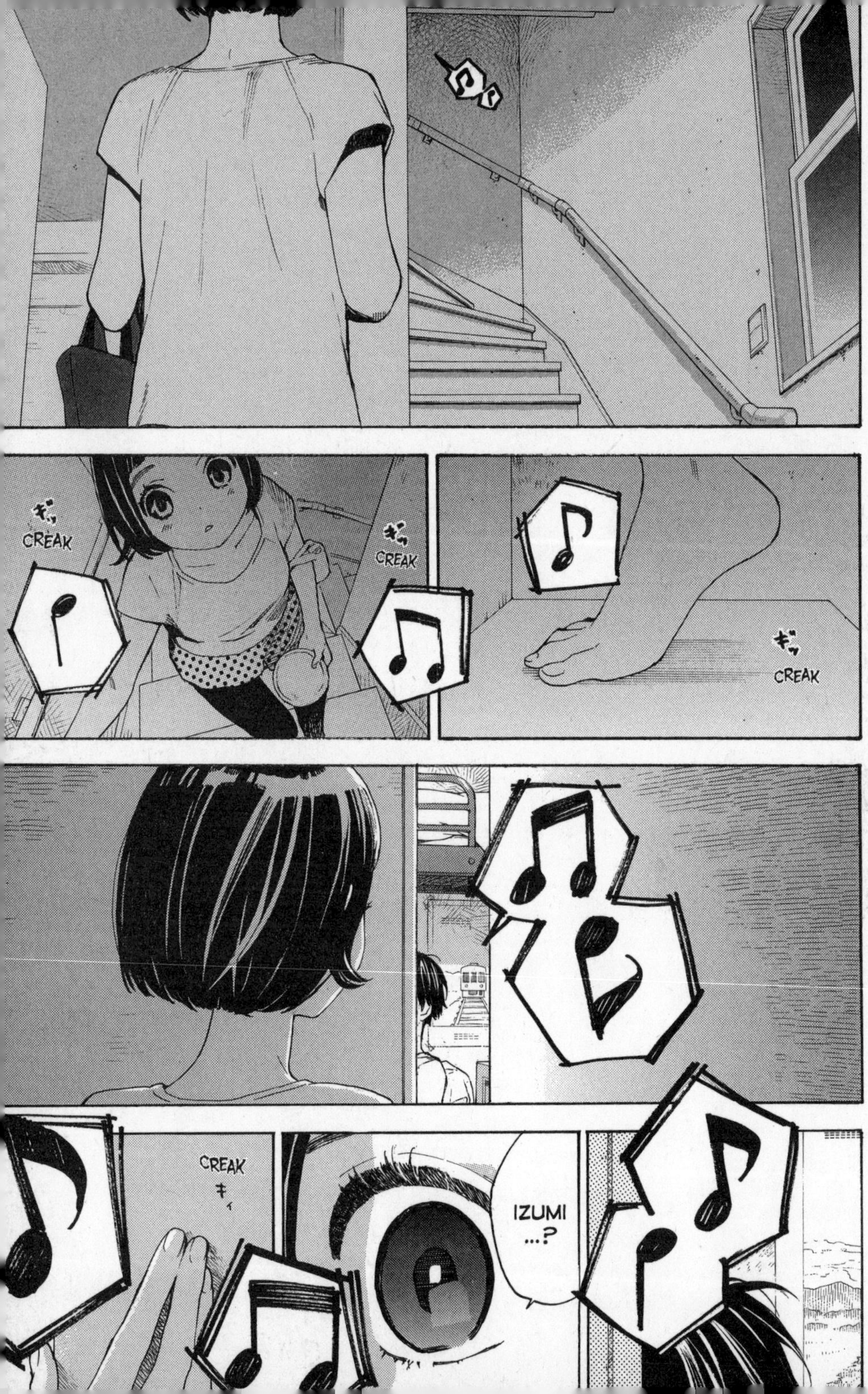

ギッ
CREAK
ギッ
CREAK
ギッ
CREAK
IZUMI ...?
CREAK
キィ

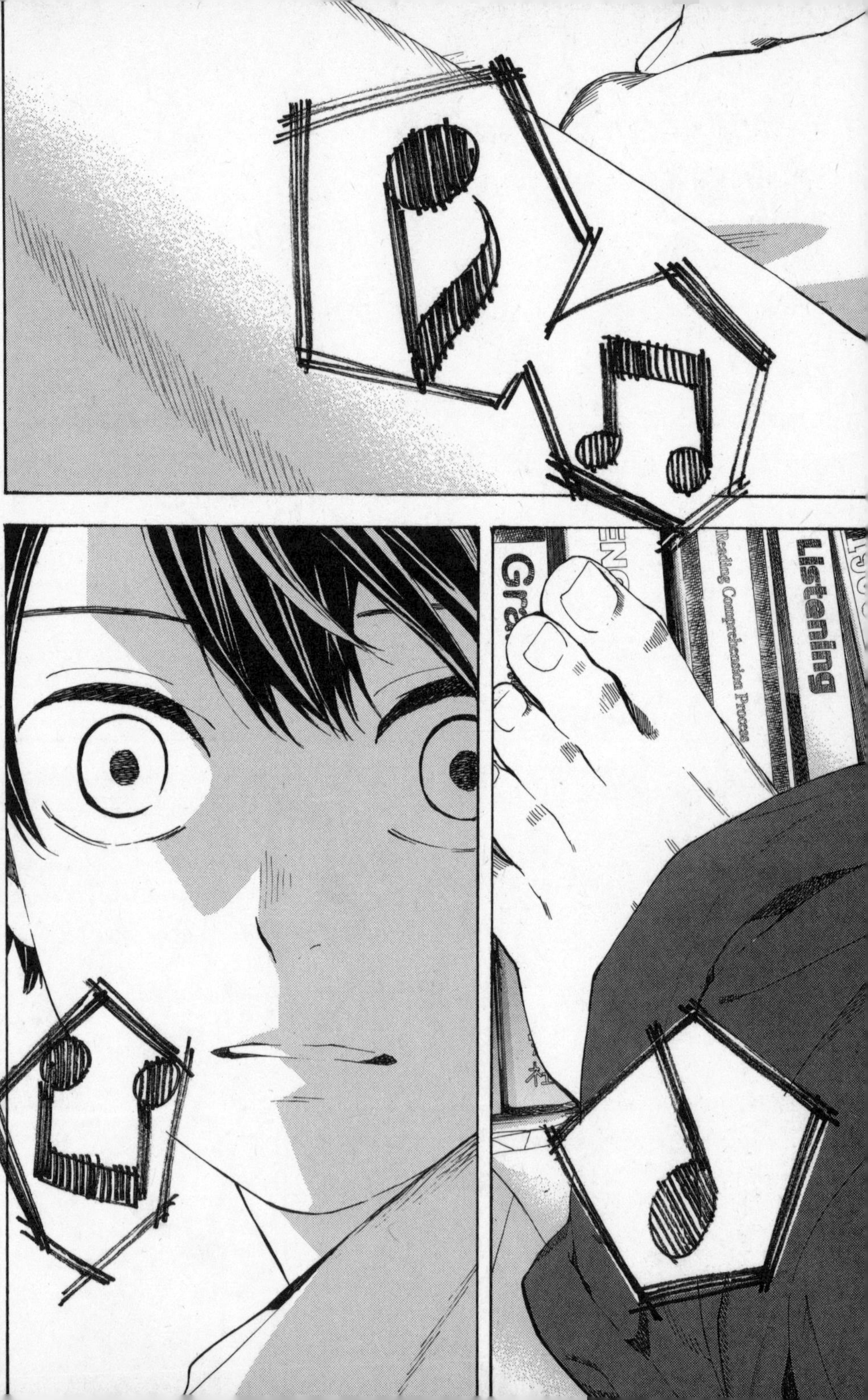
Listening
Reading Comprehension Process

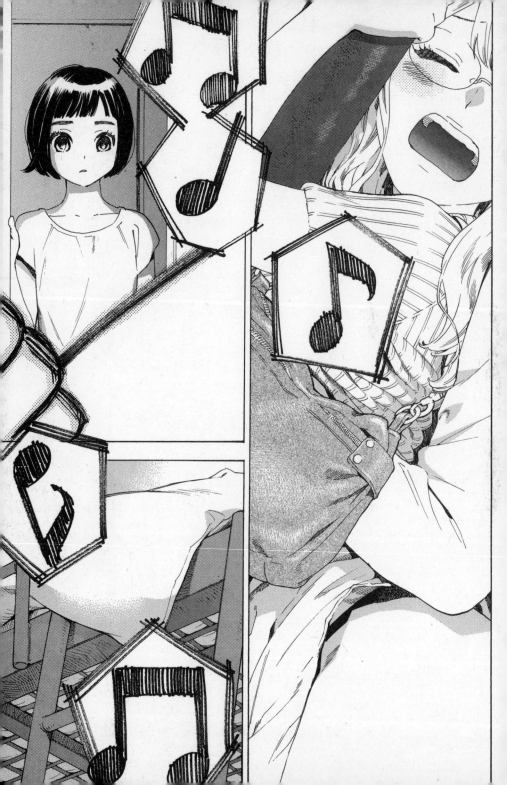

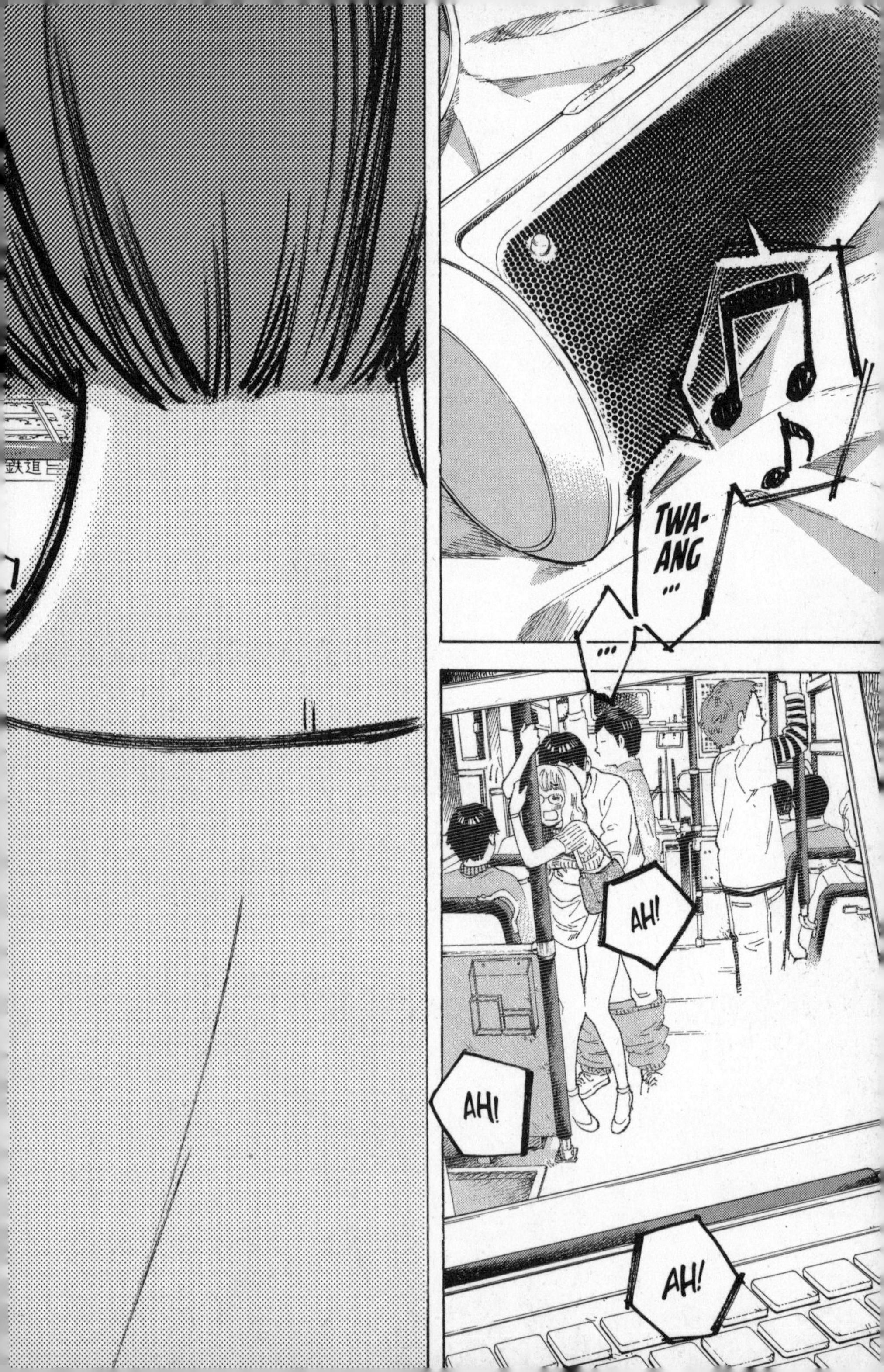
TWA-
ANG
...
...
AH!
AH!
AH!

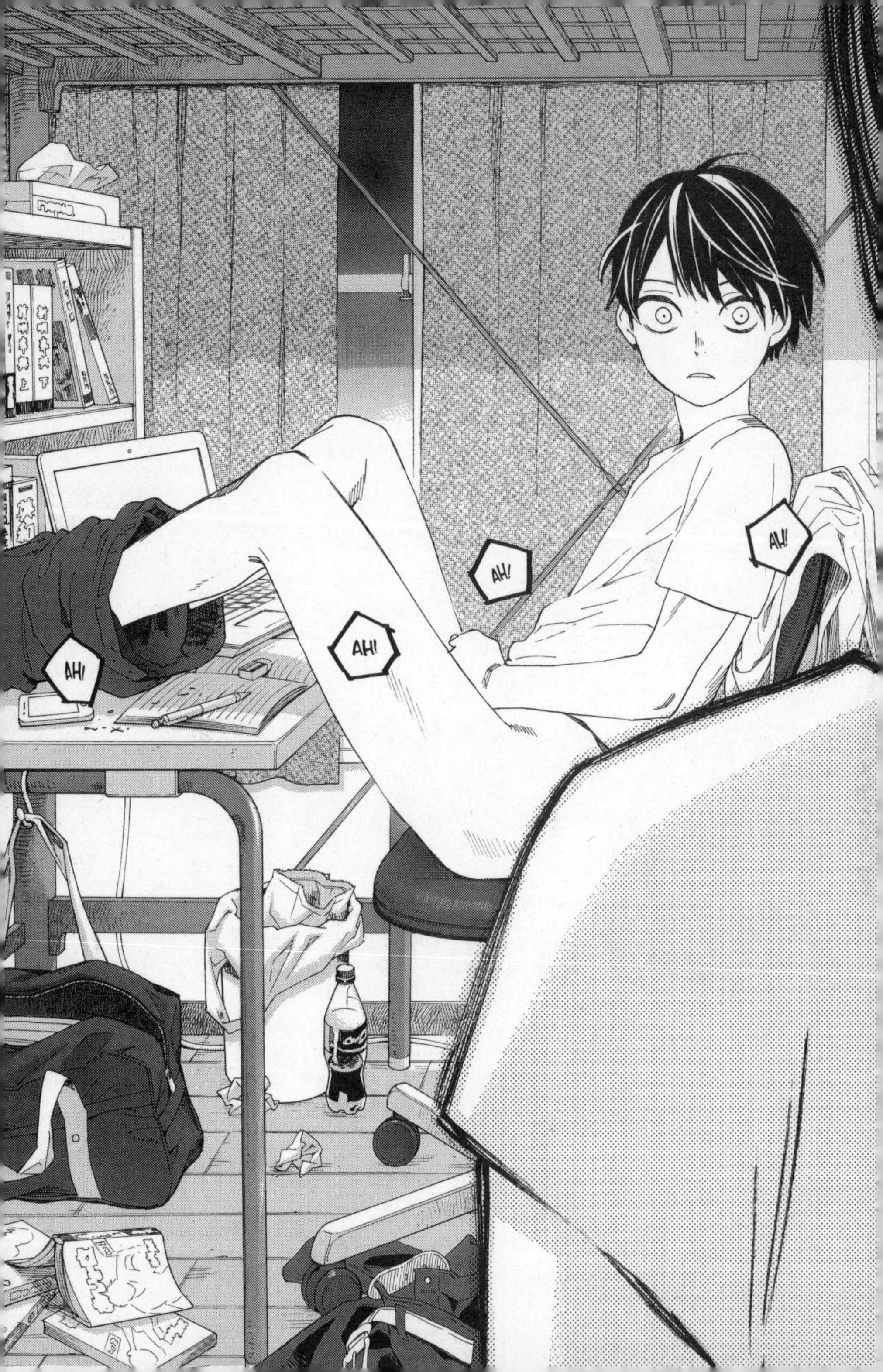
AH!
AH!
AH!
AH!

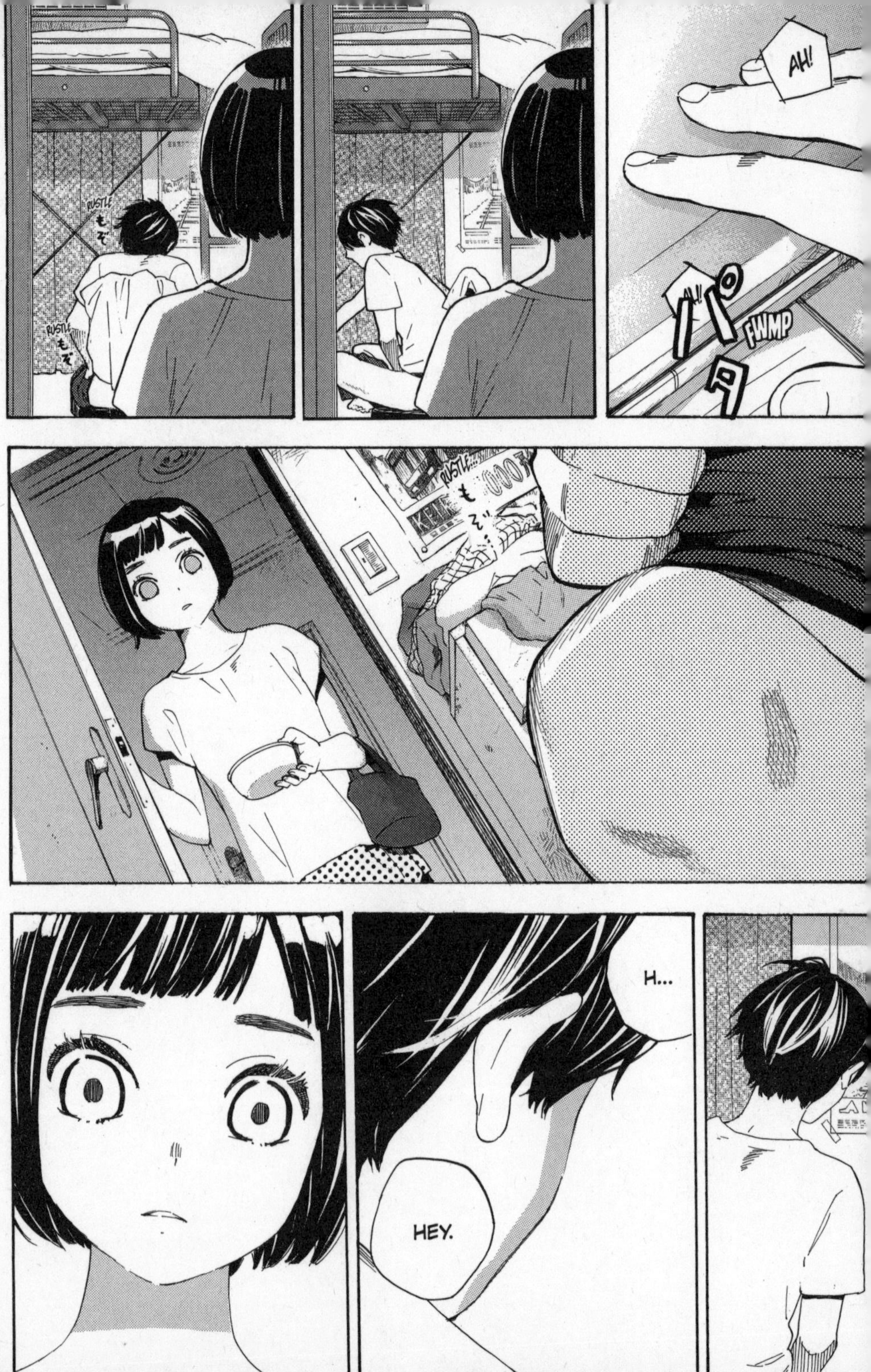
AH!
AH!
パタ
FWMP
RUSTLE
もぞ
RUSTLE
もぞ
RUSTLE...
もぞ...
H...
HEY.

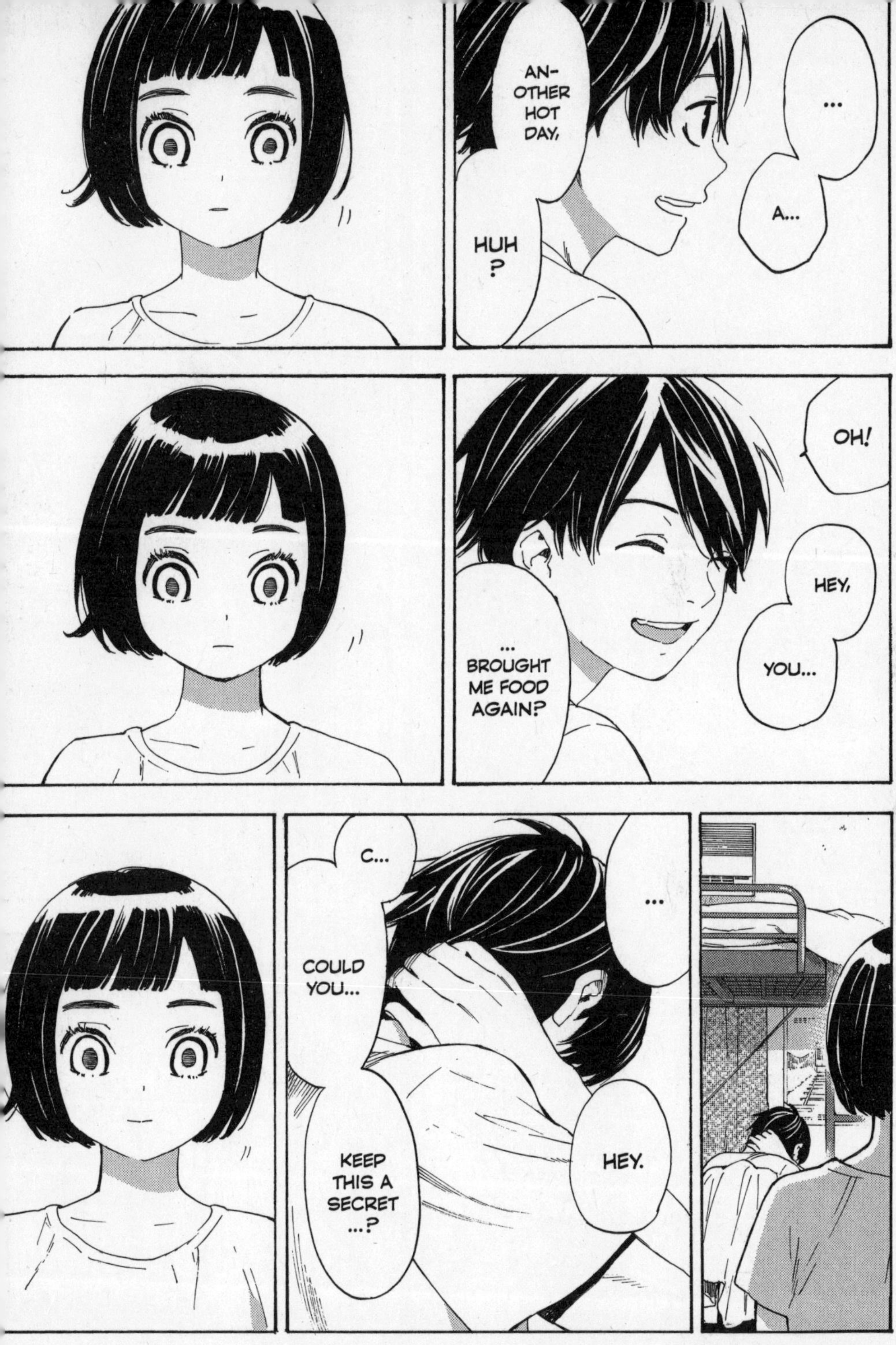
...
A...
AN-OTHER HOT DAY,
HUH?
OH!
HEY,
YOU...
... BROUGHT ME FOOD AGAIN?
...
C...
COULD YOU...
HEY.
KEEP THIS A SECRET ...?

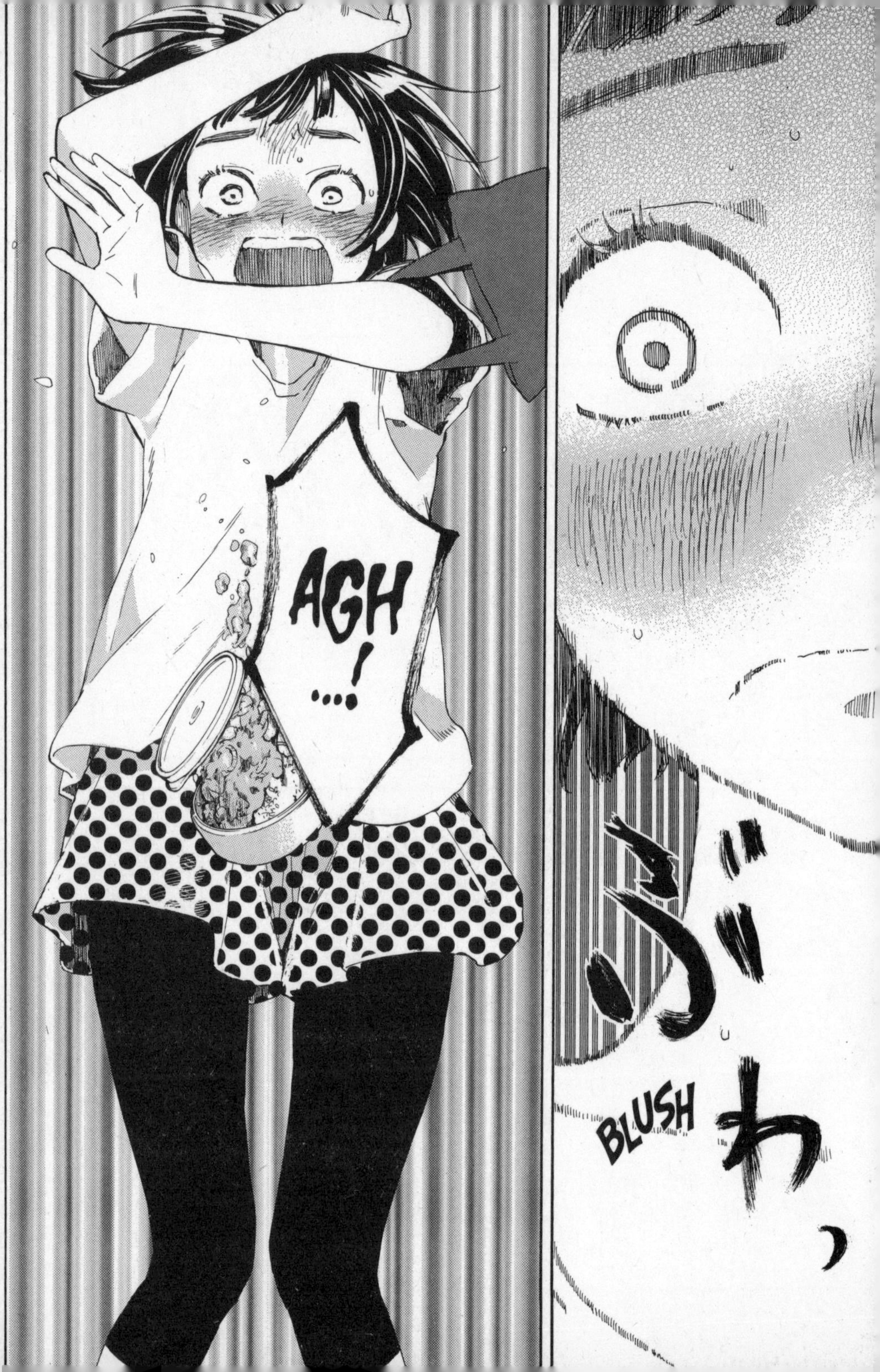
ぶわ
BLUSH
AGH ...!

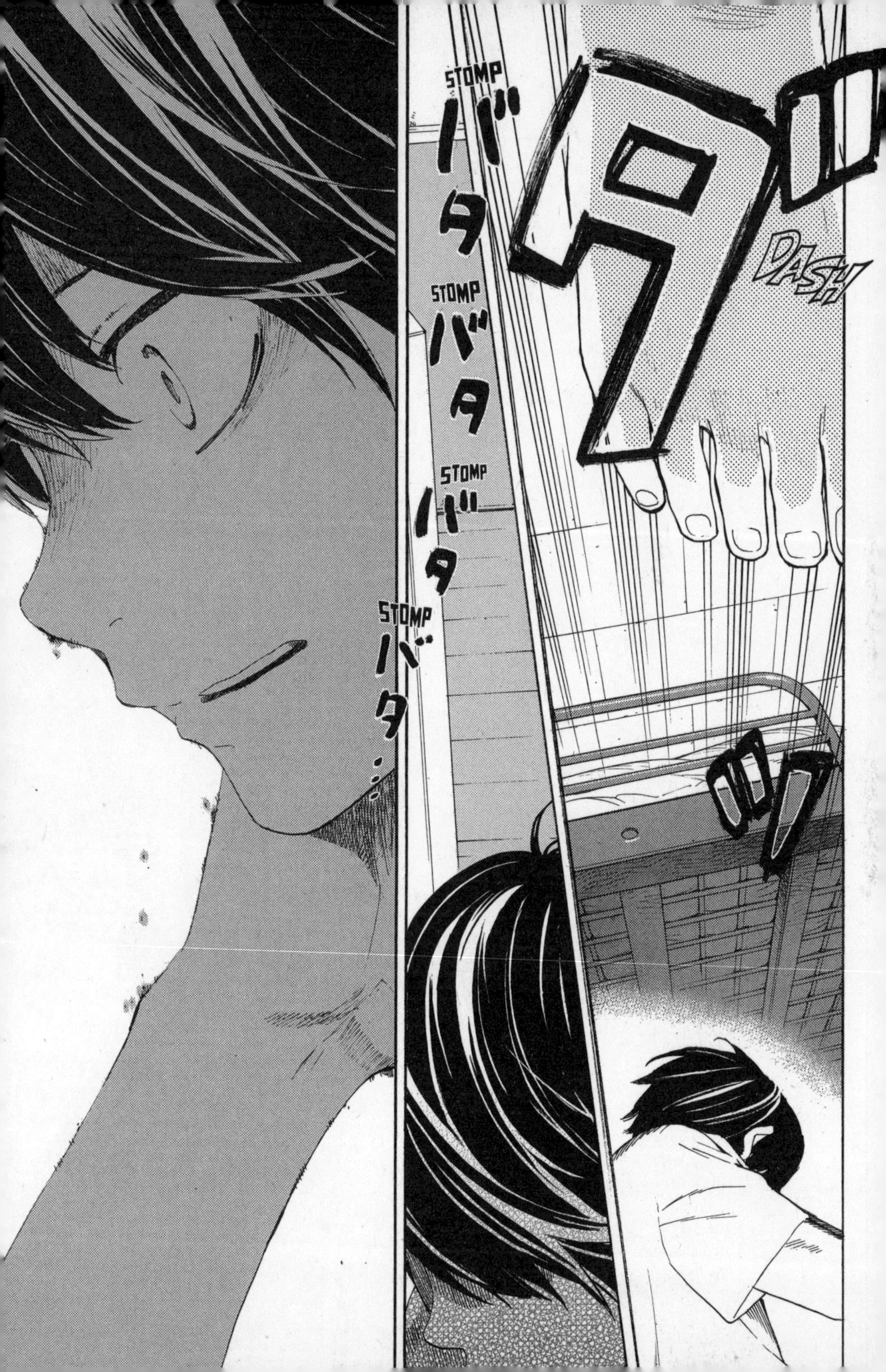
DASH!
STOMP
バタ
STOMP
バタ
STOMP
バタ
STOMP
バタ…

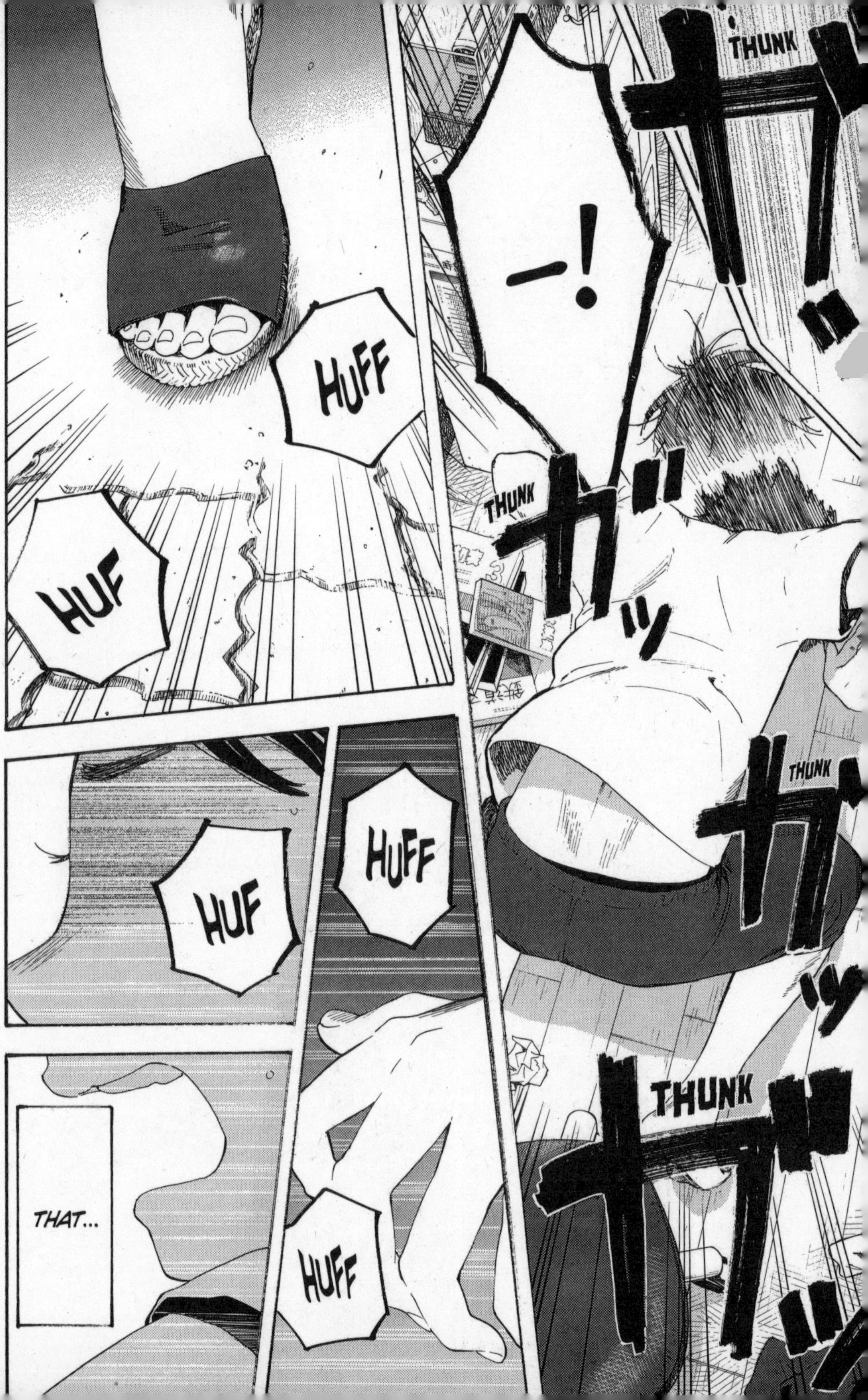
THUNK
—!
THUNK
THUNK
THUNK
HUFF
HUF
HUFF
HUF
HUFF
THAT...

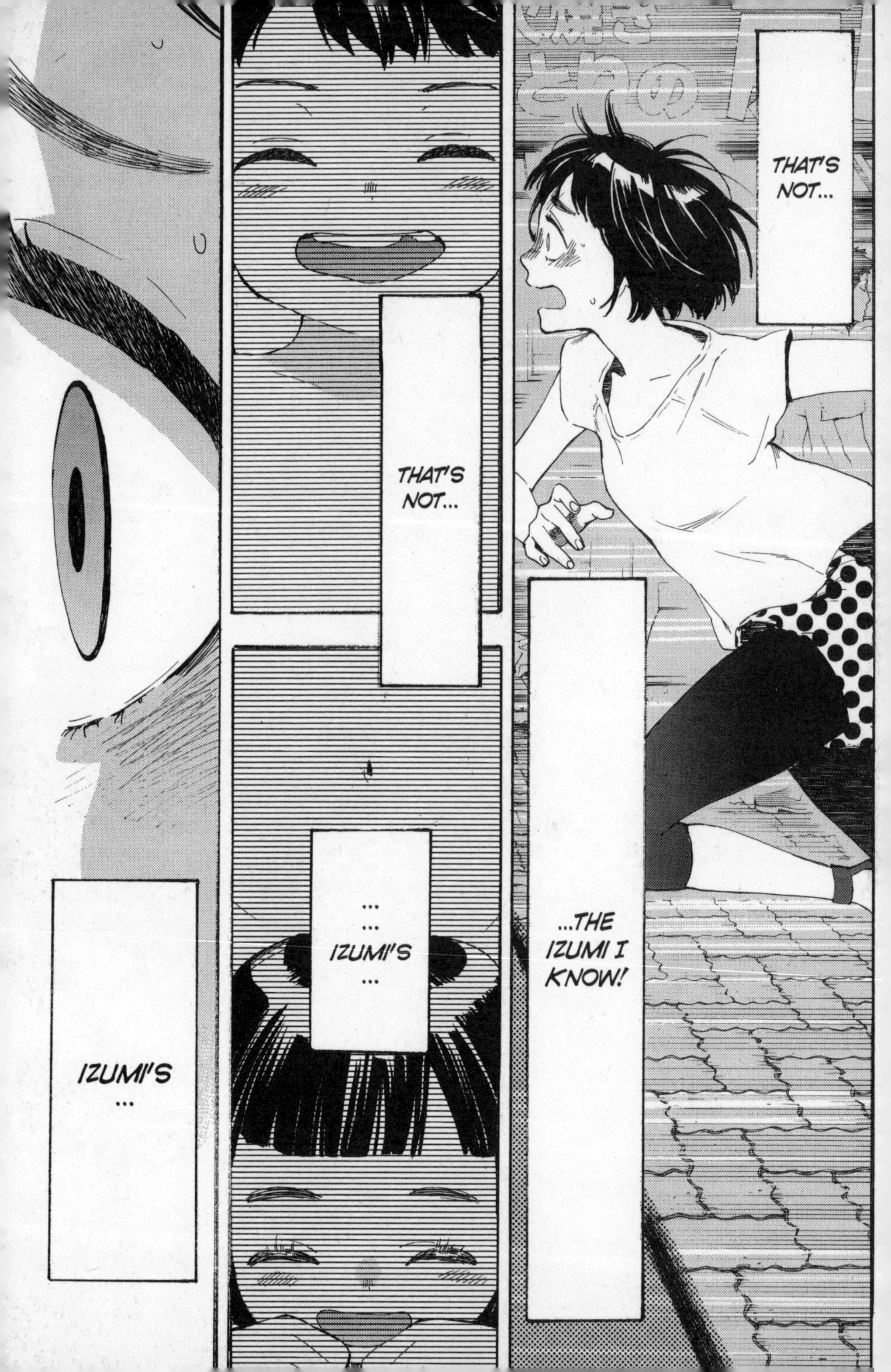
THAT'S NOT...
...THE IZUMI I KNOW!
THAT'S NOT...
... ... IZUMI'S ...
IZUMI'S ...

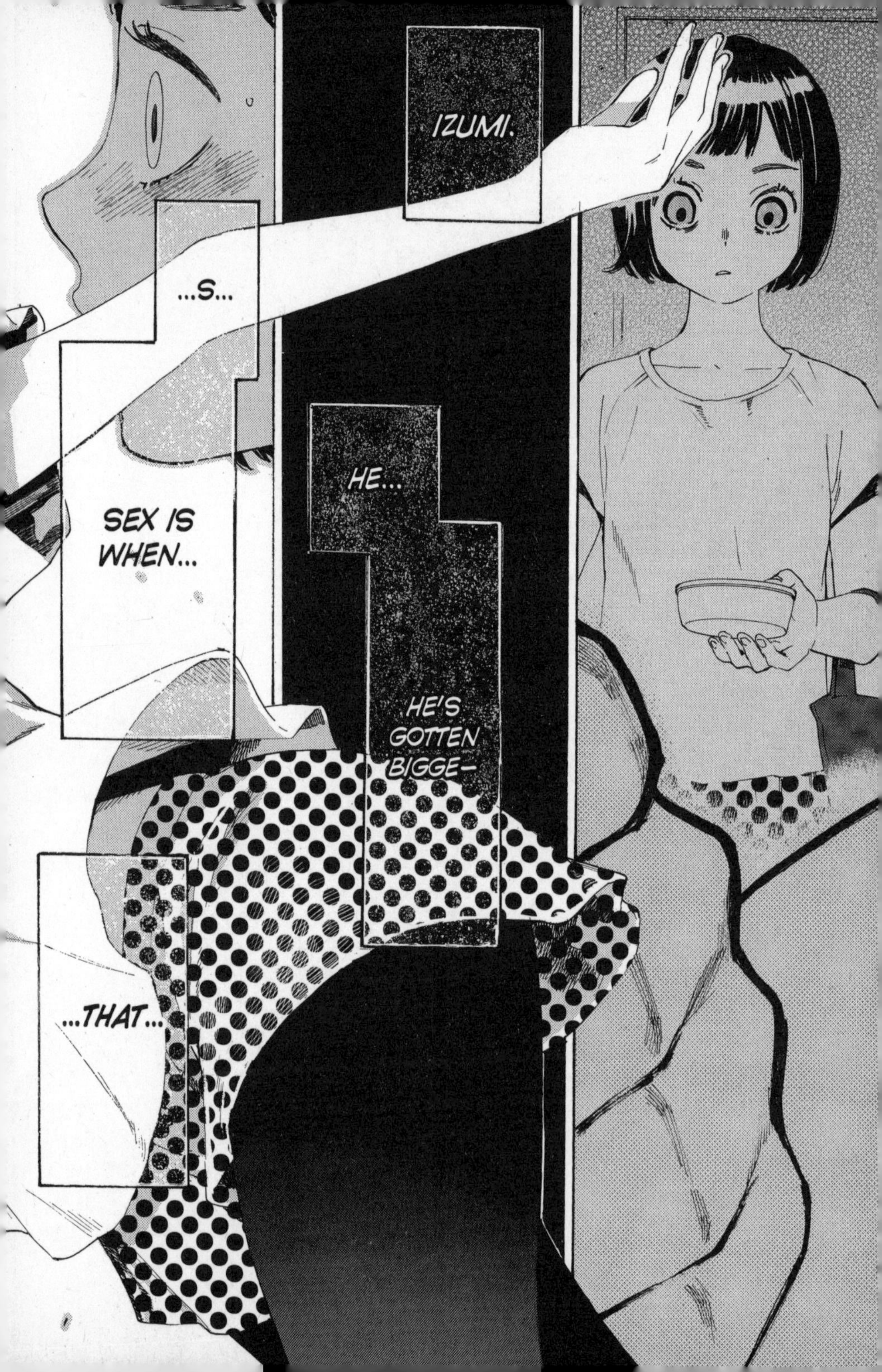
IZUMI.
HE...
HE'S GOTTEN BIGGE-
...S...
SEX IS WHEN...
...THAT...

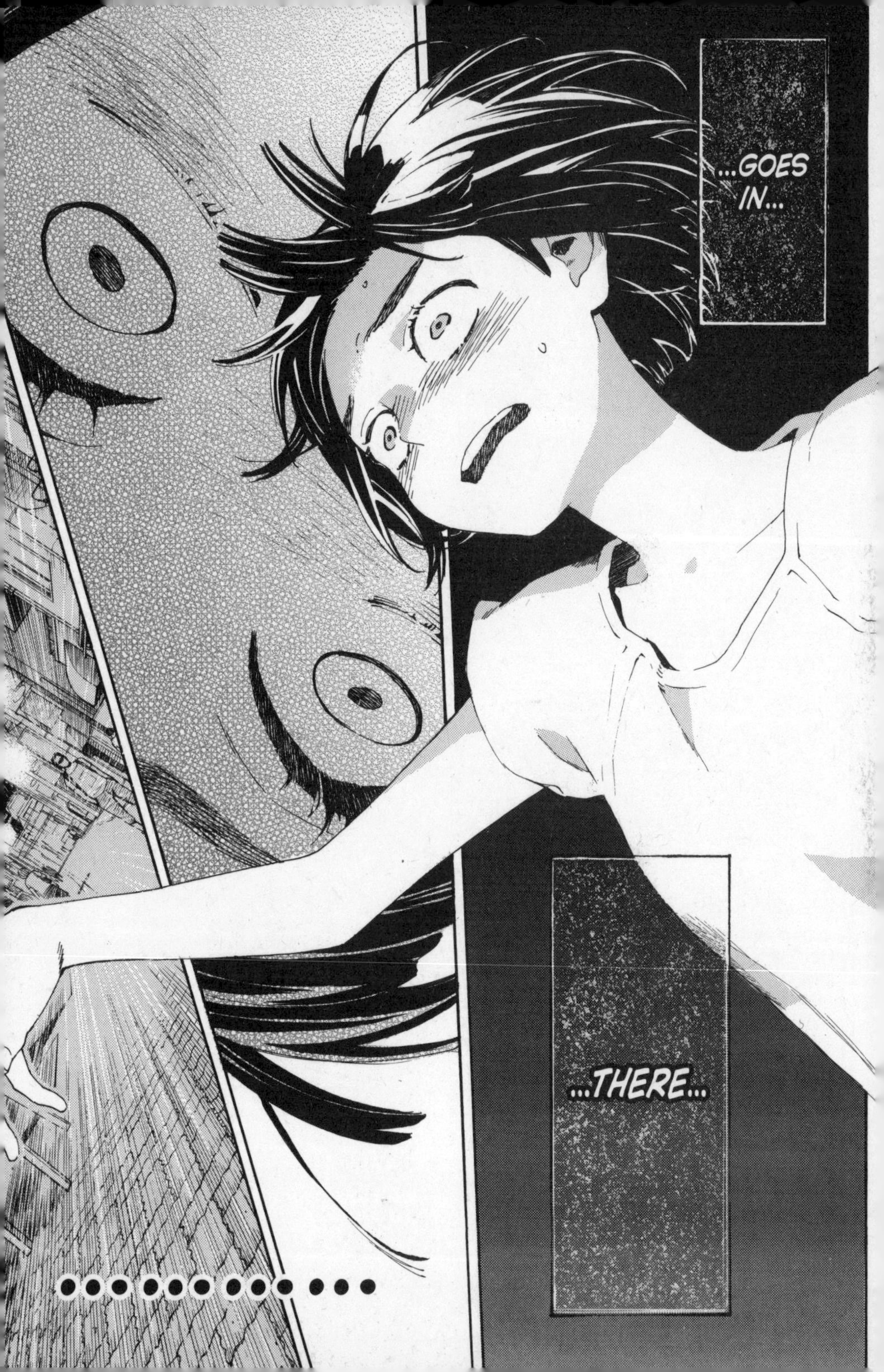
...GOES IN...
...THERE...
....

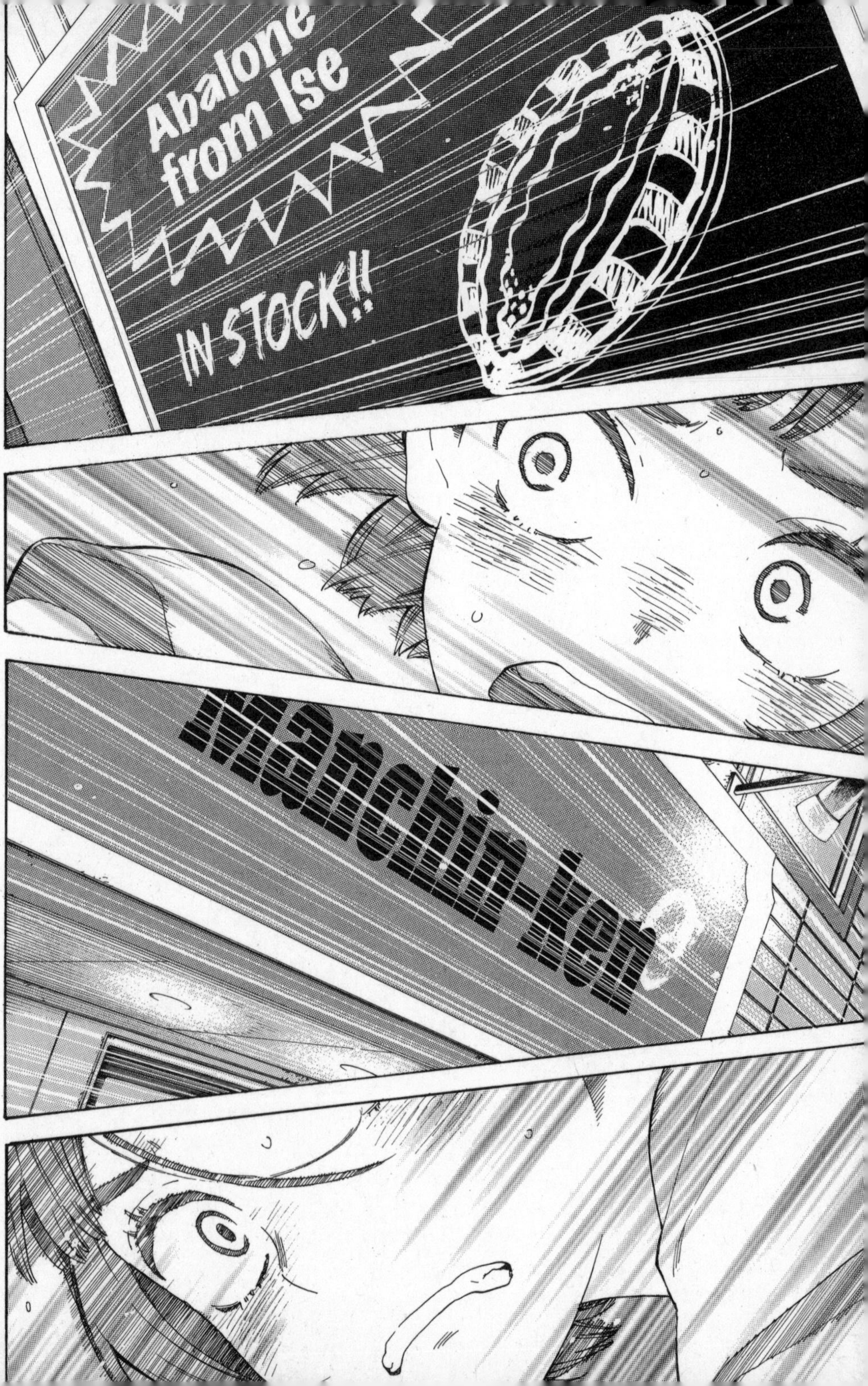
Abalone from Ise
IN STOCK!!
Manchin-ken

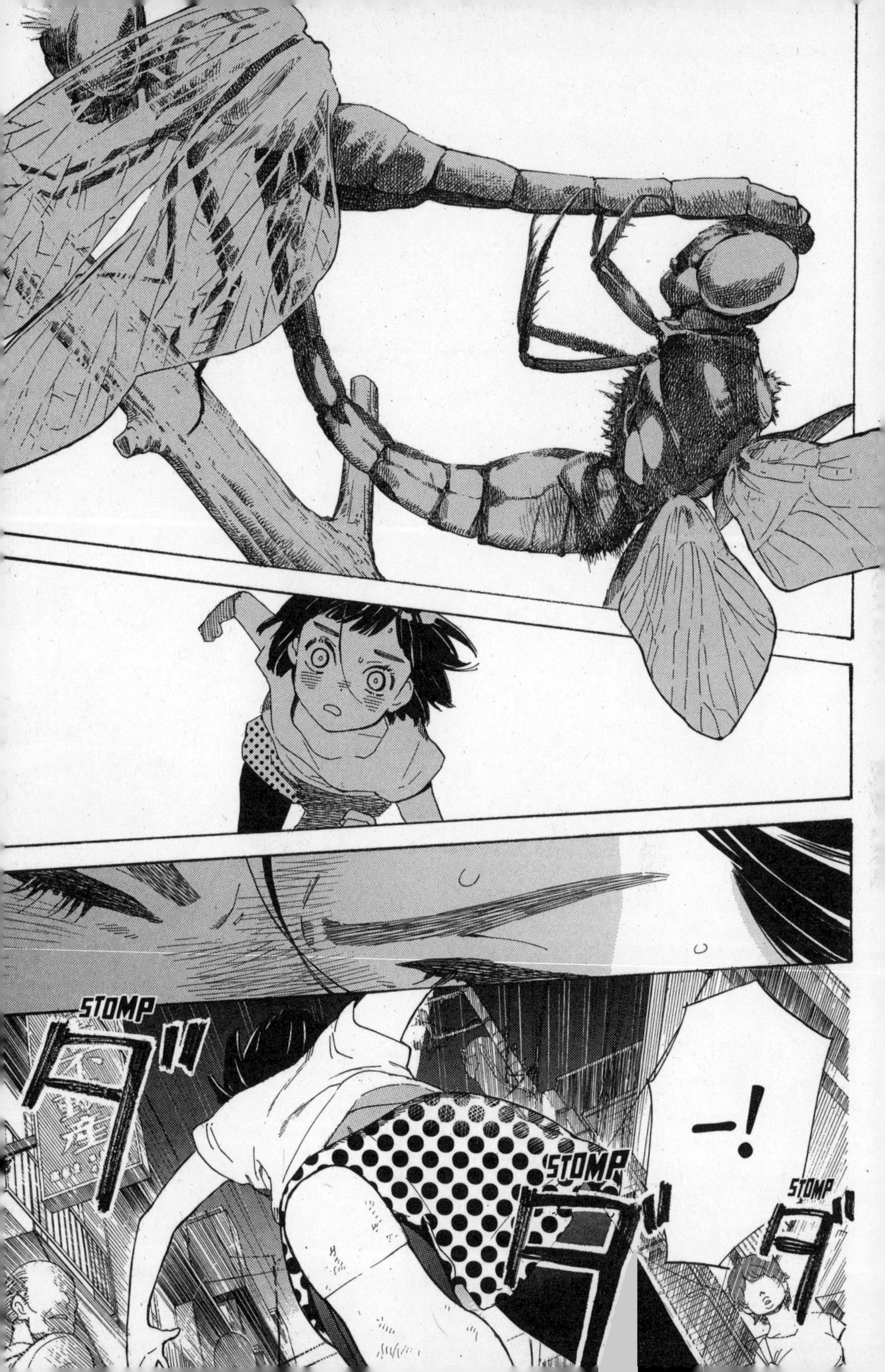
—!
STOMP
STOMP
STOMP

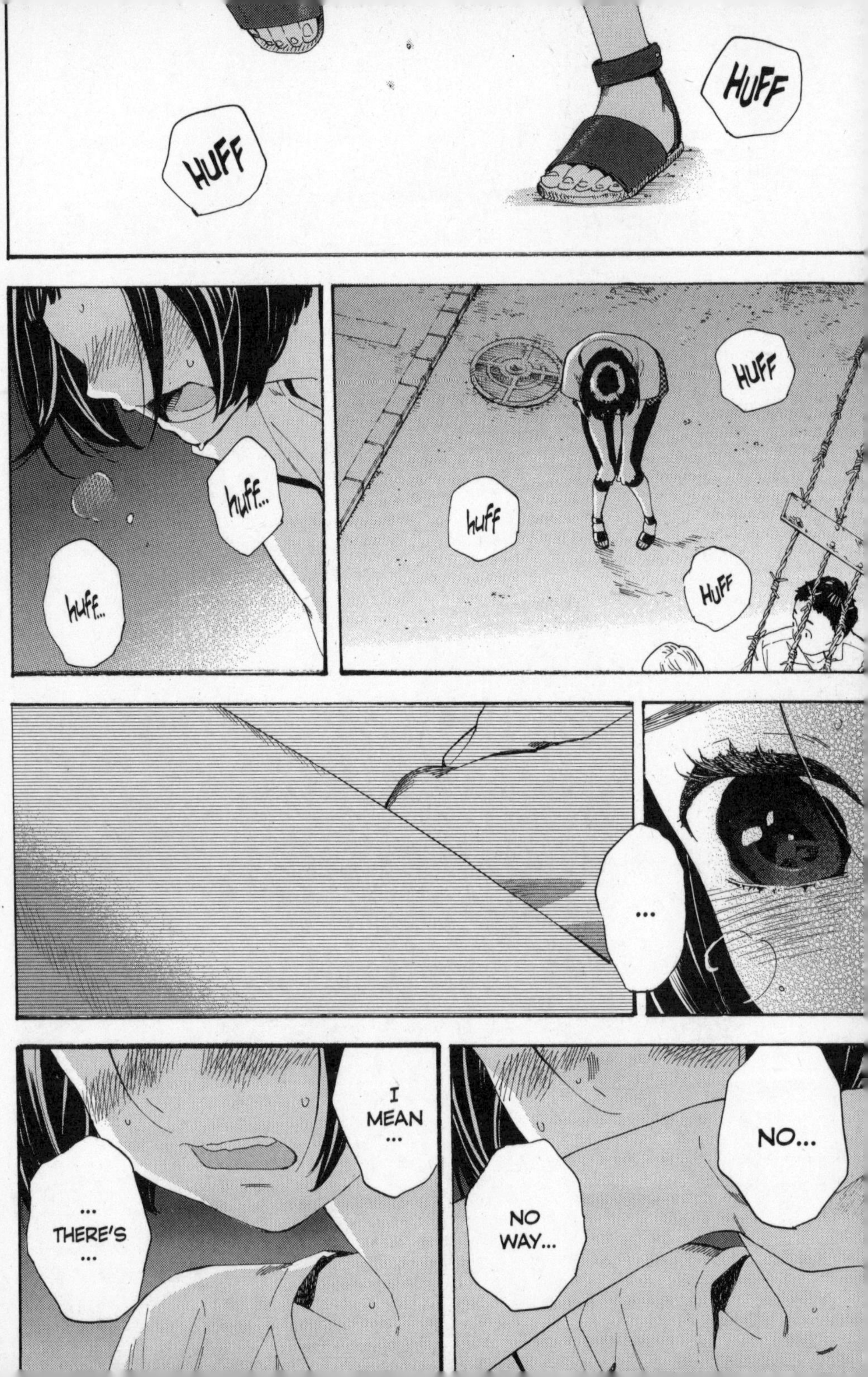
HUFF
HUFF
HUFF
huff
HUFF
huff...
huff...
...
NO...
NO WAY...
I MEAN ...
... THERE'S ...

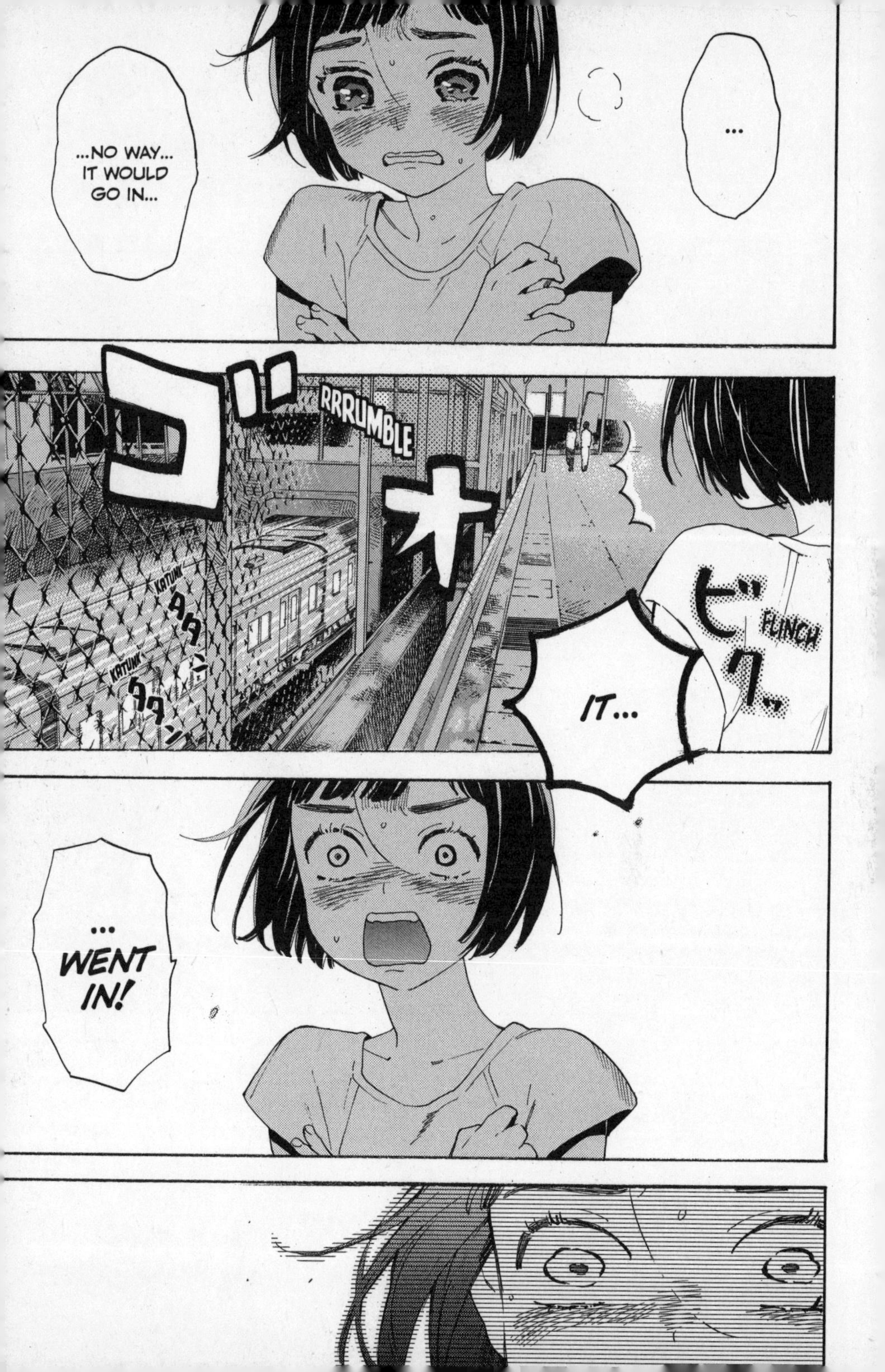
...
...NO WAY... IT WOULD GO IN...
ビクッ
FLINCH
IT...
RRRUMBLE
KATUNK
KATUNK
... WENT IN!

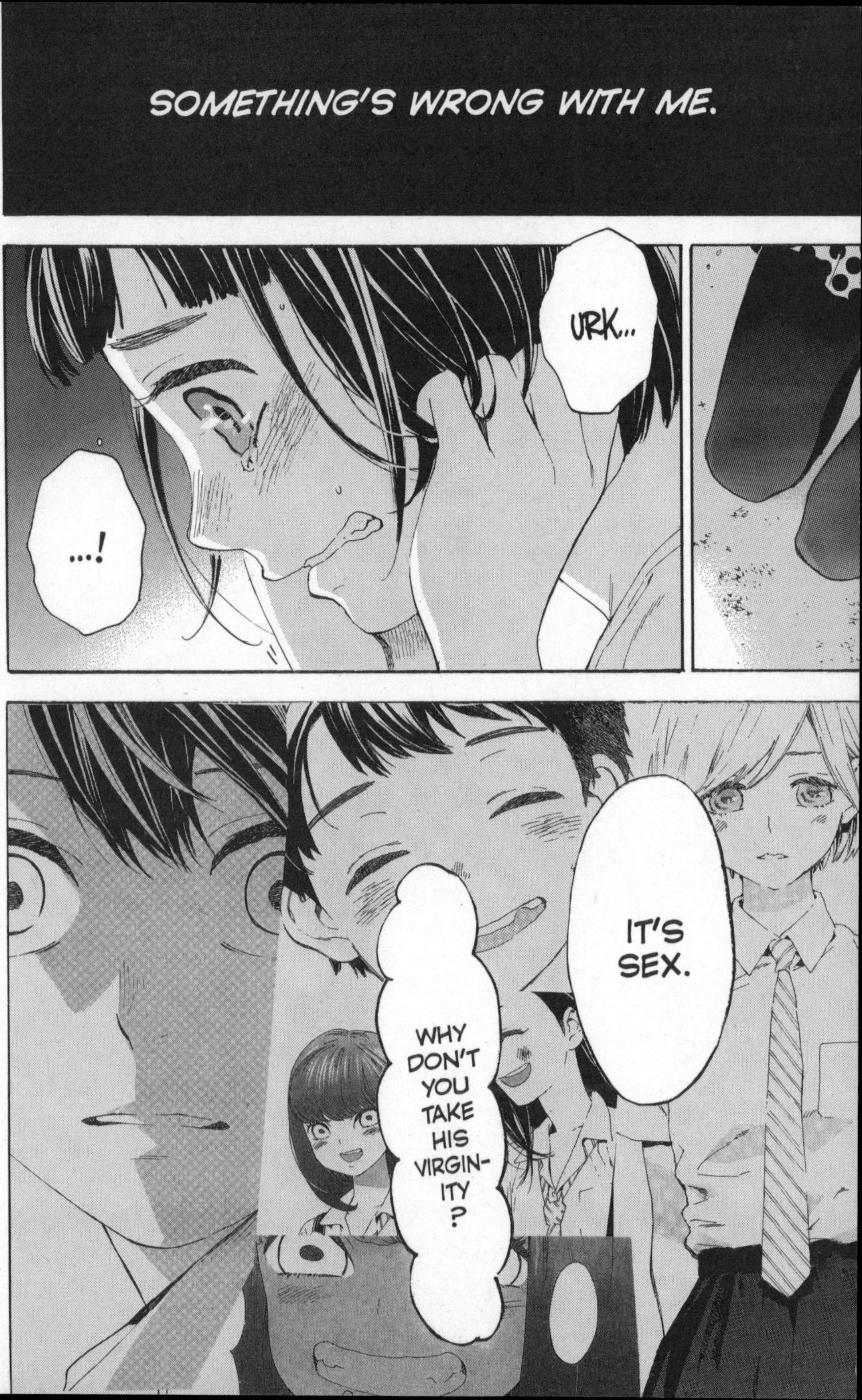
SOMETHING'S WRONG WITH ME.
URK...
...!
IT'S SEX.
WHY DON'T YOU TAKE HIS VIRGIN-ITY?

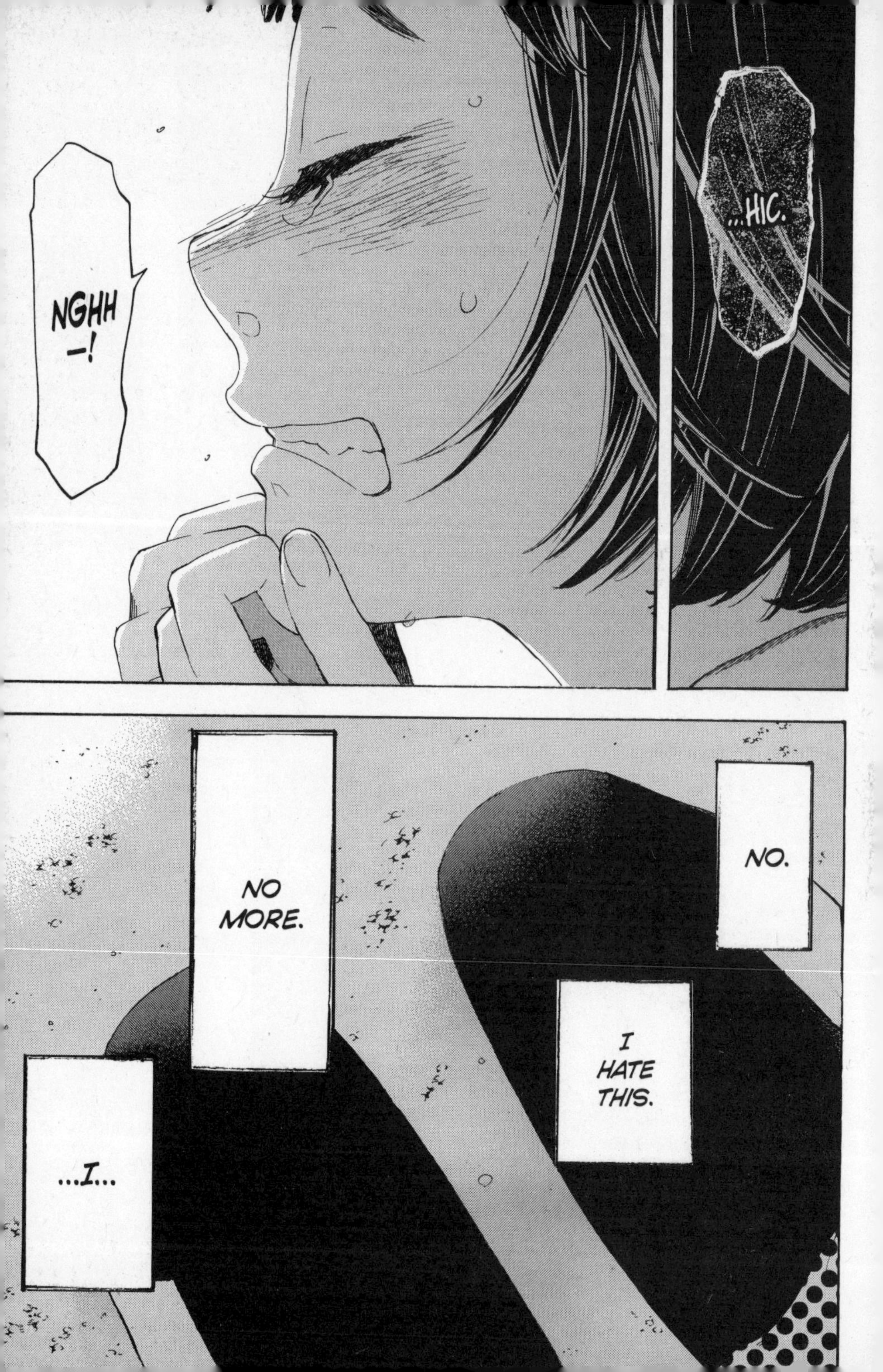
...HIC.
NGHH —!
NO.
I HATE THIS.
NO MORE.
...I...

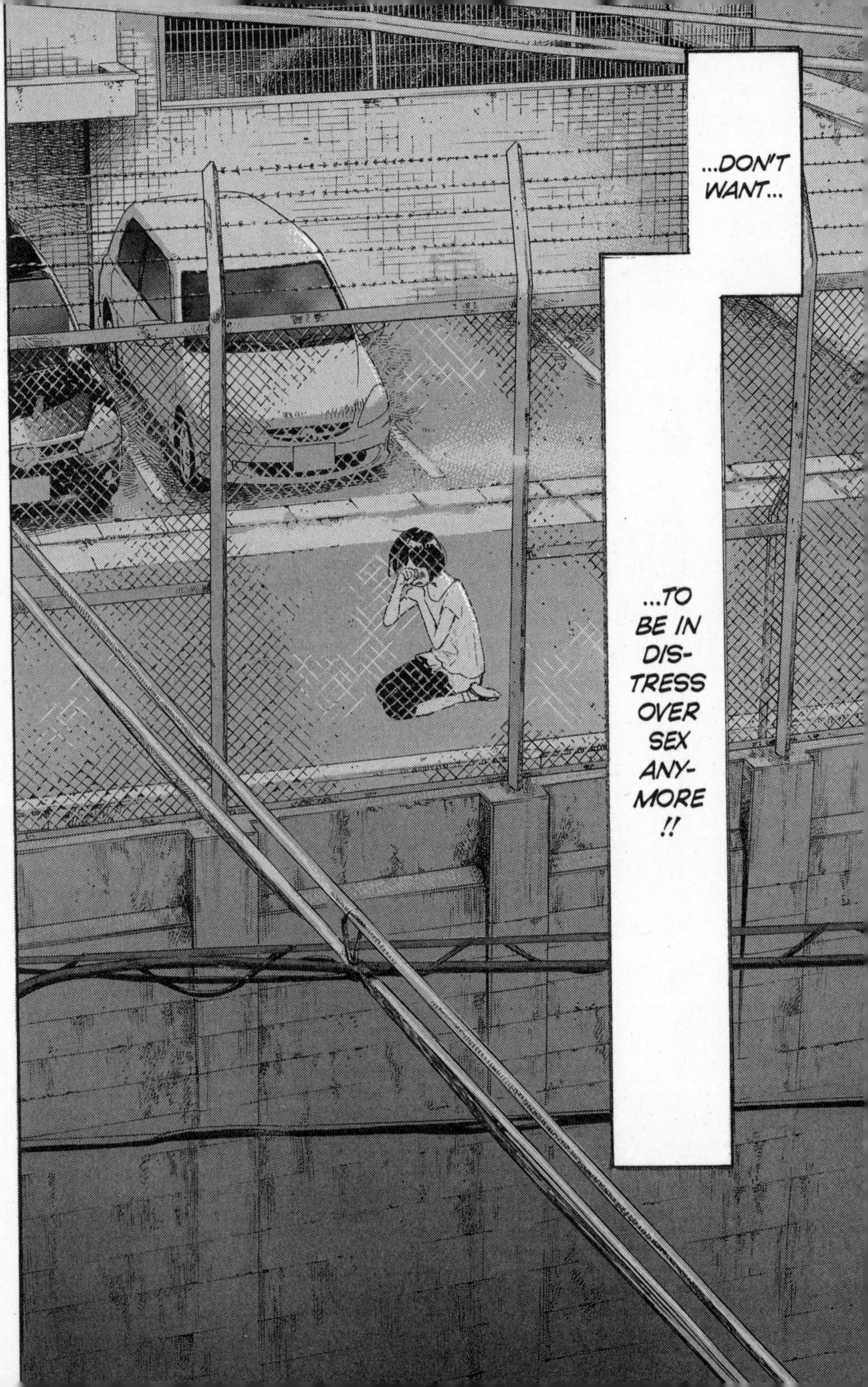
...DON'T WANT...
...TO BE IN DIS-TRESS OVER SEX ANY-MORE !!

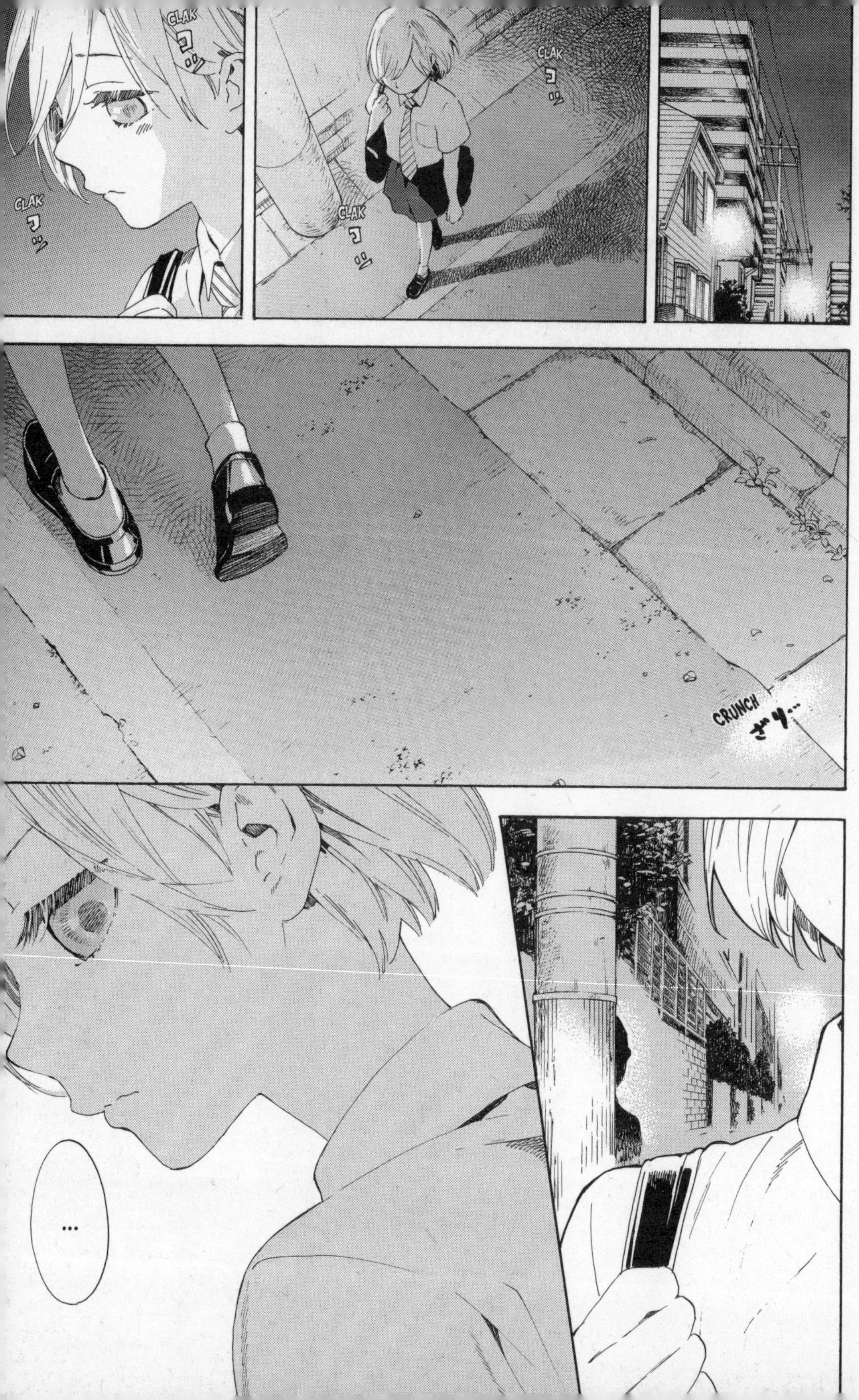
CLAK コッ
CLAK コッ
CLAK コッ
CLAK コッ
CRUNCH ざり…
...

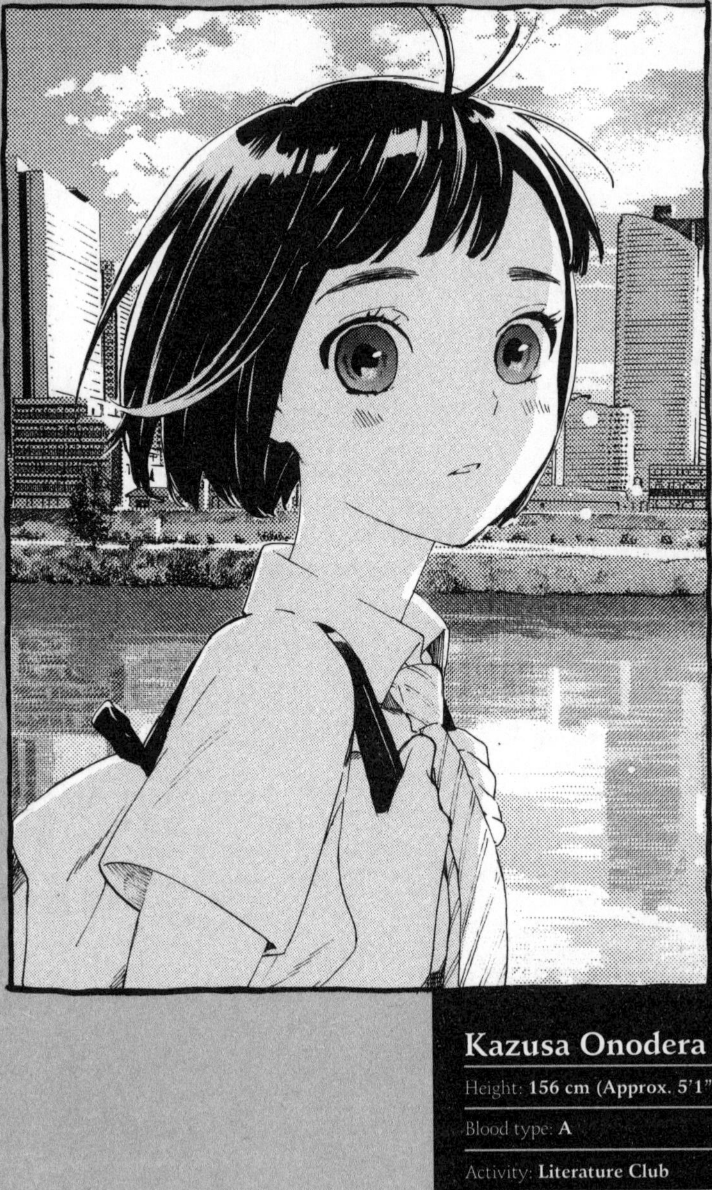

profile

Kazusa Onodera

Height: **156 cm (Approx. 5'1")**

Blood type: **A**

Activity: **Literature Club**

Favorite book: ***Momo***

Meeting 3

Boys and Sex: Being an Understanding Mother

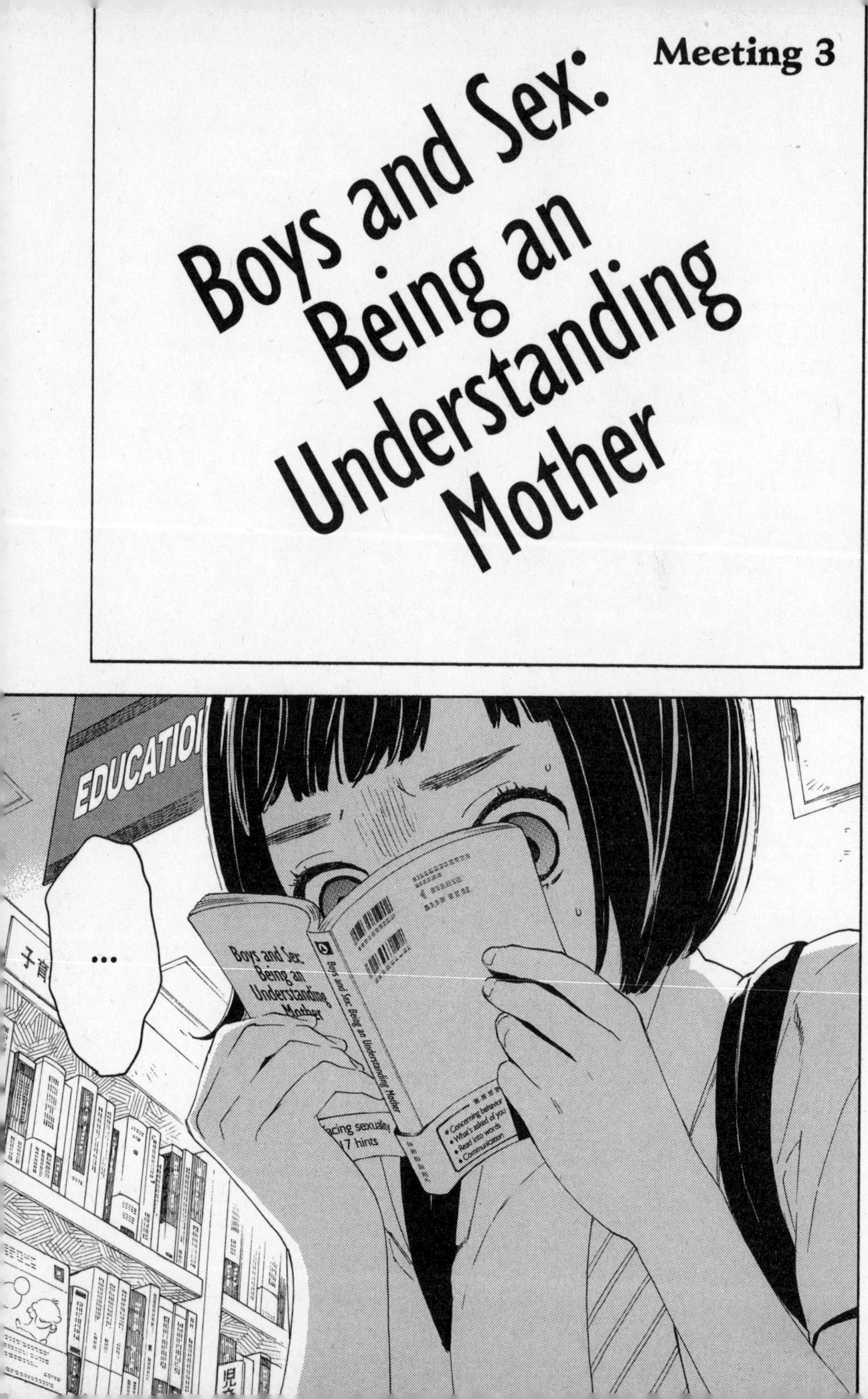

...
Boys and Sex: Being an Understanding Mother
Boys and Sex: Being an Understanding Mother
Concerning behavior
What's asked of you
Read into words
Communication

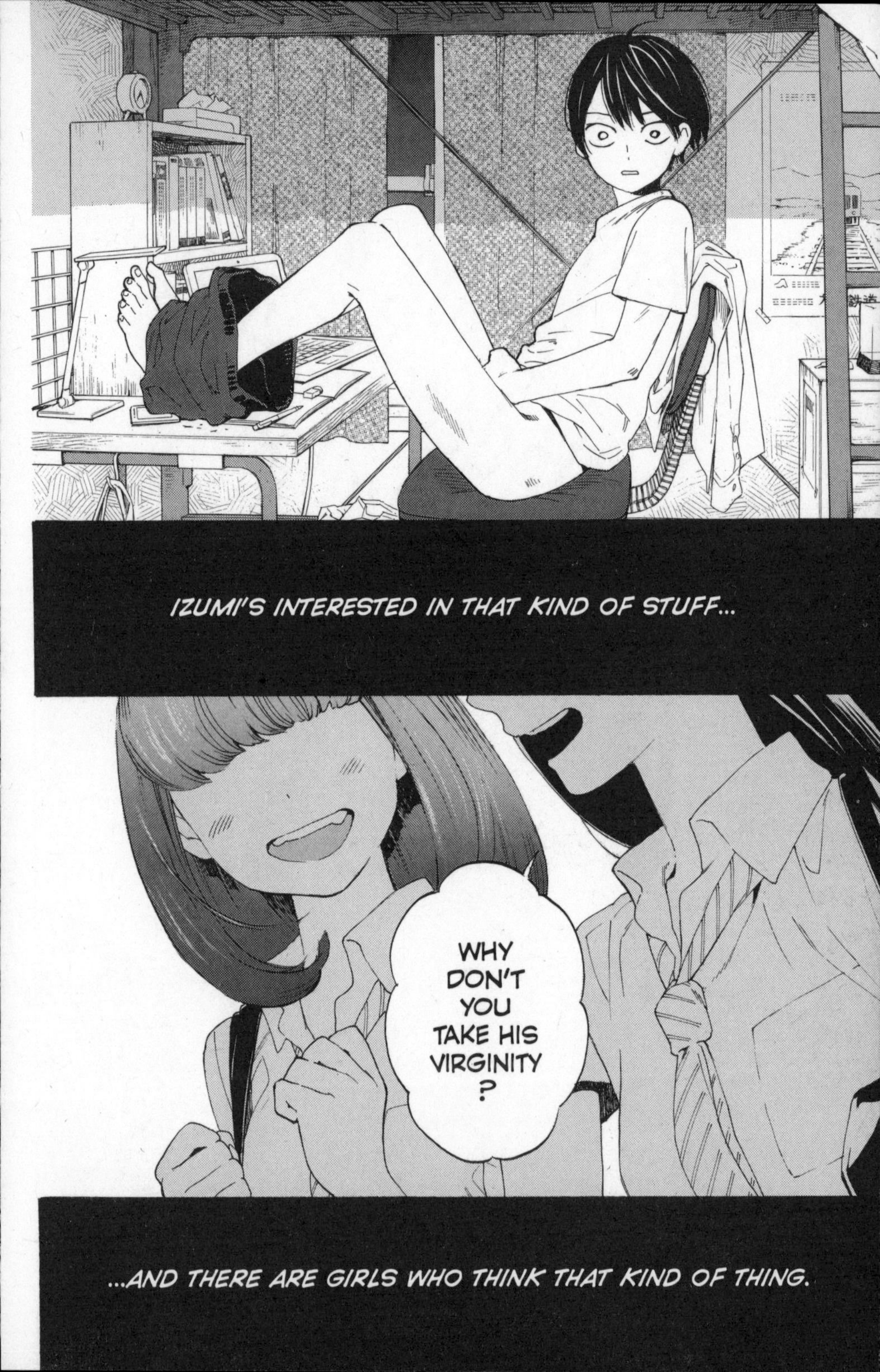
IZUMI'S INTERESTED IN THAT KIND OF STUFF...
WHY DON'T YOU TAKE HIS VIRGINITY?
...AND THERE ARE GIRLS WHO THINK THAT KIND OF THING.

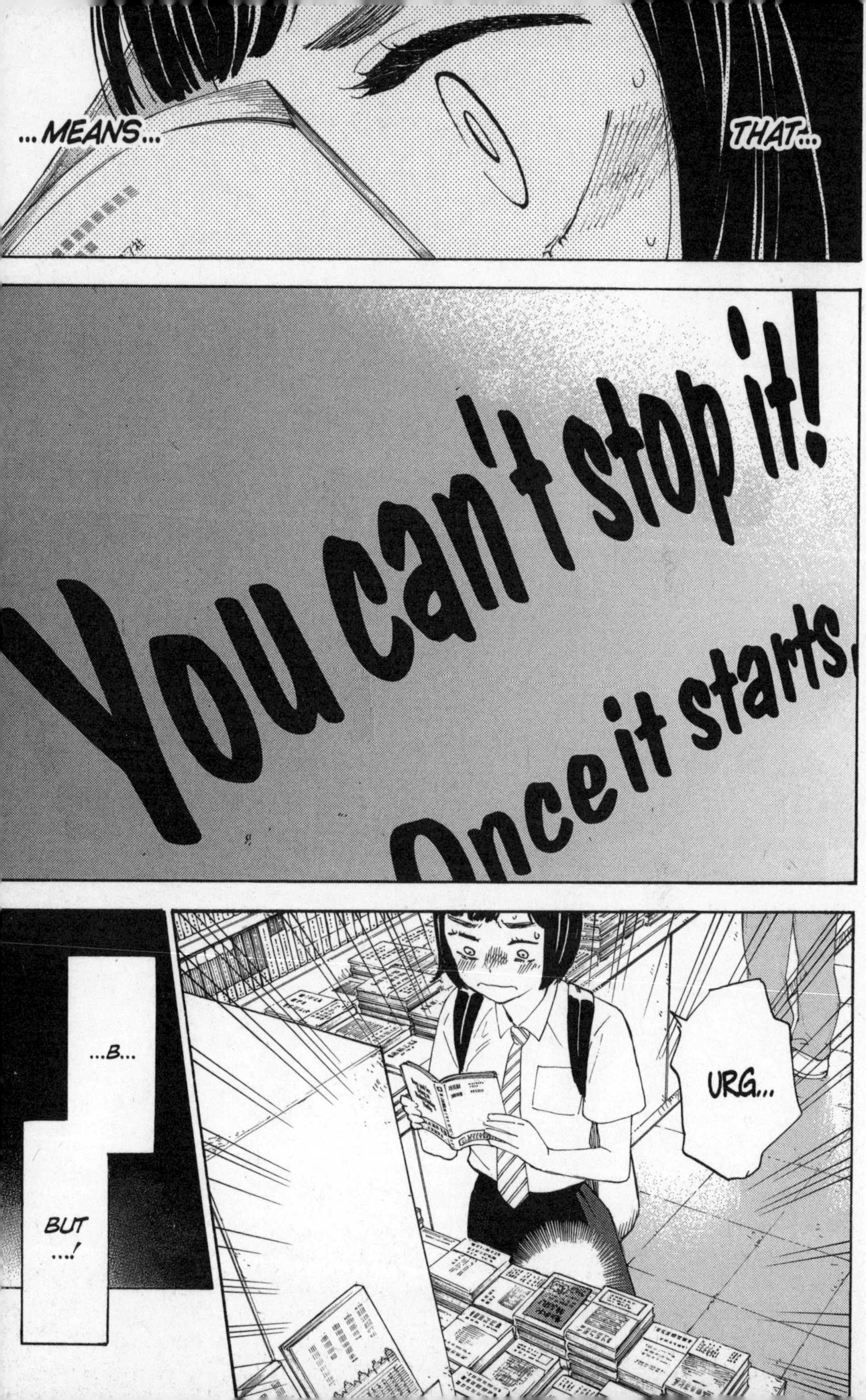
THAT...
...MEANS...
You can't stop it!
Once it starts,
URG...
...B...
BUT ...!

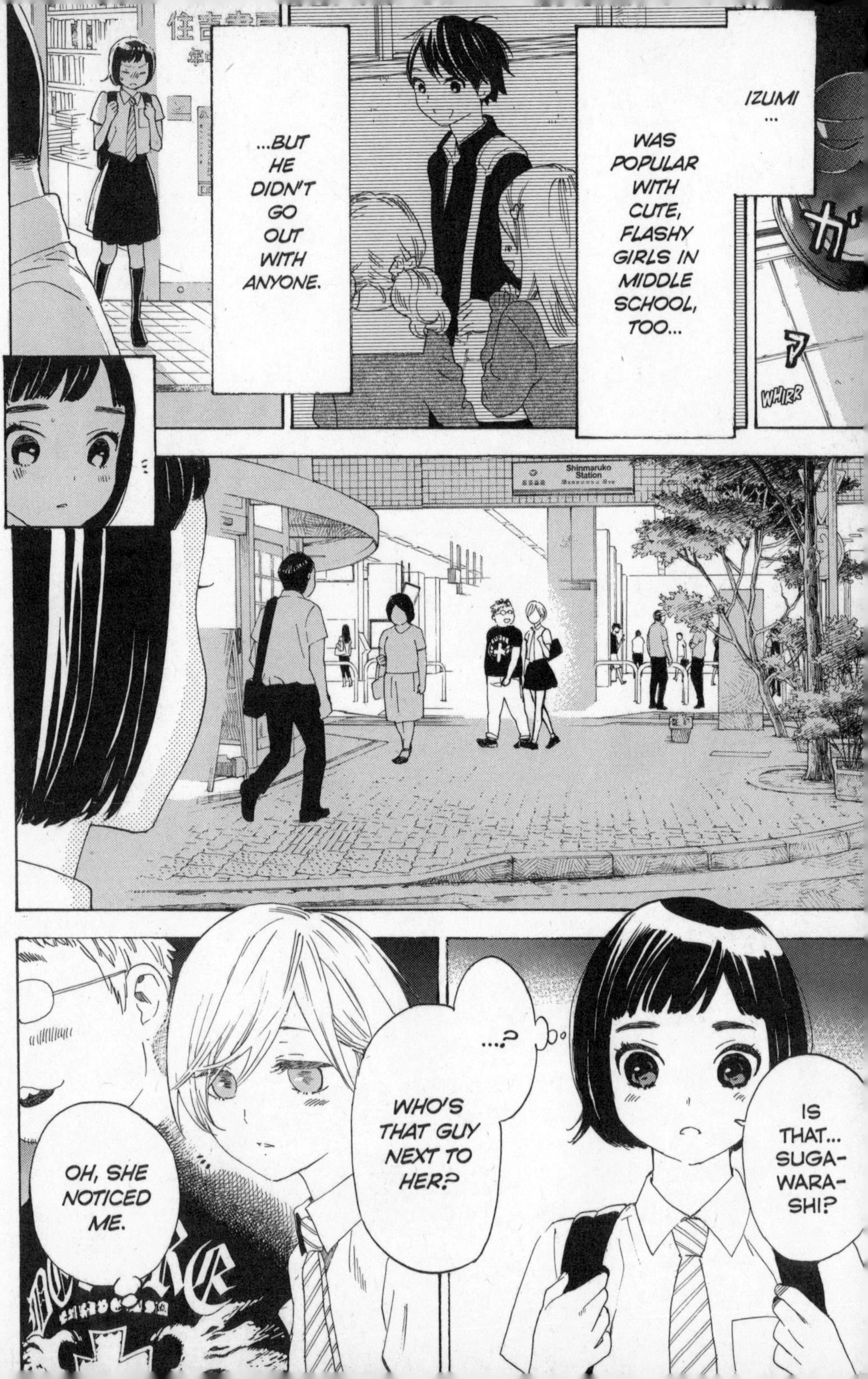

IZUMI ...
WAS POPULAR WITH CUTE, FLASHY GIRLS IN MIDDLE SCHOOL, TOO...
WHIRR
...BUT HE DIDN'T GO OUT WITH ANYONE.
Shinmaruko Station
IS THAT... SUGA-WARA-SHI?
...?
WHO'S THAT GUY NEXT TO HER?
OH, SHE NOTICED ME.

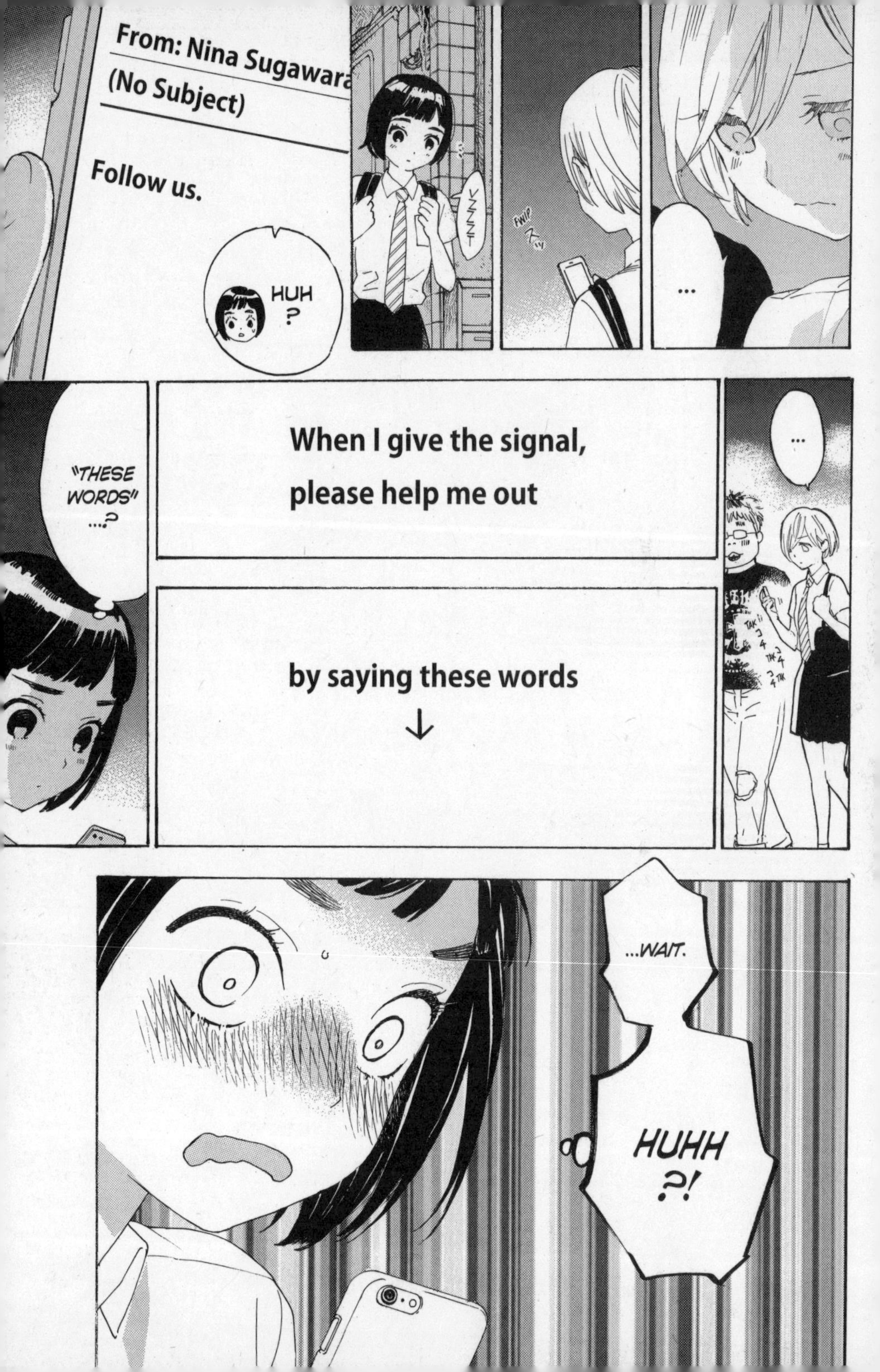
...
FWIP
VZZZT
From: Nina Sugawara
(No Subject)
Follow us.
HUH?
...
TAK TAK TAK
When I give the signal,
please help me out
by saying these words
↓
"THESE WORDS" ...?
...WAIT.
HUHH?!

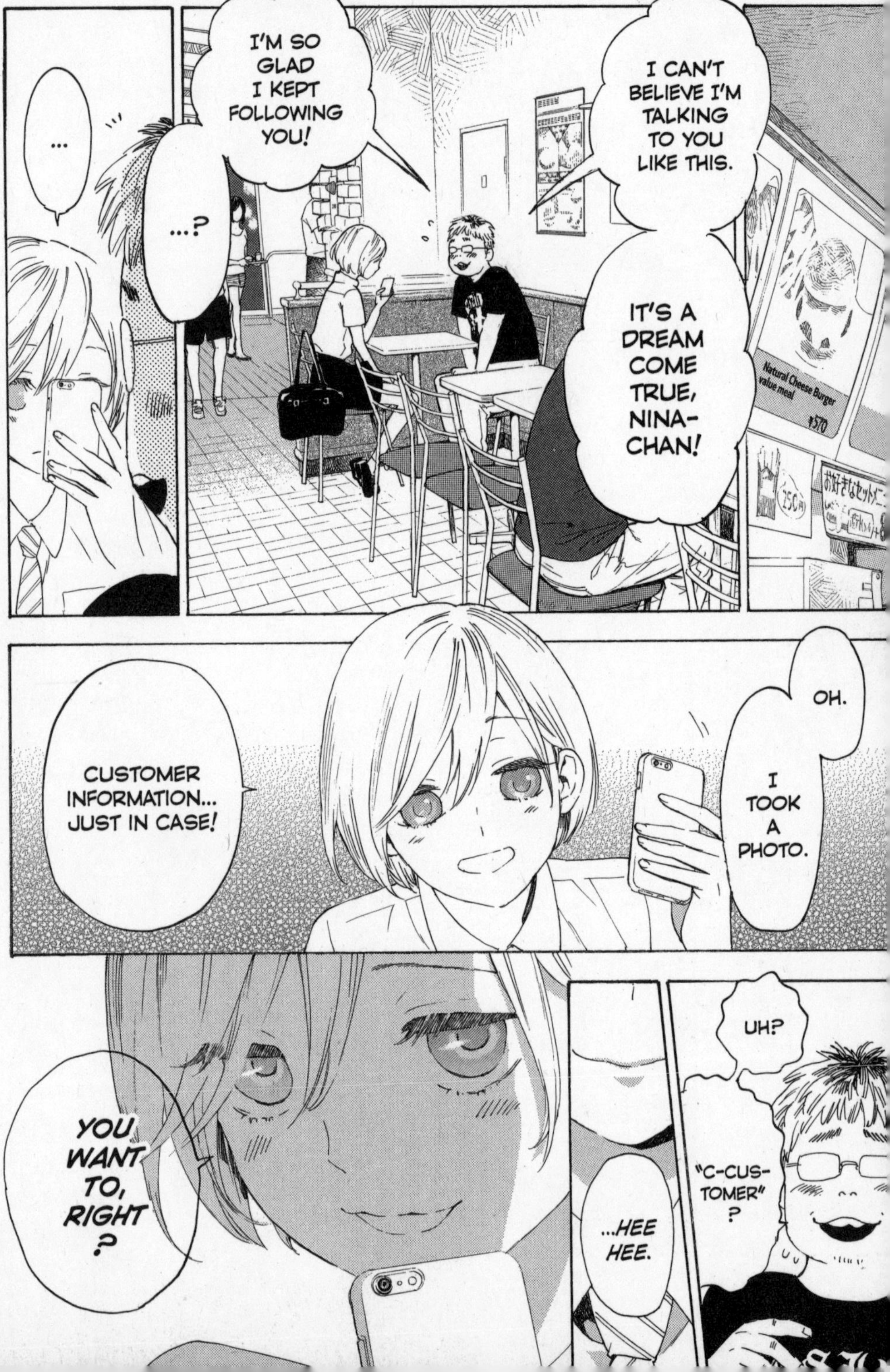
Natural Cheese Burger value meal
¥570
I CAN'T BELIEVE I'M TALKING TO YOU LIKE THIS.
IT'S A DREAM COME TRUE, NINA-CHAN!
I'M SO GLAD I KEPT FOLLOWING YOU!
...?
...
OH.
I TOOK A PHOTO.
CUSTOMER INFORMATION... JUST IN CASE!
UH?
"C-CUSTOMER"?
...HEE HEE.
YOU WANT TO, RIGHT?

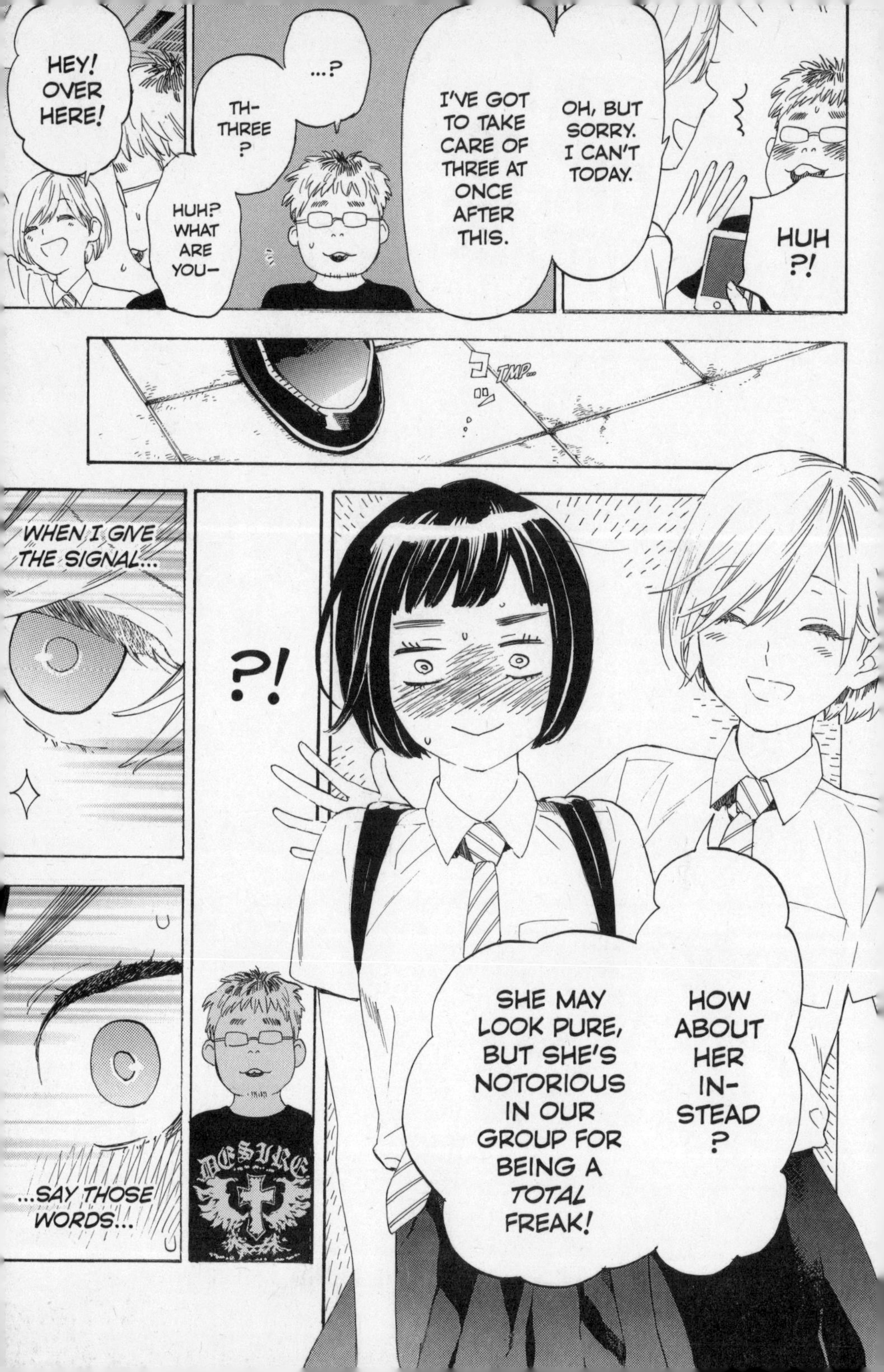
OH, BUT SORRY. I CAN'T TODAY.
I'VE GOT TO TAKE CARE OF THREE AT ONCE AFTER THIS.
HUH ?!
...?
TH- THREE ?
HUH? WHAT ARE YOU—
HEY! OVER HERE!
TMP...
HOW ABOUT HER IN- STEAD ?
SHE MAY LOOK PURE, BUT SHE'S NOTORIOUS IN OUR GROUP FOR BEING A *TOTAL* FREAK!
?!
WHEN I GIVE THE SIGNAL...
DESIRE
...SAY THOSE WORDS...

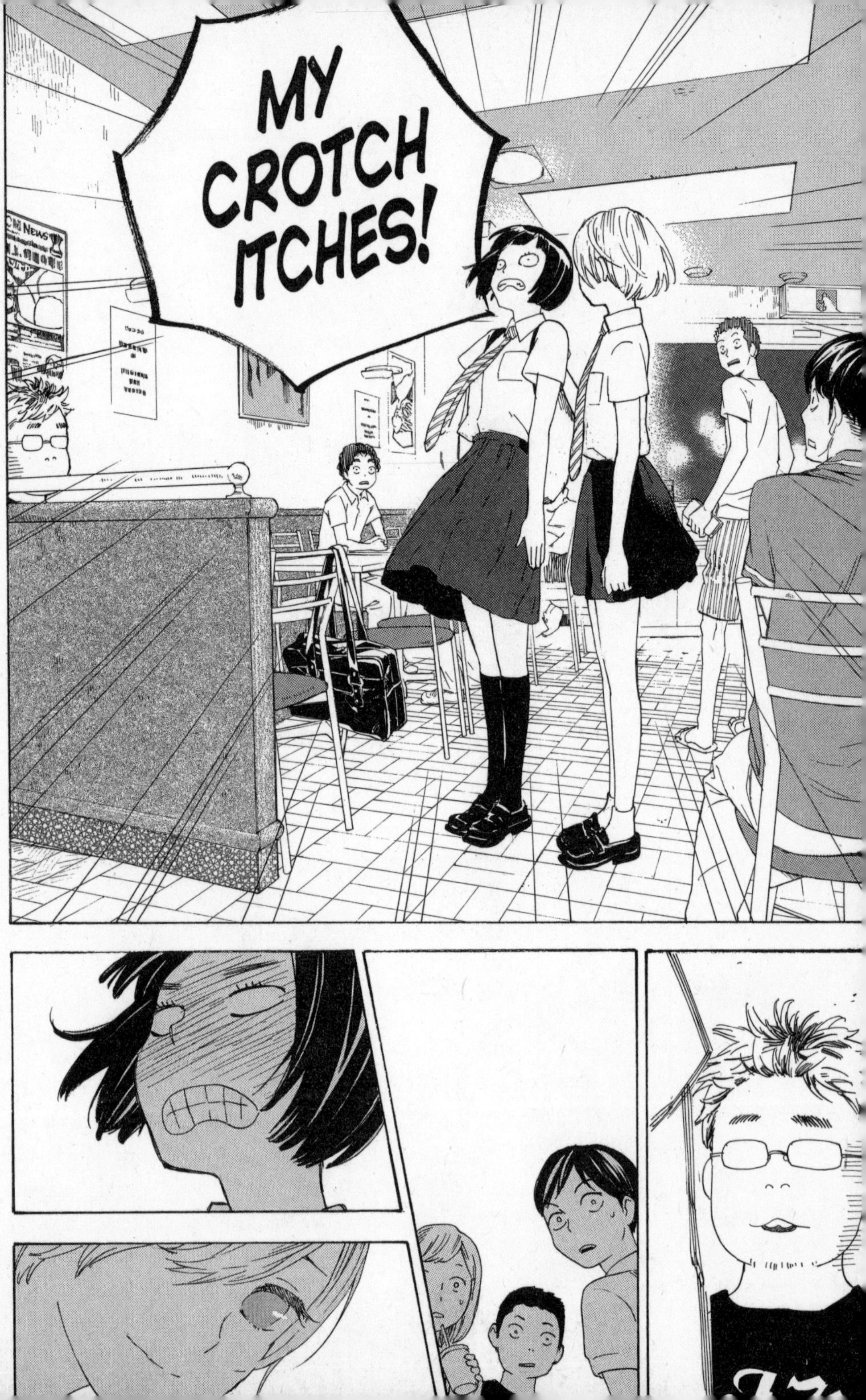
MY CROTCH ITCHES!

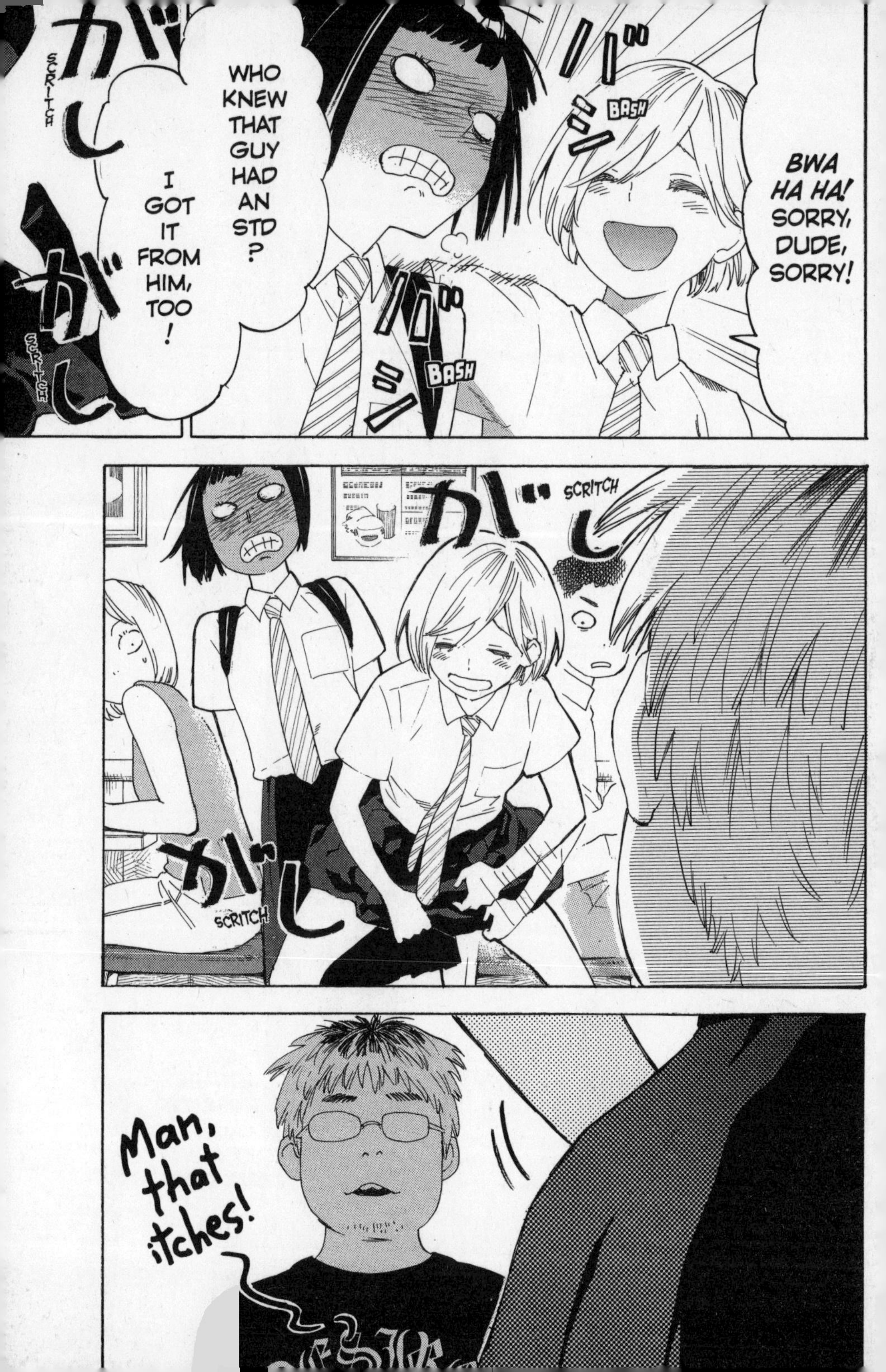
BWA HA HA! SORRY, DUDE, SORRY!
BASH
BASH
WHO KNEW THAT GUY HAD AN STD?
I GOT IT FROM HIM, TOO!
SCRITCH
SCRITCH
SCRITCH
SCRITCH
Man, that itches!

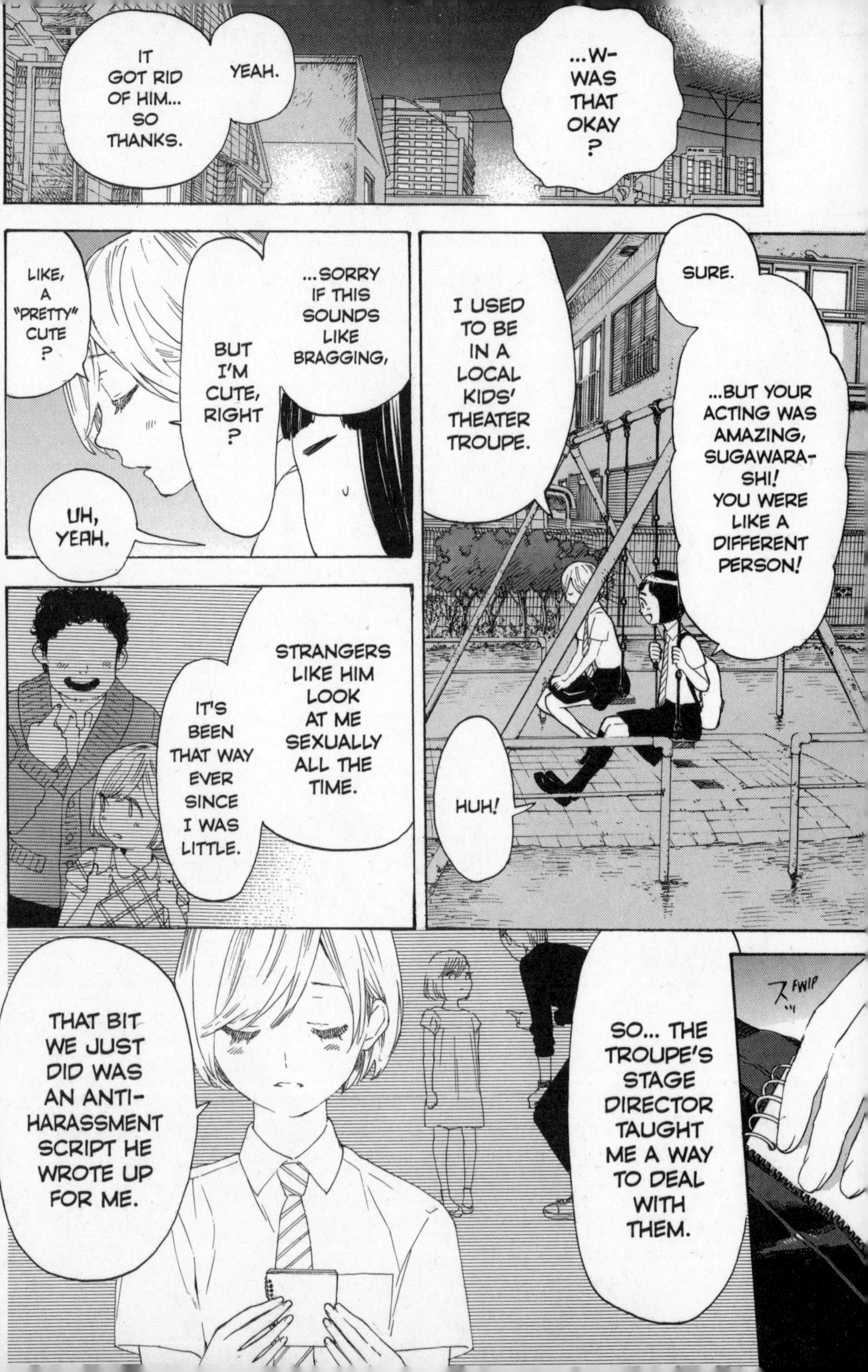
...W-WAS THAT OKAY?
YEAH.
IT GOT RID OF HIM... SO THANKS.
SURE.
...BUT YOUR ACTING WAS AMAZING, SUGAWARA-SHI! YOU WERE LIKE A DIFFERENT PERSON!
I USED TO BE IN A LOCAL KIDS' THEATER TROUPE.
HUH!
...SORRY IF THIS SOUNDS LIKE BRAGGING,
BUT I'M CUTE, RIGHT?
LIKE, A "PRETTY" CUTE?
UH, YEAH.
STRANGERS LIKE HIM LOOK AT ME SEXUALLY ALL THE TIME.
IT'S BEEN THAT WAY EVER SINCE I WAS LITTLE.
ス FWIP
SO... THE TROUPE'S STAGE DIRECTOR TAUGHT ME A WAY TO DEAL WITH THEM.
THAT BIT WE JUST DID WAS AN ANTI-HARASSMENT SCRIPT HE WROTE UP FOR ME.

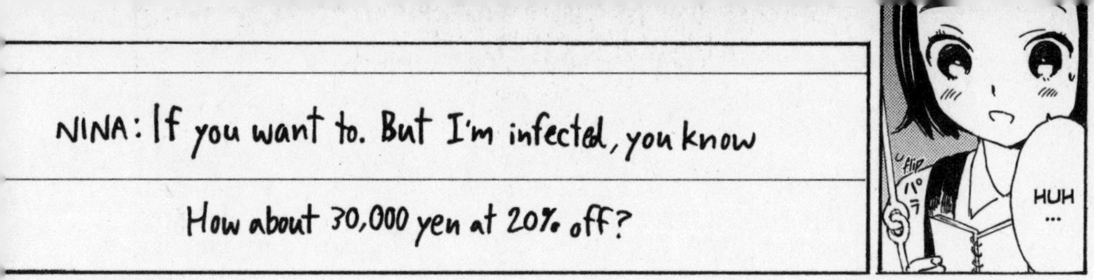
HUH...
NINA: If you want to. But I'm infected, you know
How about 30,000 yen at 20% off?
Flip

*About 300 USD.

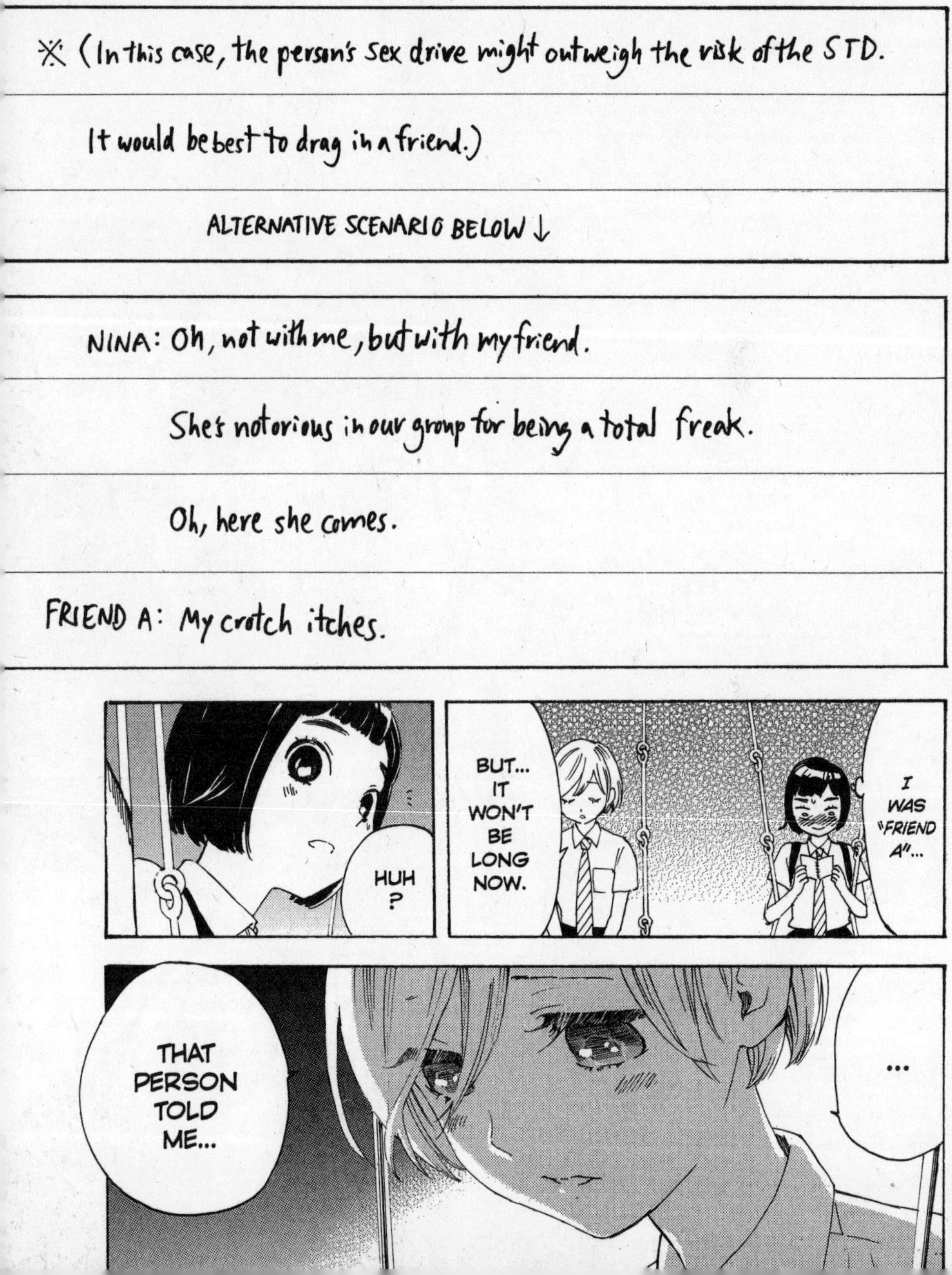
※ (In this case, the person's sex drive might outweigh the risk of the STD.
It would be best to drag in a friend.)
ALTERNATIVE SCENARIO BELOW ↓
NINA: Oh, not with me, but with my friend.
She's notorious in our group for being a total freak.
Oh, here she comes.
FRIEND A: My crotch itches.
I WAS "FRIEND A"...
BUT... IT WON'T BE LONG NOW.
HUH?
...
THAT PERSON TOLD ME...

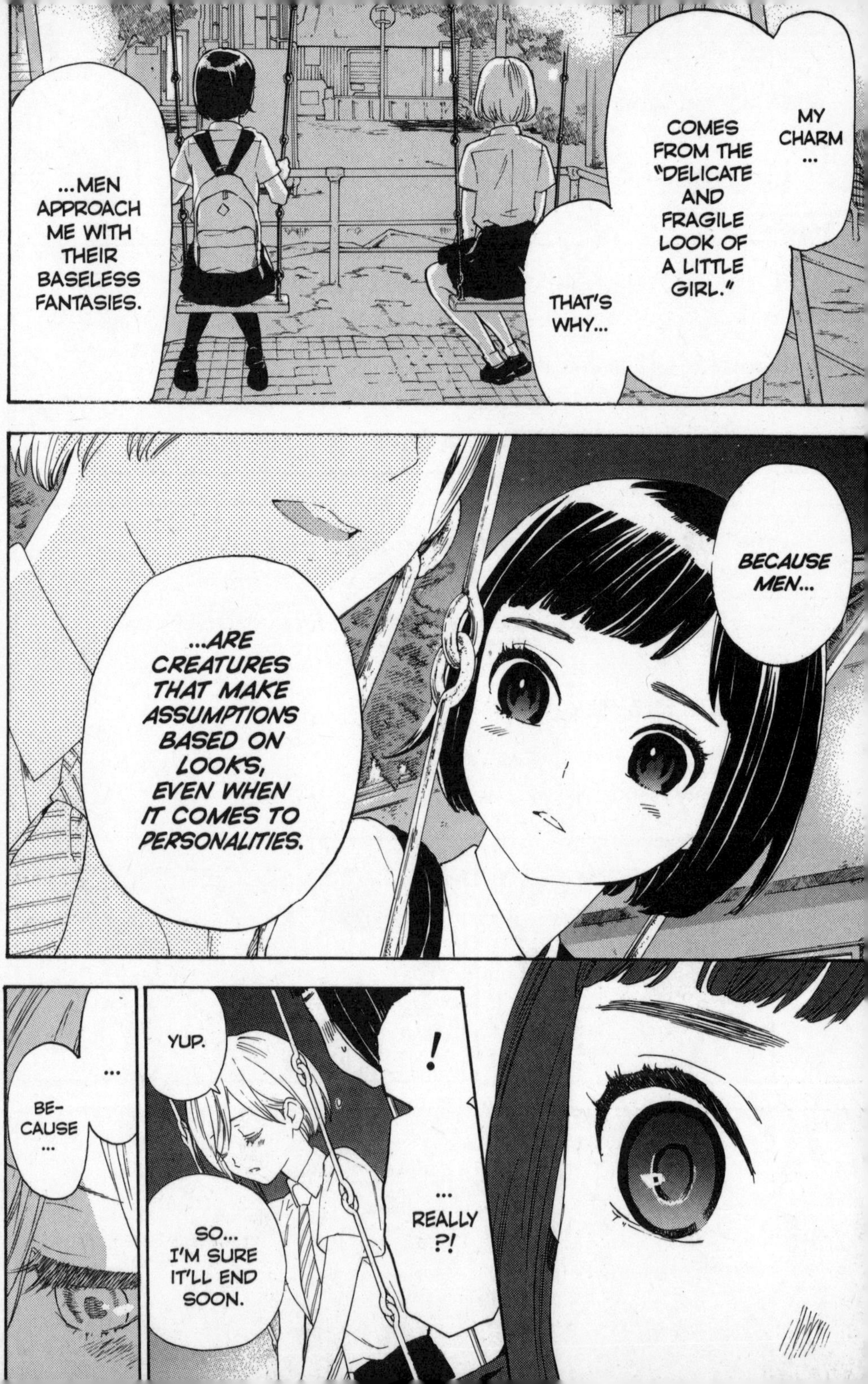
MY CHARM...
COMES FROM THE "DELICATE AND FRAGILE LOOK OF A LITTLE GIRL."
THAT'S WHY...
...MEN APPROACH ME WITH THEIR BASELESS FANTASIES.
BECAUSE MEN...
...ARE CREATURES THAT MAKE ASSUMPTIONS BASED ON LOOKS, EVEN WHEN IT COMES TO PERSONALITIES.
!
...REALLY?!
YUP.
SO... I'M SURE IT'LL END SOON.
... BE-CAUSE ...

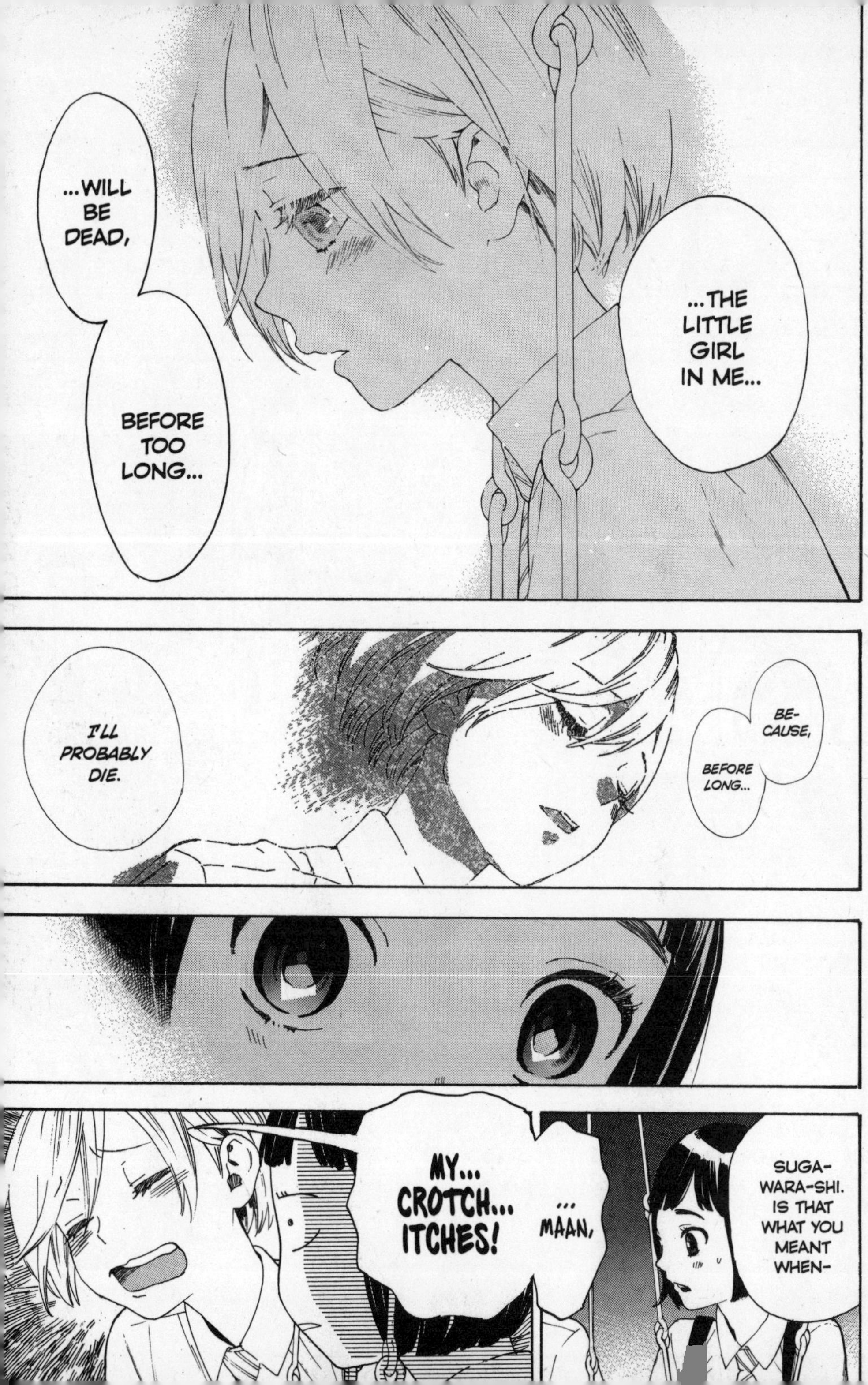
...THE LITTLE GIRL IN ME...
...WILL BE DEAD,
BEFORE TOO LONG...
BE-CAUSE,
BEFORE LONG...
I'LL PROBABLY DIE.
SUGA-WARA-SHI. IS THAT WHAT YOU MEANT WHEN-
...MAAN,
MY... CROTCH... ITCHES!

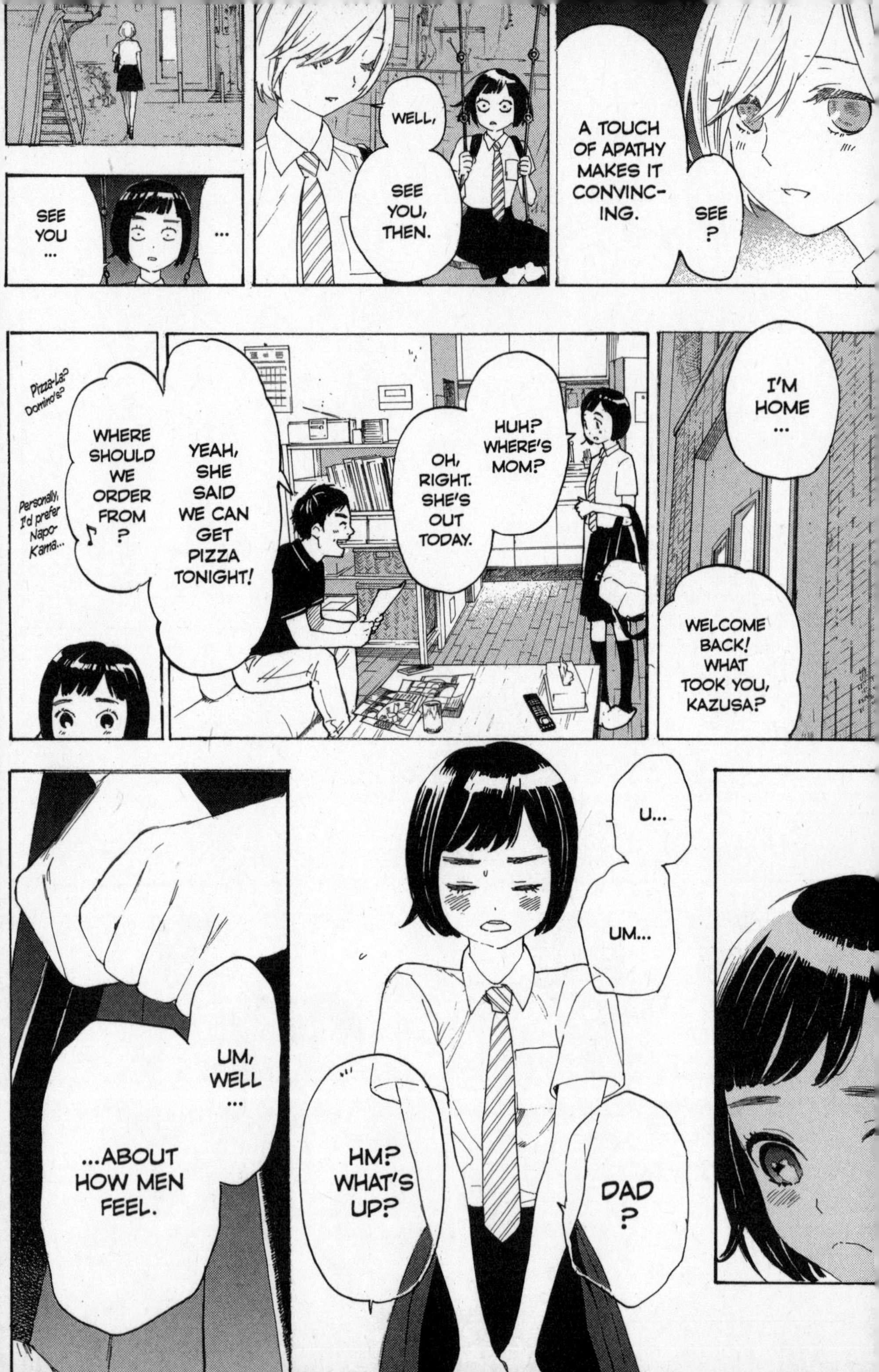
SEE ?
A TOUCH OF APATHY MAKES IT CONVINC-ING.
WELL,
SEE YOU, THEN.
...
SEE YOU ...
I'M HOME ...
WELCOME BACK! WHAT TOOK YOU, KAZUSA?
HUH? WHERE'S MOM?
OH, RIGHT. SHE'S OUT TODAY.
YEAH, SHE SAID WE CAN GET PIZZA TONIGHT!
WHERE SHOULD WE ORDER FROM ?
Pizza-La? Domino's?
Personally, I'd prefer Napo-Kama...
U...
UM...
DAD ?
HM? WHAT'S UP?
UM, WELL ...
...ABOUT HOW MEN FEEL.

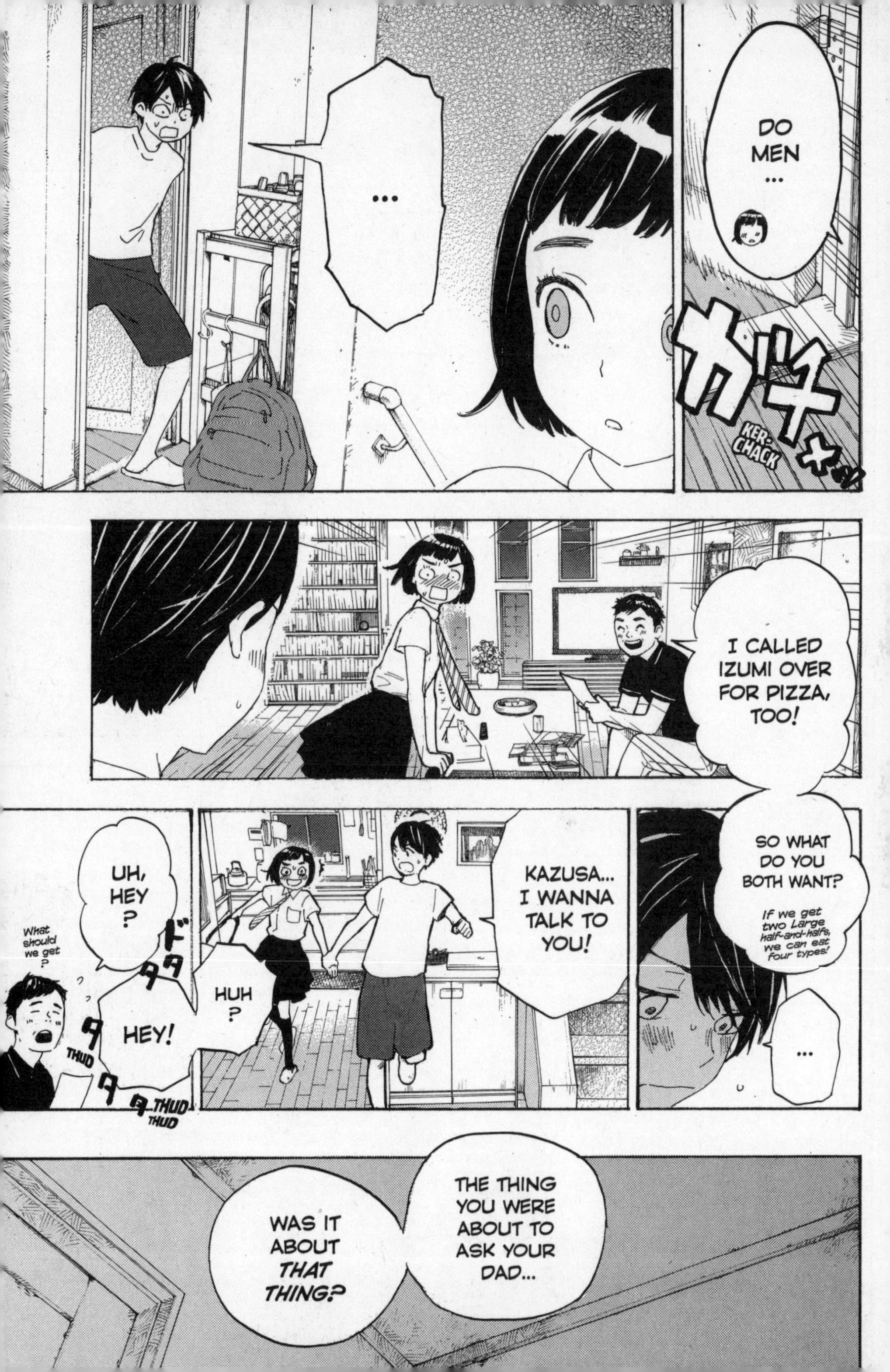
DO MEN ...
KER-CHACK
...
I CALLED IZUMI OVER FOR PIZZA, TOO!
SO WHAT DO YOU BOTH WANT?
If we get two Large half-and-halfs, we can eat four types!
...
KAZUSA... I WANNA TALK TO YOU!
HUH?
UH, HEY?
HEY!
What should we get?
THUD THUD THUD
THE THING YOU WERE ABOUT TO ASK YOUR DAD...
WAS IT ABOUT THAT THING?

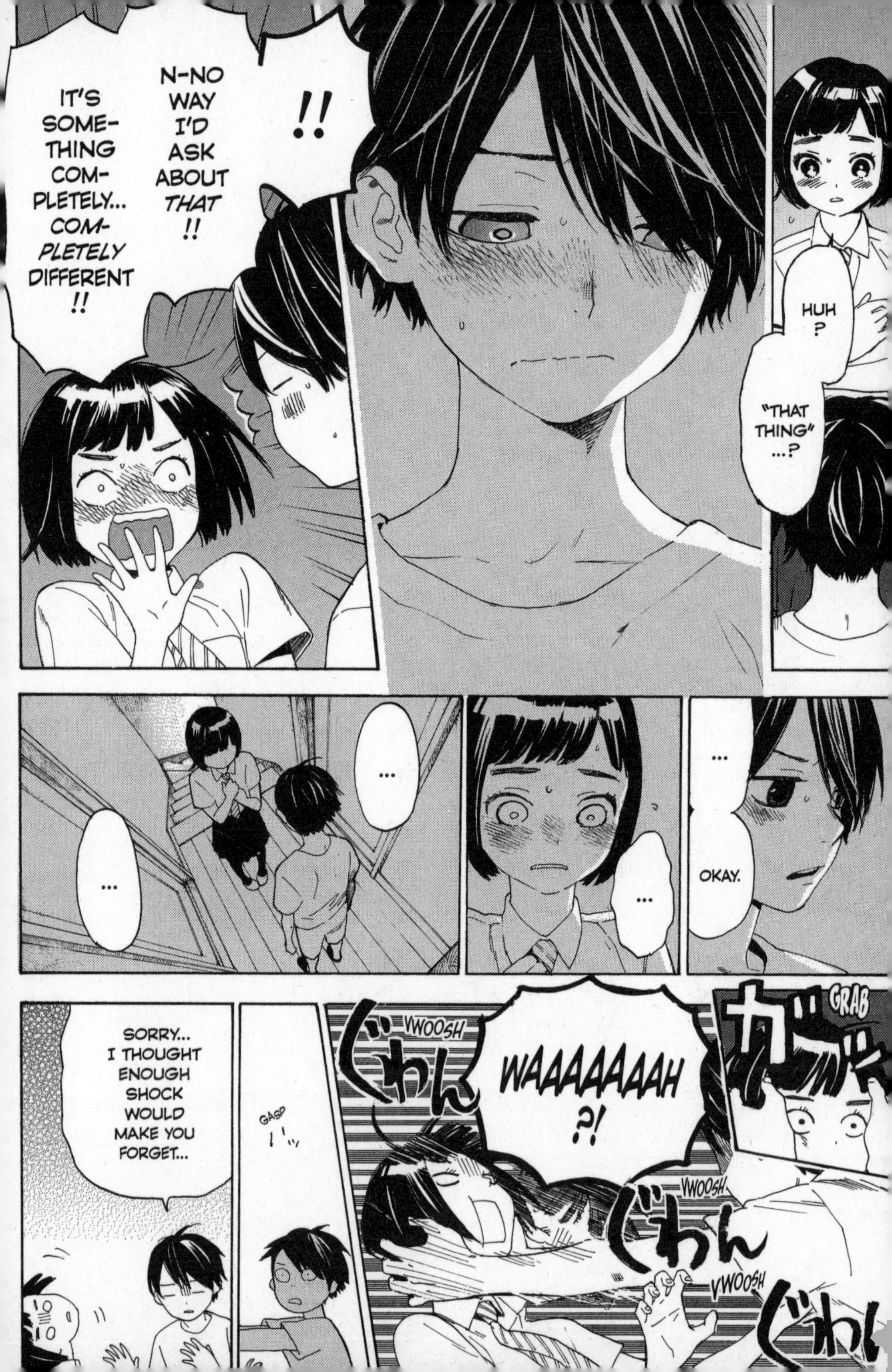
HUH?
"THAT THING"...?
!!
N-NO WAY I'D ASK ABOUT *THAT*!!
IT'S SOMETHING COMPLETELY... *COMPLETELY* DIFFERENT!!
...
OKAY.
...
...
...
GRAB
WAAAAAAAH?!
VWOOSH
ぐわん
VWOOSH
ぐわん
VWOOSH
ぐわん
GASP
SORRY... I THOUGHT ENOUGH SHOCK WOULD MAKE YOU FORGET...

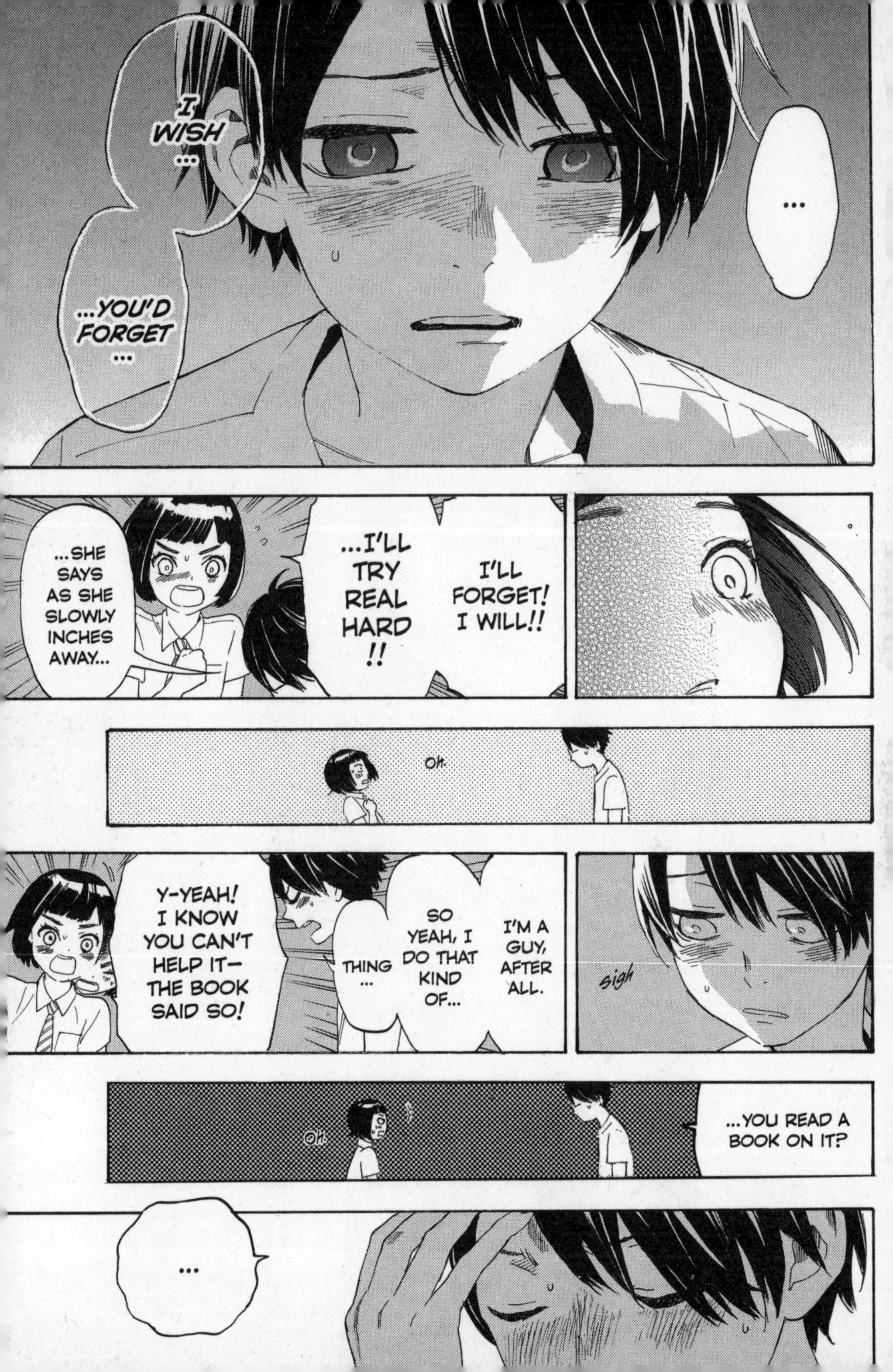
...
I WISH ...
...YOU'D FORGET ...
I'LL FORGET! I WILL!!
...I'LL TRY REAL HARD!!
...SHE SAYS AS SHE SLOWLY INCHES AWAY...
Oh.
sigh
I'M A GUY, AFTER ALL.
SO YEAH, I DO THAT KIND OF...
THING ...
Y-YEAH! I KNOW YOU CAN'T HELP IT— THE BOOK SAID SO!
...YOU READ A BOOK ON IT?
Oh.
...

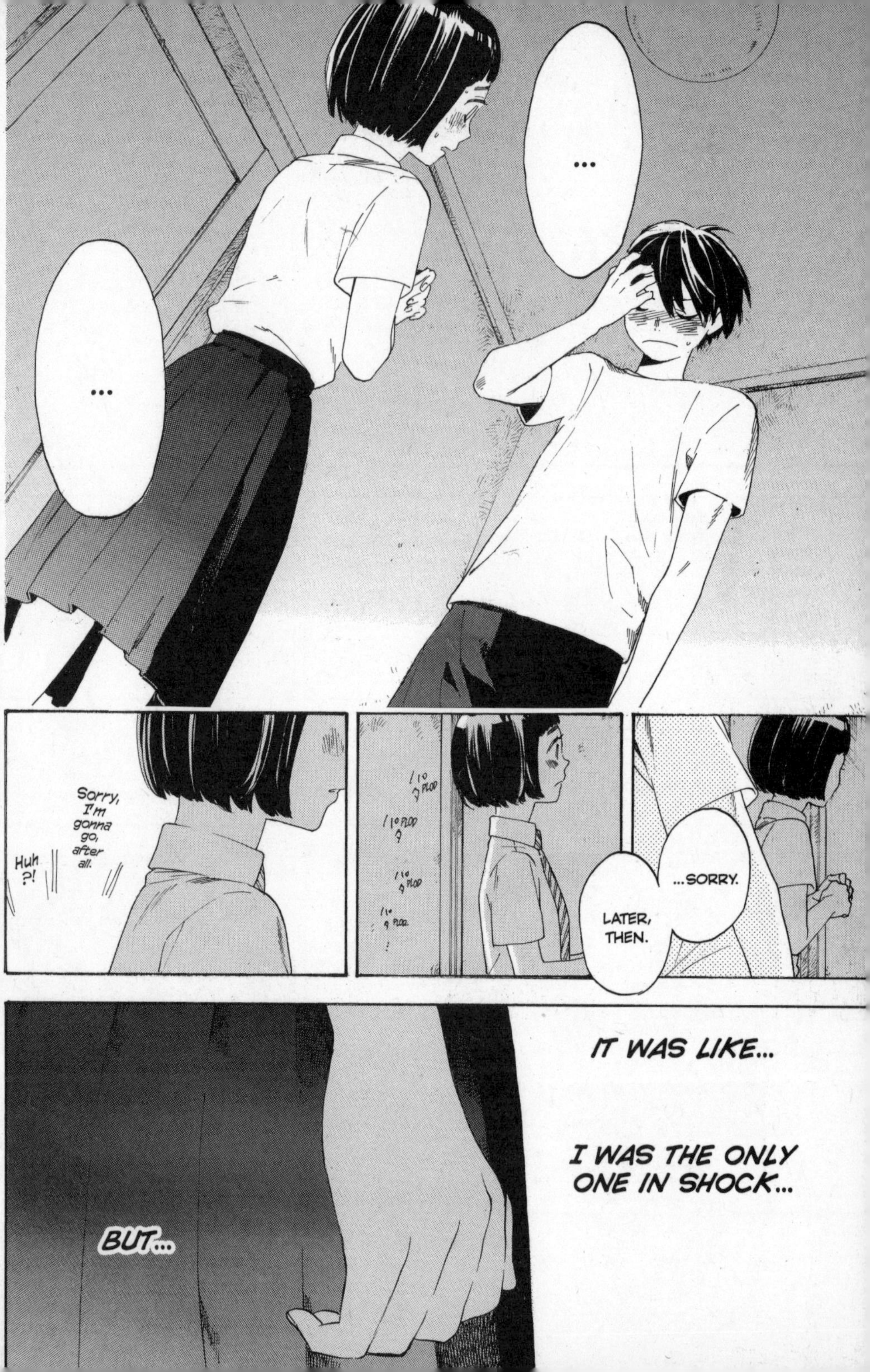
...
...
...SORRY.
LATER, THEN.
PLOD
PLOD
PLOD
PLOD
Sorry, I'm gonna go, after all.
Huh ?!
IT WAS LIKE...
I WAS THE ONLY ONE IN SHOCK...
BUT...

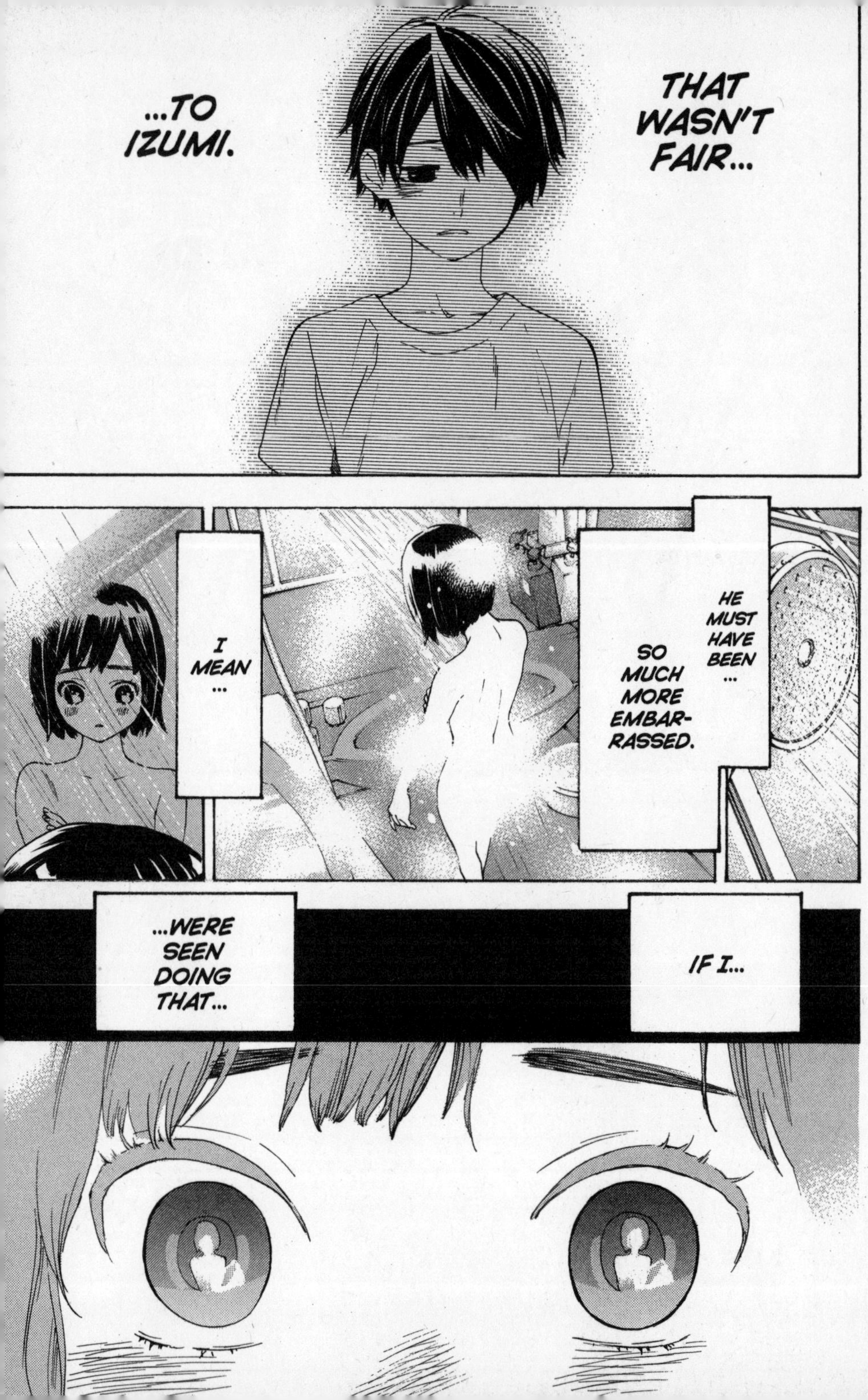
THAT WASN'T FAIR...
...TO IZUMI.
HE MUST HAVE BEEN...
SO MUCH MORE EMBARRASSED.
I MEAN...
IF I...
...WERE SEEN DOING THAT...

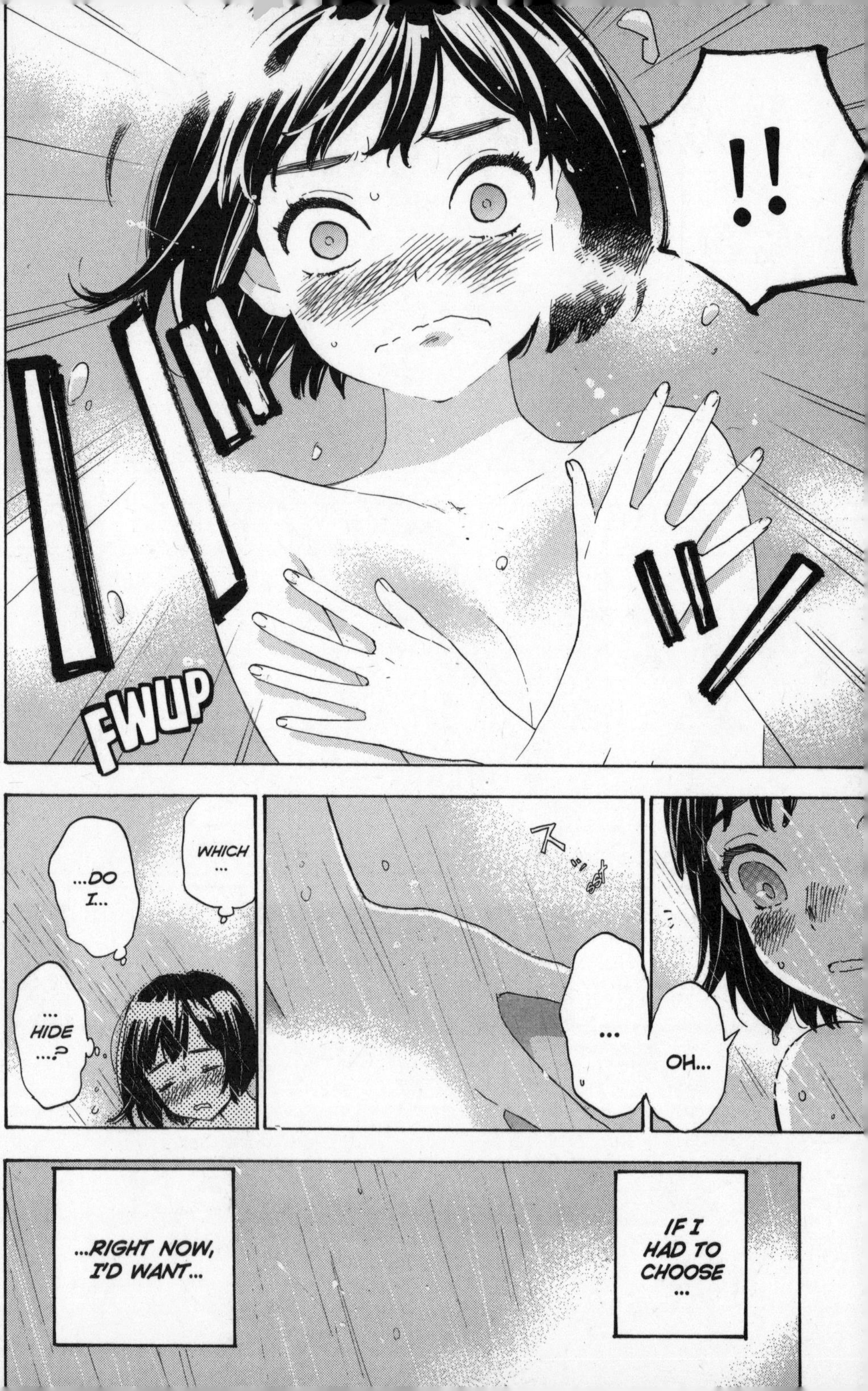
!!
FWUP
OH...
...
スッ
sst
WHICH ...
...DO I...
... HIDE ...?
IF I HAD TO CHOOSE ...
...RIGHT NOW, I'D WANT...

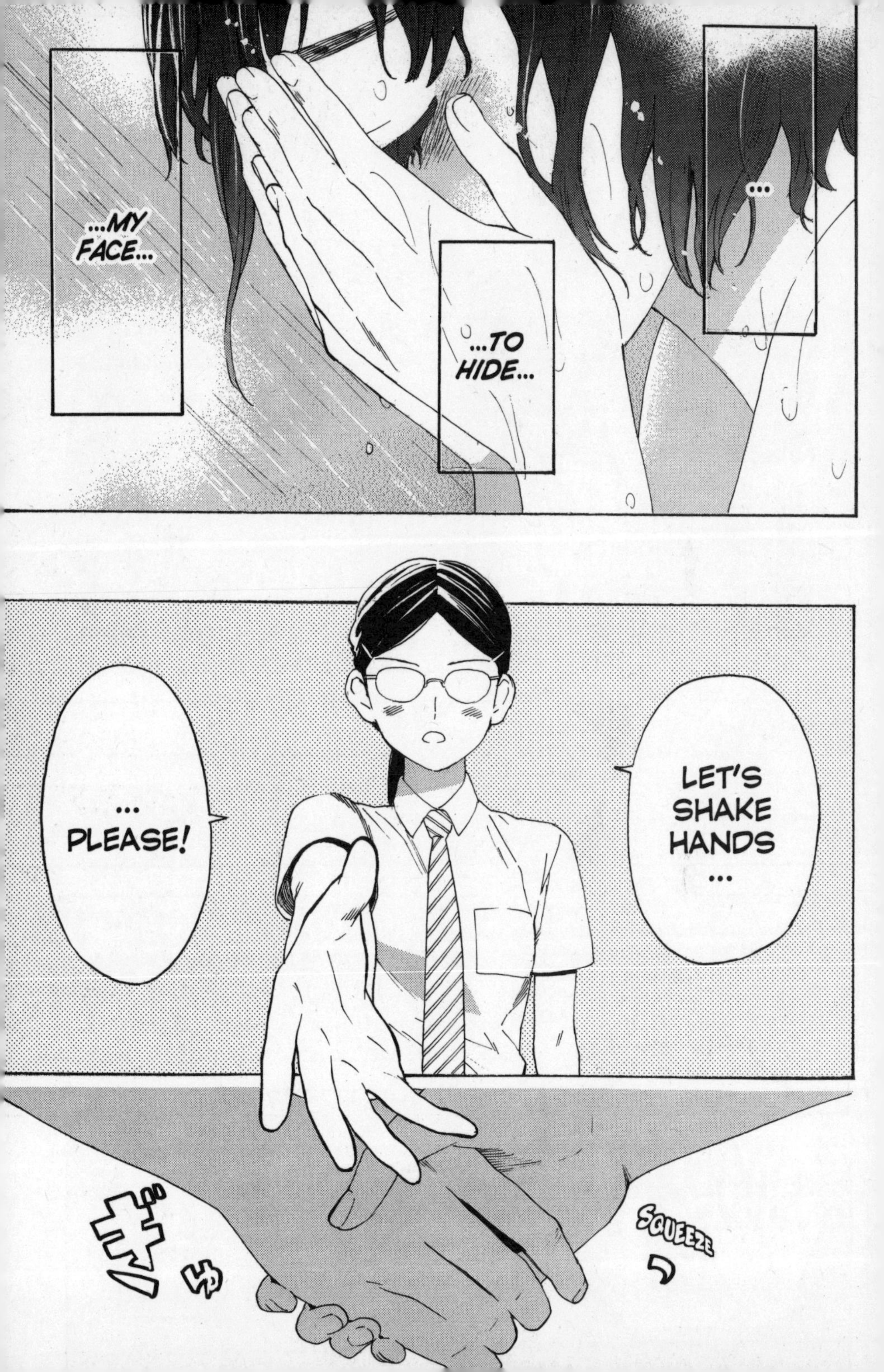
...
...TO HIDE...
...MY FACE...
LET'S SHAKE HANDS ...
... PLEASE!
SQUEEZE

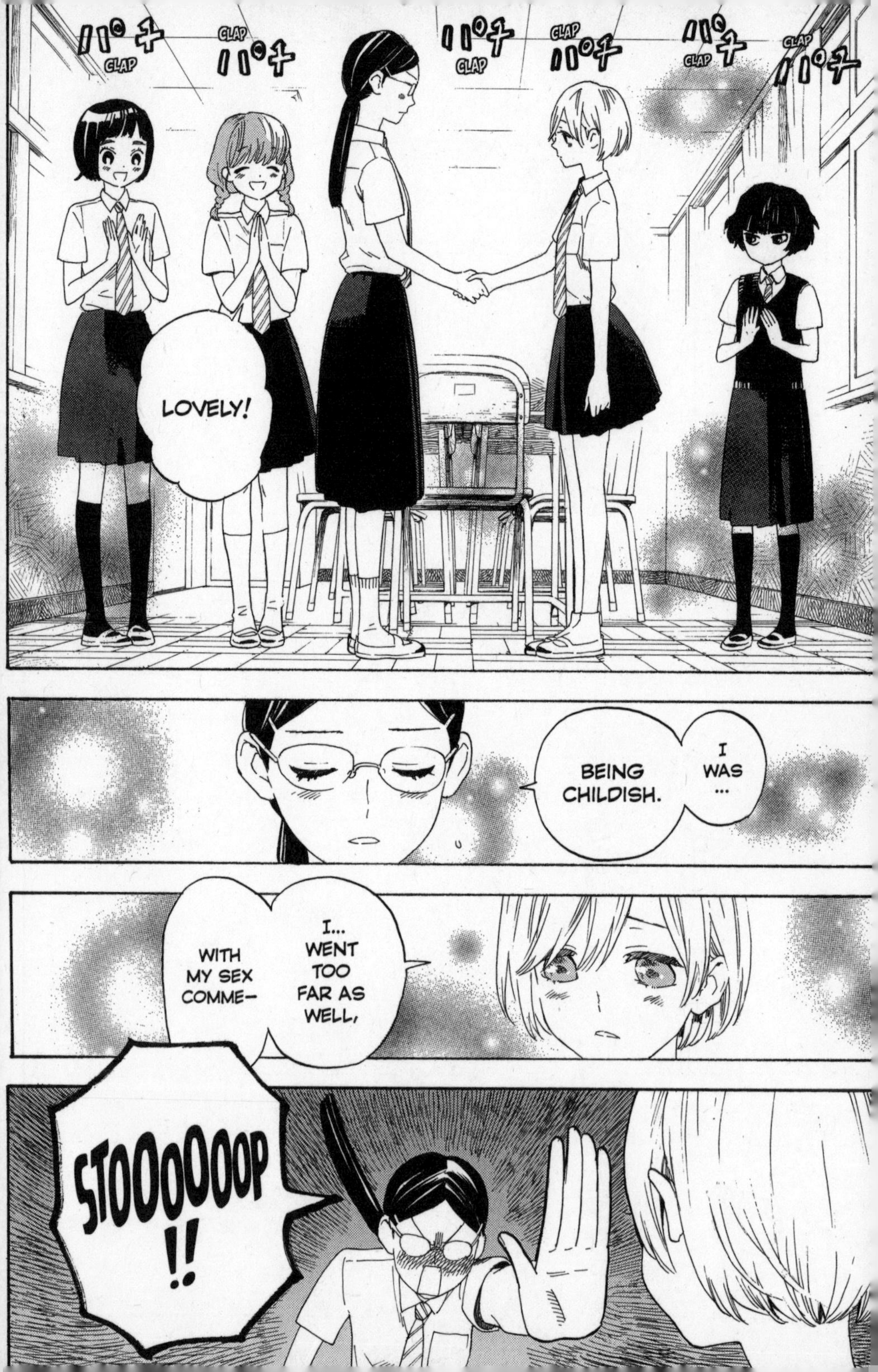
パチ CLAP
パチ CLAP
パチ CLAP
パチ CLAP
パチ CLAP
パチ CLAP
LOVELY!
I WAS...
BEING CHILDISH.
I... WENT TOO FAR AS WELL,
WITH MY SEX COMME—
STOOOOOP!!

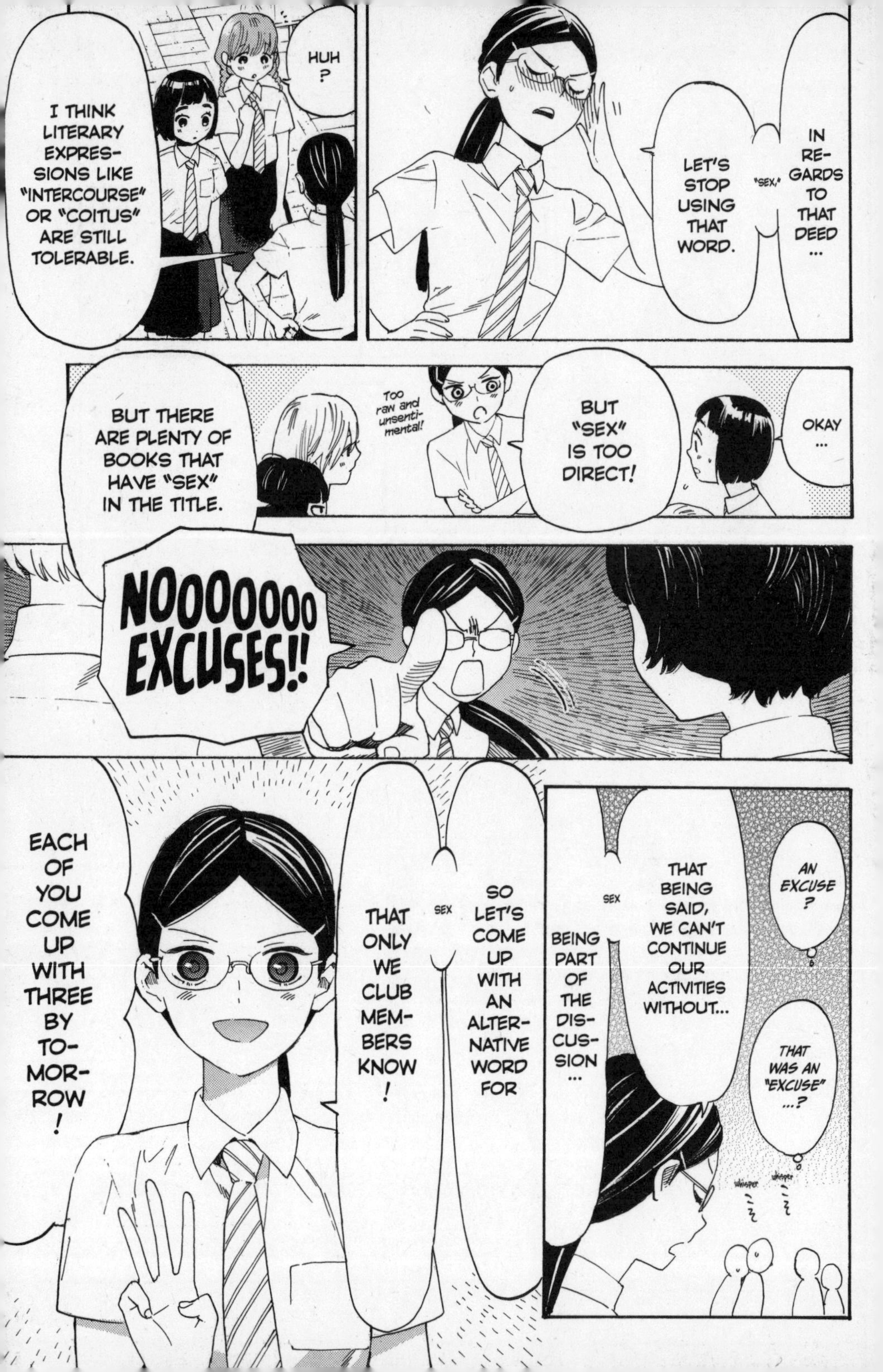
IN REGARDS TO THAT DEED...
"SEX,"
LET'S STOP USING THAT WORD.
HUH?
I THINK LITERARY EXPRESSIONS LIKE "INTERCOURSE" OR "COITUS" ARE STILL TOLERABLE.
OKAY...
BUT "SEX" IS TOO DIRECT!
Too raw and unsentimental!
BUT THERE ARE PLENTY OF BOOKS THAT HAVE "SEX" IN THE TITLE.
NOOOOOOO EXCUSES!!
AN EXCUSE?
THAT WAS AN "EXCUSE"...?
whisper whisper
THAT BEING SAID, WE CAN'T CONTINUE OUR ACTIVITIES WITHOUT...
SEX
BEING PART OF THE DISCUSSION...
SO LET'S COME UP WITH AN ALTERNATIVE WORD FOR
SEX
THAT ONLY WE CLUB MEMBERS KNOW!
EACH OF YOU COME UP WITH THREE BY TOMORROW!

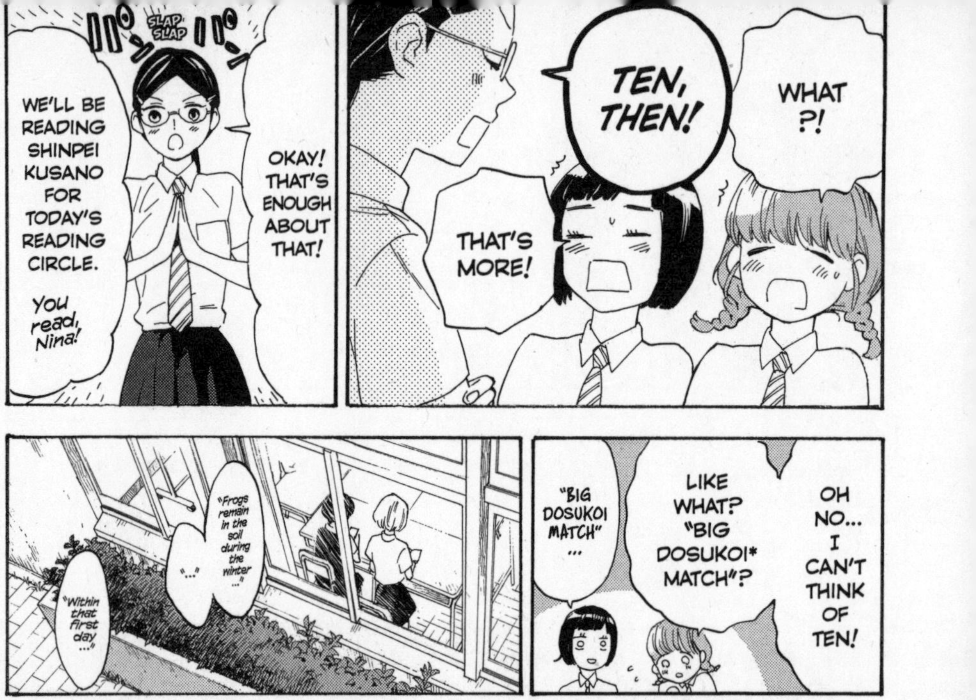
TEN, THEN!
WHAT ?!
THAT'S MORE!
SLAP SLAP
OKAY! THAT'S ENOUGH ABOUT THAT!
WE'LL BE READING SHINPEI KUSANO FOR TODAY'S READING CIRCLE.
You read, Nina!
OH NO... I CAN'T THINK OF TEN!
LIKE WHAT? "BIG DOSUKOI* MATCH"?
"BIG DOSUKOI MATCH" ...
"Frogs remain in the soil during the winter ..."
"..."
"Within that first day ..."

*A sumo wrestler's shout to 'bring it on.'

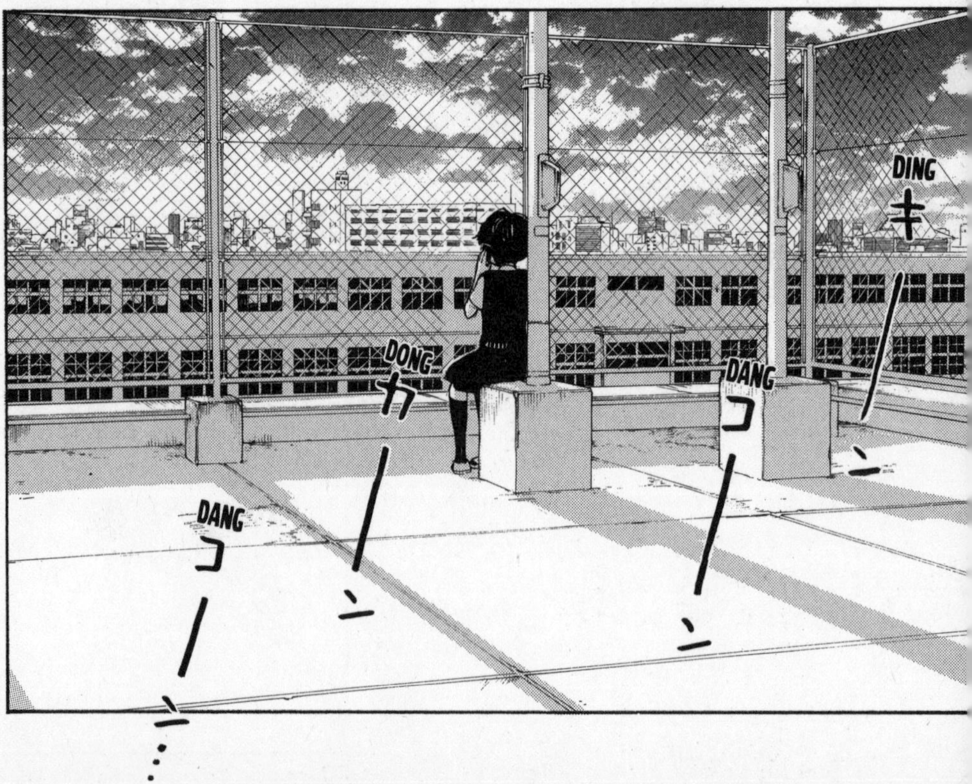
DING
DANG
DONG
DANG

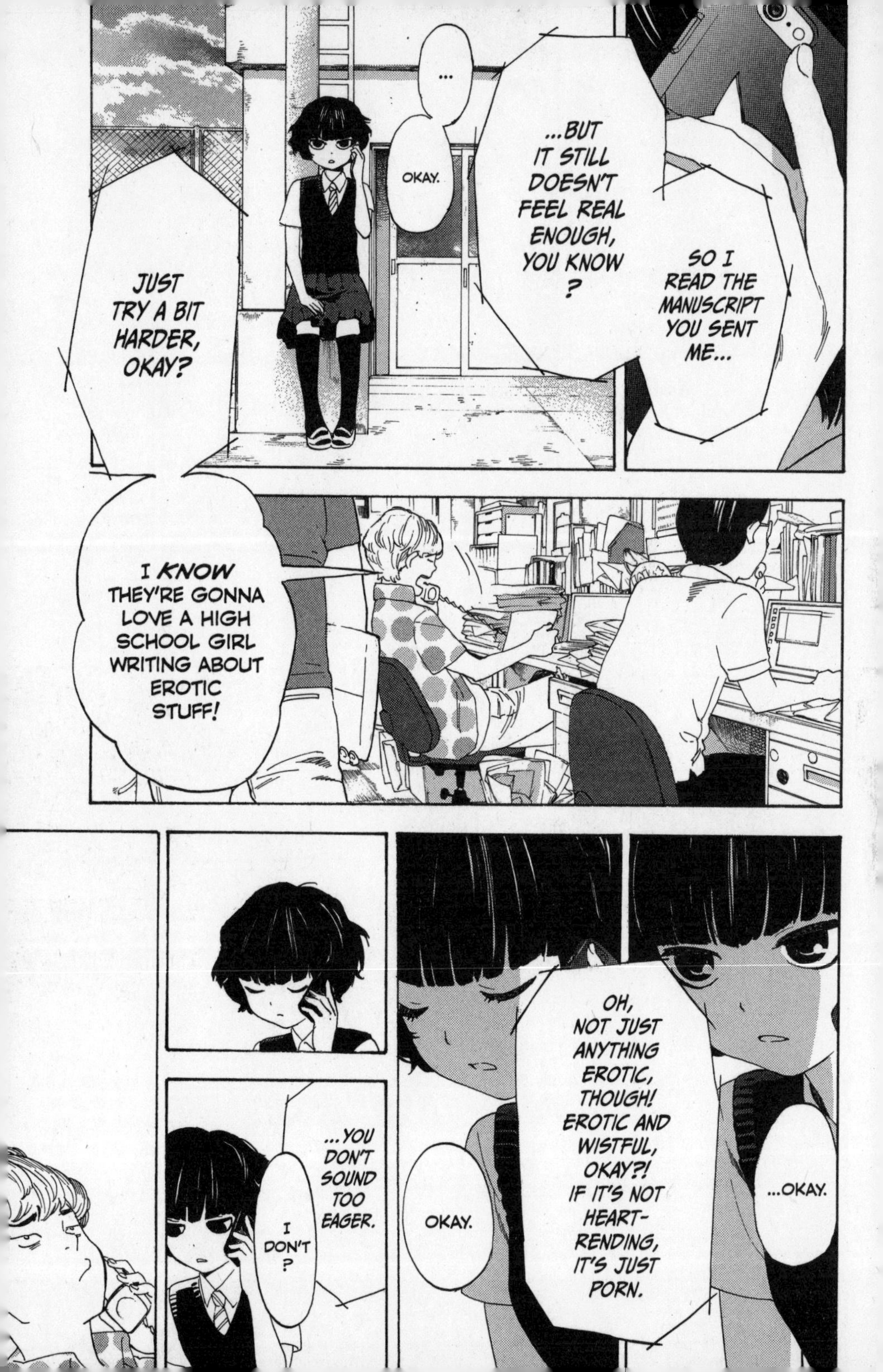
SO I READ THE MANUSCRIPT YOU SENT ME...
...BUT IT STILL DOESN'T FEEL REAL ENOUGH, YOU KNOW?
...
OKAY.
JUST TRY A BIT HARDER, OKAY?
I *KNOW* THEY'RE GONNA LOVE A HIGH SCHOOL GIRL WRITING ABOUT EROTIC STUFF!
OH, NOT JUST ANYTHING EROTIC, THOUGH! EROTIC AND WISTFUL, OKAY?! IF IT'S NOT HEART-RENDING, IT'S JUST PORN.
...OKAY.
OKAY.
...YOU DON'T SOUND TOO EAGER.
I DON'T?

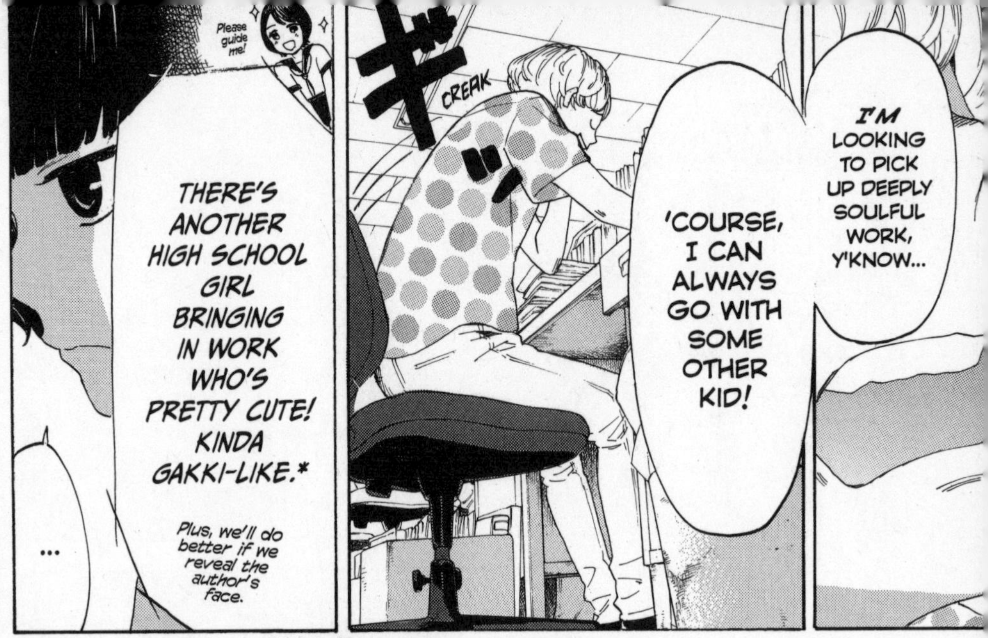
I'M LOOKING TO PICK UP DEEPLY SOULFUL WORK, Y'KNOW...
CREAK
'COURSE, I CAN ALWAYS GO WITH SOME OTHER KID!
Please guide me!
THERE'S ANOTHER HIGH SCHOOL GIRL BRINGING IN WORK WHO'S PRETTY CUTE! KINDA GAKKI-LIKE.*
Plus, we'll do better if we reveal the author's face.
...

*Model-turned-actress-and-singer Yui Aragaki.

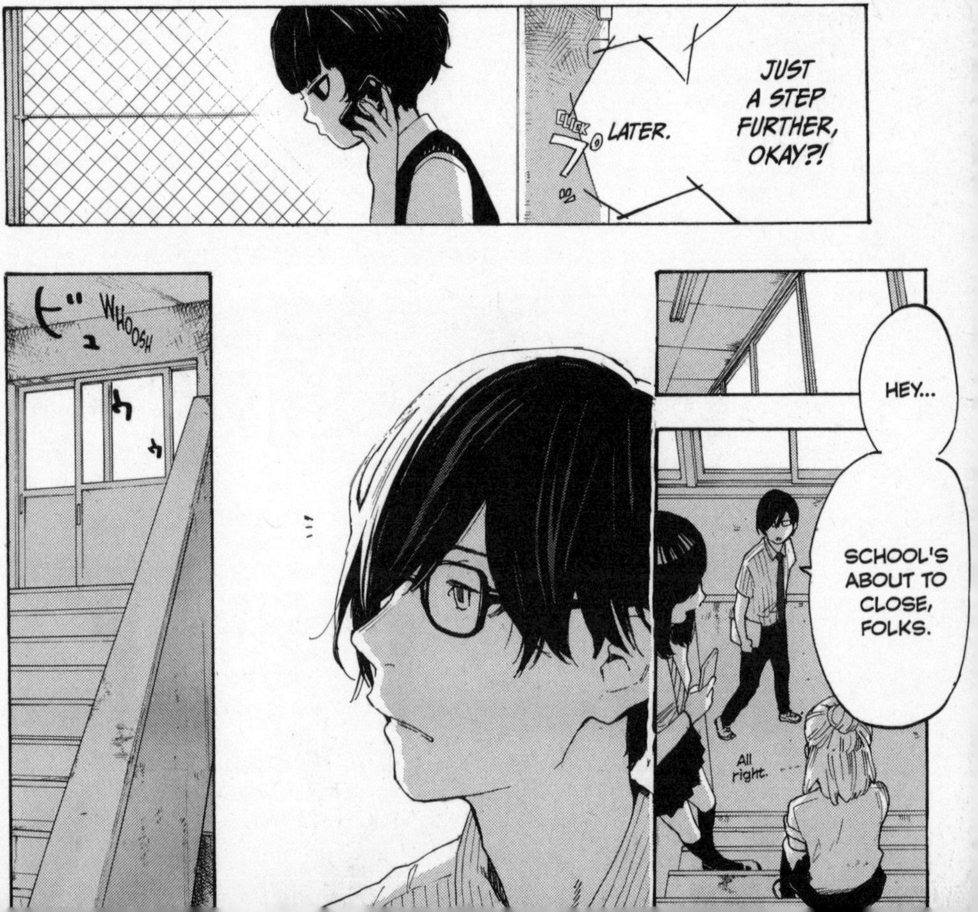
JUST A STEP FURTHER, OKAY?!
CLICK
LATER.
HEY...
SCHOOL'S ABOUT TO CLOSE, FOLKS.
All right.
WHOOSH

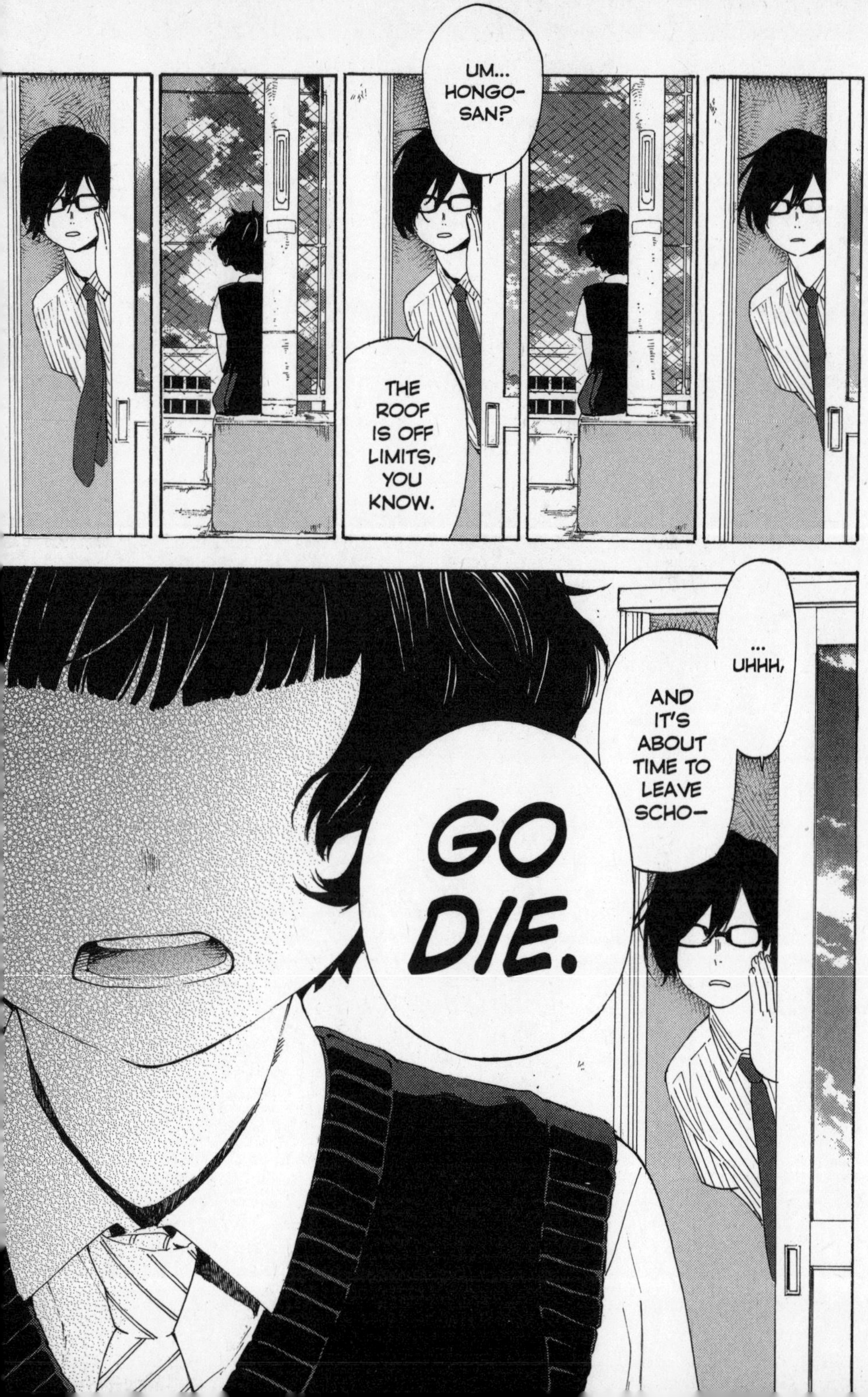
UM... HONGO-SAN?
THE ROOF IS OFF LIMITS, YOU KNOW.
... UHHH,
AND IT'S ABOUT TIME TO LEAVE SCHO—
GO DIE.

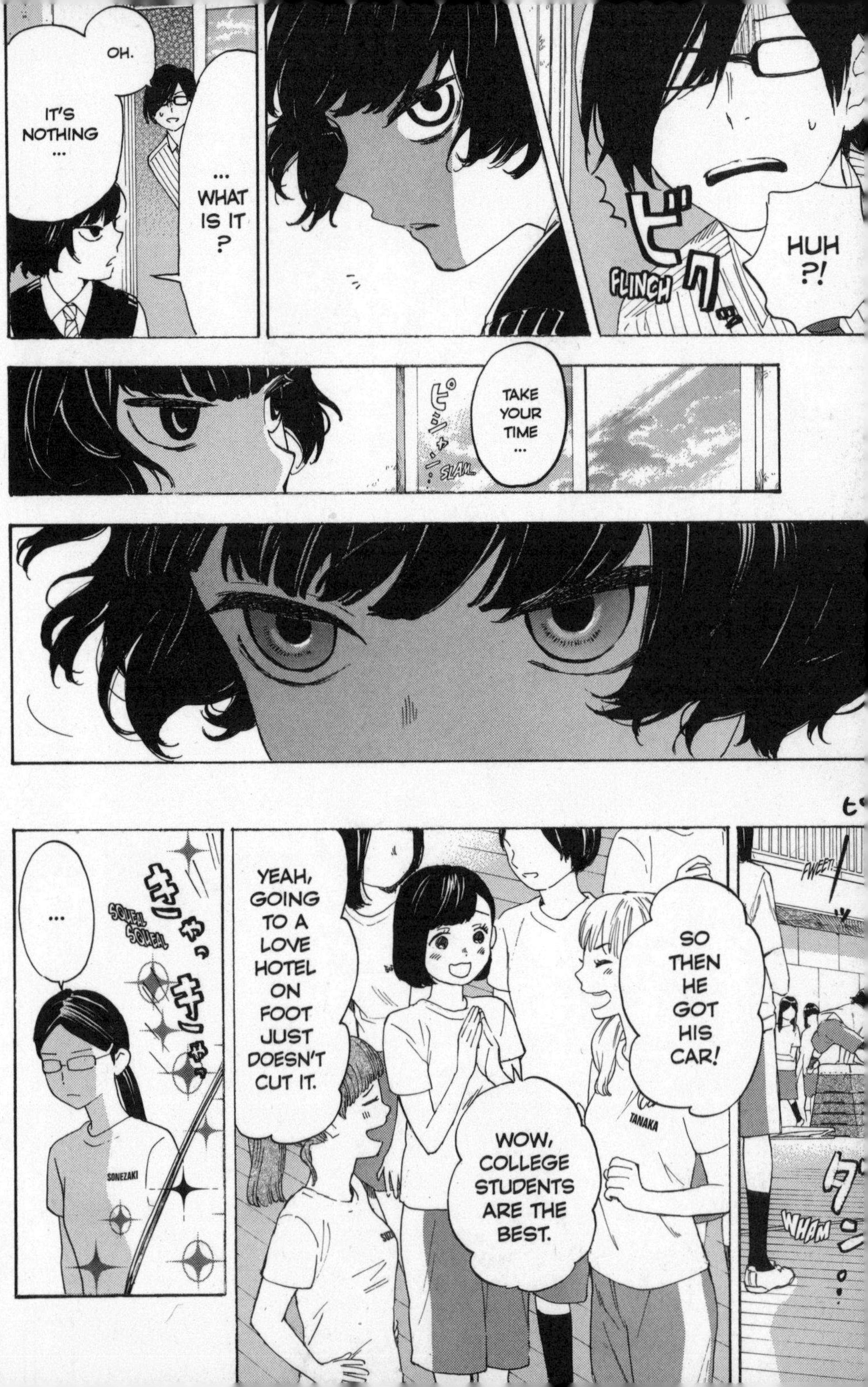
HUH ?!
FLINCH
... WHAT IS IT ?
OH.
IT'S NOTHING ...
TAKE YOUR TIME ...
SLAM...
FWEET!
WHAM
SO THEN HE GOT HIS CAR!
TANAKA
YEAH, GOING TO A LOVE HOTEL ON FOOT JUST DOESN'T CUT IT.
WOW, COLLEGE STUDENTS ARE THE BEST.
SQUEAL SQUEAL
...
SONEZAKI

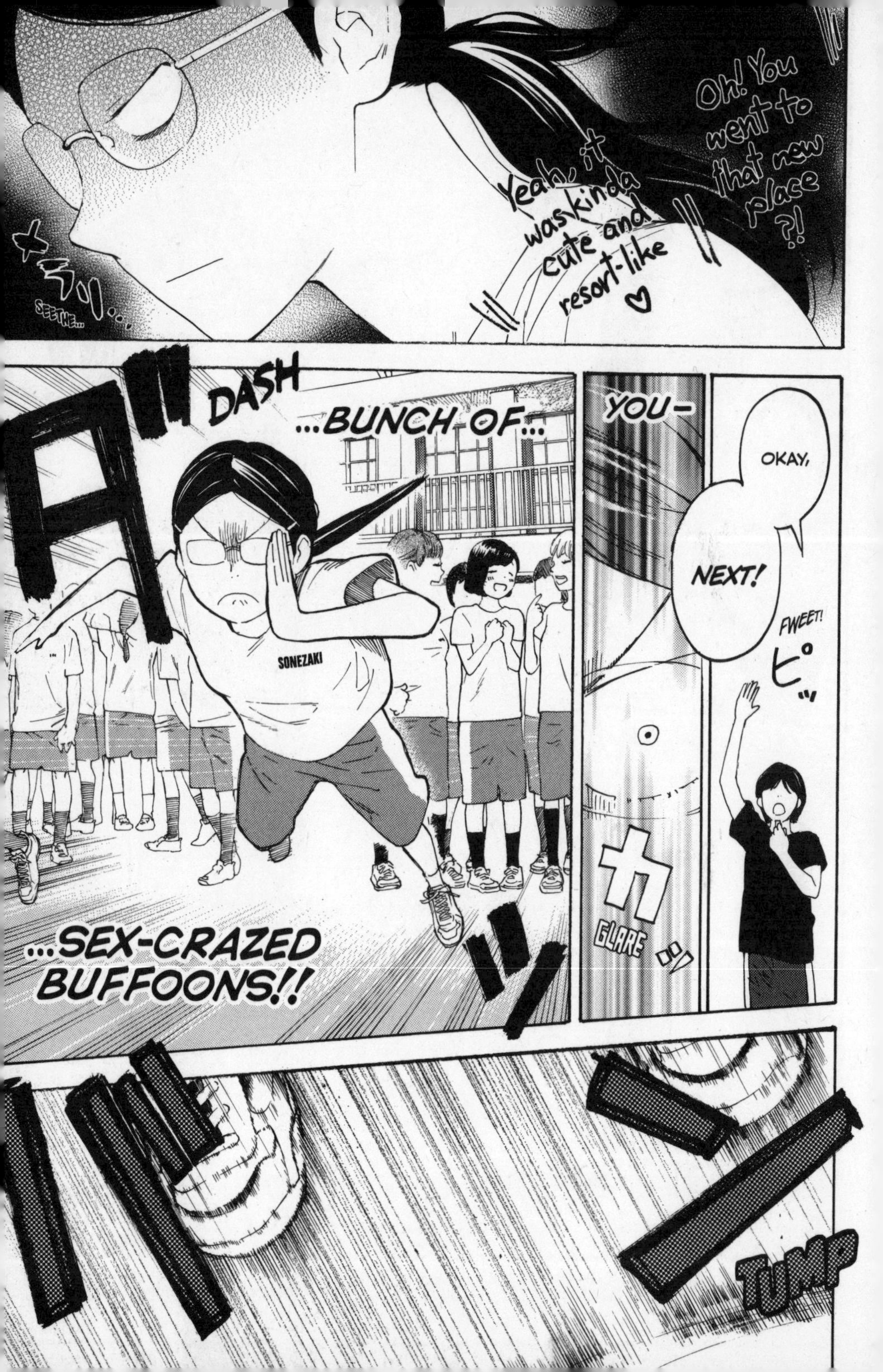
Oh! You went to that new place?!
Yeah, it was kinda cute and resort-like ♥
SEETHE...
OKAY, NEXT!
FWEET!
ピッ
YOU-
カ
GLARE
DASH
...BUNCH OF...
SONEZAKI
...SEX-CRAZED BUFFOONS!!
TUMP

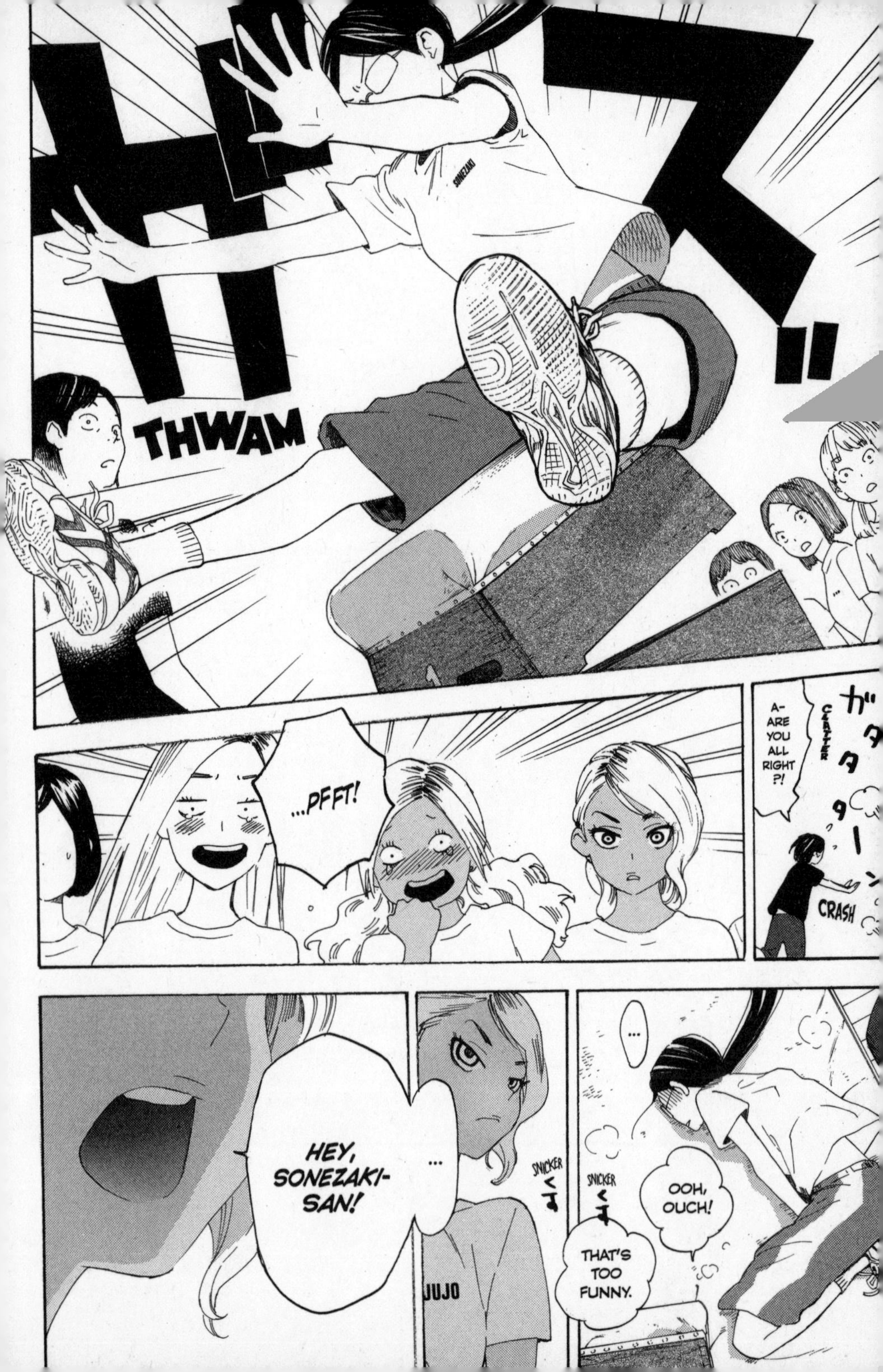
THWAM
SONEZAKI
A-ARE YOU ALL RIGHT?!
CLATTER
CRASH
...PFFT!
...
OOH, OUCH!
SNICKER
THAT'S TOO FUNNY.
SNICKER
...
JUJO
HEY, SONEZAKI-SAN!

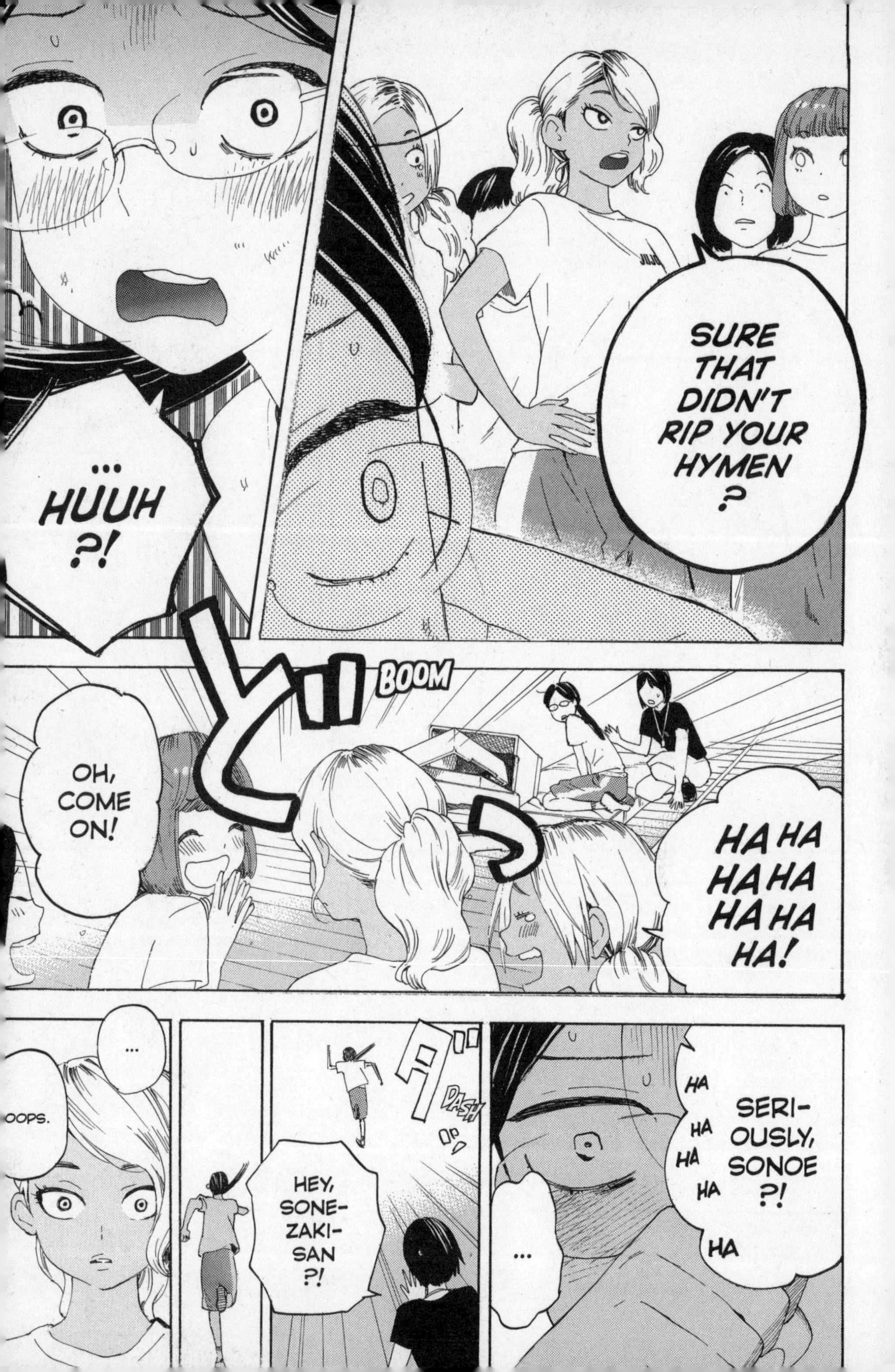
SURE THAT DIDN'T RIP YOUR HYMEN?
...HUUH?!
BOOM
HA HA HA HA HA HA HA!
OH, COME ON!
HA HA HA HA HA
SERIOUSLY, SONOE?!
...
DASH
HEY, SONE-ZAKI-SAN?!
...
OOPS.

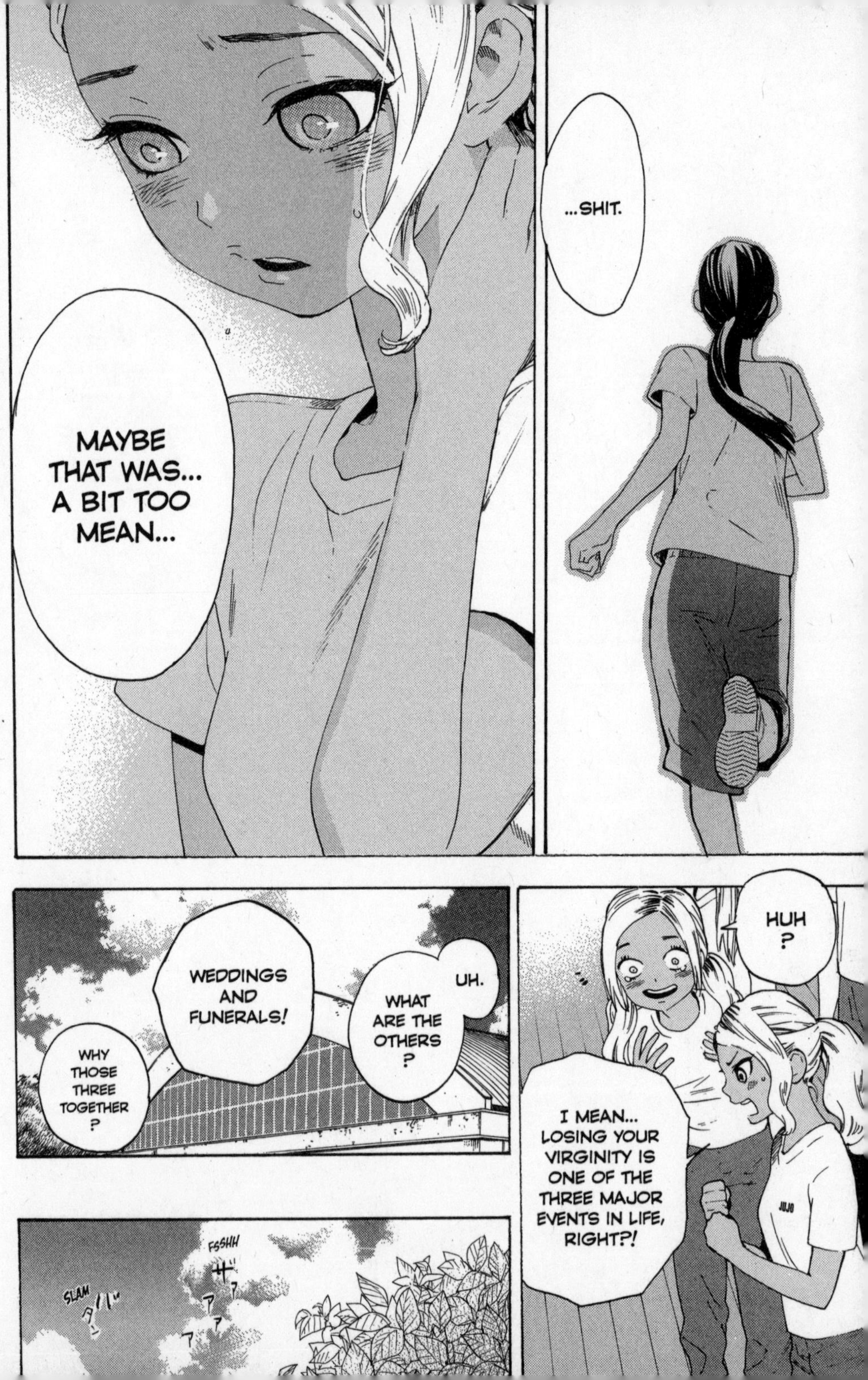
...SHIT.
MAYBE THAT WAS... A BIT TOO MEAN...
HUH?
I MEAN... LOSING YOUR VIRGINITY IS ONE OF THE THREE MAJOR EVENTS IN LIFE, RIGHT?!
JUJO
UH.
WHAT ARE THE OTHERS?
WEDDINGS AND FUNERALS!
WHY THOSE THREE TOGETHER?
FSSHH
SLAM

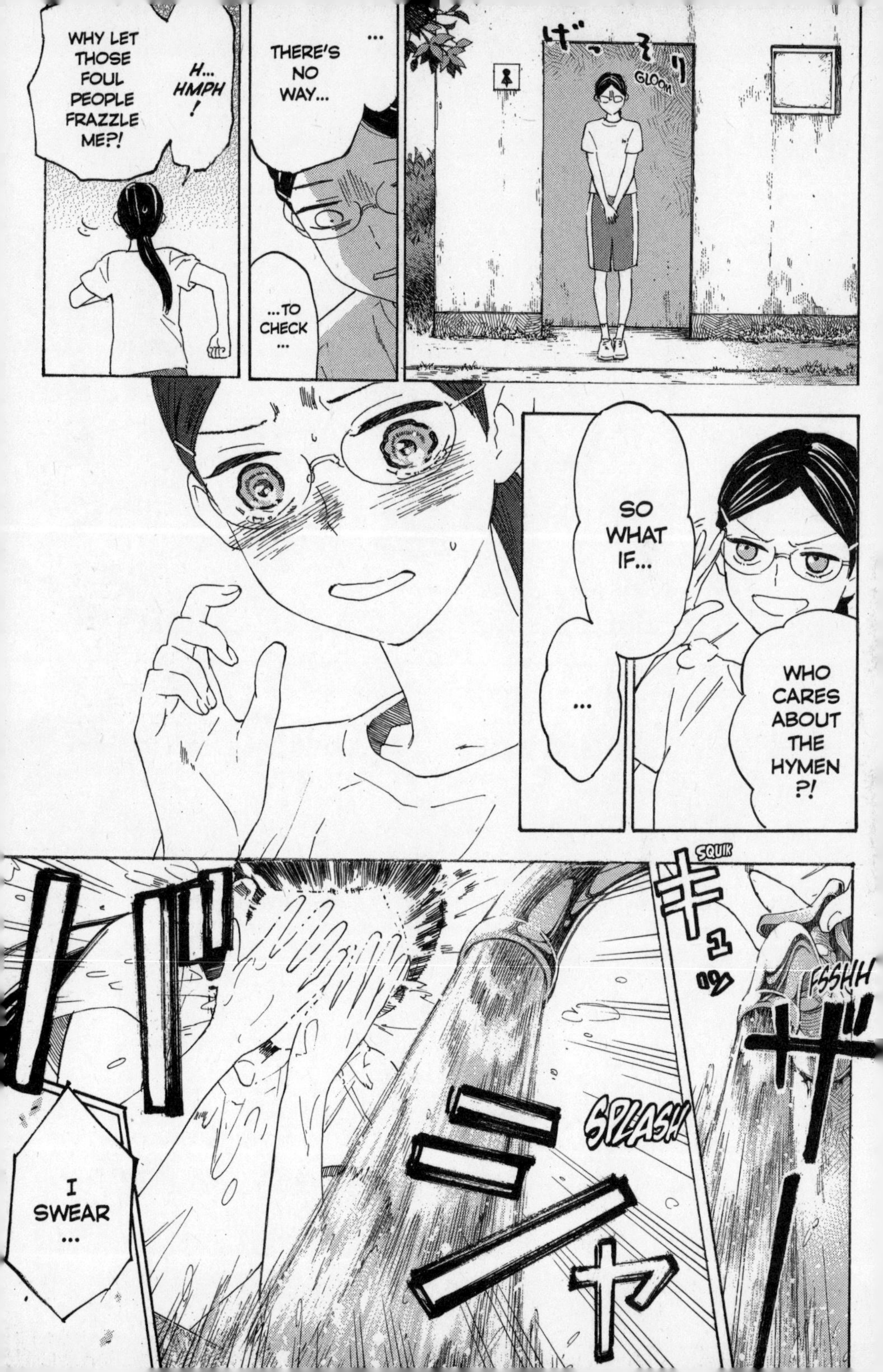
げっそり
GLOOM
...
THERE'S NO WAY...
...TO CHECK ...
WHY LET THOSE FOUL PEOPLE FRAZZLE ME?!
H... HMPH!
SO WHAT IF...
WHO CARES ABOUT THE HYMEN?!
...
SQUIK
FSSHH
SPLASH
I SWEAR ...

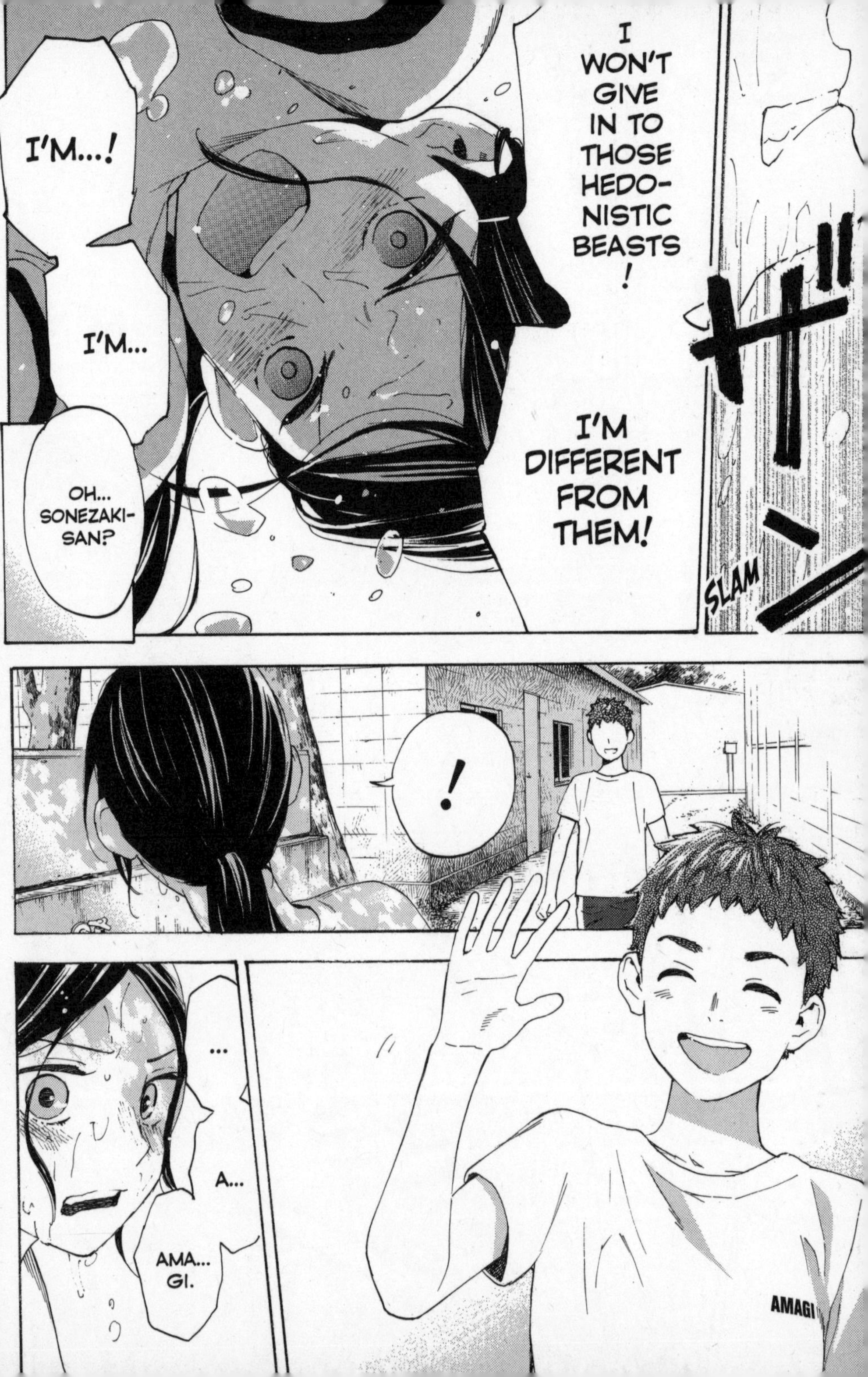
SLAM
I WON'T GIVE IN TO THOSE HEDO-NISTIC BEASTS!
I'M DIFFERENT FROM THEM!
I'M...!
I'M...
OH... SONEZAKI-SAN?
!
AMAGI
...
A...
AMA... GI.

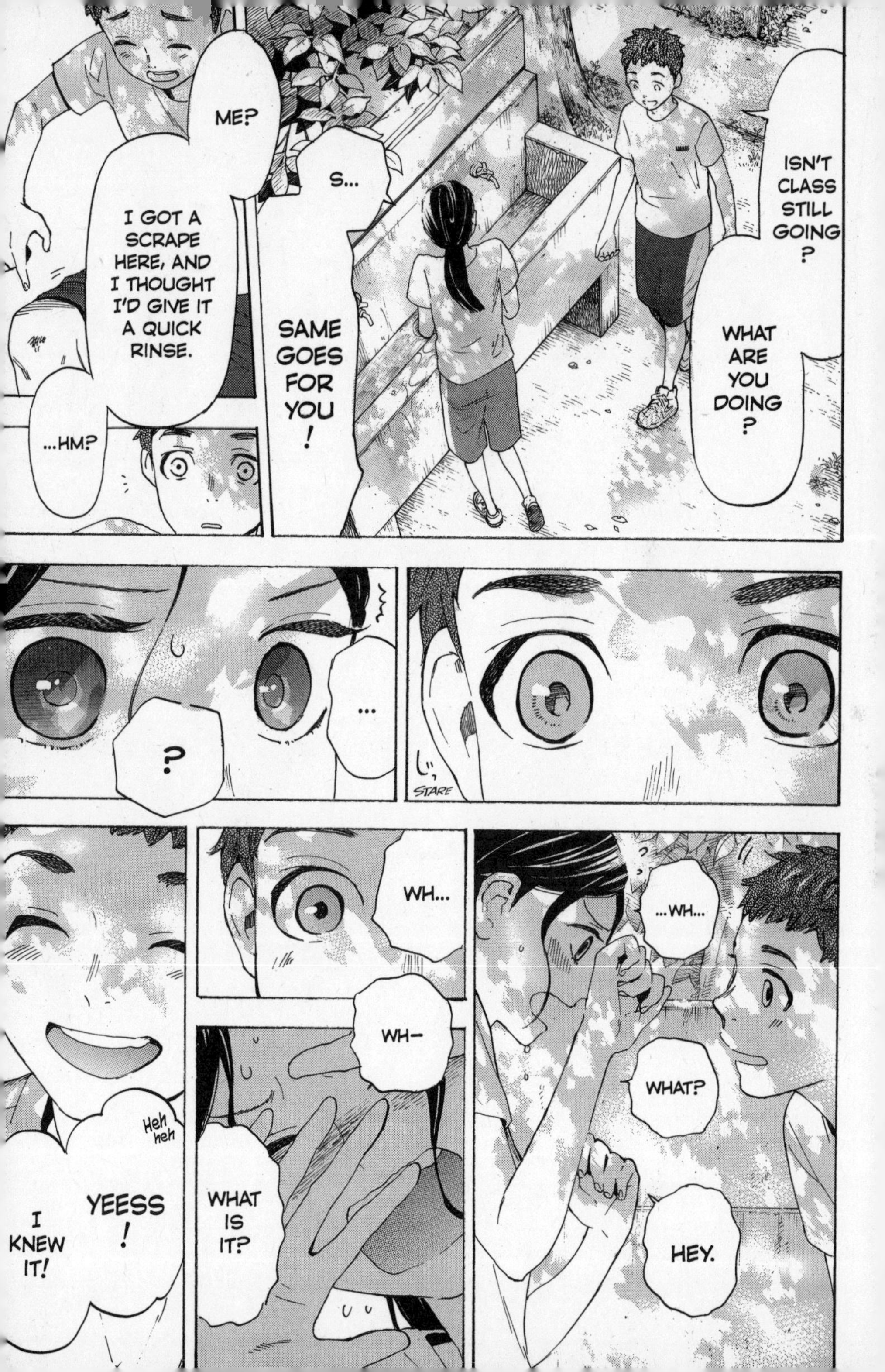
ISN'T CLASS STILL GOING?
WHAT ARE YOU DOING?
S...
SAME GOES FOR YOU!
ME?
I GOT A SCRAPE HERE, AND I THOUGHT I'D GIVE IT A QUICK RINSE.
...HM?
じっ
STARE
...
?
...WH...
WHAT?
HEY.
WH...
WH-
WHAT IS IT?
Heh heh
YEESS!
I KNEW IT!

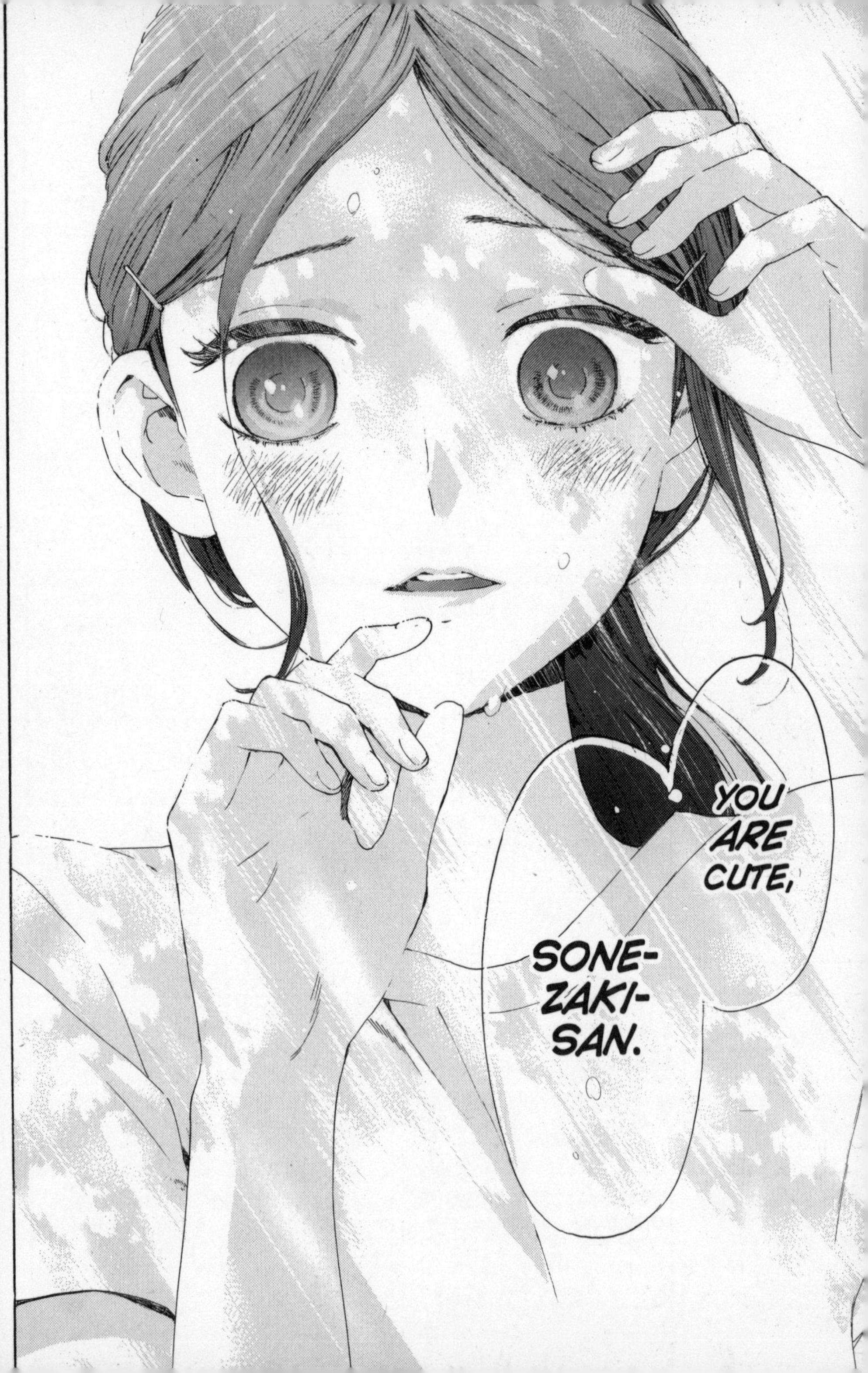
YOU ARE CUTE,
SONE-ZAKI-SAN.

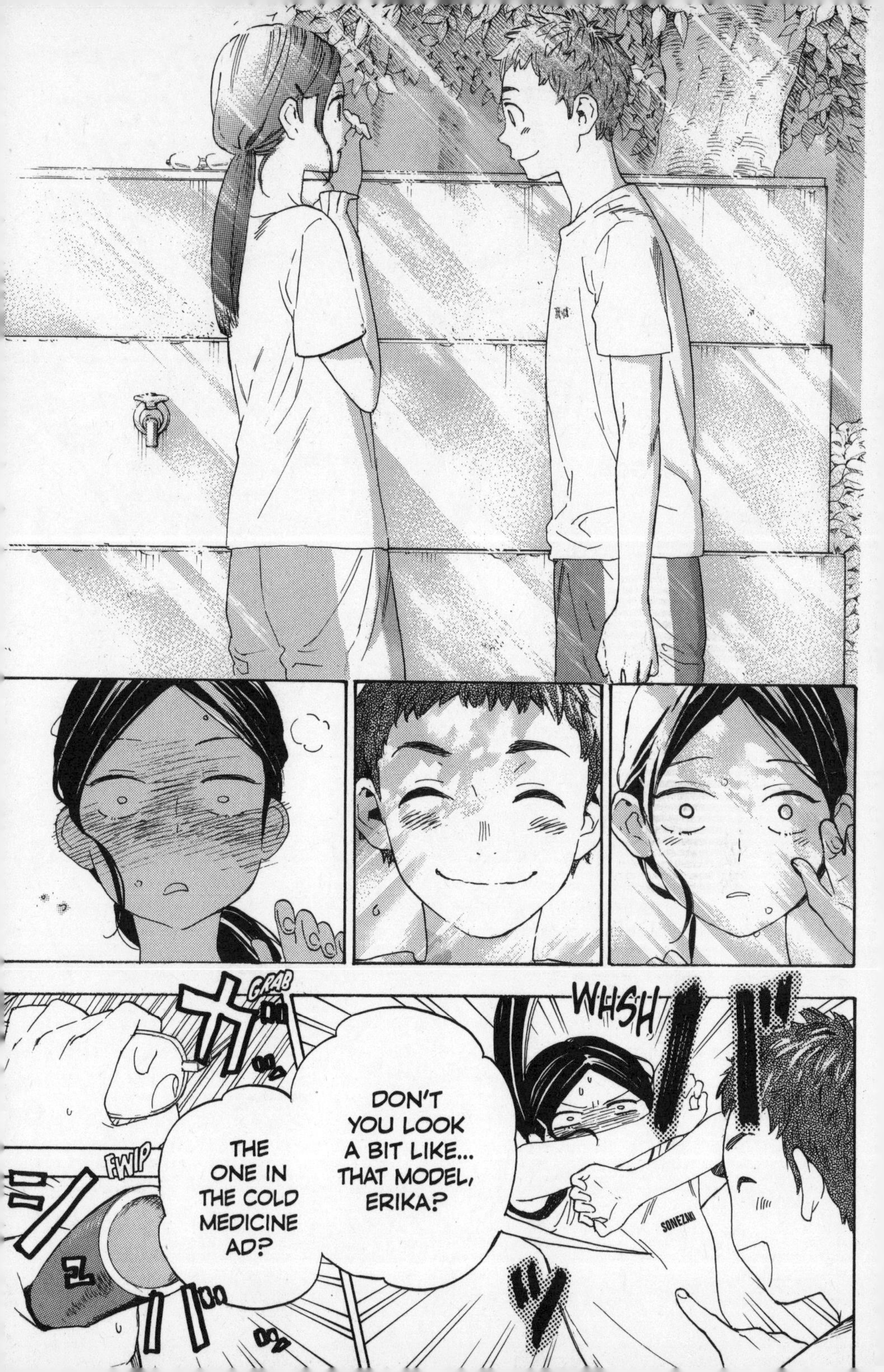
WHSH
GRAB
DON'T YOU LOOK A BIT LIKE... THAT MODEL, ERIKA?
THE ONE IN THE COLD MEDICINE AD?
SONEZAKI
FWIP

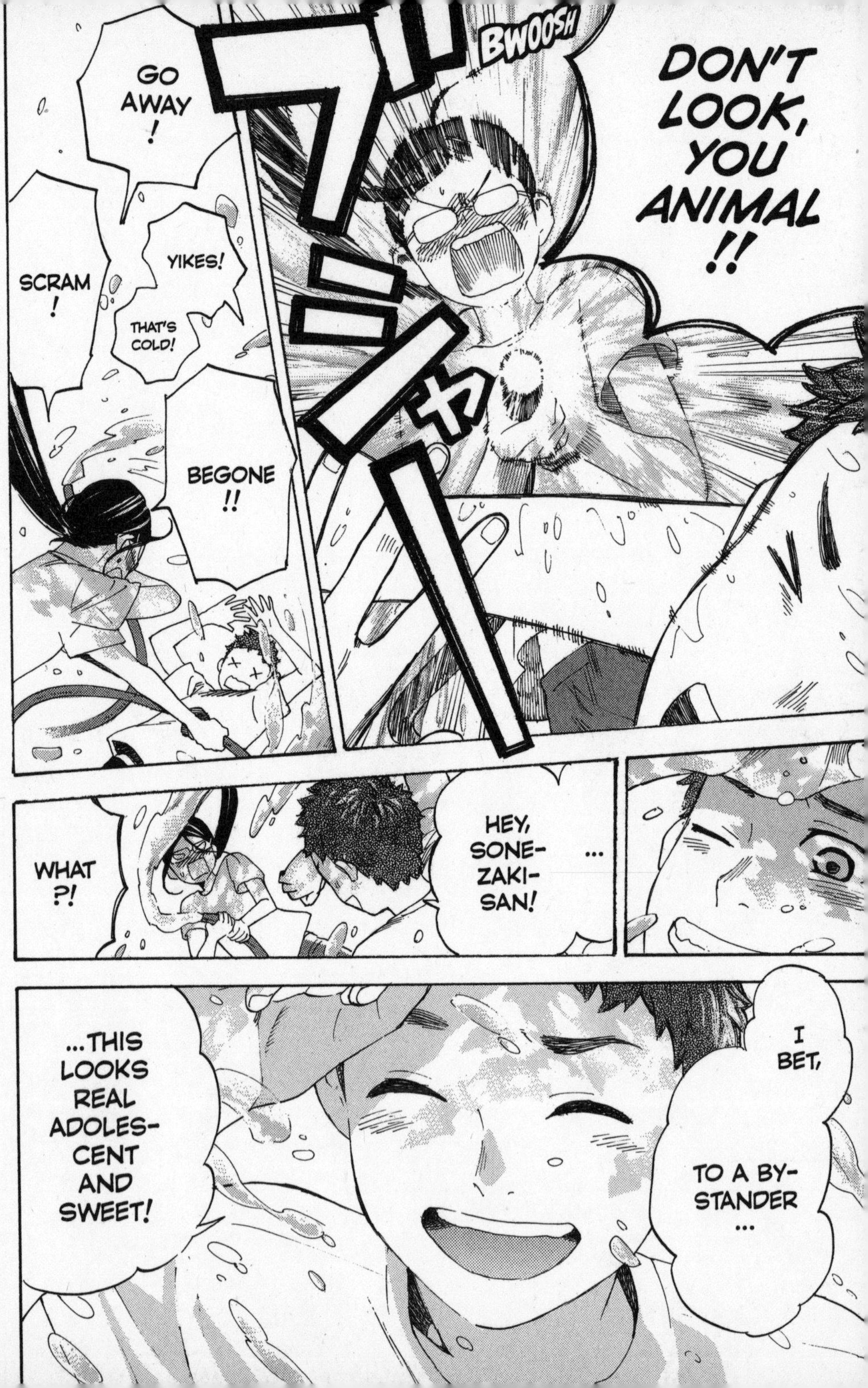
BWOOSH
DON'T LOOK, YOU ANIMAL!!
GO AWAY!
YIKES!
THAT'S COLD!
SCRAM!
BEGONE!!
...
HEY, SONE-ZAKI-SAN!
WHAT?!
I BET,
TO A BY-STANDER...
...THIS LOOKS REAL ADOLES-CENT AND SWEET!

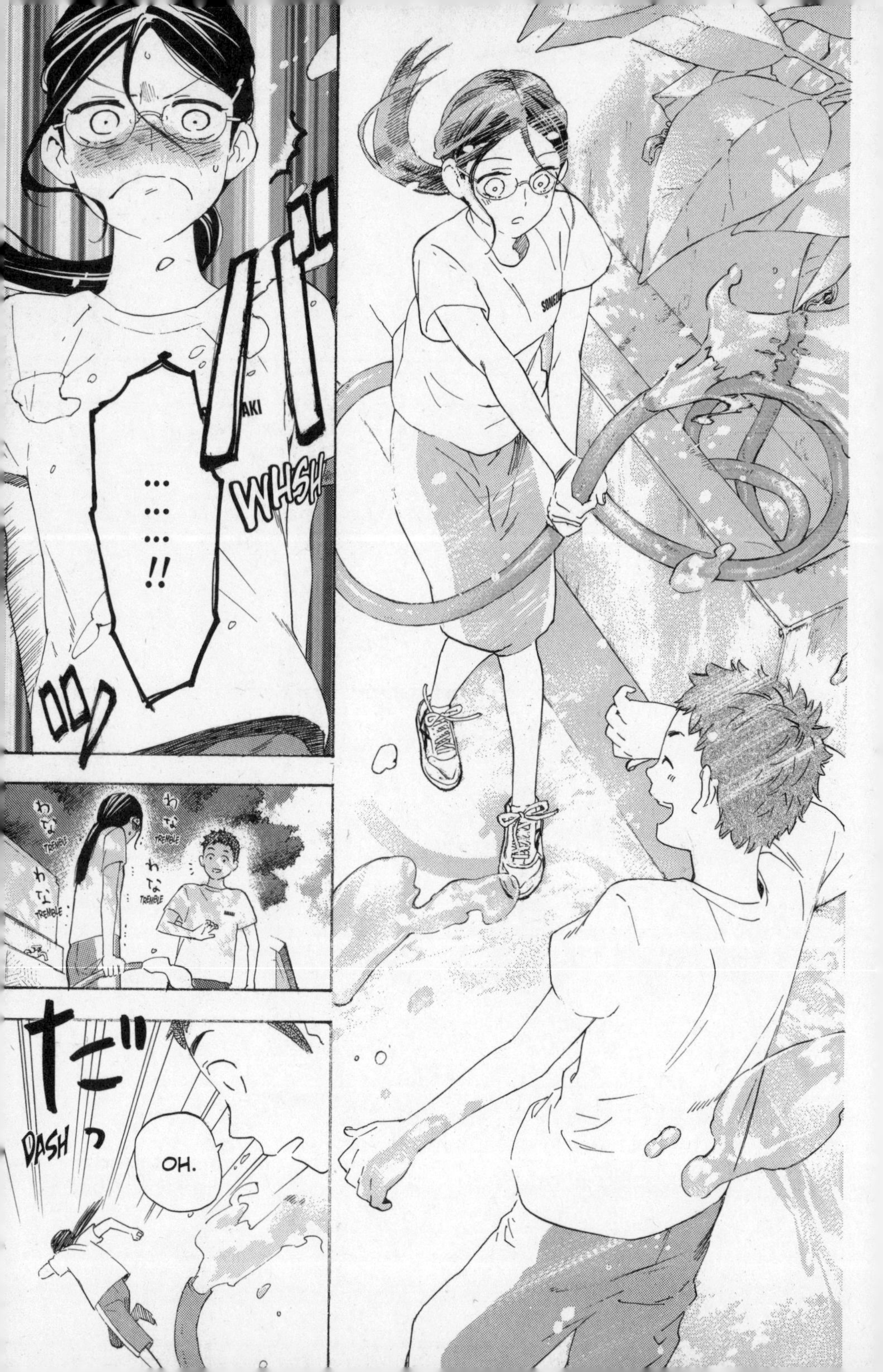

......
......
......!!
WHSH
わな TREMBLE
わな TREMBLE
わな TREMBLE
OH.
だっ DASH

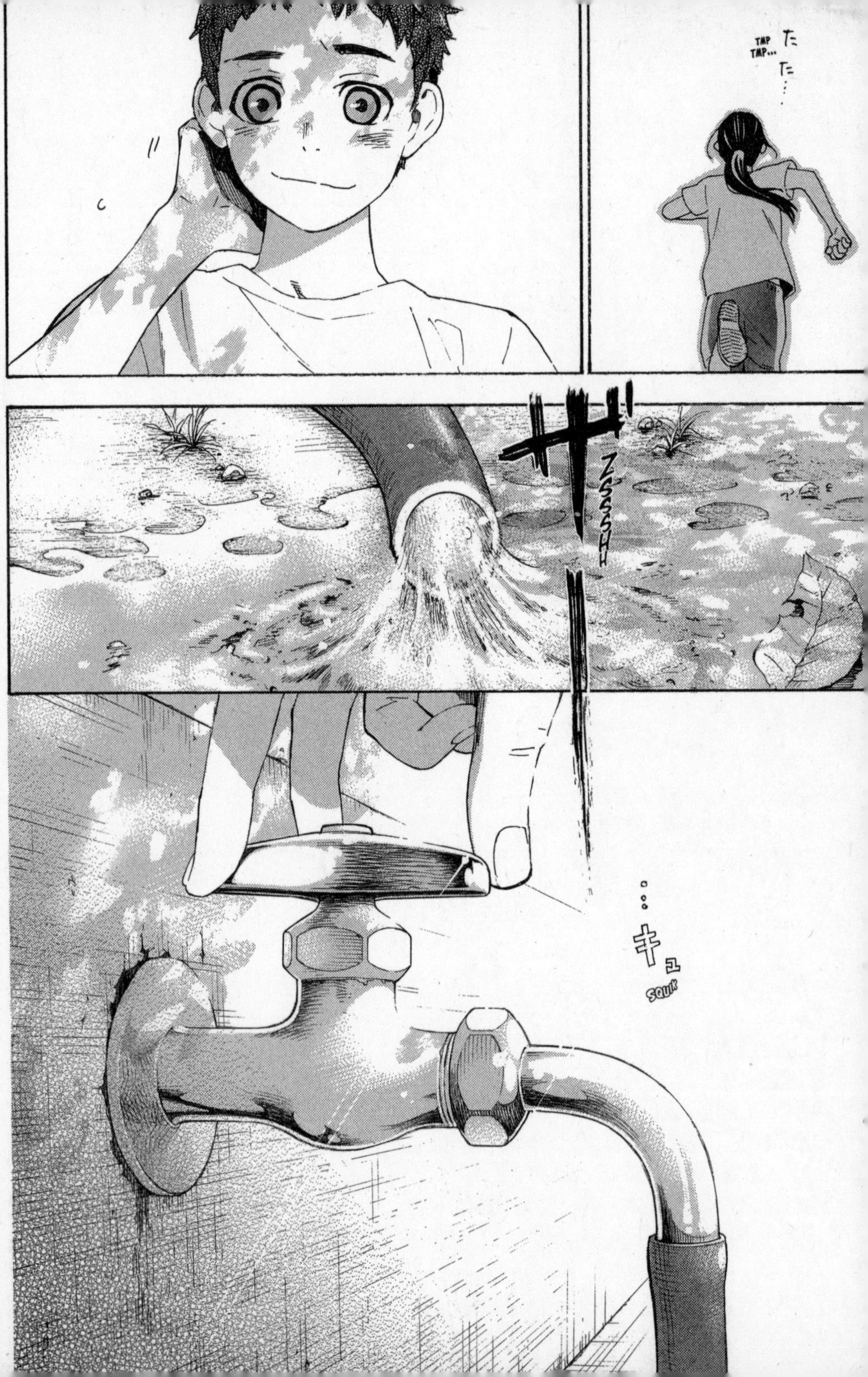
TMP TMP...
たた…
ザ
ZSSSHH
…キュ
SQUIK

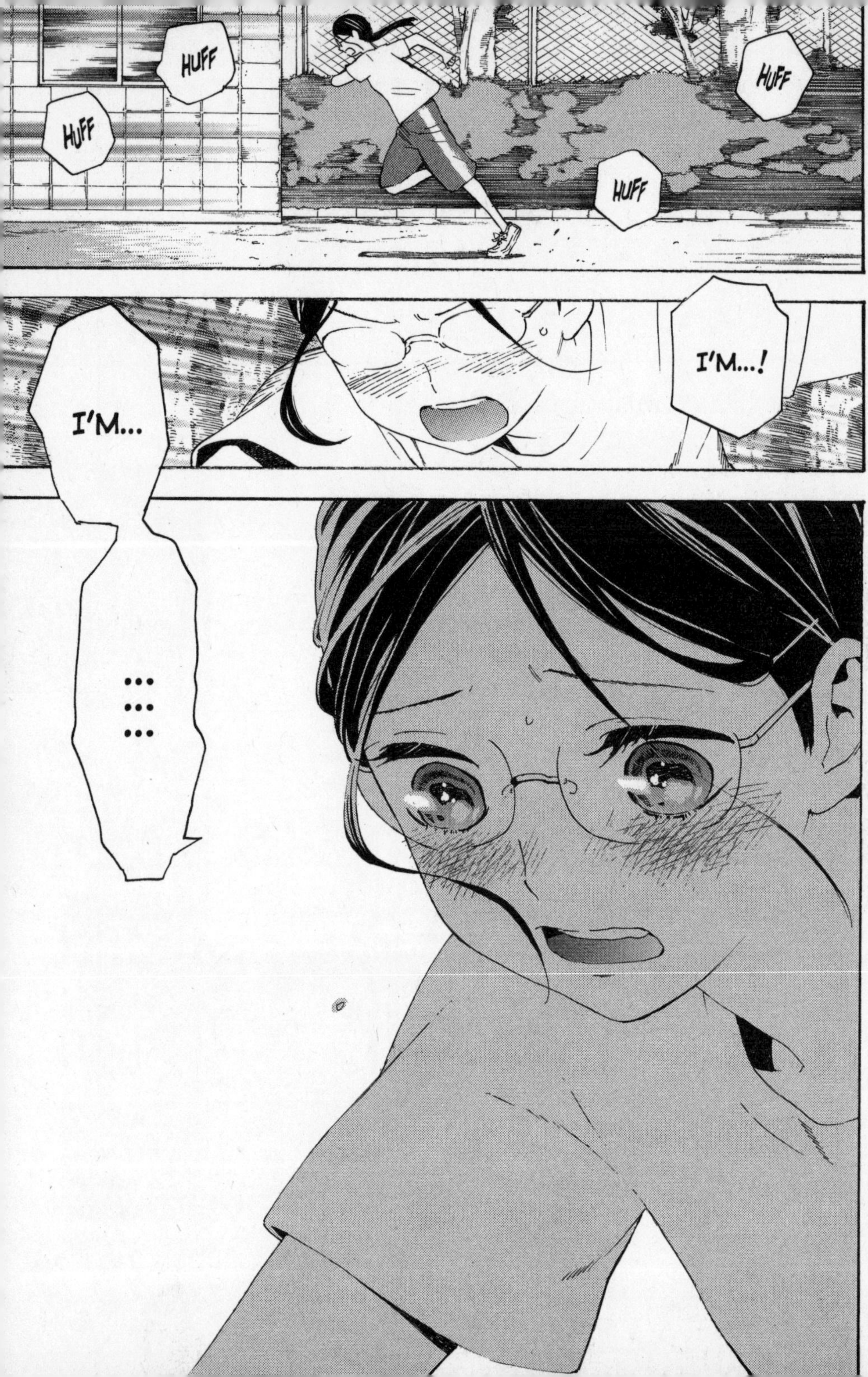
HUFF
HUFF
HUFF
HUFF
I'M...!
I'M... ... ...

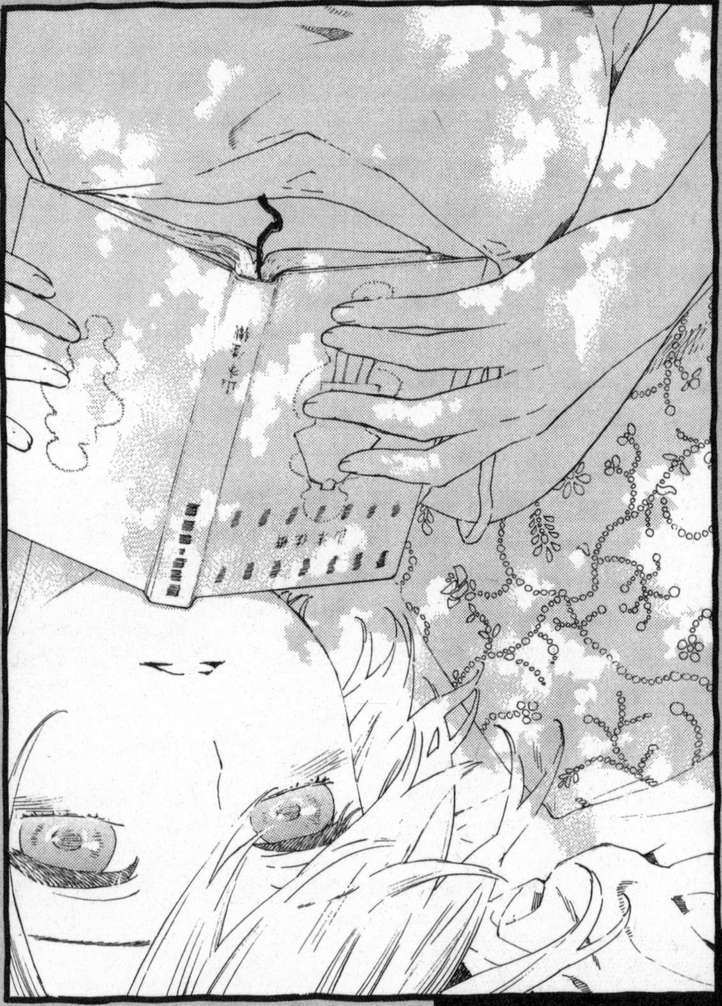

profile

Nina Sugawara

Height: **160 cm (Approx. 5'3")**

Blood type: **B**

Activity: **Literature Club**

Favorite book: ***Story of the Eye***

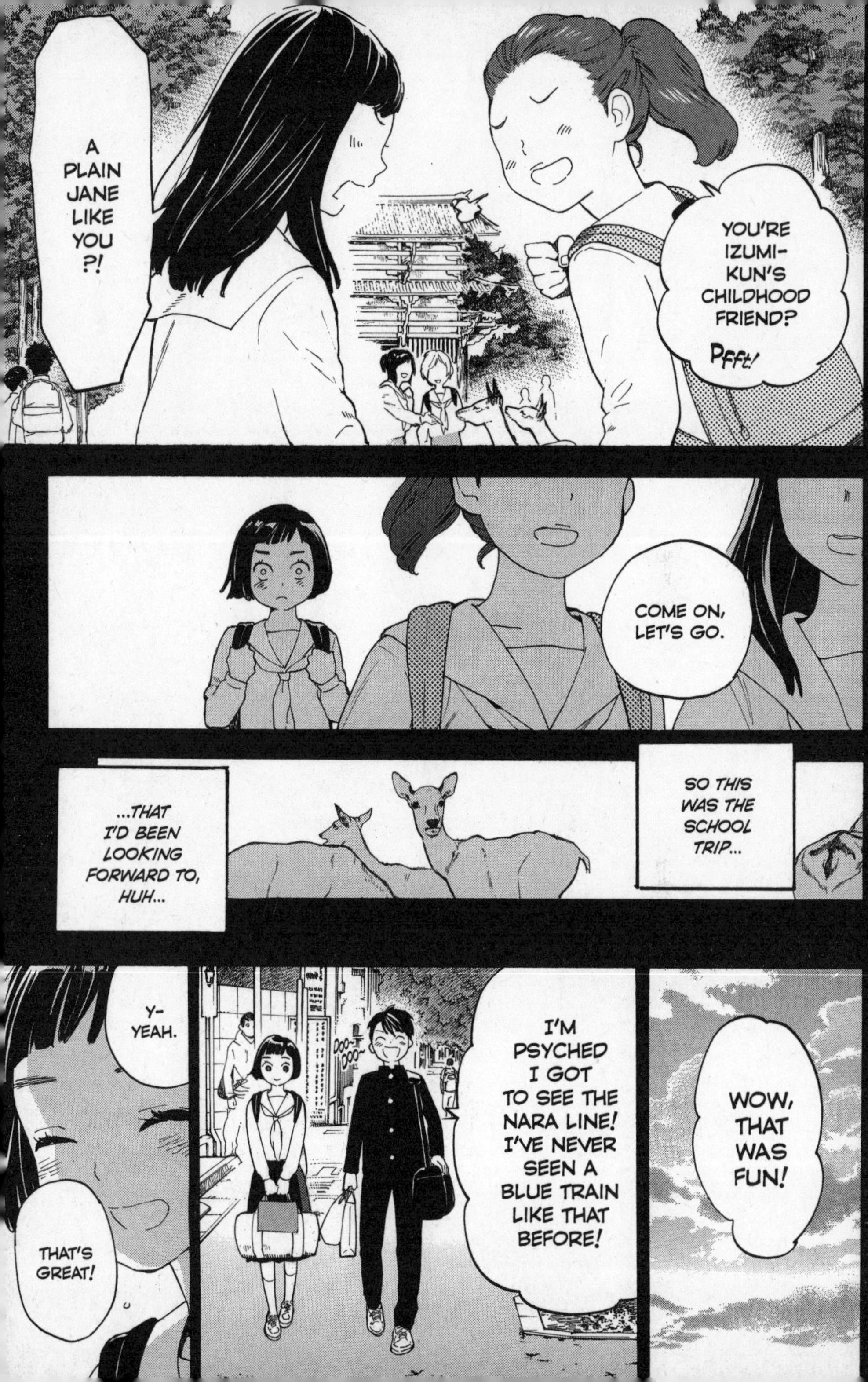
YOU'RE IZUMI-KUN'S CHILDHOOD FRIEND?
Pfft!
A PLAIN JANE LIKE YOU?!
COME ON, LET'S GO.
SO THIS WAS THE SCHOOL TRIP...
...THAT I'D BEEN LOOKING FORWARD TO, HUH...
WOW, THAT WAS FUN!
I'M PSYCHED I GOT TO SEE THE NARA LINE! I'VE NEVER SEEN A BLUE TRAIN LIKE THAT BEFORE!
DOO~ DOO~
Y-YEAH.
THAT'S GREAT!

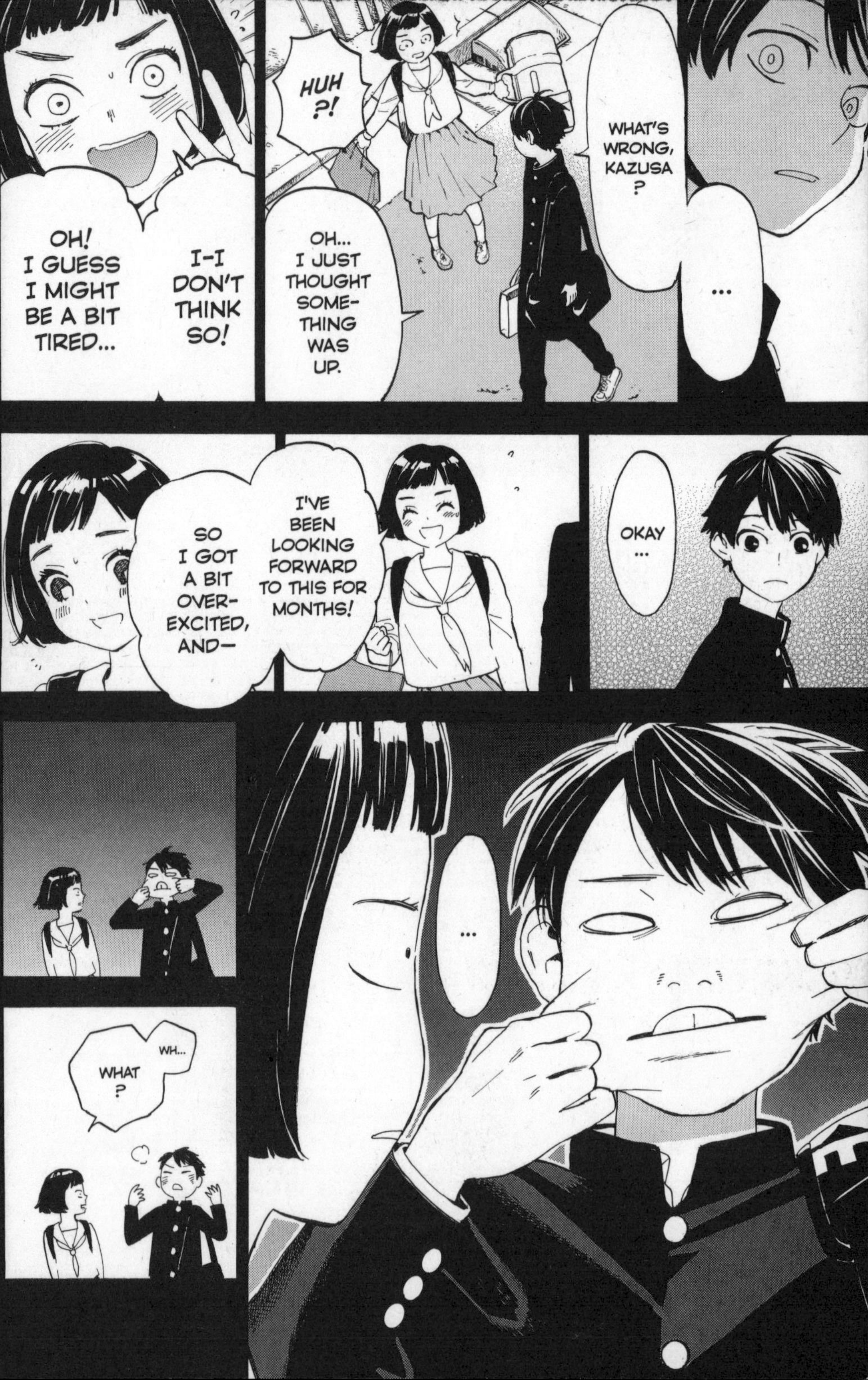
...
WHAT'S WRONG, KAZUSA?
HUH?!
OH... I JUST THOUGHT SOME-THING WAS UP.
I-I DON'T THINK SO!
OH! I GUESS I MIGHT BE A BIT TIRED...
OKAY...
I'VE BEEN LOOKING FORWARD TO THIS FOR MONTHS!
SO I GOT A BIT OVER-EXCITED, AND—
...
WH... WHAT?

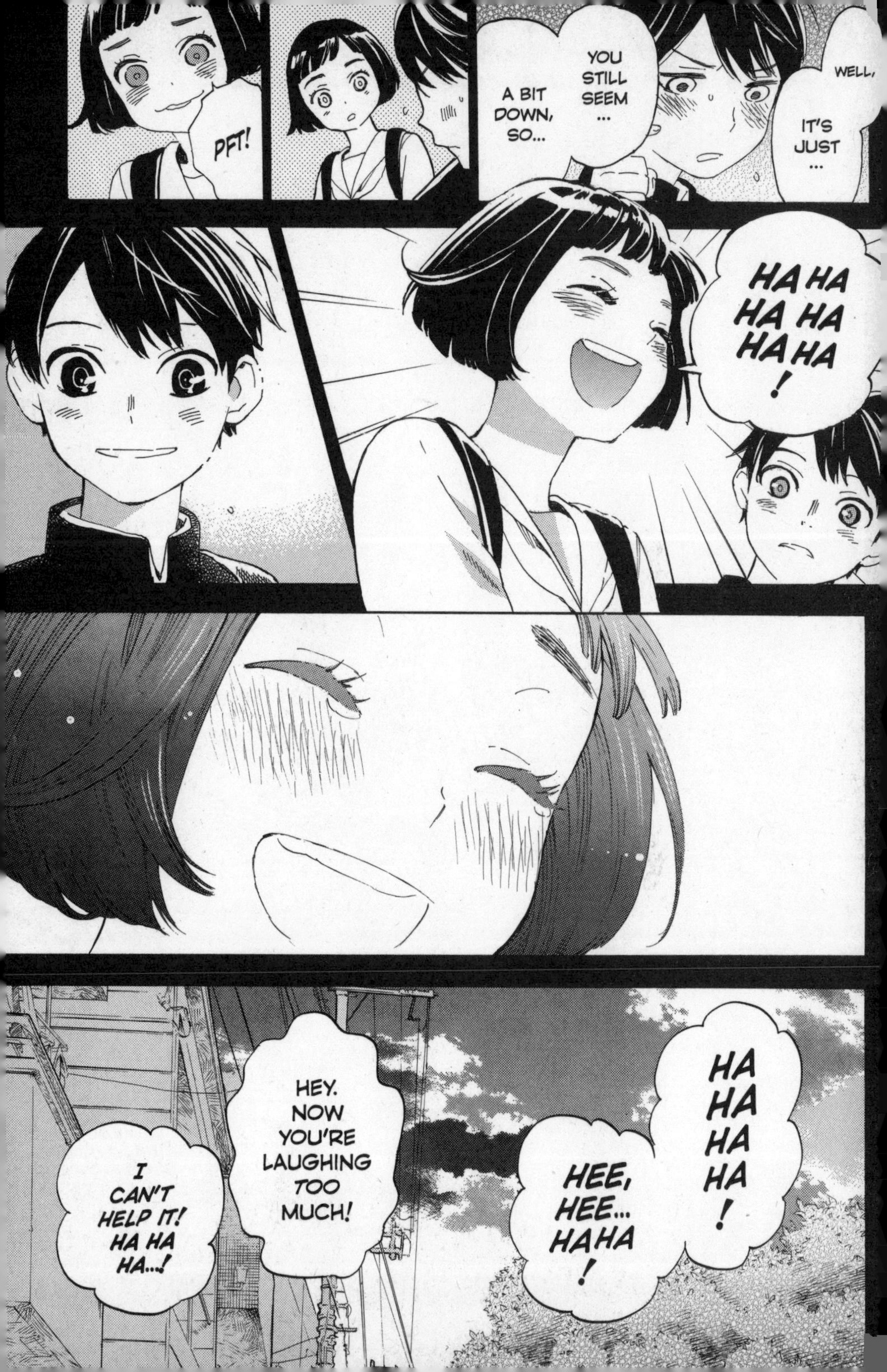
WELL, IT'S JUST ...
YOU STILL SEEM ... A BIT DOWN, SO...
PFT!
HA HA HA HA HA HA!
HA HA HA HA!
HEE, HEE... HAHA!
HEY. NOW YOU'RE LAUGHING TOO MUCH!
I CAN'T HELP IT! HA HA HA...!

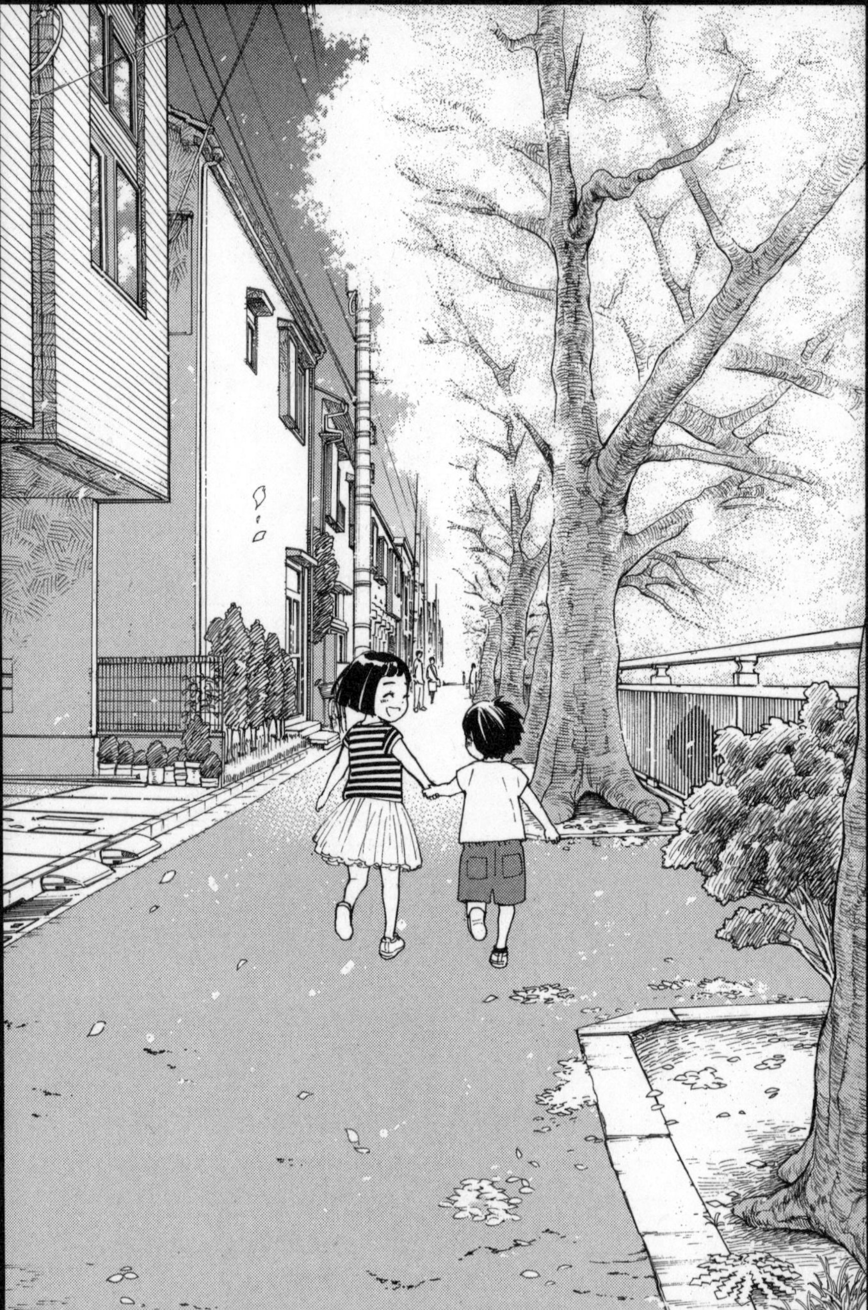

Meeting 4

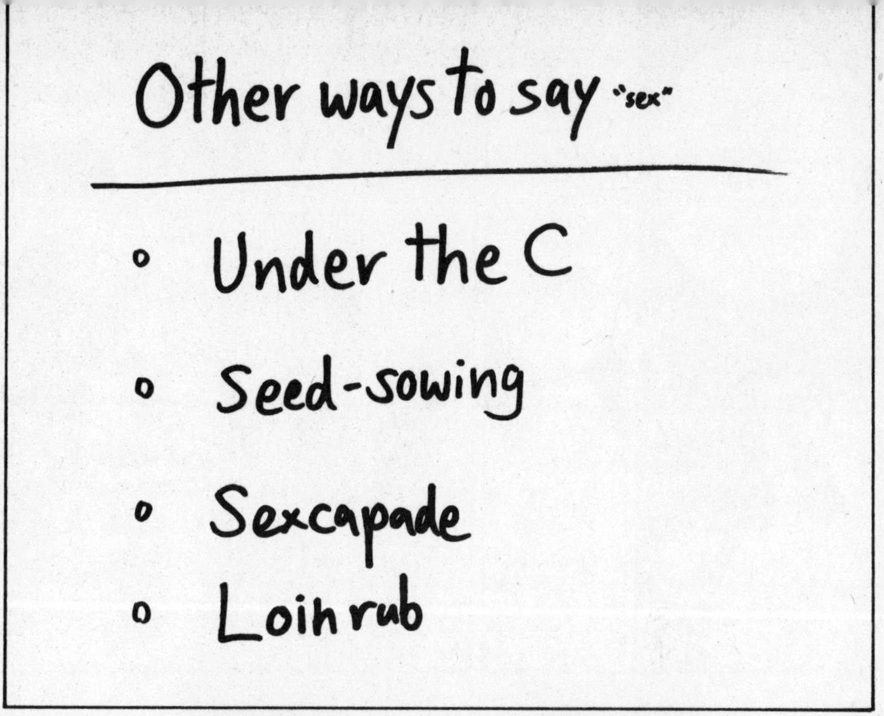
Other ways to say "sex"
Under the C
Seed-sowing
Sexcapade
Loin rub
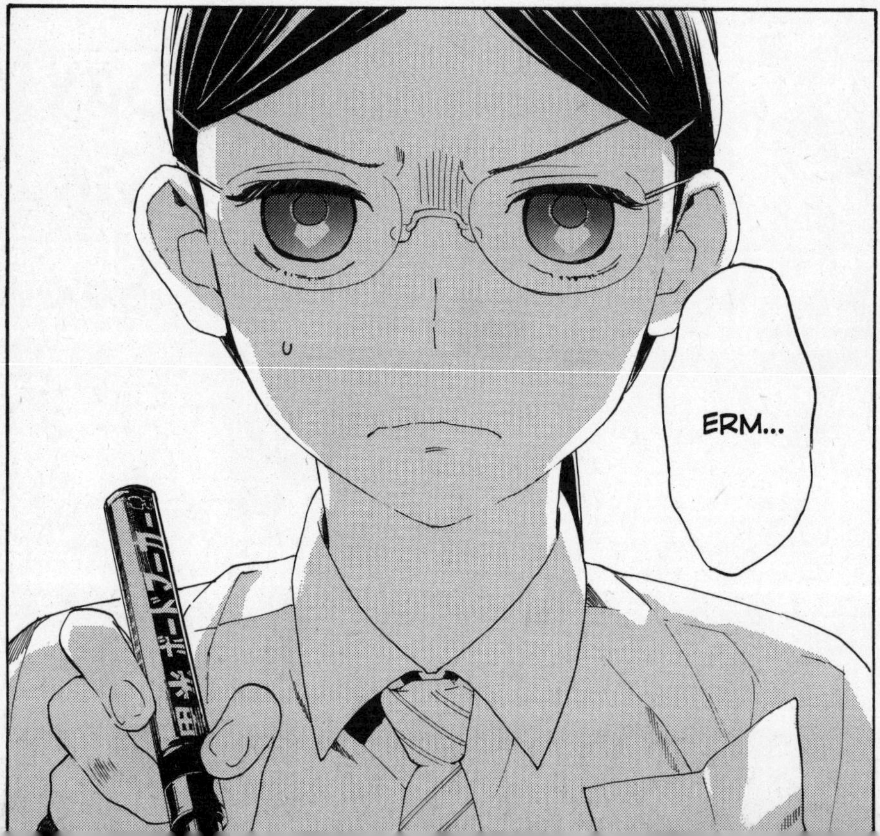
ERM...

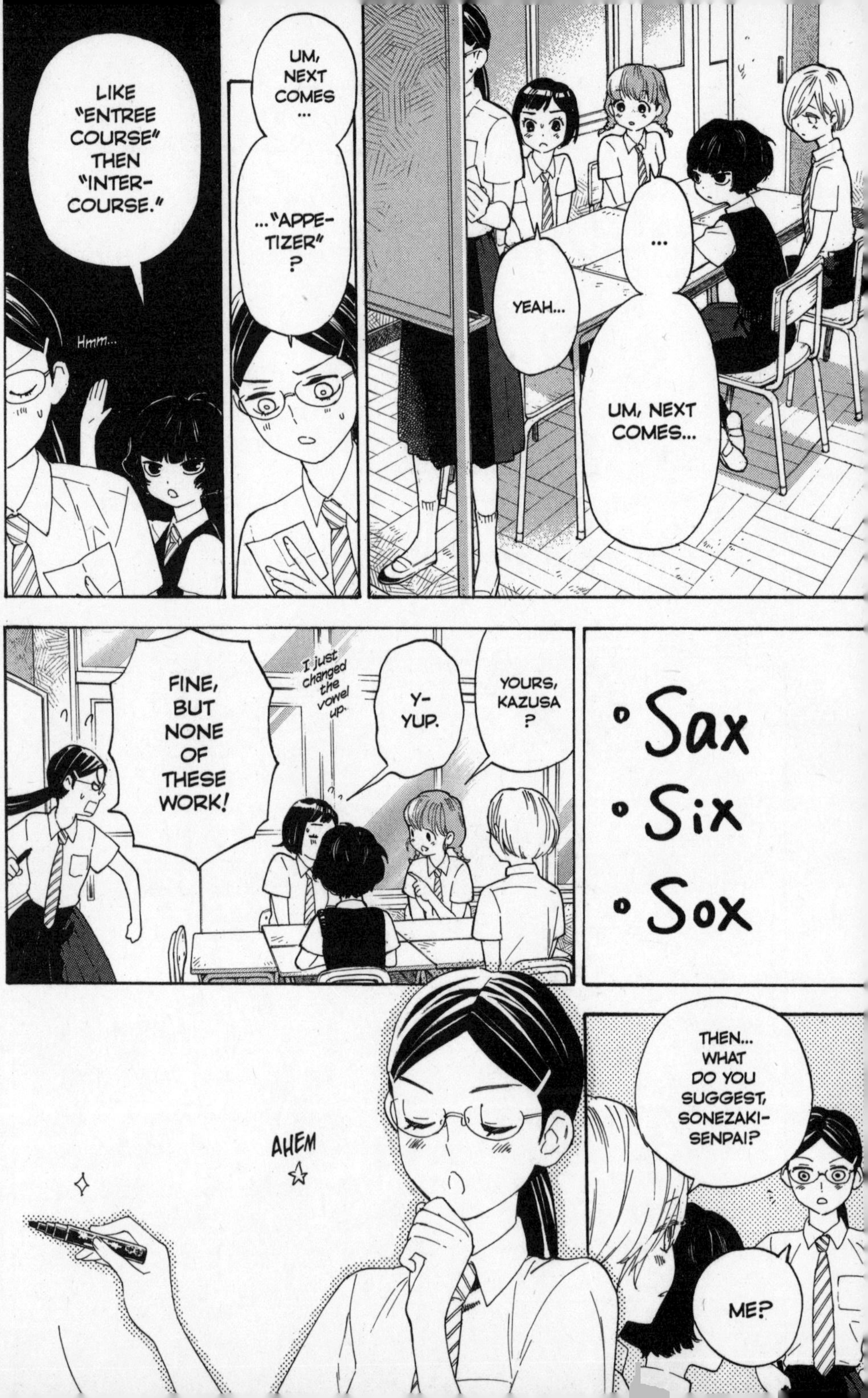
...
UM, NEXT COMES...
YEAH...
UM, NEXT COMES ...
..."APPE-TIZER" ?
LIKE "ENTREE COURSE" THEN "INTER-COURSE."
Hmm...
• Sax
• Six
• Sox
YOURS, KAZUSA ?
Y-YUP.
I just changed the vowel up.
FINE, BUT NONE OF THESE WORK!
THEN... WHAT DO YOU SUGGEST, SONEZAKI-SENPAI?
ME?
AHEM

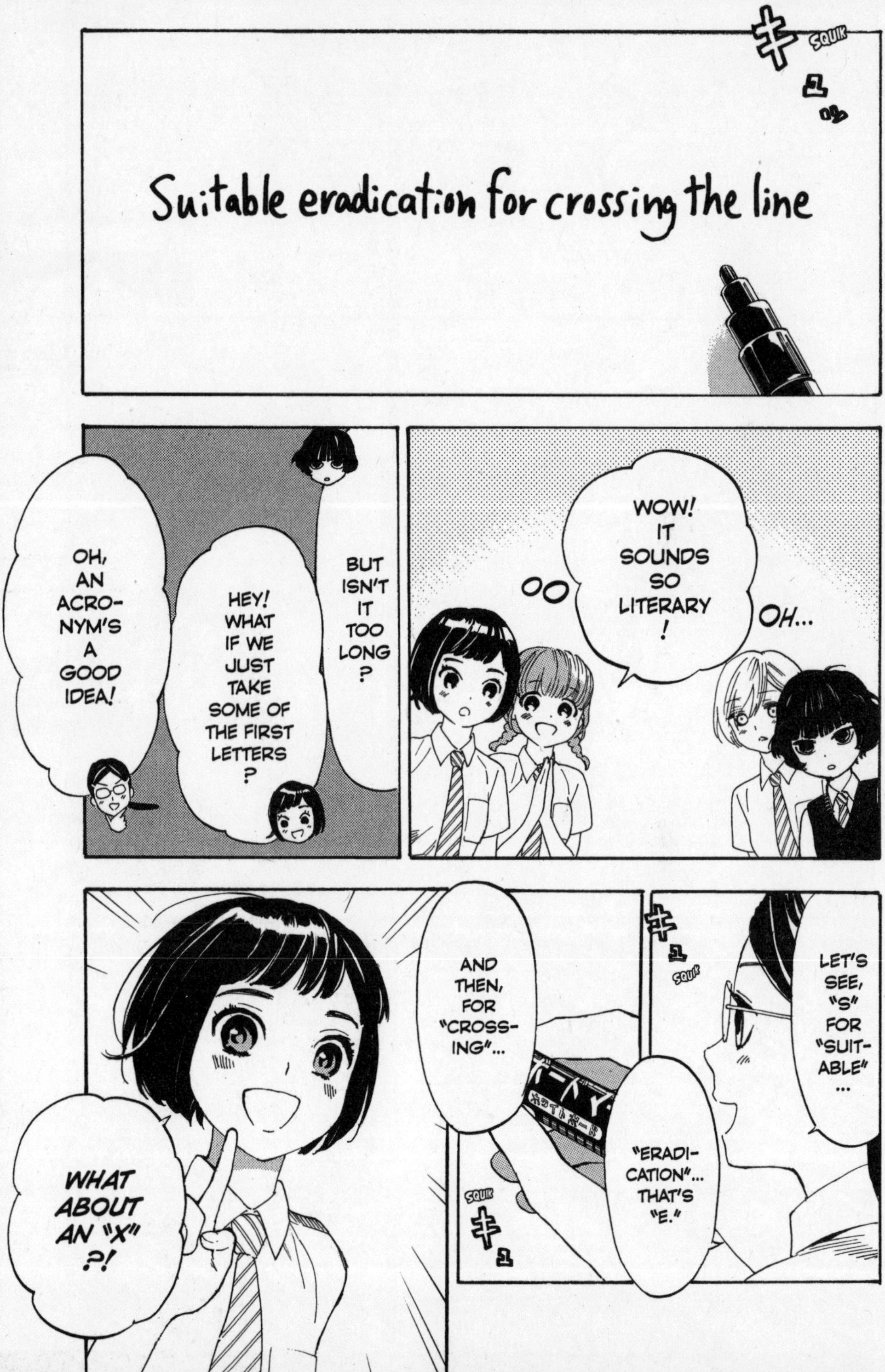
SQUIK
Suitable eradication for crossing the line
WOW! IT SOUNDS SO LITERARY!
OH...
OO
BUT ISN'T IT TOO LONG?
HEY! WHAT IF WE JUST TAKE SOME OF THE FIRST LETTERS?
OH, AN ACRONYM'S A GOOD IDEA!
SQUIK
LET'S SEE, "S" FOR "SUITABLE"...
"ERADICATION"... THAT'S "E."
SQUIK
AND THEN, FOR "CROSSING"...
WHAT ABOUT AN "X"?!

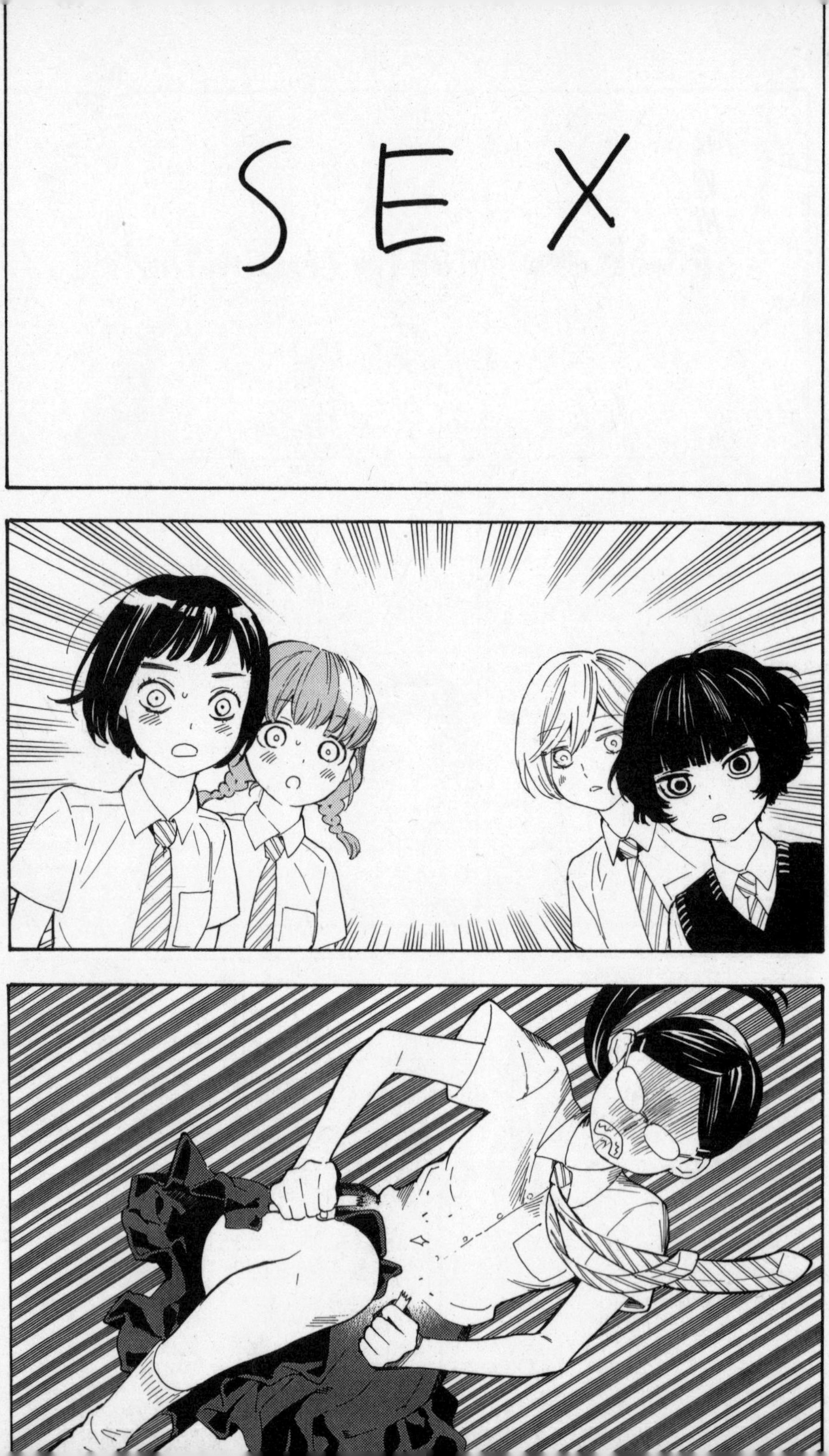
SEX

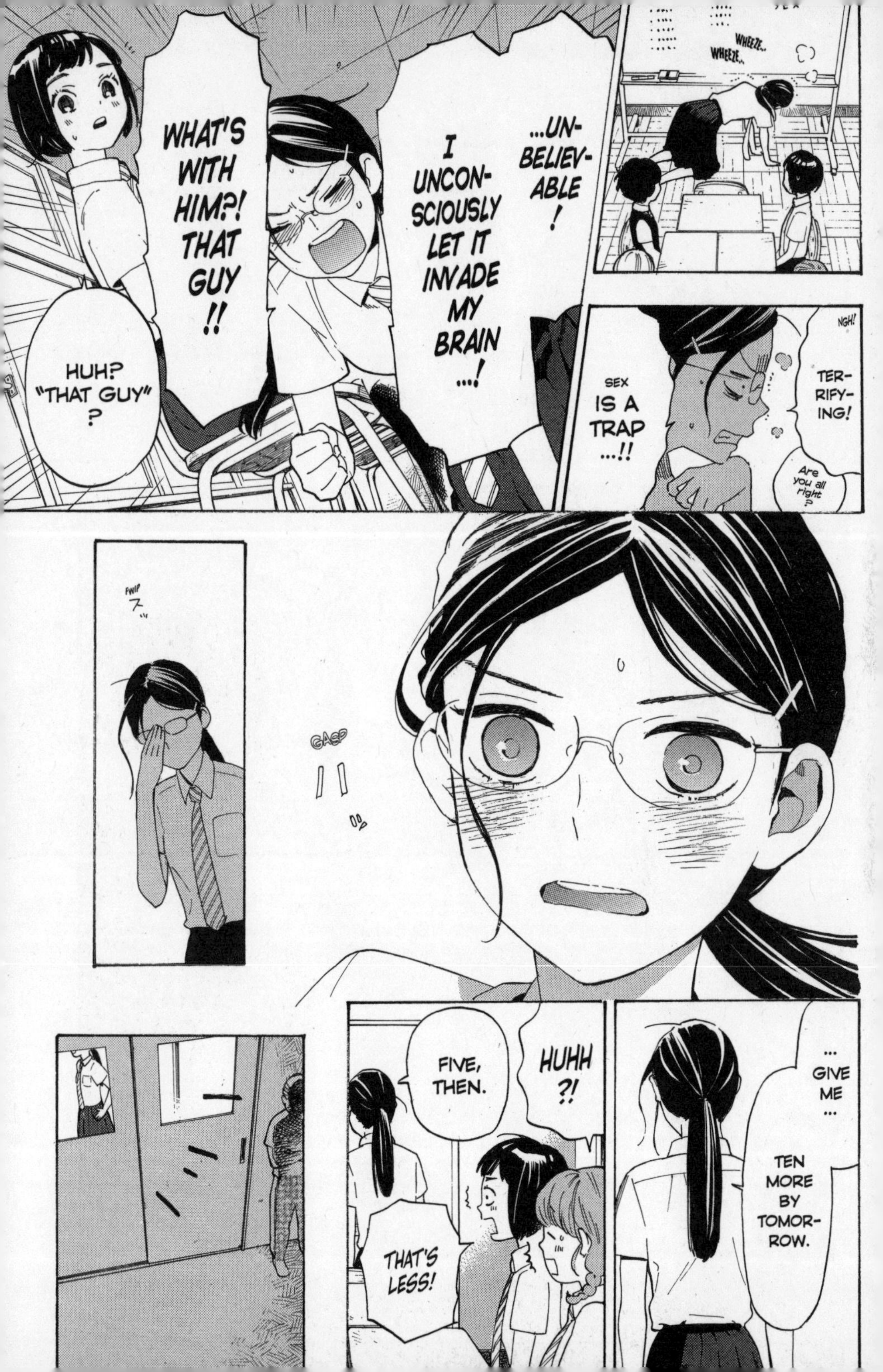
WHEEZE..
WHEEZE..
NGH!
TER-RIFYING!
SEX IS A TRAP ...!!
Are you all right?
...UN-BELIEV-ABLE!
I UNCON-SCIOUSLY LET IT INVADE MY BRAIN ...!
WHAT'S WITH HIM?! THAT GUY!!
HUH? "THAT GUY"?
GASP
FWIP
ス
... GIVE ME ... TEN MORE BY TOMOR-ROW.
HUHH?!
FIVE, THEN.
THAT'S LESS!

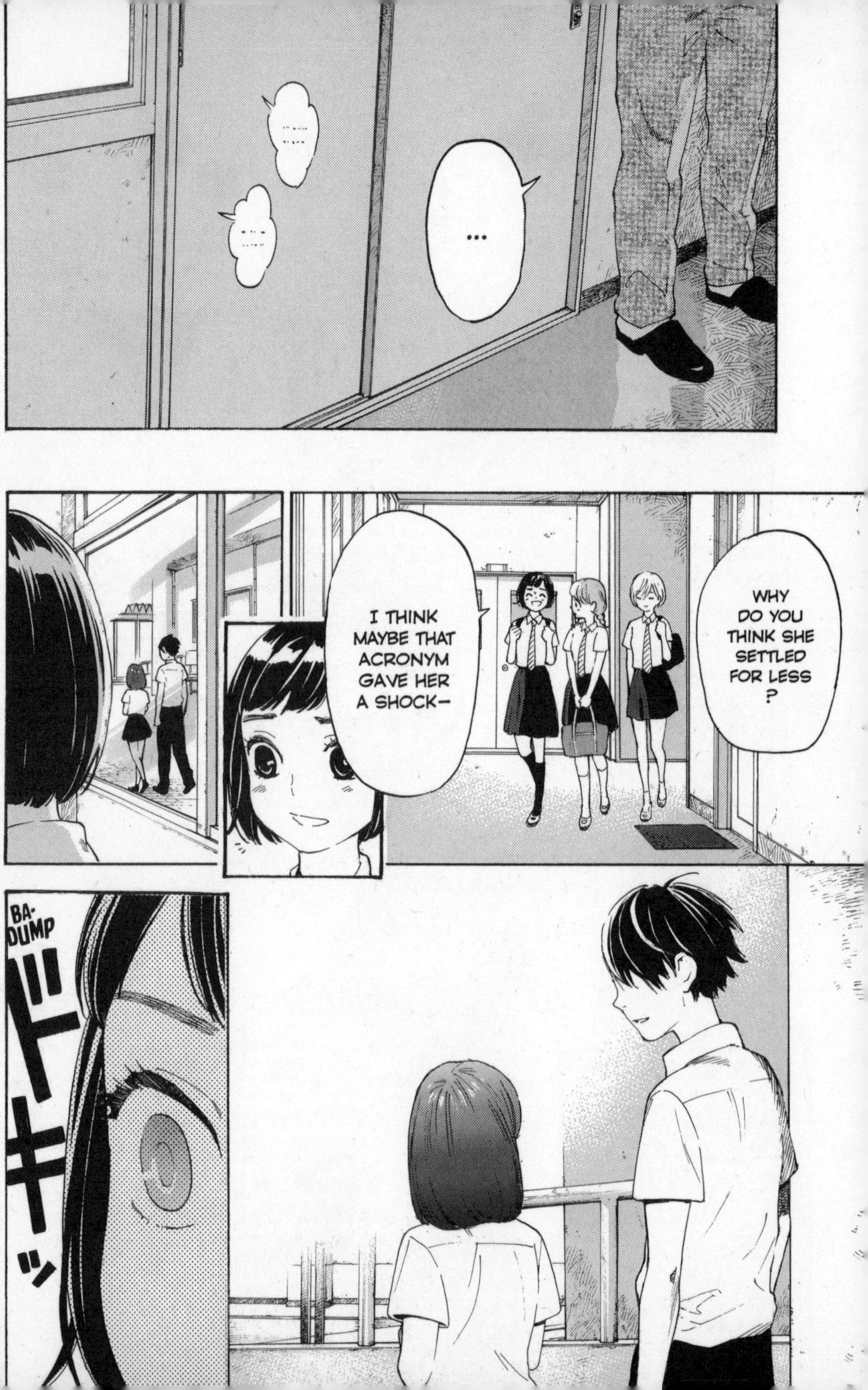
...
WHY DO YOU THINK SHE SETTLED FOR LESS?
I THINK MAYBE THAT ACRONYM GAVE HER A SHOCK—
BA-DUMP
ドキッ

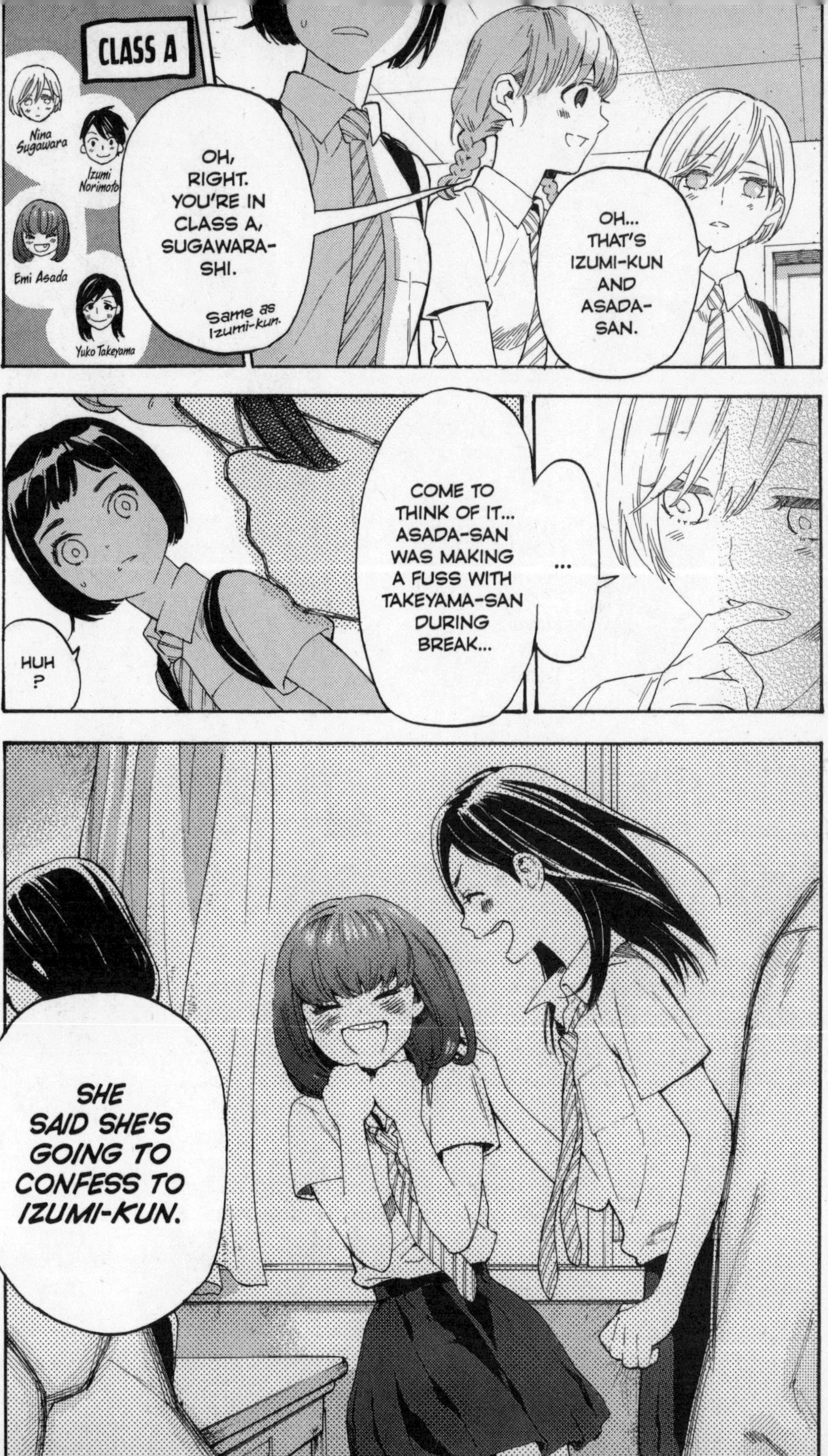
OH... THAT'S IZUMI-KUN AND ASADA-SAN.
OH, RIGHT. YOU'RE IN CLASS A, SUGAWARA-SHI.
Same as Izumi-kun.
CLASS A
Nina Sugawara
Izumi Norimoto
Emi Asada
Yuko Takeyama
...
COME TO THINK OF IT... ASADA-SAN WAS MAKING A FUSS WITH TAKEYAMA-SAN DURING BREAK...
HUH?
SHE SAID SHE'S GOING TO CONFESS TO IZUMI-KUN.

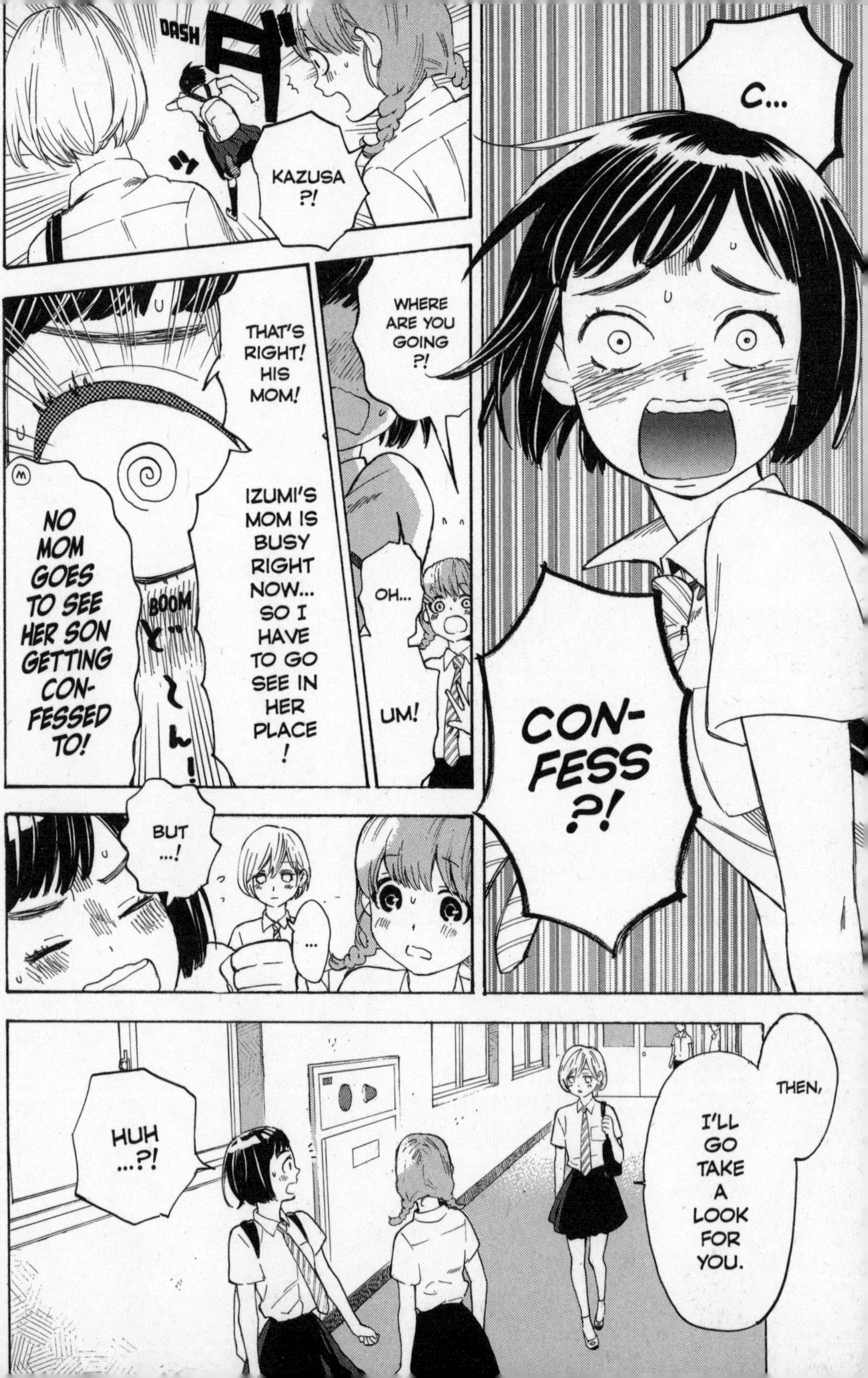
C...
CON-FESS?!
DASH
KAZUSA?!
WHERE ARE YOU GOING?!
OH...
UM!
THAT'S RIGHT! HIS MOM!
IZUMI'S MOM IS BUSY RIGHT NOW... SO I HAVE TO GO SEE IN HER PLACE!
NO MOM GOES TO SEE HER SON GETTING CON-FESSED TO!
BOOM
BUT...!
...
THEN, I'LL GO TAKE A LOOK FOR YOU.
HUH...?!

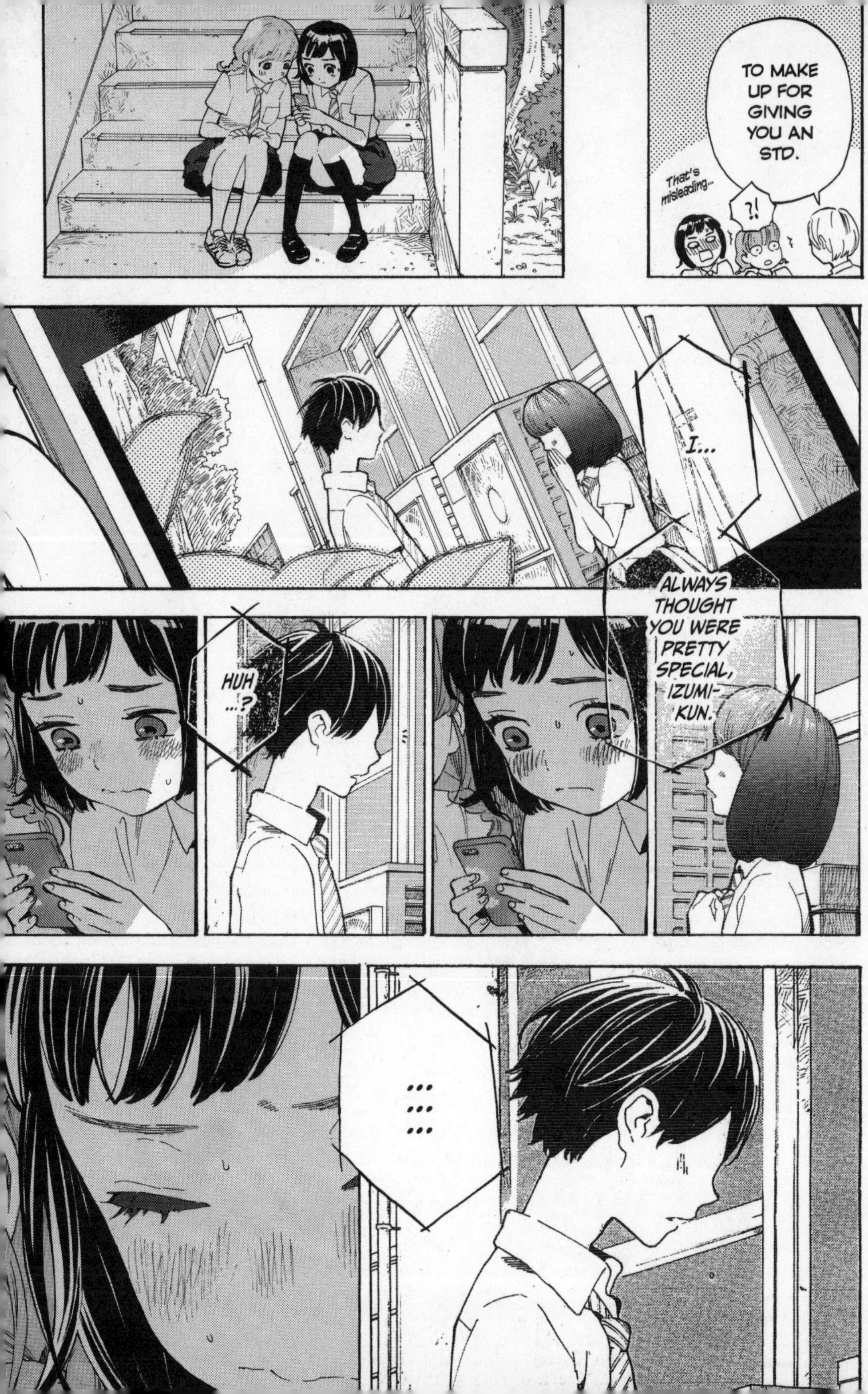
TO MAKE UP FOR GIVING YOU AN STD.
That's misleading...
?!
I...
ALWAYS THOUGHT YOU WERE PRETTY SPECIAL, IZUMI-KUN.
HUH ...?
...
...
...

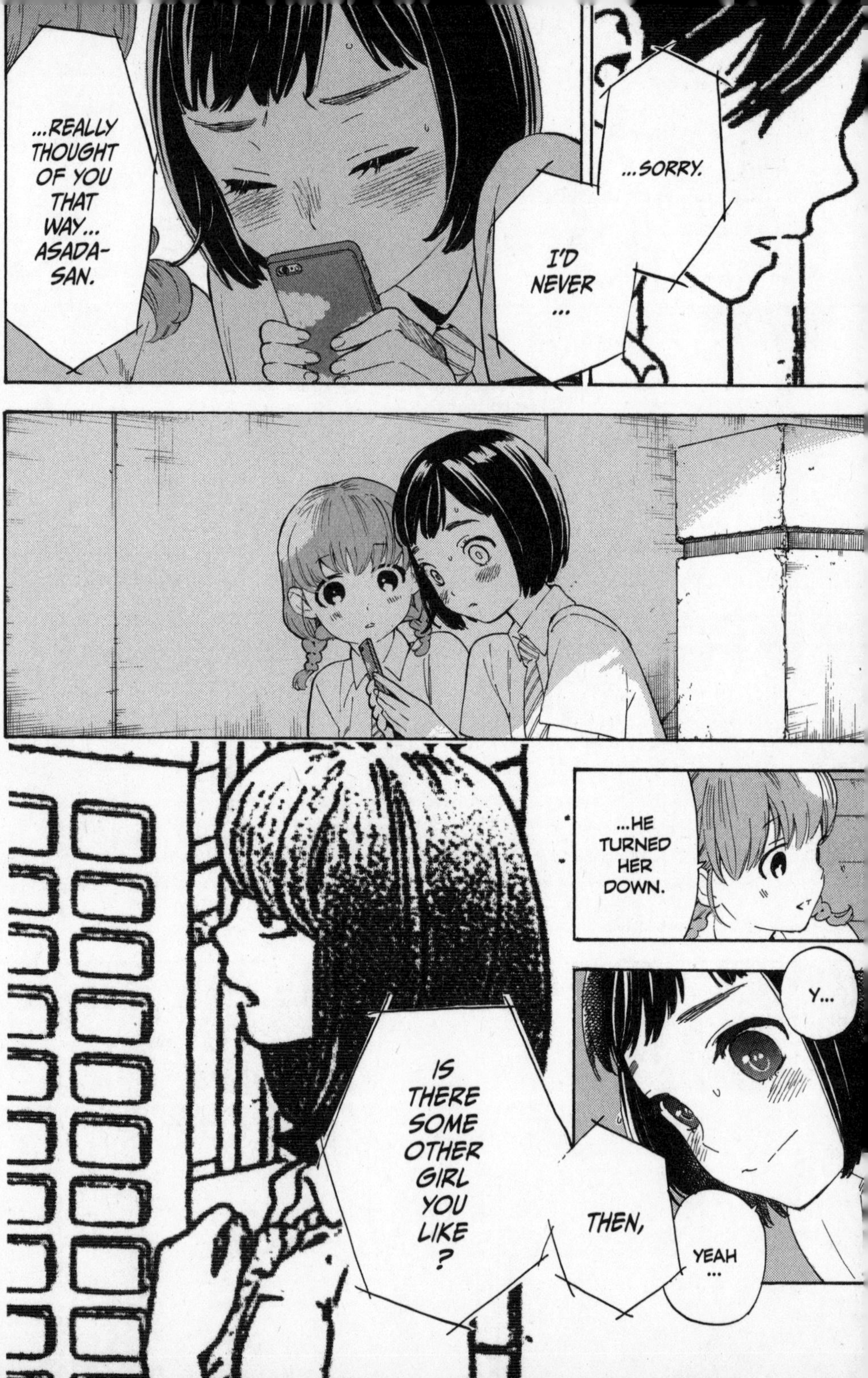
...SORRY.
I'D NEVER ...
...REALLY THOUGHT OF YOU THAT WAY... ASADA-SAN.
...HE TURNED HER DOWN.
Y...
THEN,
IS THERE SOME OTHER GIRL YOU LIKE?
YEAH ...

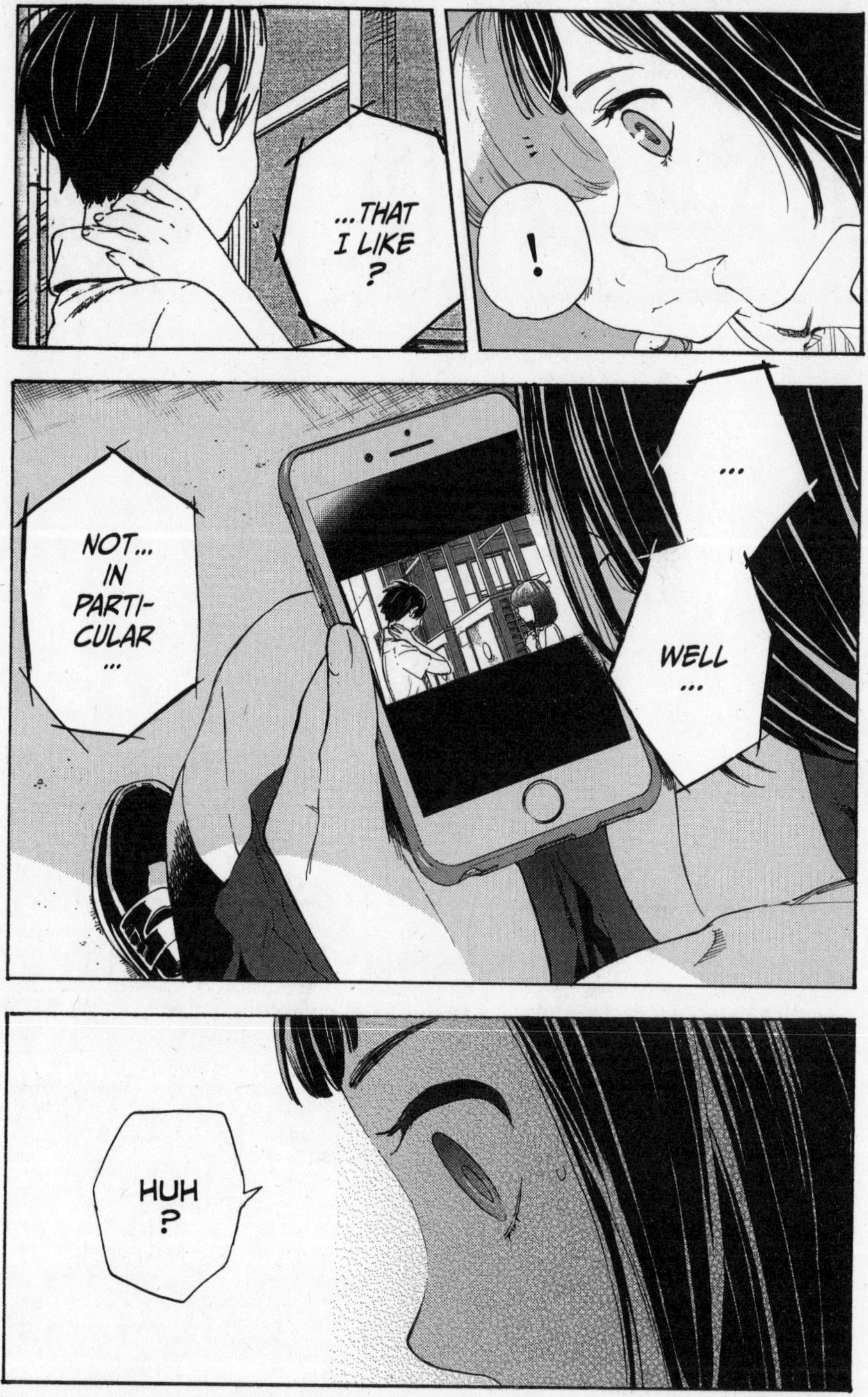
!
...THAT I LIKE ?
...
WELL ...
NOT... IN PARTICULAR ...
HUH ?

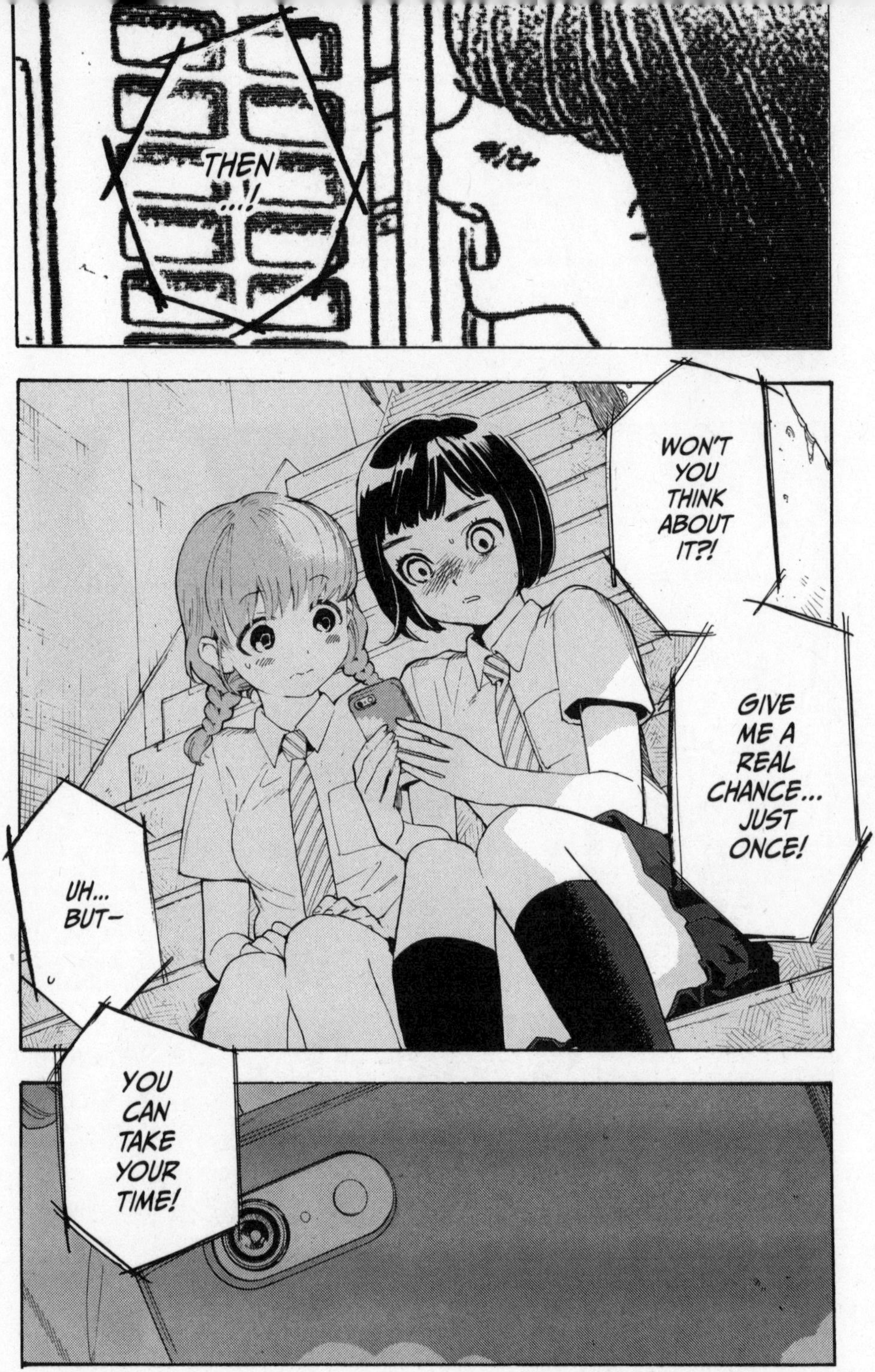
THEN ...!
WON'T YOU THINK ABOUT IT?!
GIVE ME A REAL CHANCE... JUST ONCE!
UH... BUT–
YOU CAN TAKE YOUR TIME!

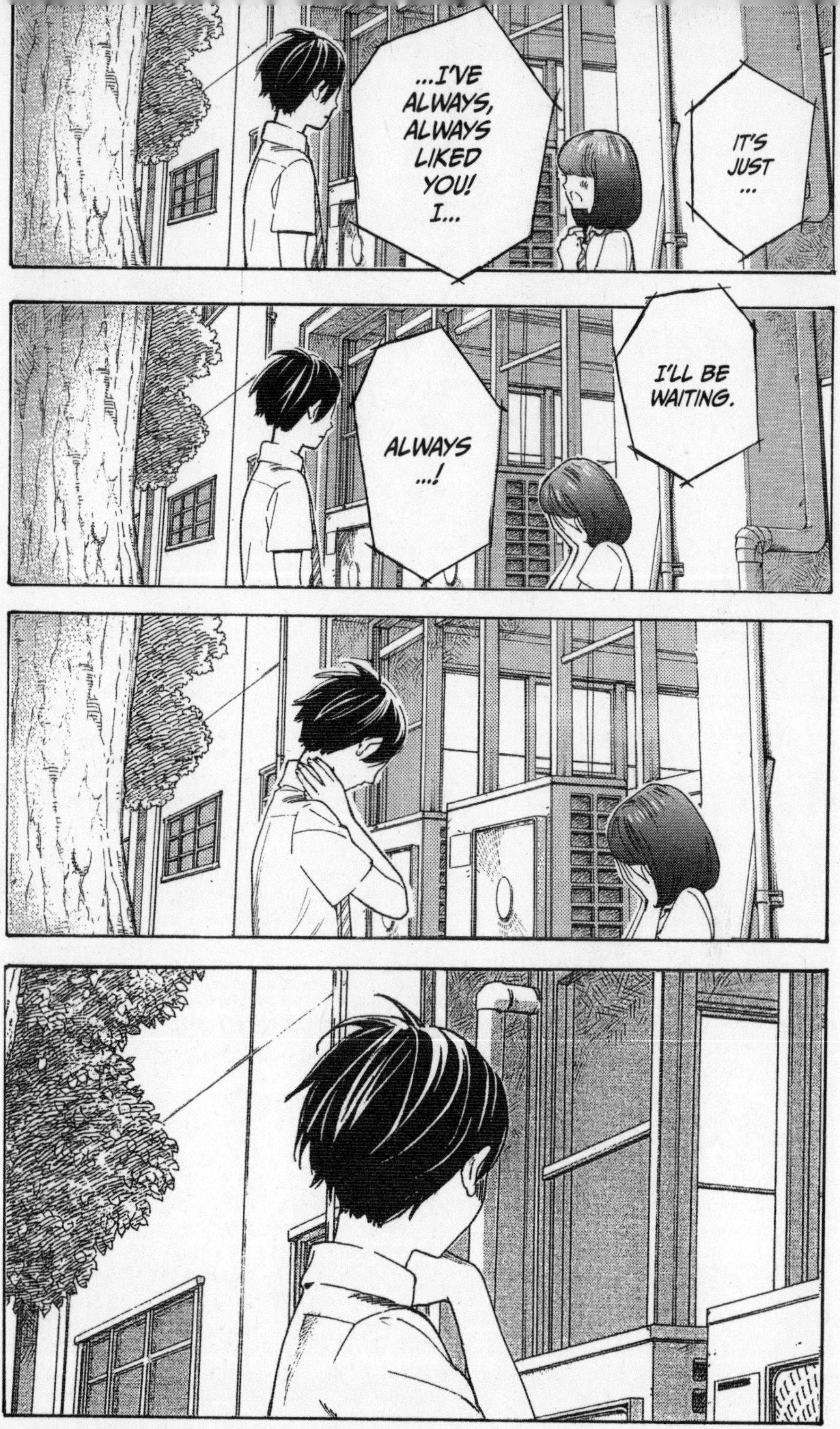
IT'S JUST ...
...I'VE ALWAYS, ALWAYS LIKED YOU! I...
I'LL BE WAITING.
ALWAYS ...!

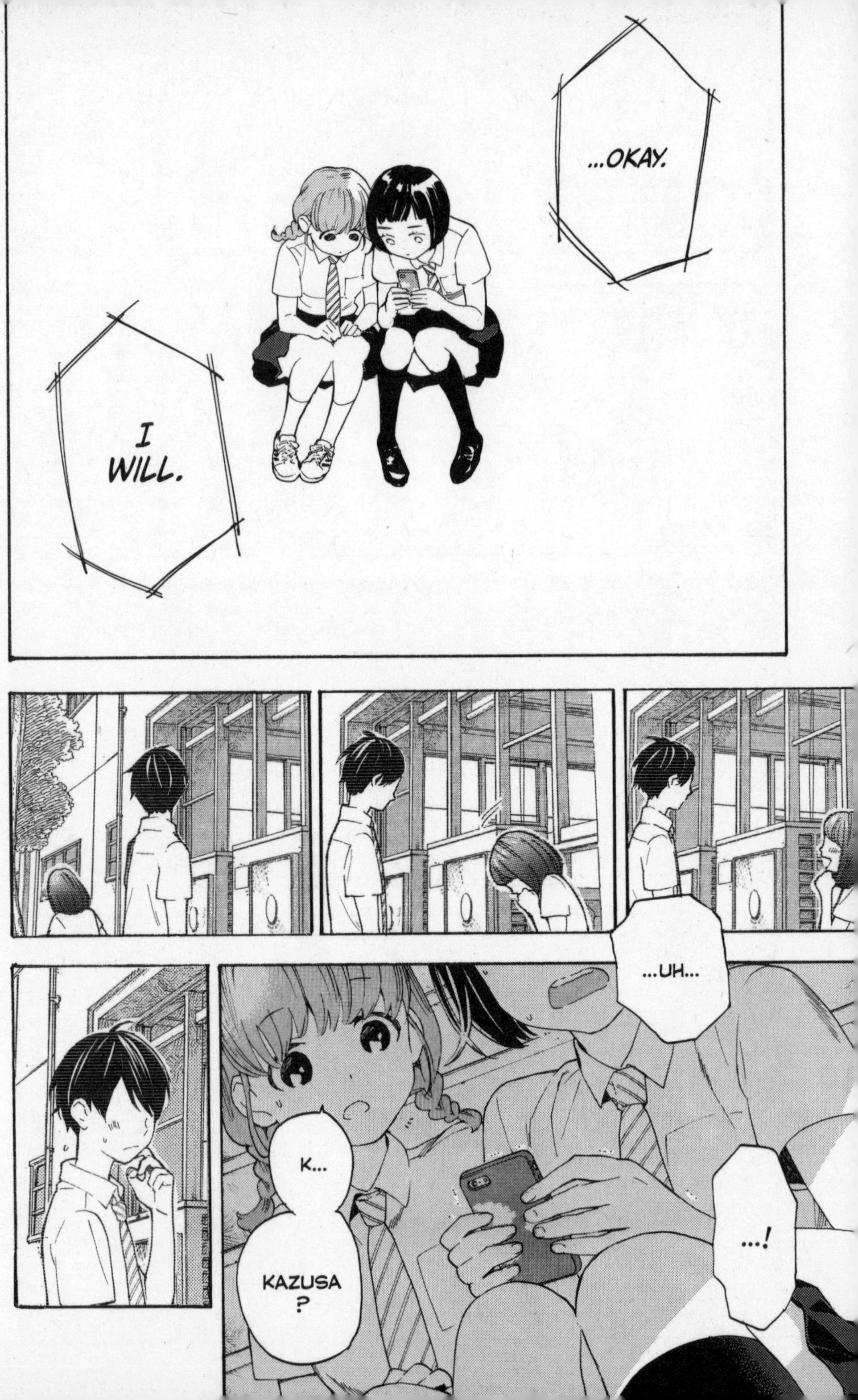
...OKAY.
I WILL.
...UH...
K... KAZUSA?
...!

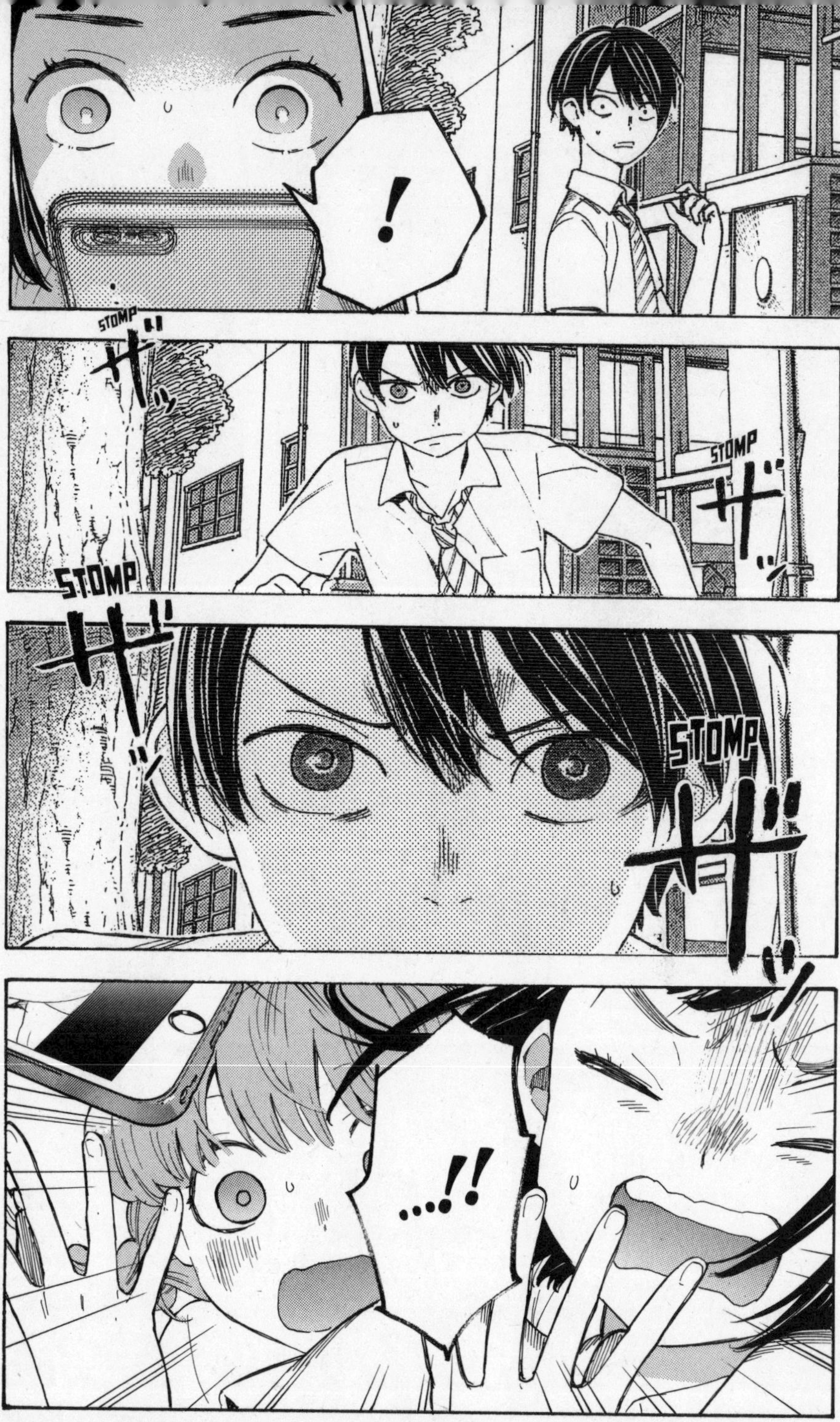

!
STOMP
ザッ
STOMP
ザッ
STOMP
ザッ
STOMP
ザッ
...!!

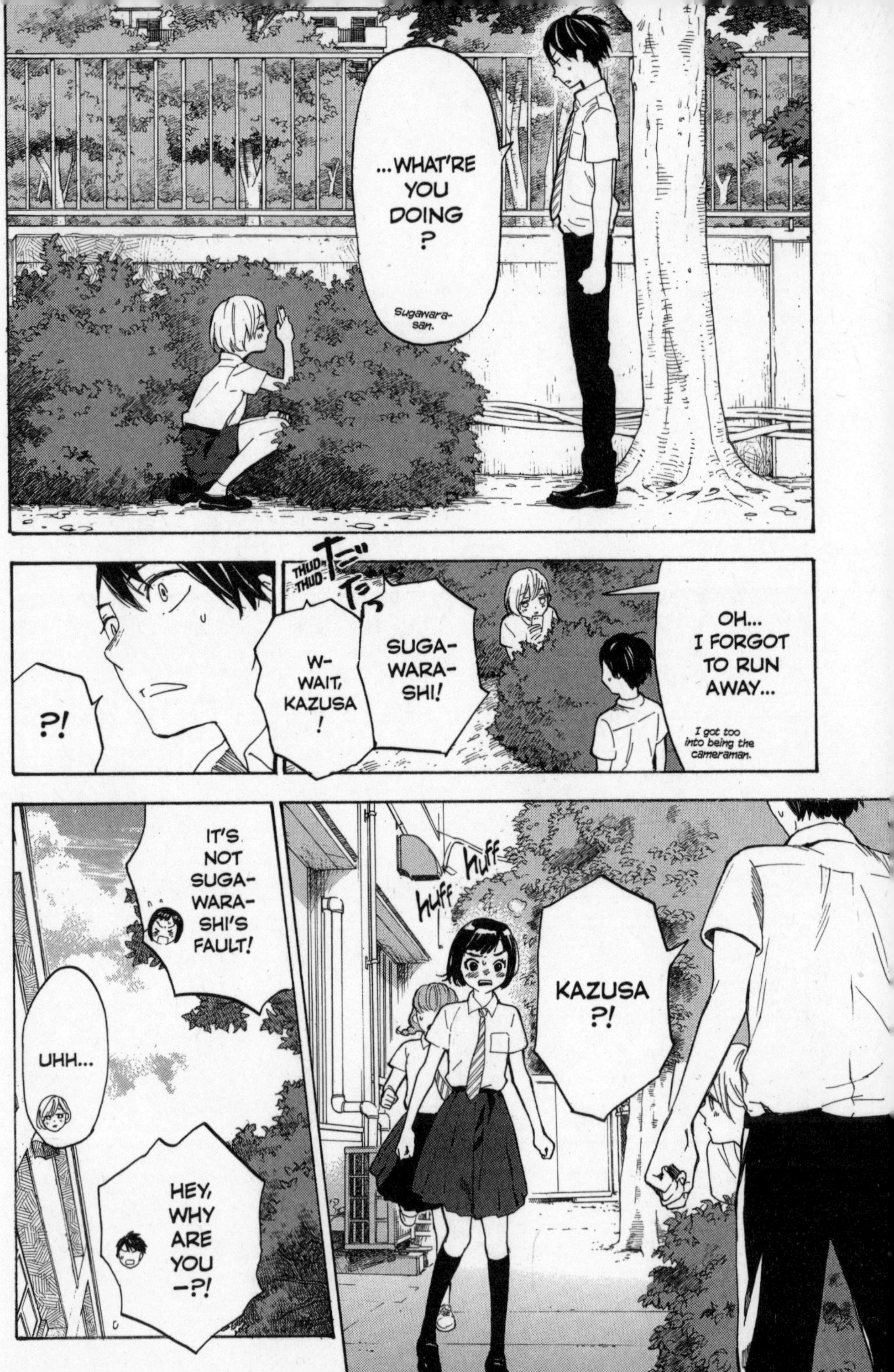
...WHAT'RE YOU DOING?
Sugawara-san.
OH... I FORGOT TO RUN AWAY...
I got too into being the cameraman.
THUD THUD
SUGA-WARA-SHI!
W-WAIT, KAZUSA!
?!
huff huff
KAZUSA?!
IT'S NOT SUGA-WARA-SHI'S FAULT!
UHH...
HEY, WHY ARE YOU-?!

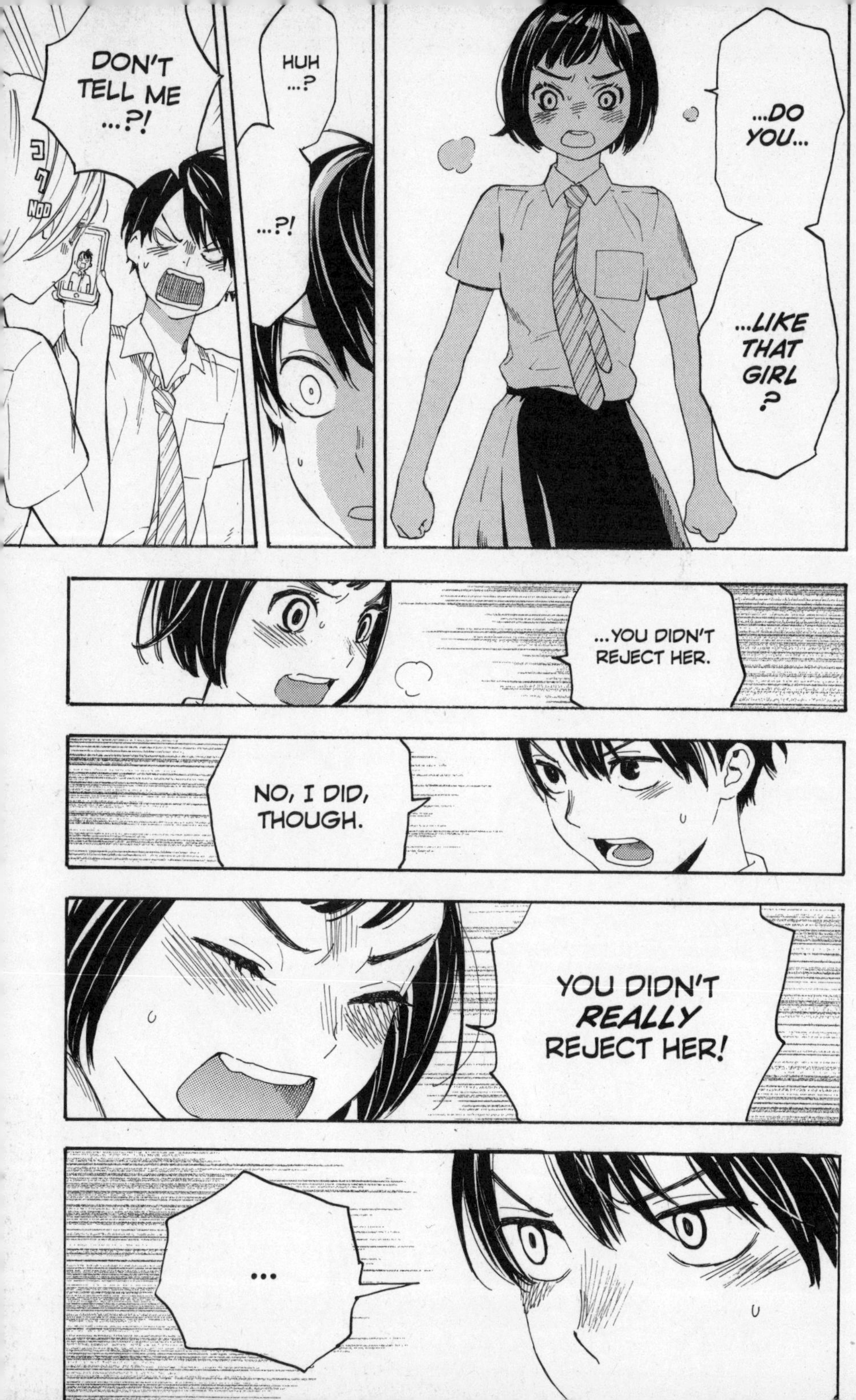
...DO YOU...
...LIKE THAT GIRL?
HUH ...?
...?!
DON'T TELL ME ...?!
コク NOD
...YOU DIDN'T REJECT HER.
NO, I DID, THOUGH.
YOU DIDN'T REALLY REJECT HER!
...

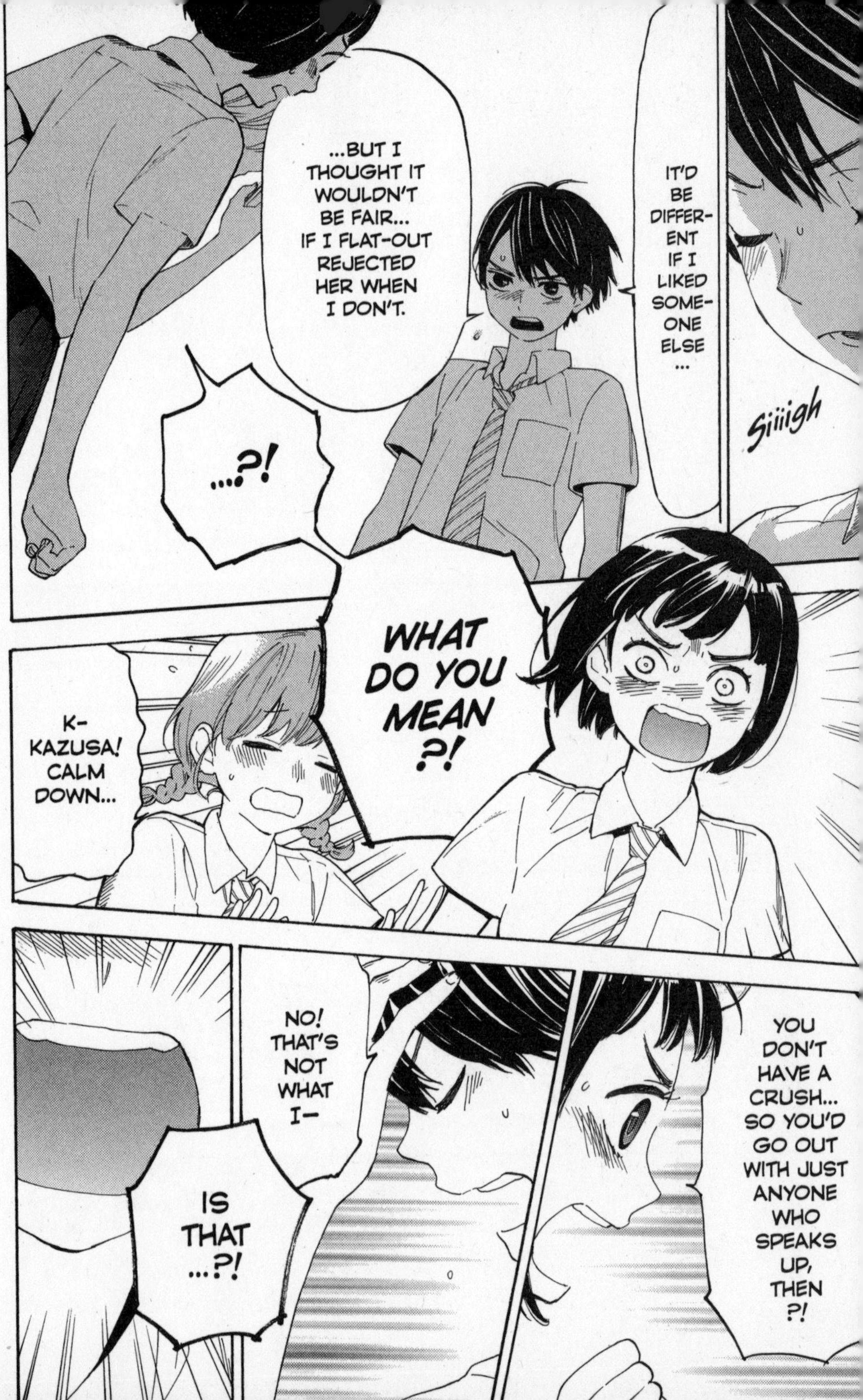
IT'D BE DIFFERENT IF I LIKED SOMEONE ELSE...
Siiiigh
...BUT I THOUGHT IT WOULDN'T BE FAIR... IF I FLAT-OUT REJECTED HER WHEN I DON'T.
...?!
WHAT DO YOU MEAN?!
K-KAZUSA! CALM DOWN...
YOU DON'T HAVE A CRUSH... SO YOU'D GO OUT WITH JUST ANYONE WHO SPEAKS UP, THEN?!
NO! THAT'S NOT WHAT I—
IS THAT...?!

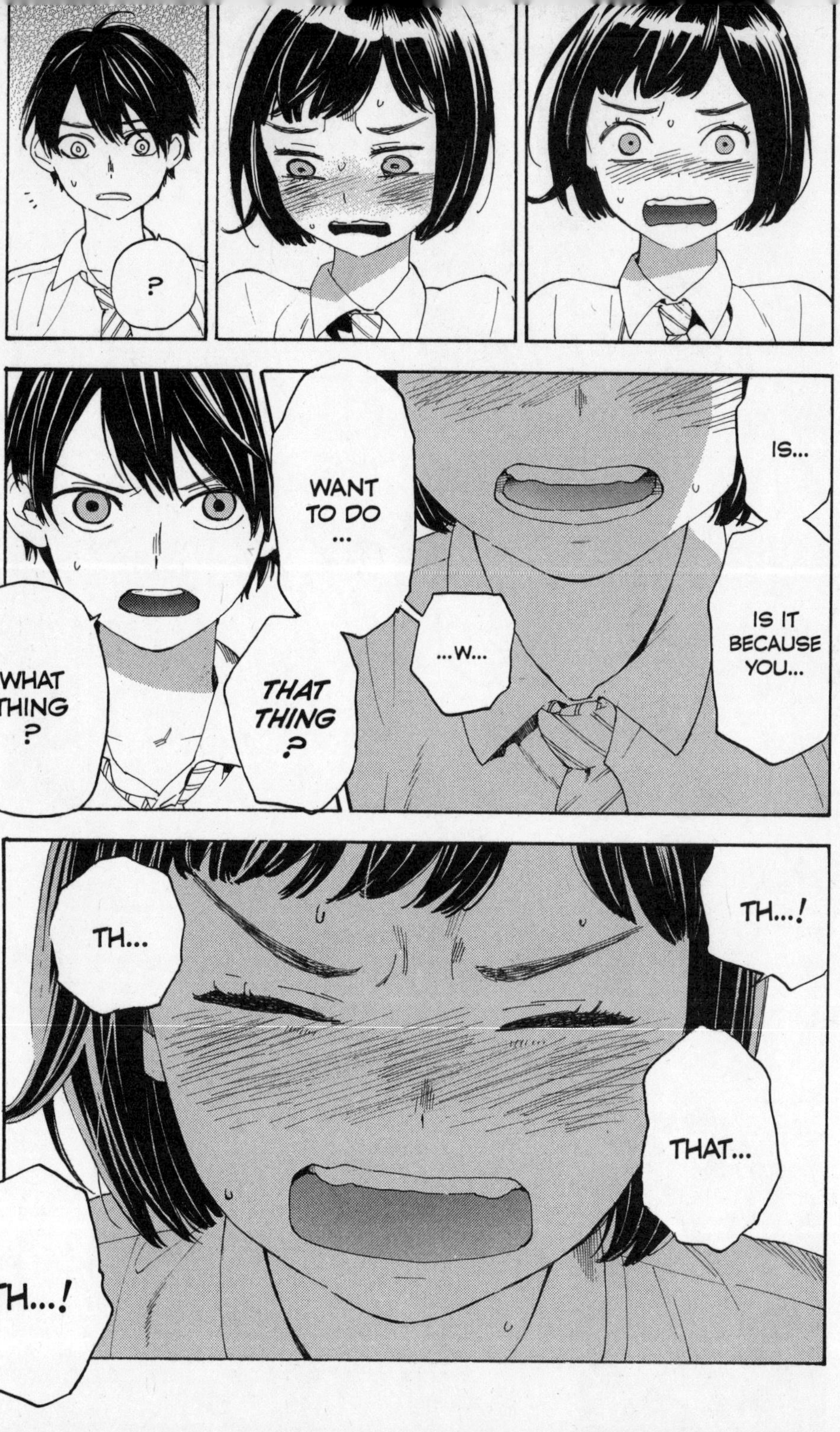
?
IS...
IS IT BECAUSE YOU...
...W...
WANT TO DO ...
THAT THING?
WHAT THING?
TH...!
TH...
THAT...
TH...!

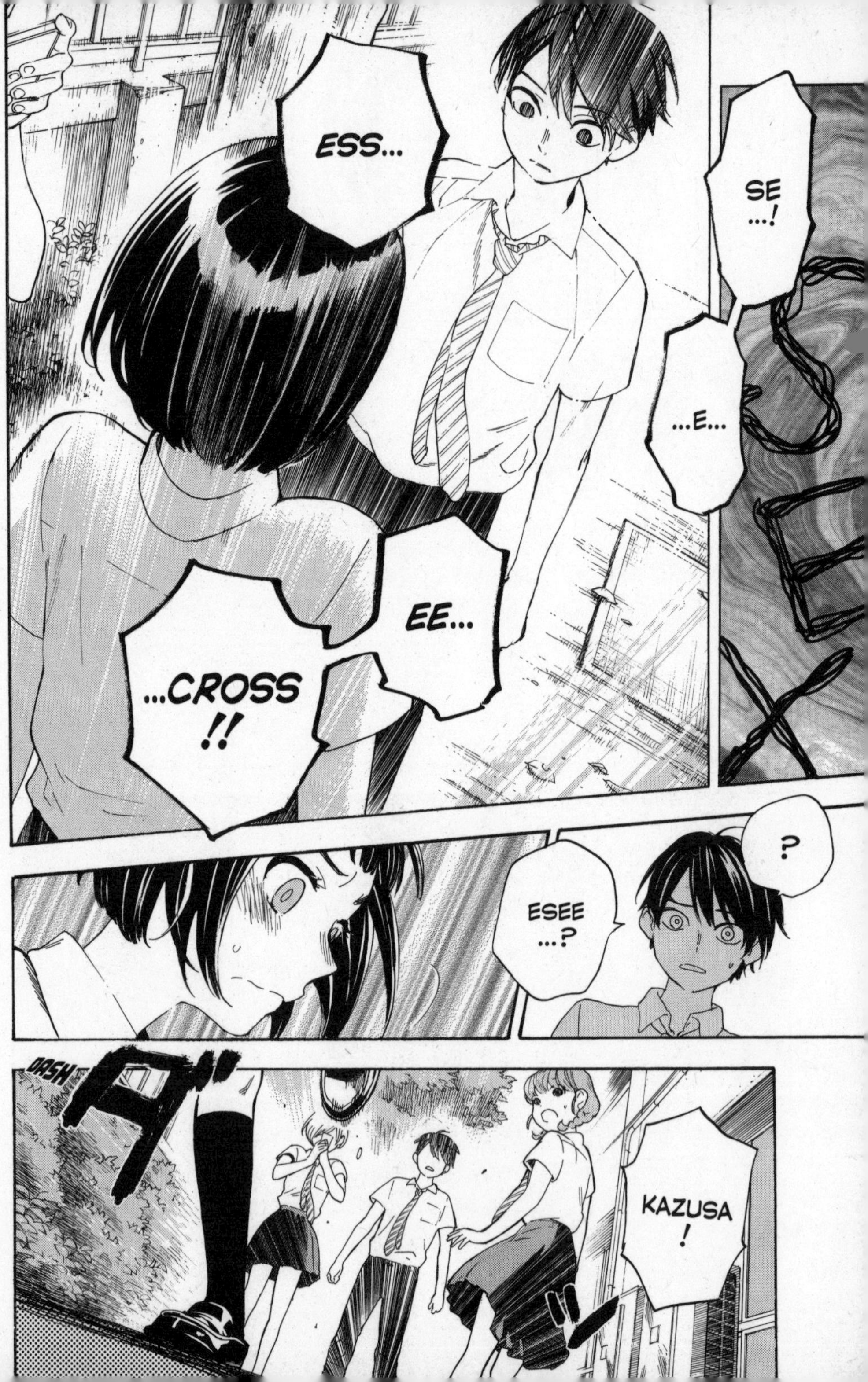
SE ...!
...E...
ESS...
EE...
...CROSS !!
?
ESEE ...?
DASH
KAZUSA !

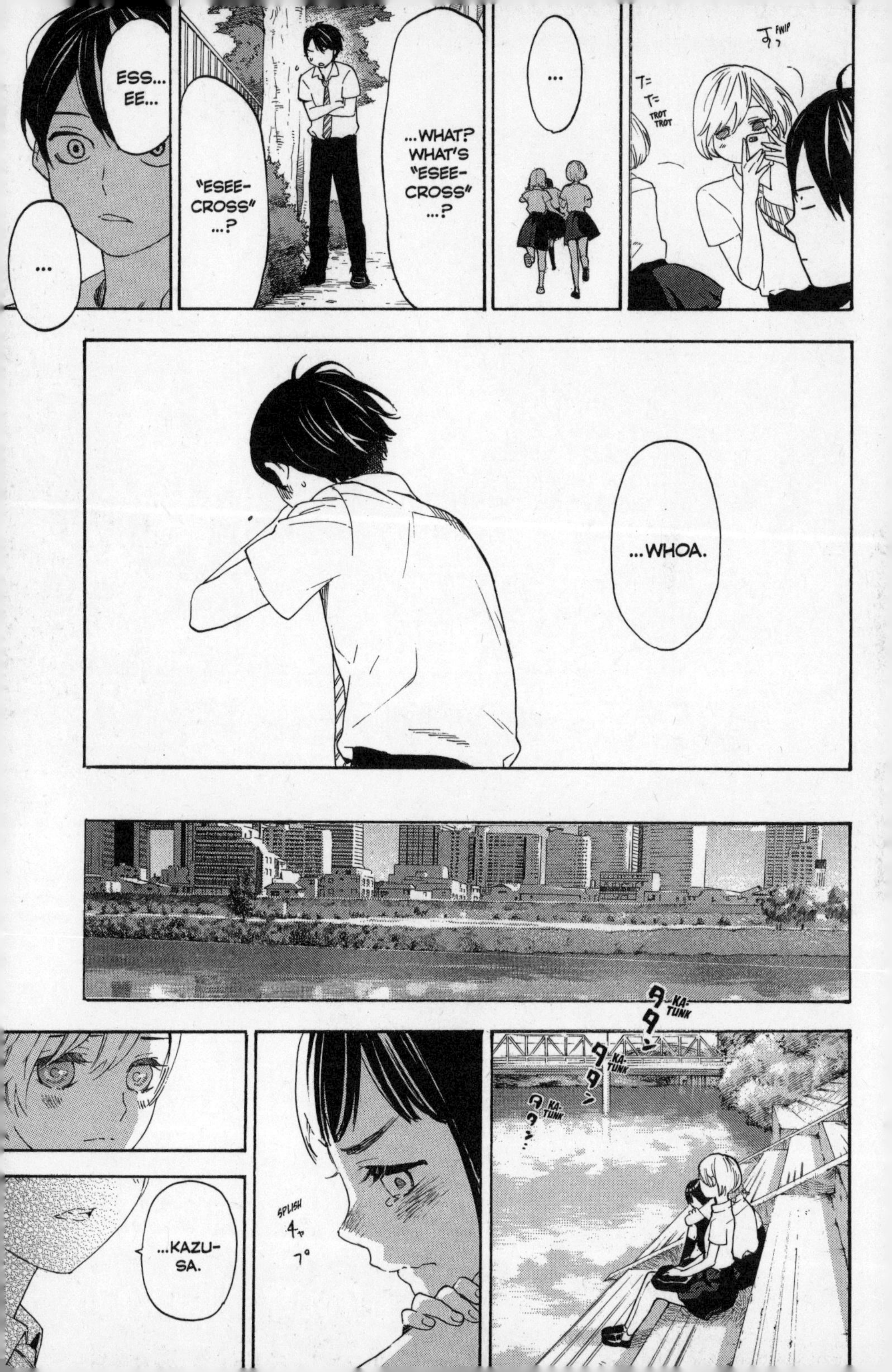
FWIP
TROT TROT
...
...WHAT? WHAT'S "ESEE-CROSS" ...?
"ESEE-CROSS" ...?
ESS... EE...
...
...WHOA.
KA-TUNK
KA-TUNK
KA-TUNK
SPLISH
...KAZU-SA.

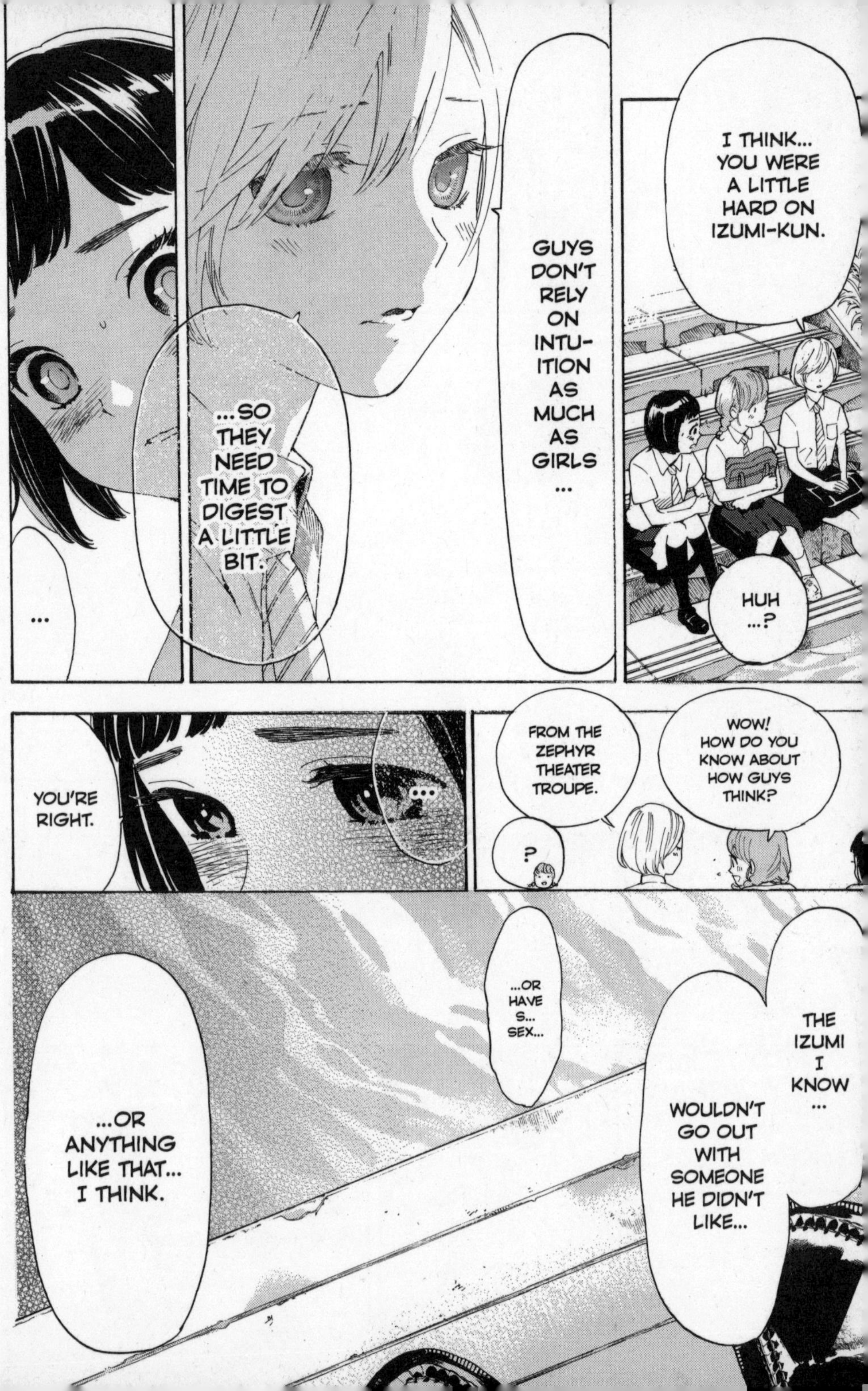
I THINK... YOU WERE A LITTLE HARD ON IZUMI-KUN.
HUH ...?
GUYS DON'T RELY ON INTU-ITION AS MUCH AS GIRLS ...
...SO THEY NEED TIME TO DIGEST A LITTLE BIT.
...
WOW! HOW DO YOU KNOW ABOUT HOW GUYS THINK?
FROM THE ZEPHYR THEATER TROUPE.
?
...
YOU'RE RIGHT.
THE IZUMI I KNOW ...
WOULDN'T GO OUT WITH SOMEONE HE DIDN'T LIKE...
...OR HAVE S... SEX...
...OR ANYTHING LIKE THAT... I THINK.

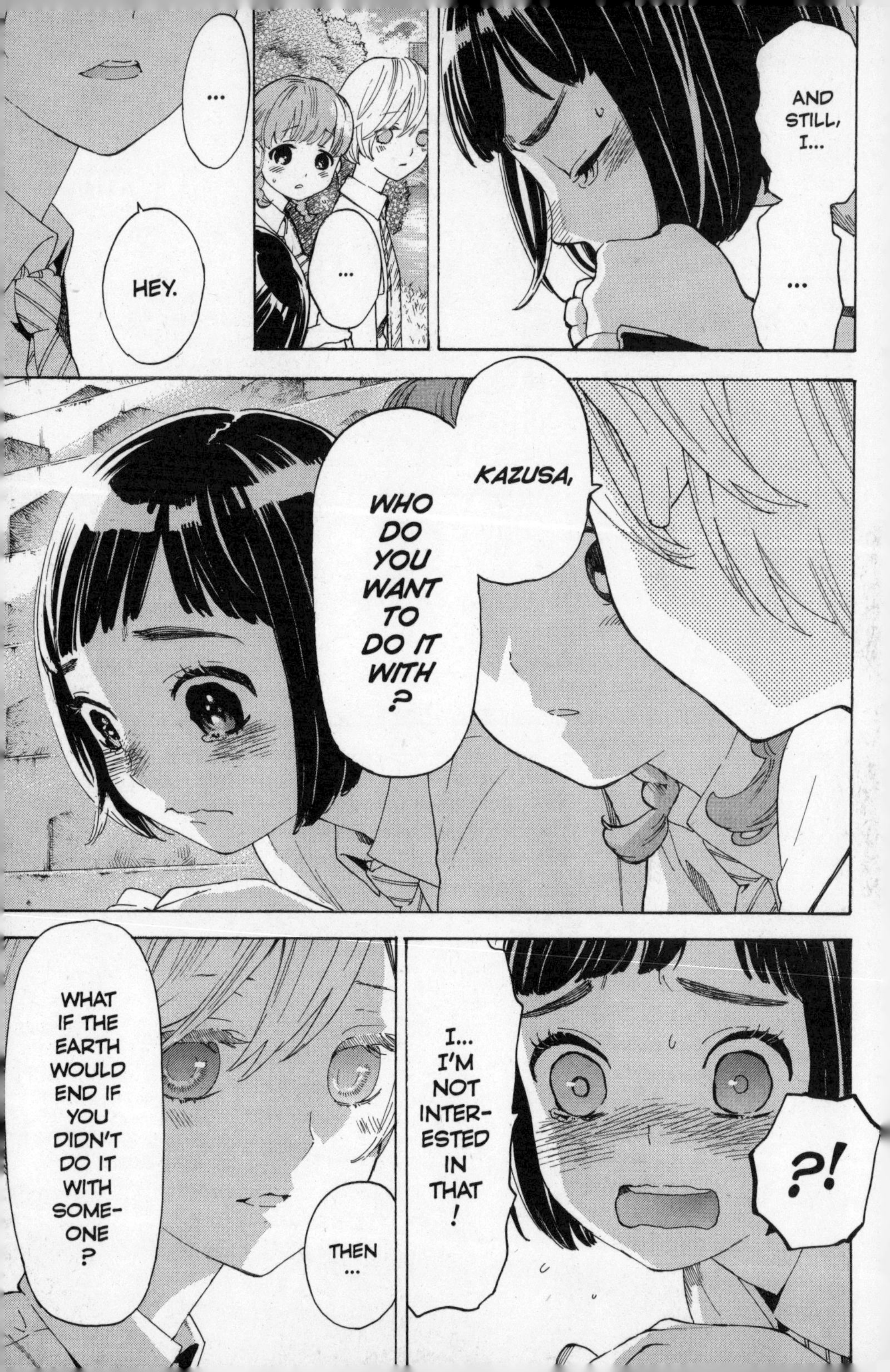
AND STILL, I...
...
...
...
HEY.
KAZUSA, WHO DO YOU WANT TO DO IT WITH?
?!
I... I'M NOT INTER-ESTED IN THAT!
THEN...
WHAT IF THE EARTH WOULD END IF YOU DIDN'T DO IT WITH SOME-ONE?

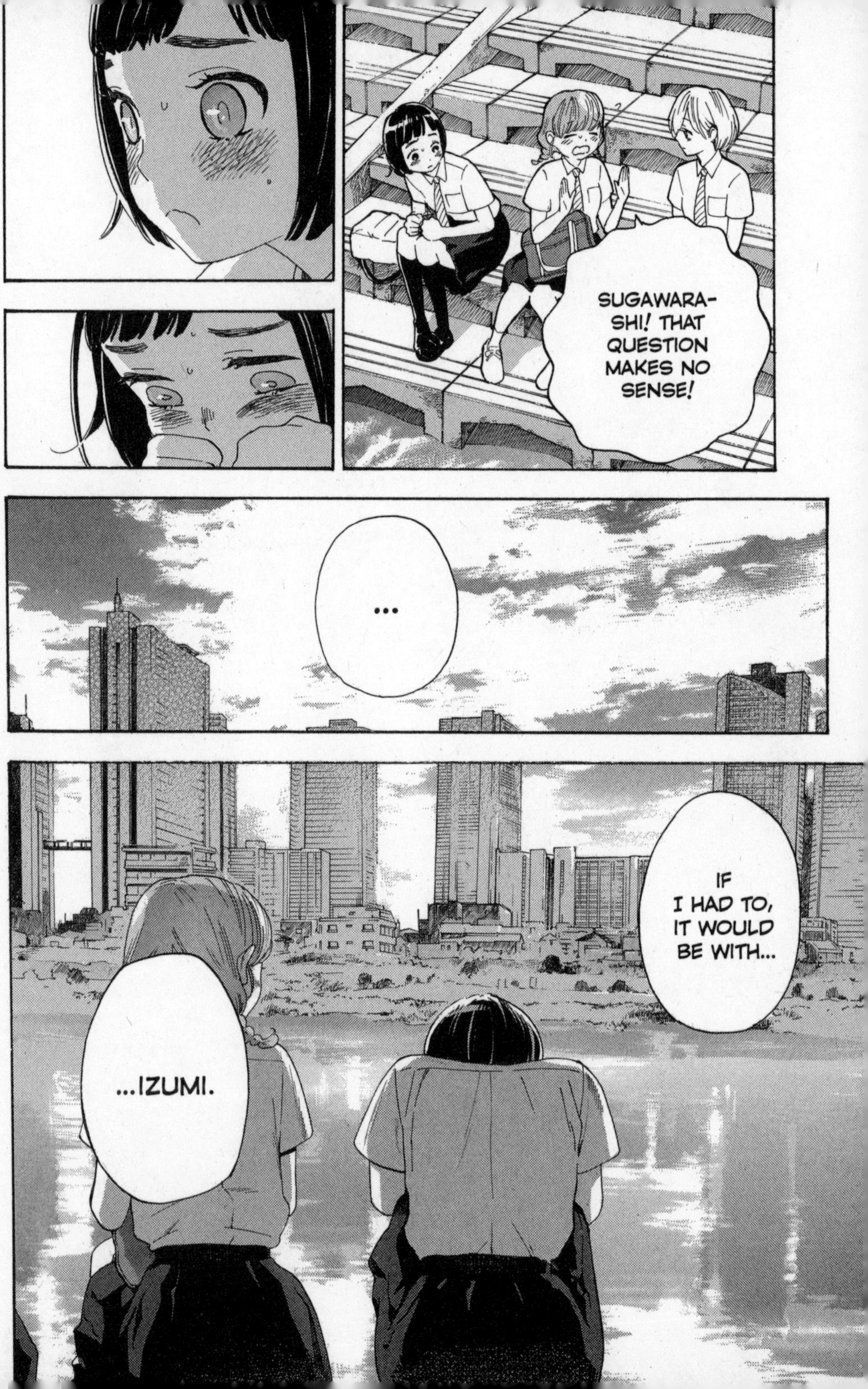
SUGAWARA-SHI! THAT QUESTION MAKES NO SENSE!
...
IF I HAD TO, IT WOULD BE WITH...
...IZUMI.

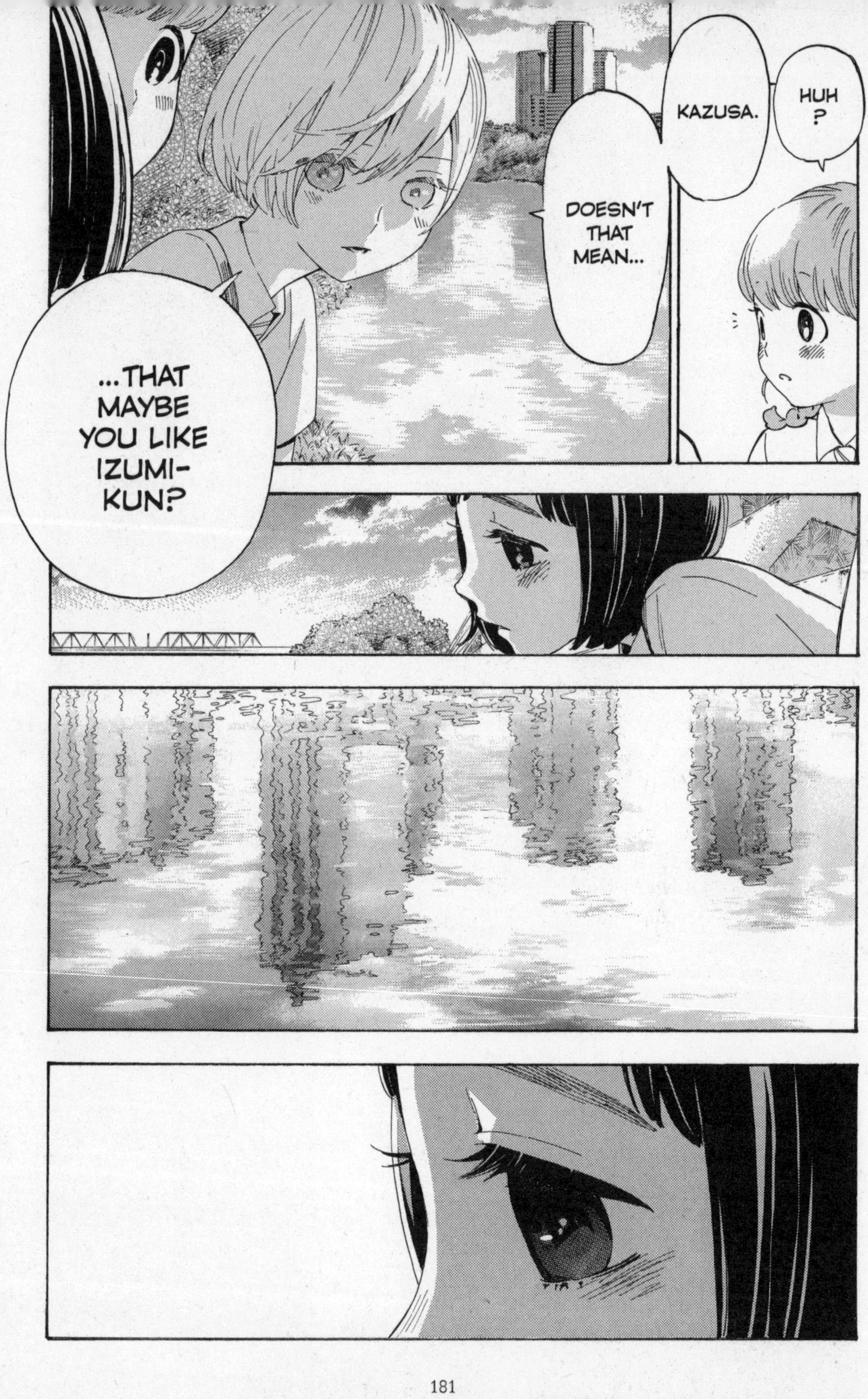
KAZUSA.
HUH?
DOESN'T THAT MEAN...
...THAT MAYBE YOU LIKE IZUMI-KUN?

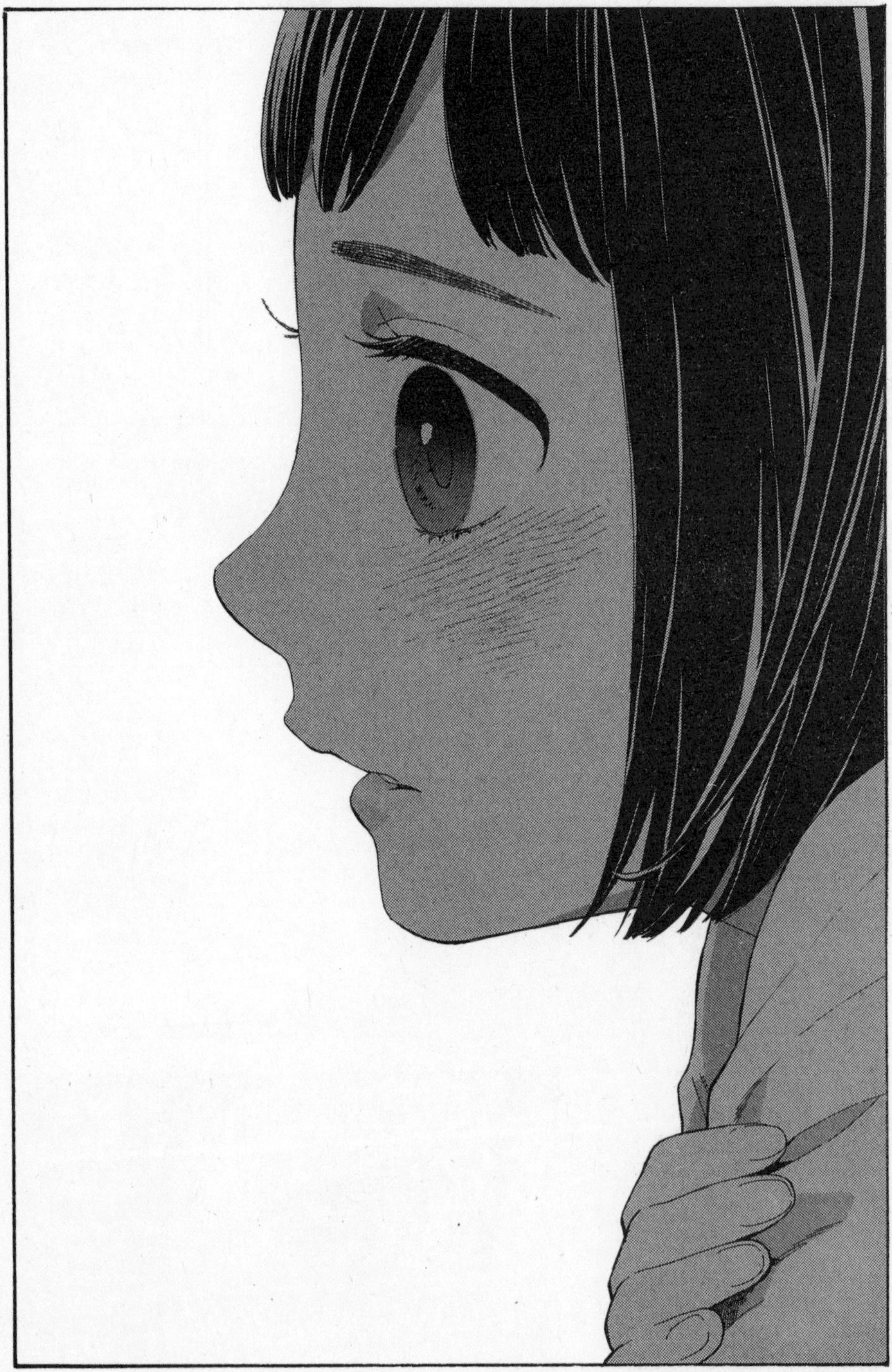

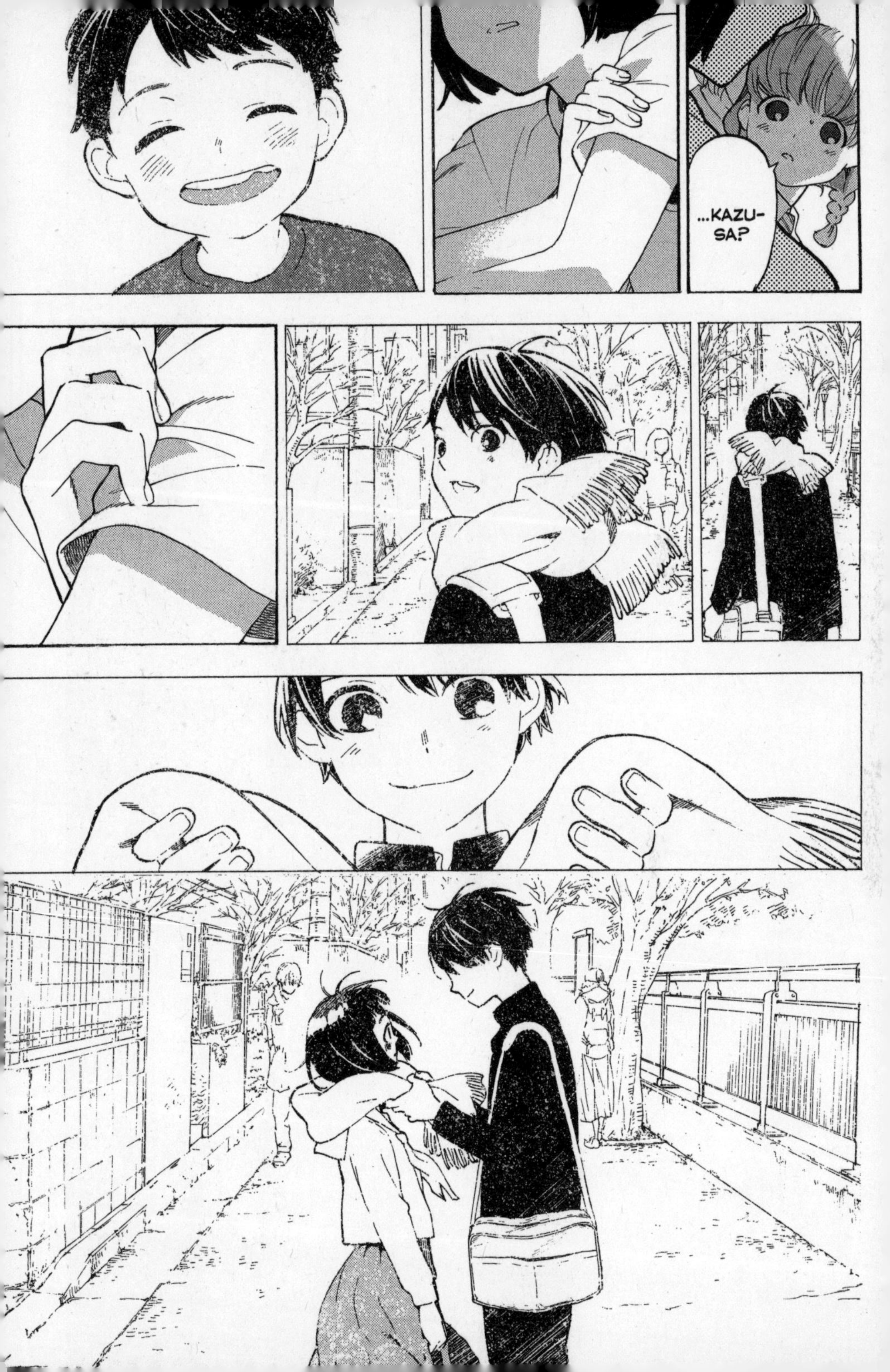
...KAZU-SA?

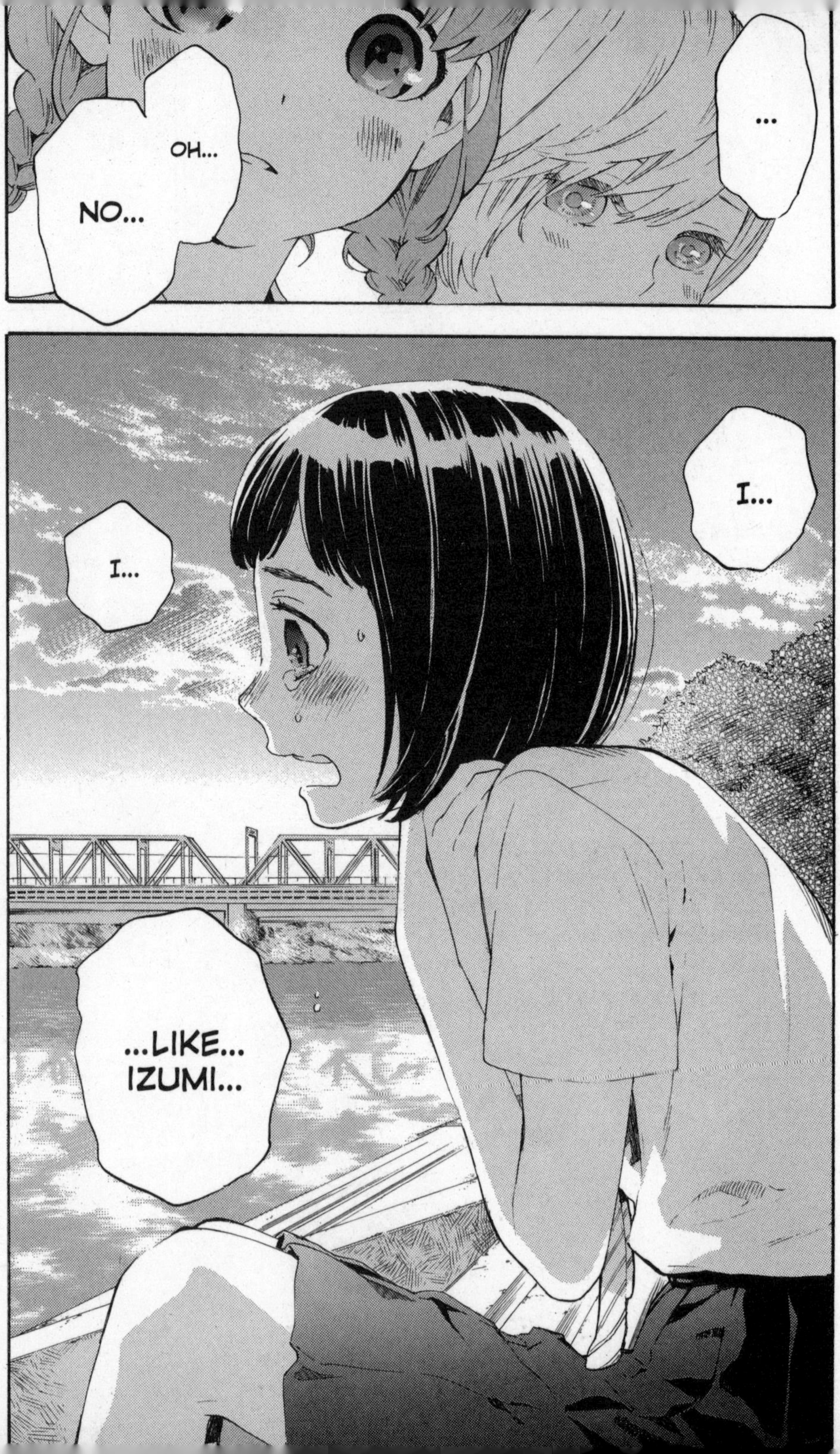
...
OH... NO...
I...
I...
...LIKE... IZUMI...

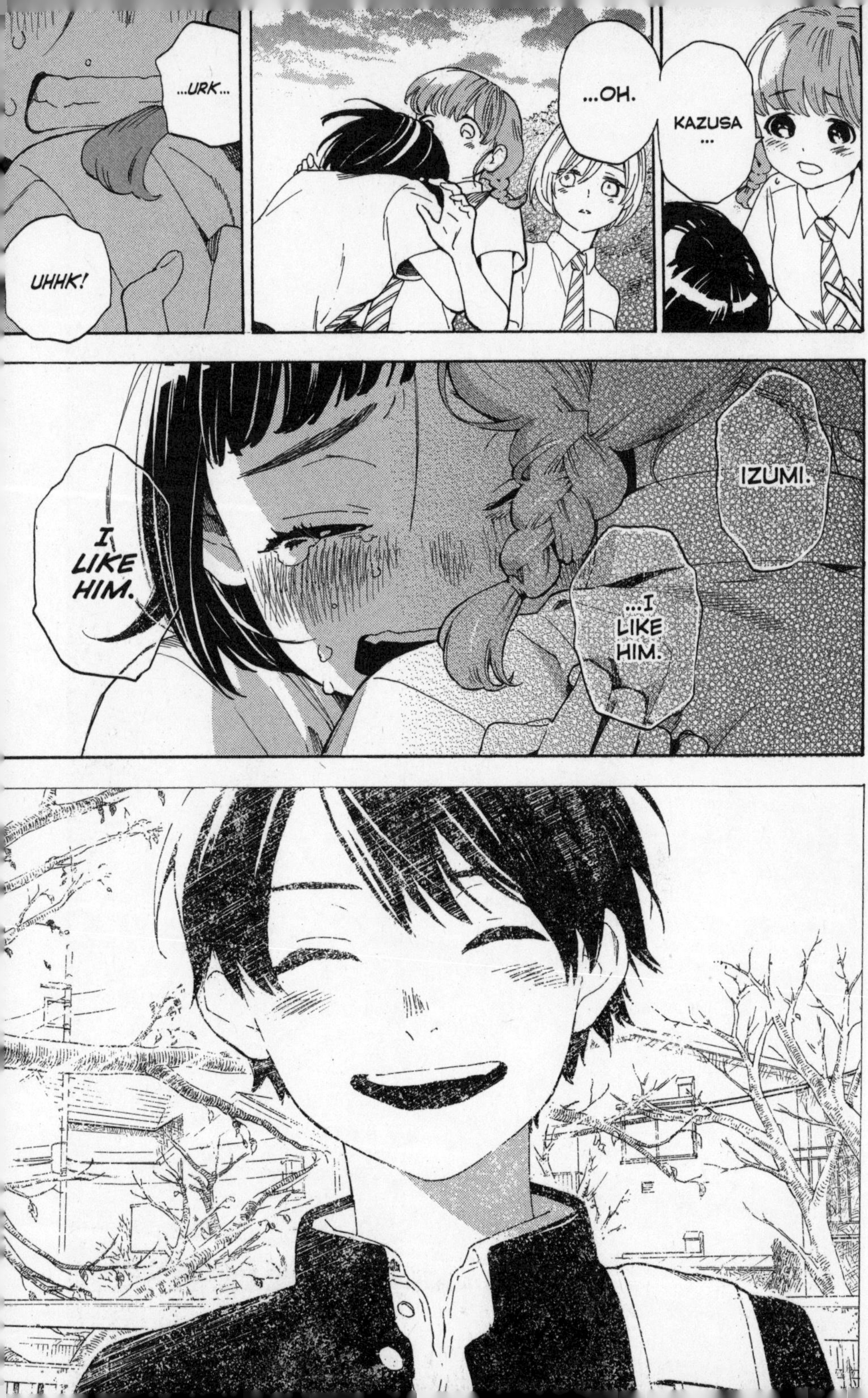

KAZUSA ...
...OH.
...URK...
UHHK!
IZUMI.
...I LIKE HIM.
I LIKE HIM.

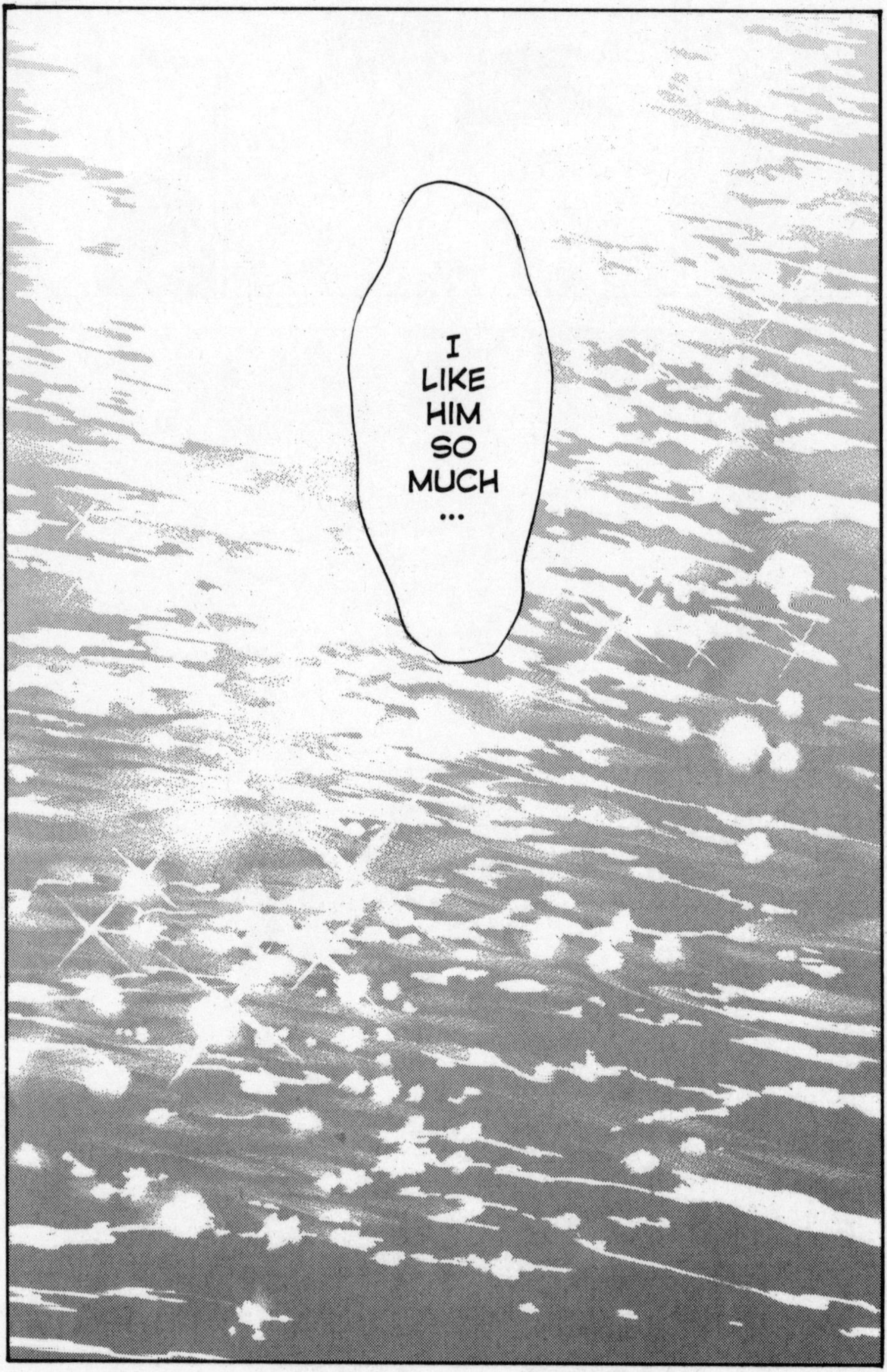
I LIKE HIM SO MUCH...

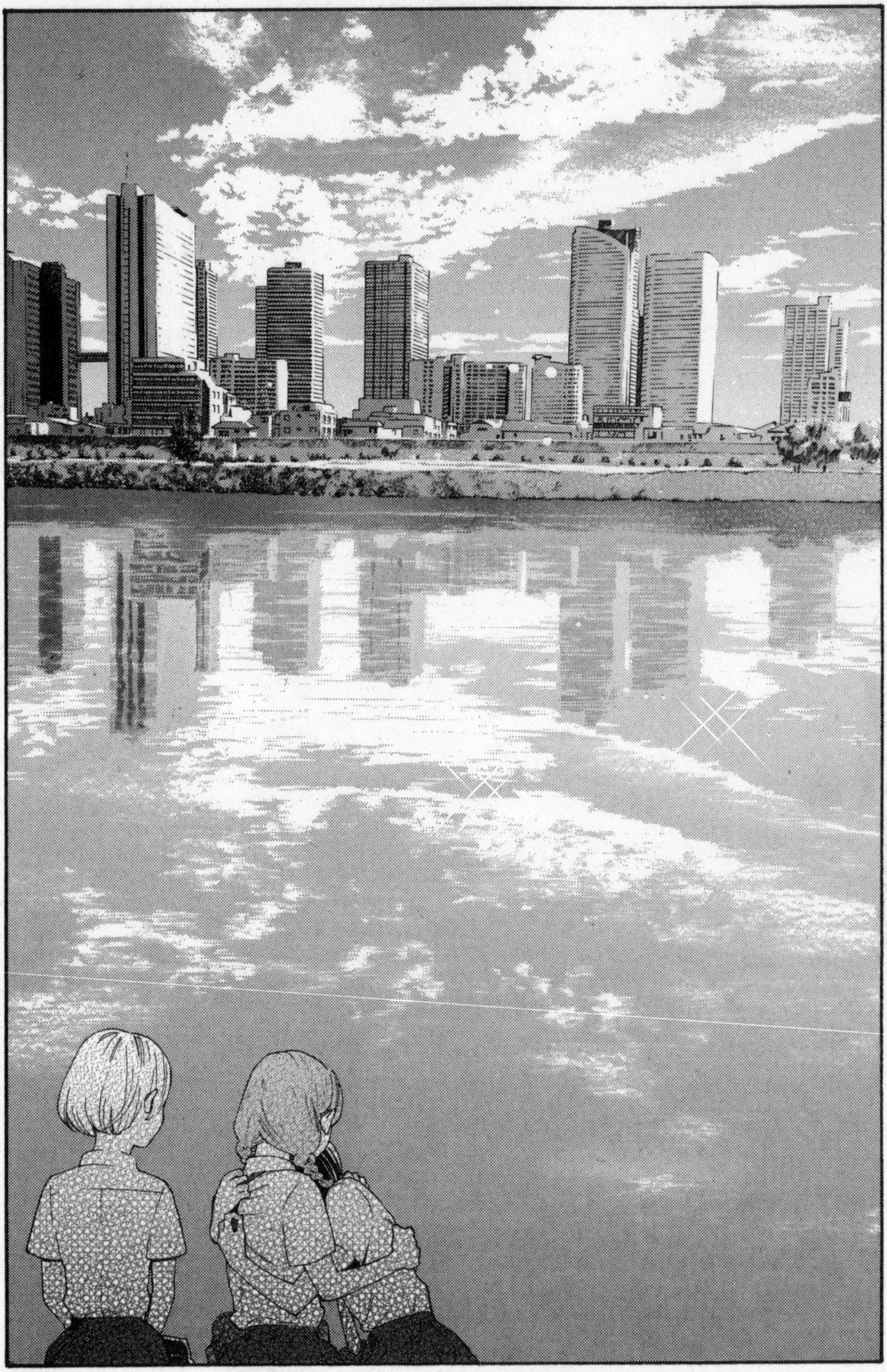

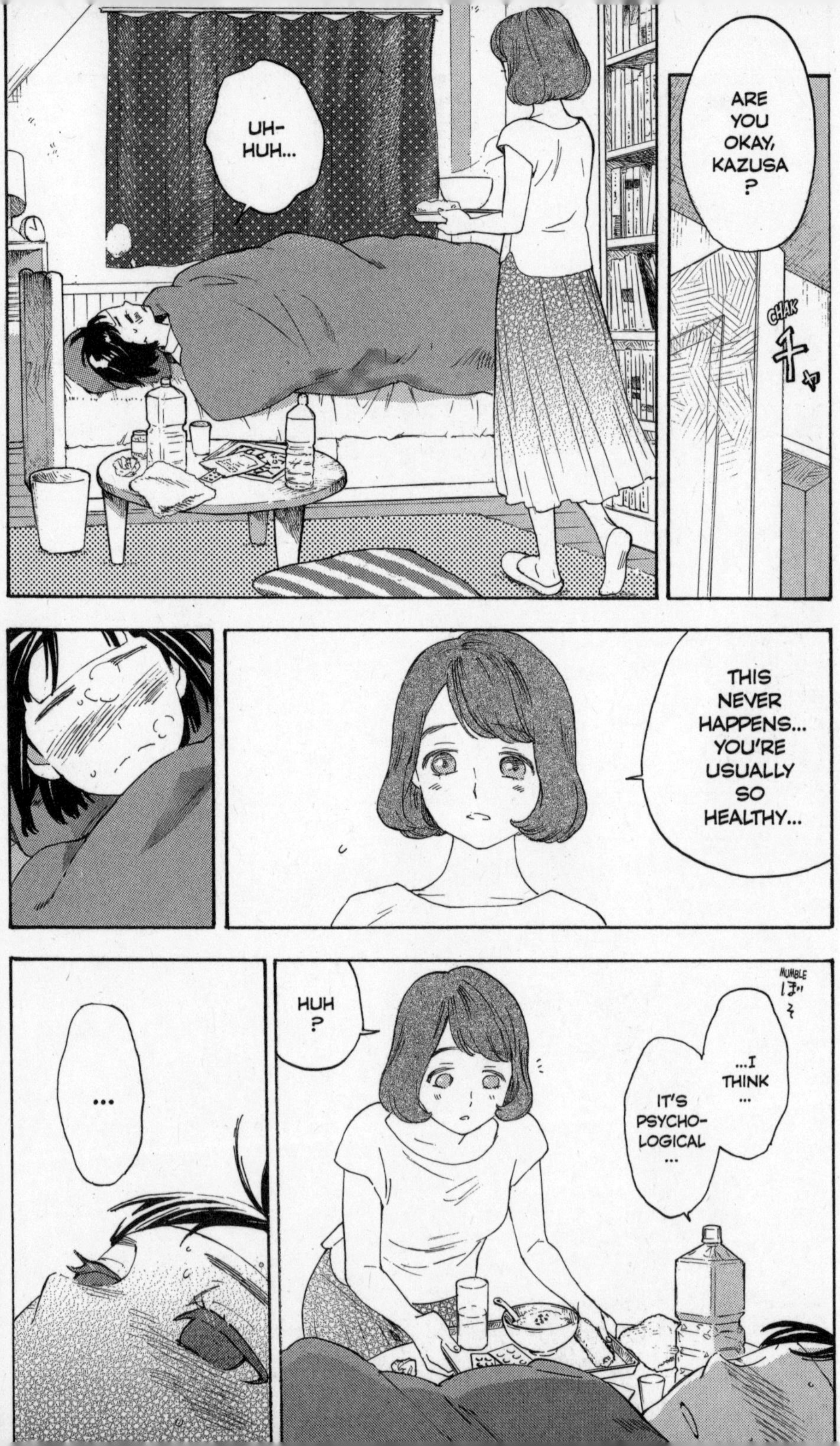
ARE YOU OKAY, KAZUSA?
CHAK
UH-HUH...
THIS NEVER HAPPENS... YOU'RE USUALLY SO HEALTHY...
MUMBLE
...I THINK... IT'S PSYCHOLOGICAL...
HUH?
...

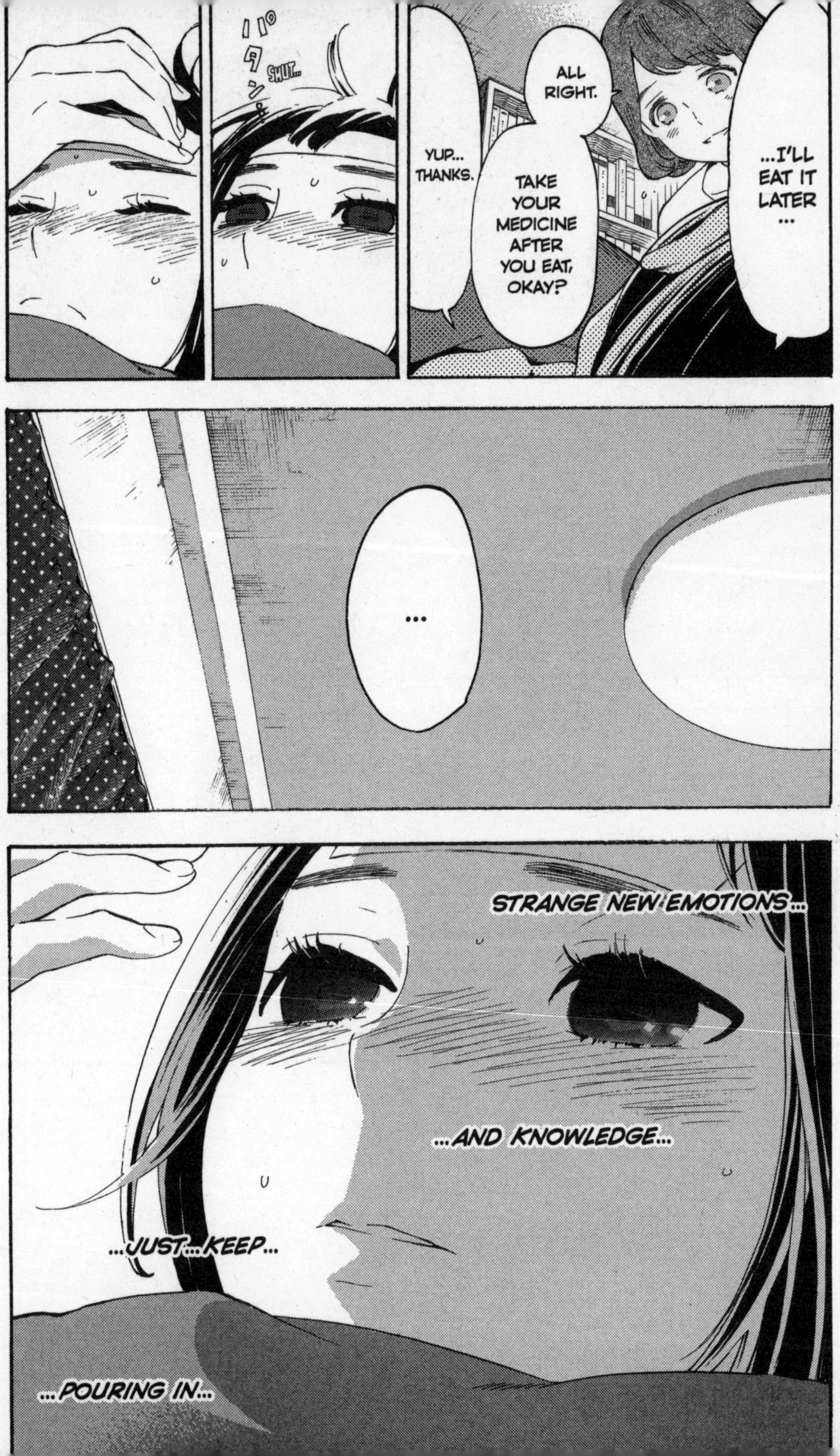
...I'LL EAT IT LATER...
ALL RIGHT.
TAKE YOUR MEDICINE AFTER YOU EAT, OKAY?
YUP... THANKS.
パタン
SHUT...
...
STRANGE NEW EMOTIONS...
...AND KNOWLEDGE...
...JUST...KEEP...
...POURING IN...

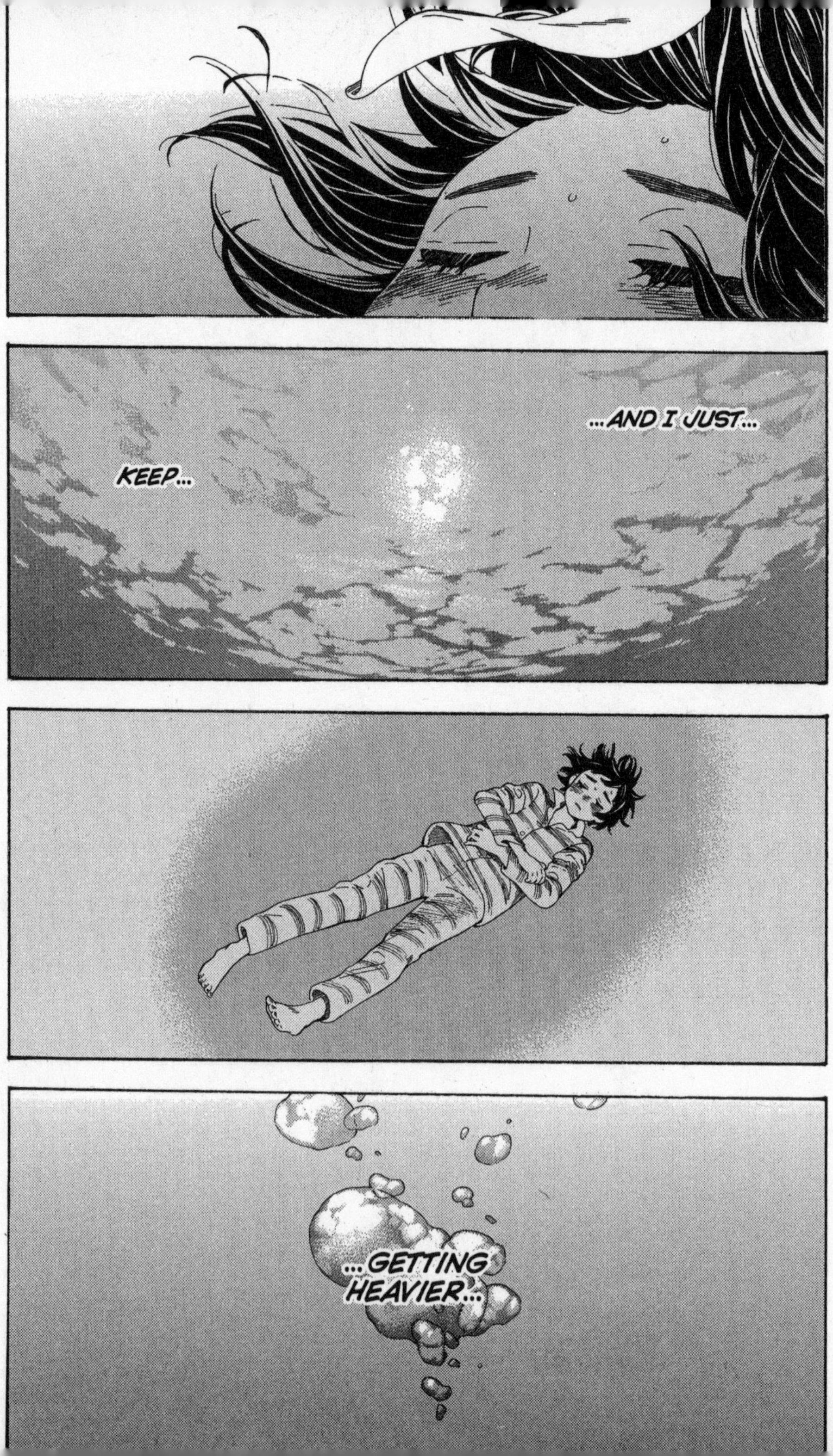
...AND I JUST...
KEEP...
...GETTING HEAVIER...

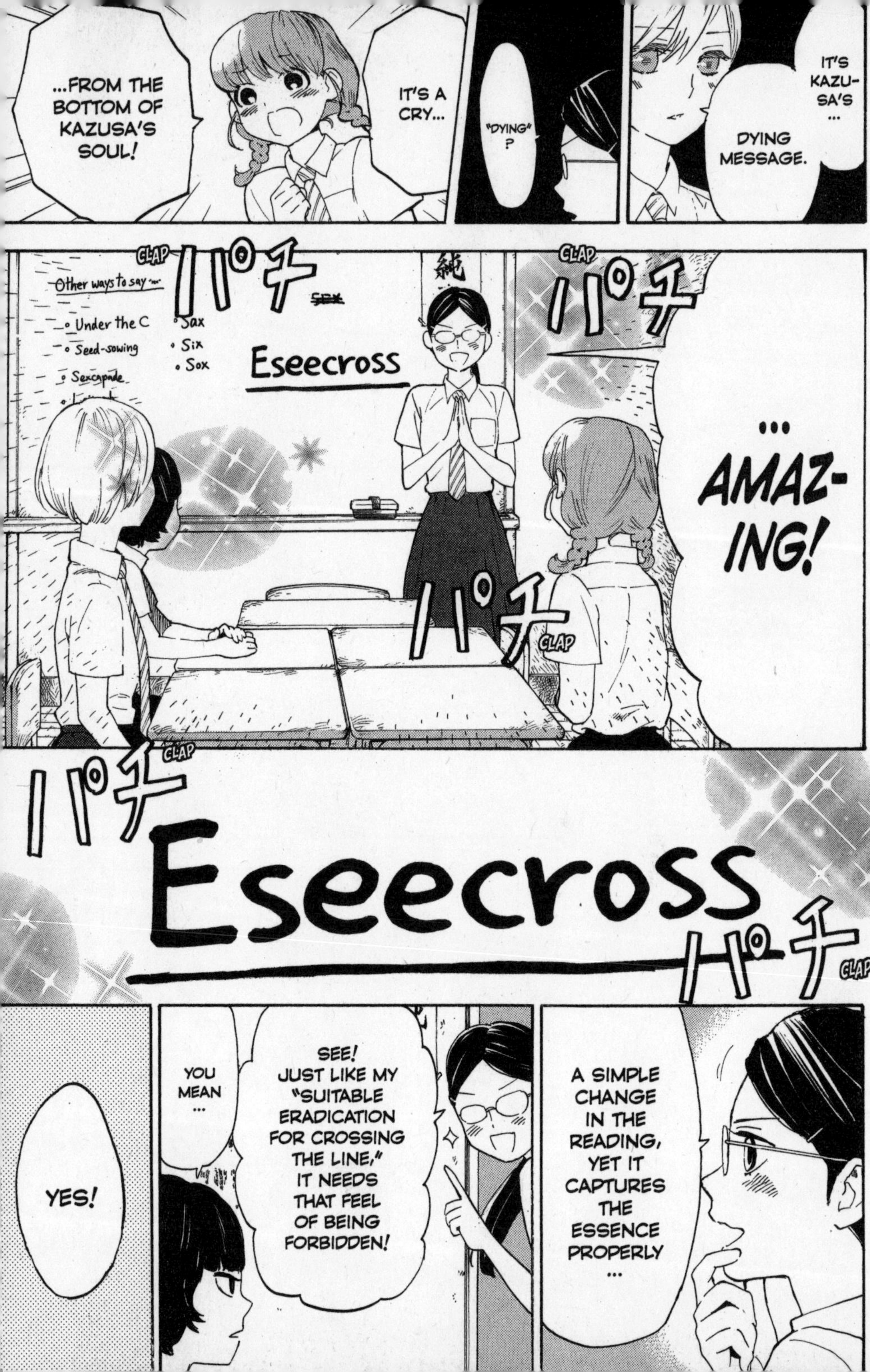
IT'S KAZUSA'S ... DYING MESSAGE.
"DYING"?
IT'S A CRY...
...FROM THE BOTTOM OF KAZUSA'S SOUL!
CLAP パチ
CLAP パチ
Other ways to say ~
Under the C
Seed-sowing
Sexcapade
Sax
Six
Sox
Eseecross
... AMAZING!
パチ CLAP
パチ CLAP
Eseecross
パチ CLAP
A SIMPLE CHANGE IN THE READING, YET IT CAPTURES THE ESSENCE PROPERLY ...
SEE! JUST LIKE MY "SUITABLE ERADICATION FOR CROSSING THE LINE," IT NEEDS THAT FEEL OF BEING FORBIDDEN!
YOU MEAN ...
YES!

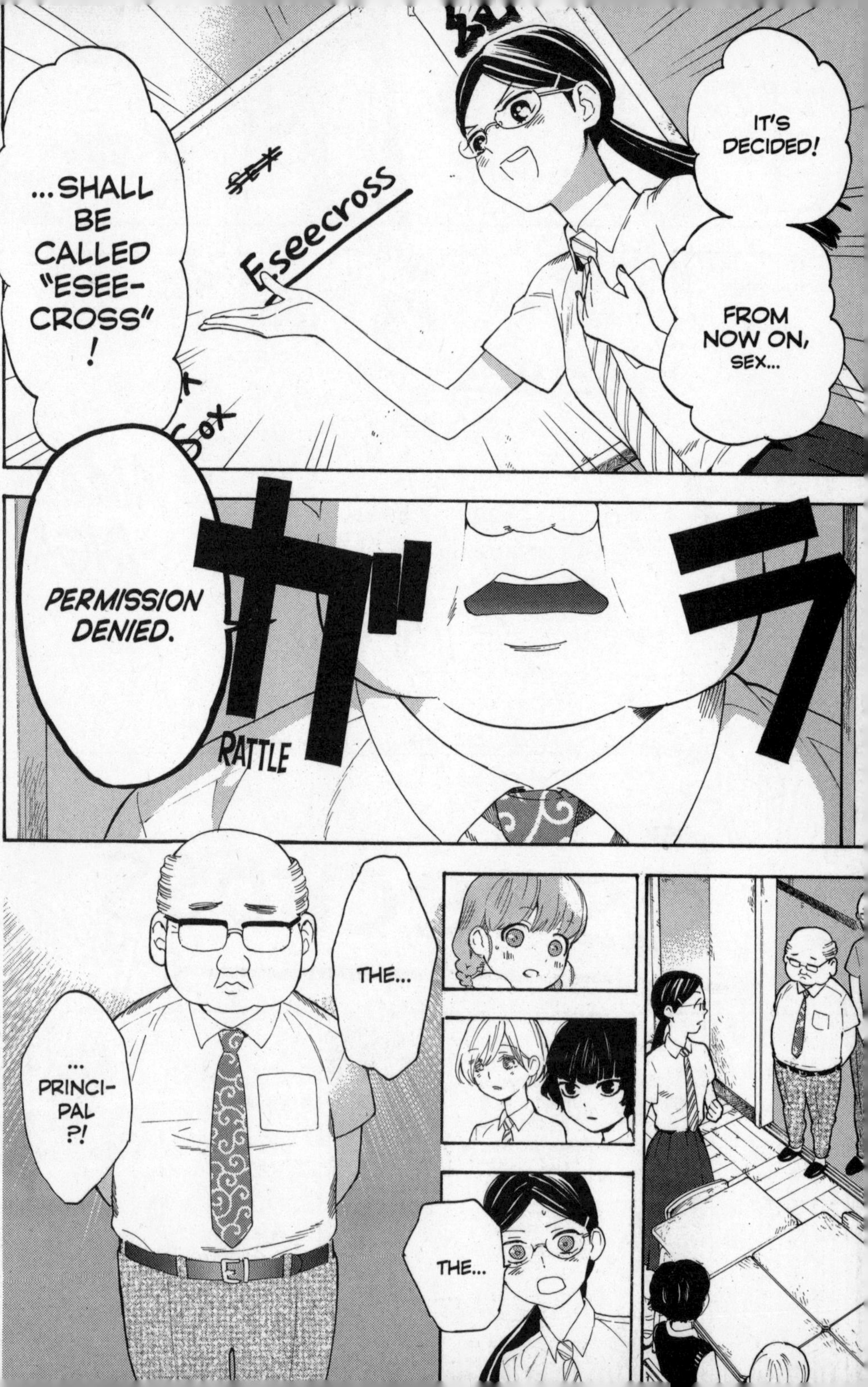

IT'S DECIDED!
FROM NOW ON, SEX...
SEX
Eseecross
...SHALL BE CALLED "ESEE-CROSS"!
ガラ
RATTLE
PERMISSION DENIED.
THE...
THE...
...PRINCIPAL?!

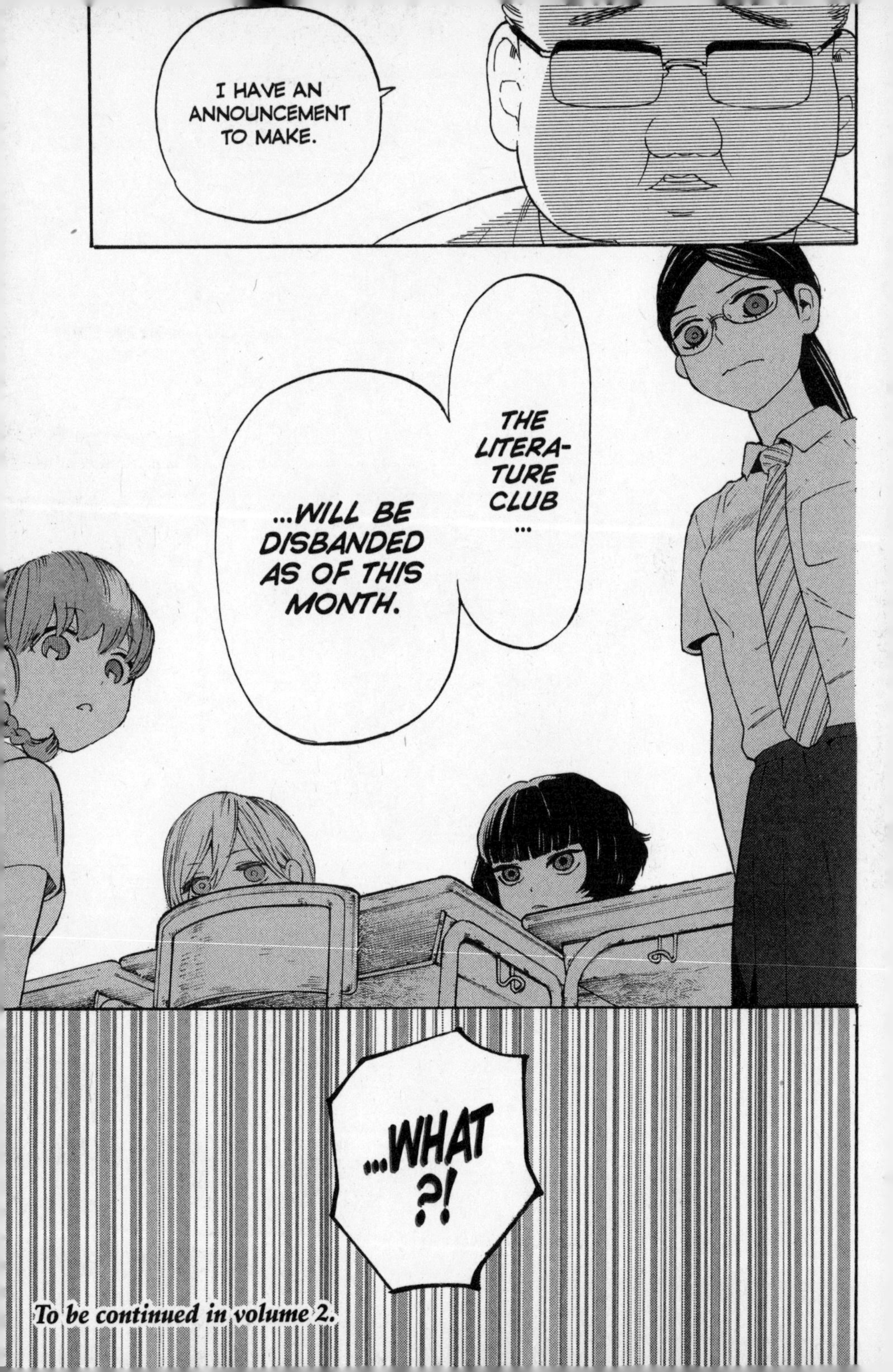
I HAVE AN ANNOUNCEMENT TO MAKE.
THE LITERATURE CLUB...
...WILL BE DISBANDED AS OF THIS MONTH.
...WHAT?!

To be continued in volume 2.

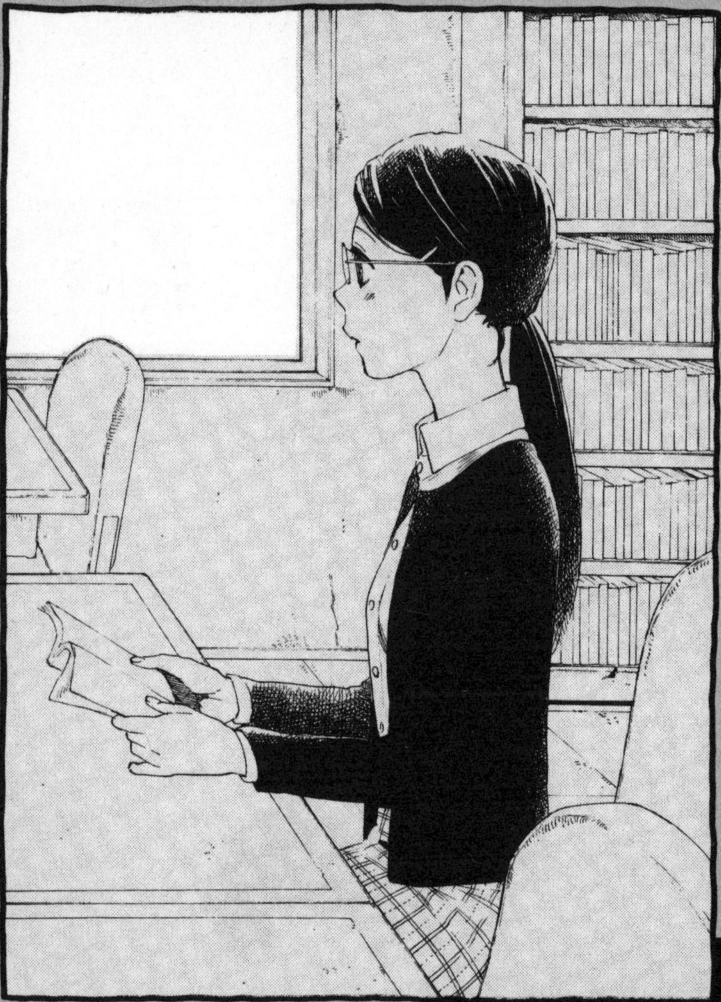

profile

Rika Sonezaki

Height: **170 cm (Approx. 5'6")**

Blood type: **O**

Activity: **Literature Club**

Favorite book: ***The Twelve Kingdoms* series**

Momoko Sudo

Height: **154 cm (Approx. 5')**

Blood type: **AB**

Activity: **Literature Club**

Favorite book: ***Flowers for Algernon***

profile

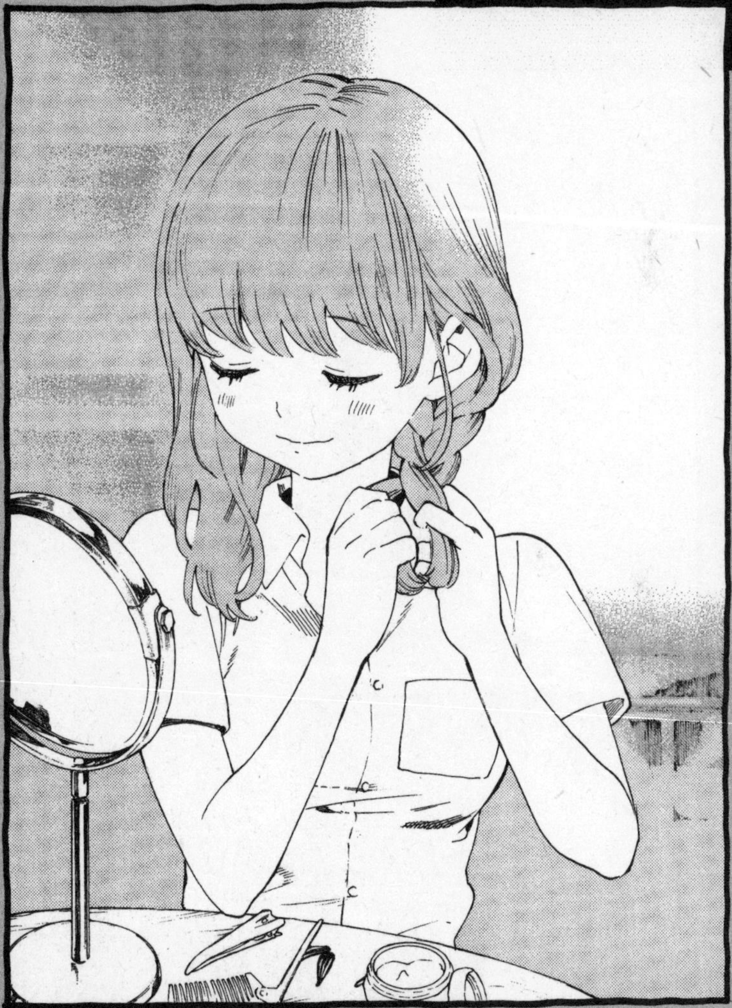

Hitoha Hongo

Height: **141 cm (Approx. 4'6")**

Blood type: **B**

Activity: **Literature Club**

Favorite book: *Coin Locker Babies*

profile

O Maidens in Your Savage Season

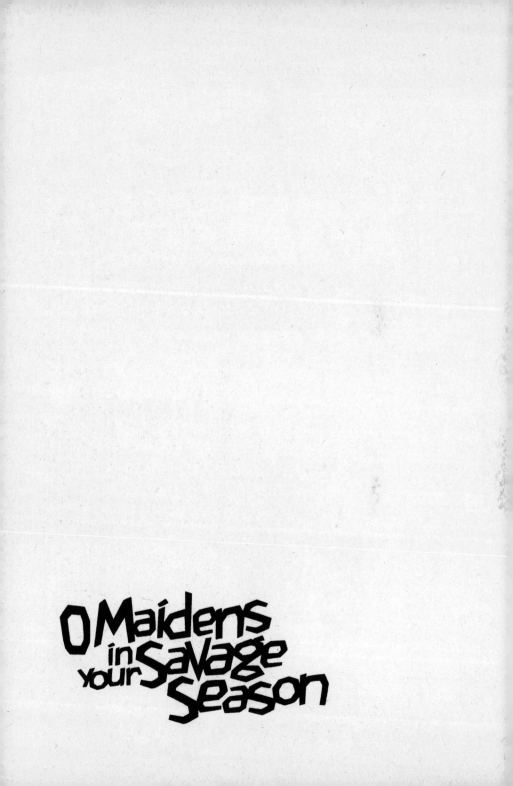

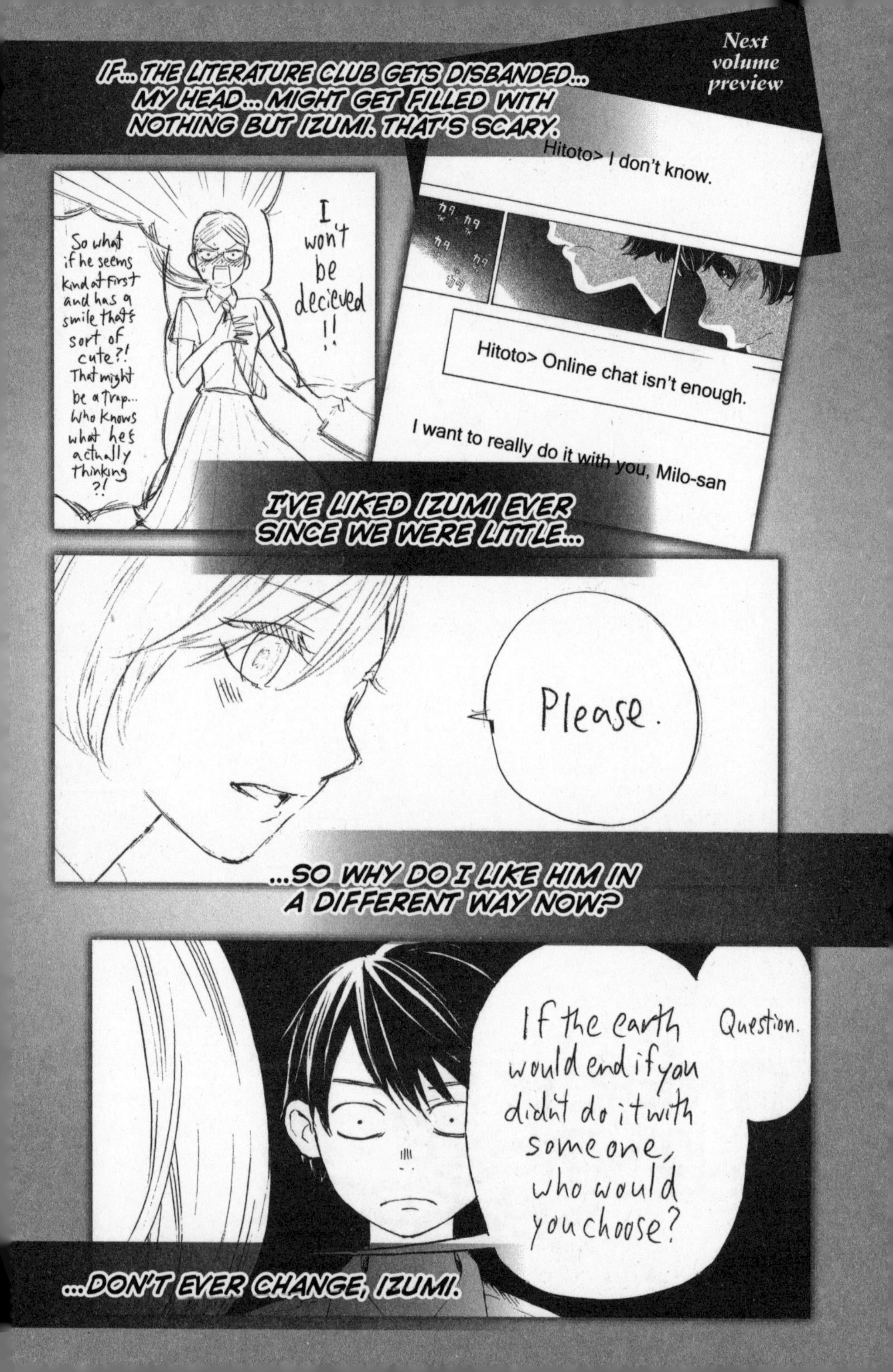
Next volume preview
IF... THE LITERATURE CLUB GETS DISBANDED... MY HEAD... MIGHT GET FILLED WITH NOTHING BUT IZUMI. THAT'S SCARY.
Hitoto> I don't know.
Hitoto> Online chat isn't enough.
I want to really do it with you, Milo-san
I won't be decieved!!
So what if he seems kind at first and has a smile that's sort of cute?! That might be a trap... Who knows what he's actually thinking?!
I'VE LIKED IZUMI EVER SINCE WE WERE LITTLE...
Please.
...SO WHY DO I LIKE HIM IN A DIFFERENT WAY NOW?
Question.
If the earth would end if you didn't do it with someone, who would you choose?
...DON'T EVER CHANGE, IZUMI.

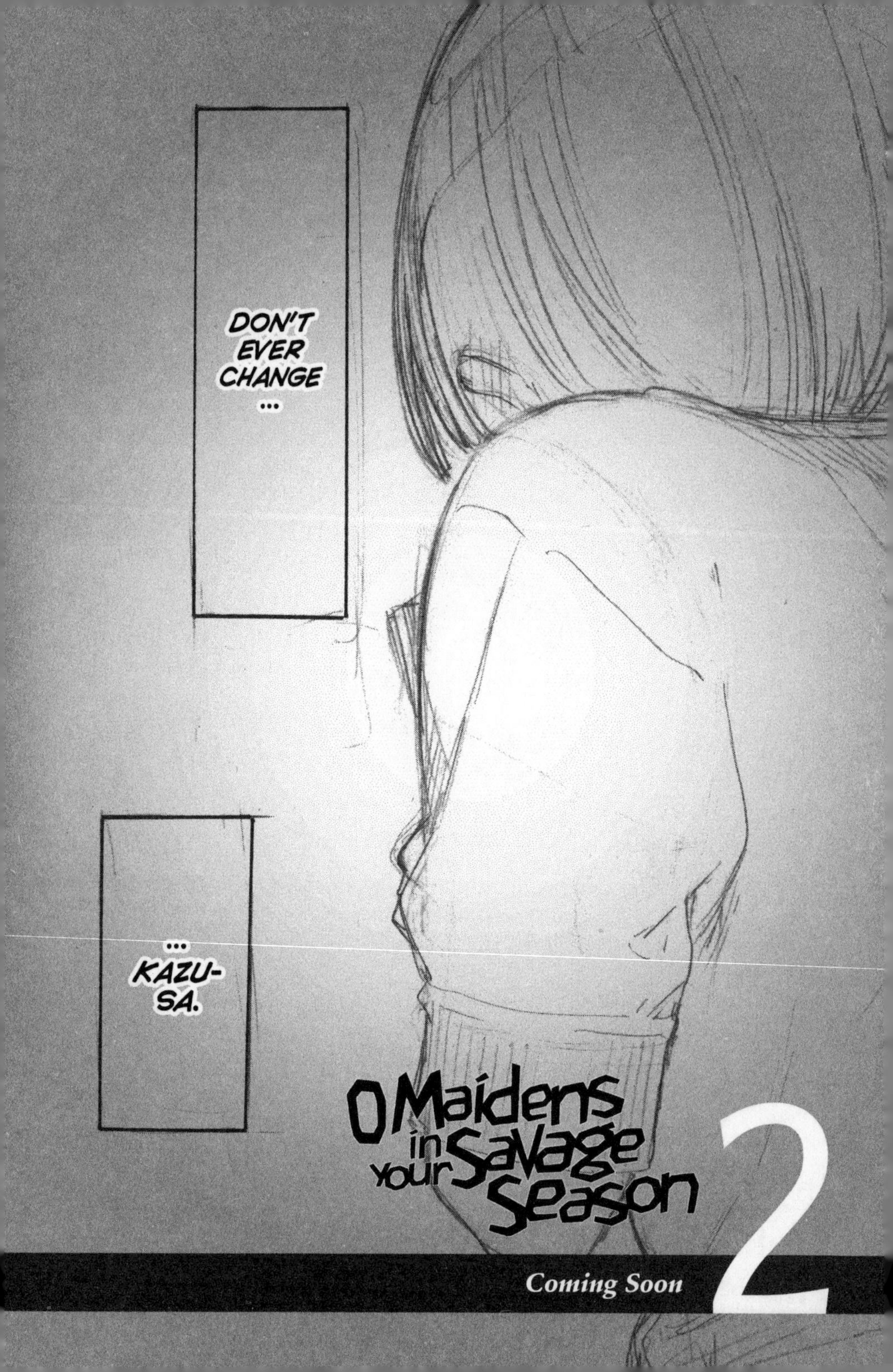
DON'T EVER CHANGE ...
... KAZU-SA.
O Maidens in Your Savage Season
2
Coming Soon

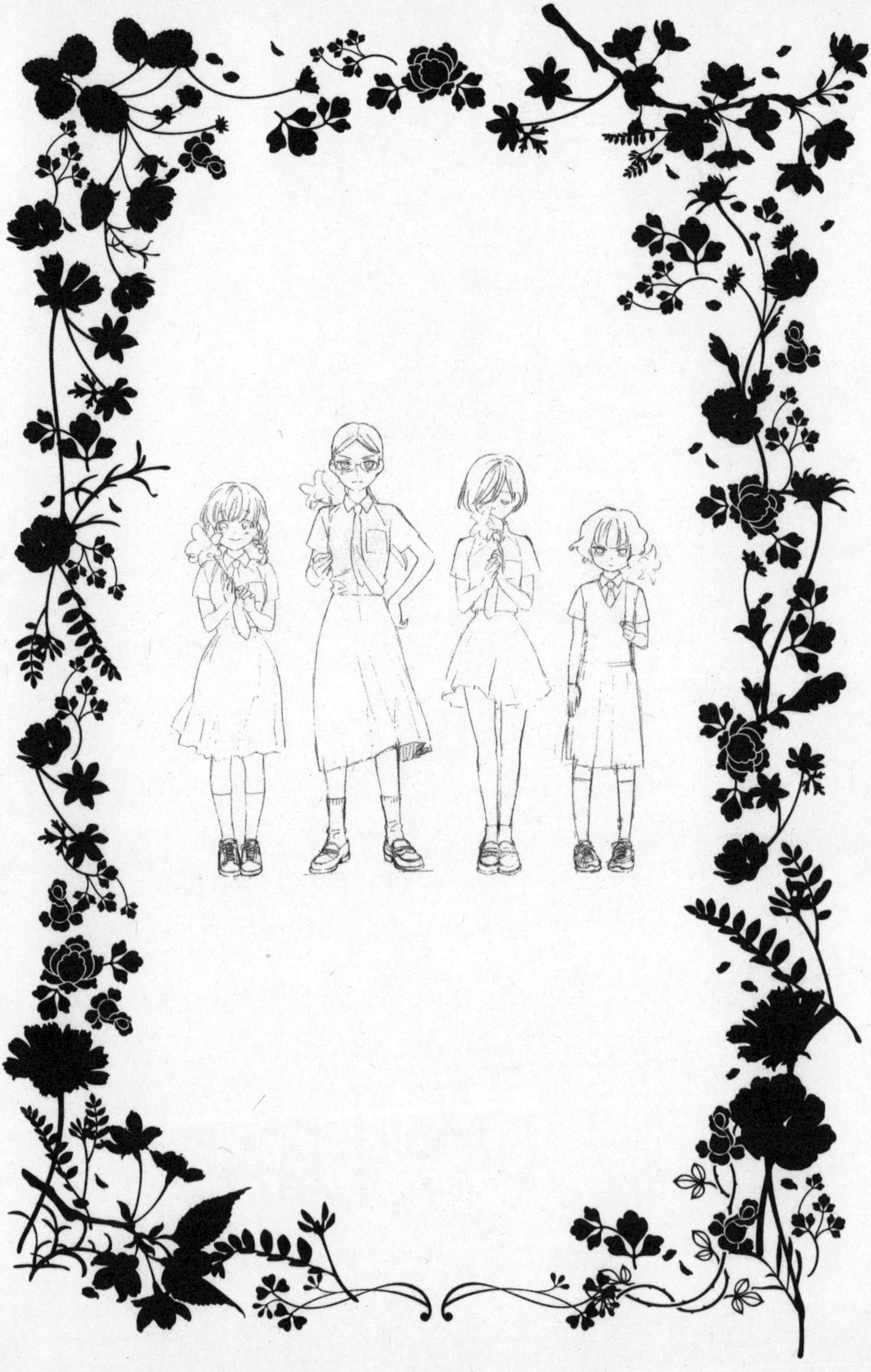

荒ぶる季節の乙女どもよ。

1

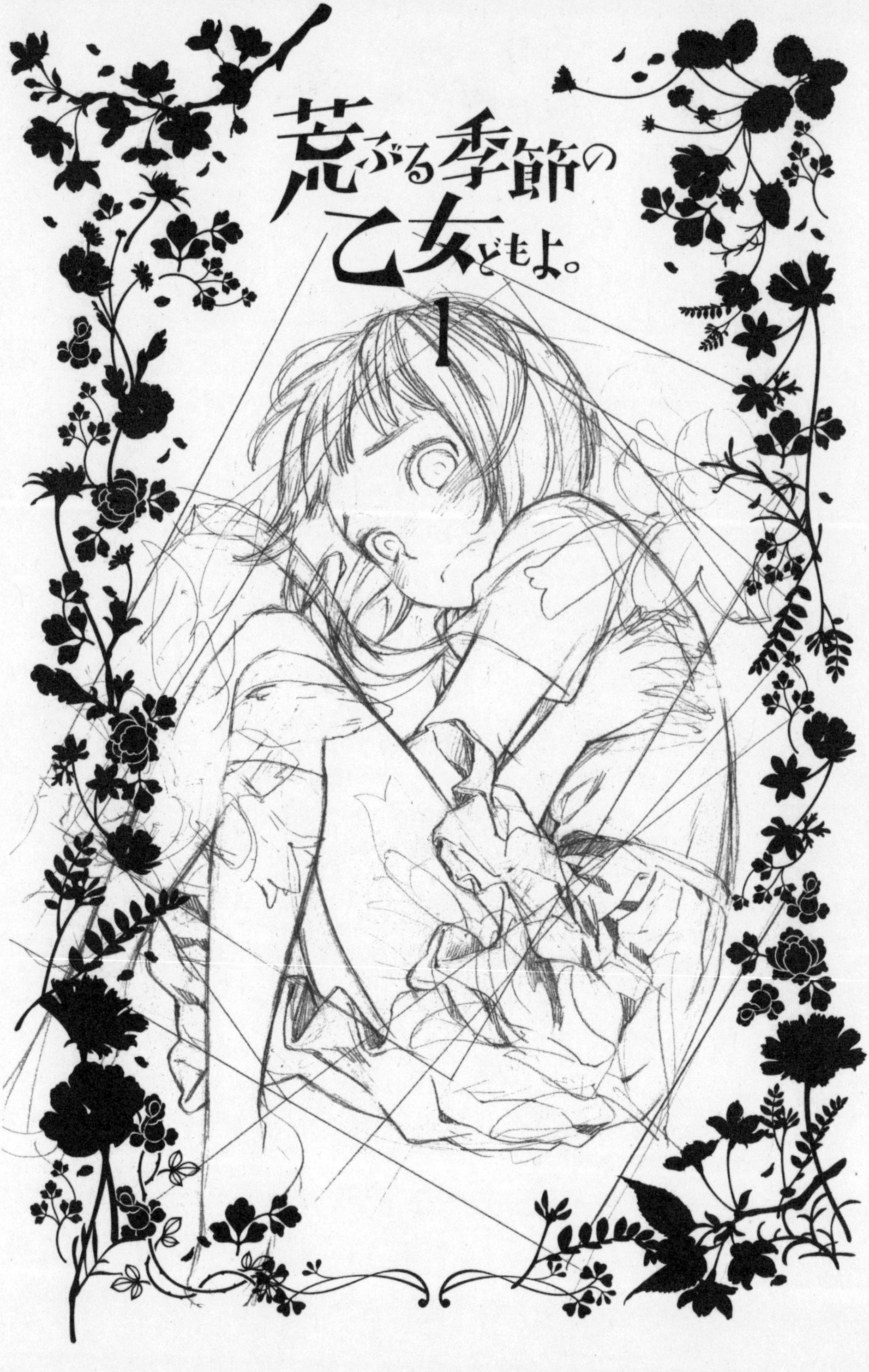

Why does everyone want to know about *that?*

I don't want to think about it.

I don't want to be in distress over it.

But I don't want to be the only one
left behind, either...

Listen.
If only we could all hold hands
and avoid taking the first step,
and never have to know
about *that* at all...

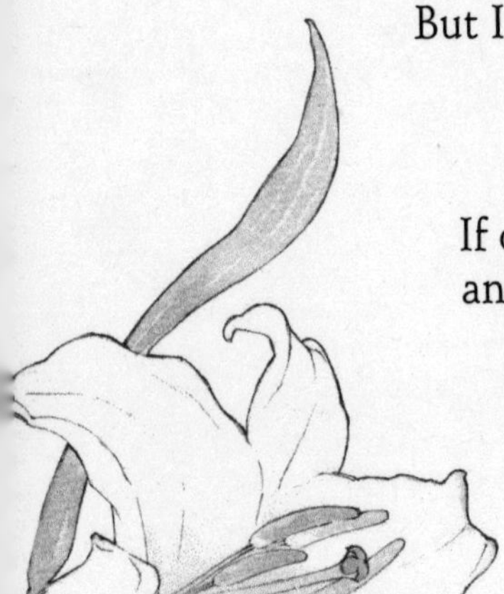

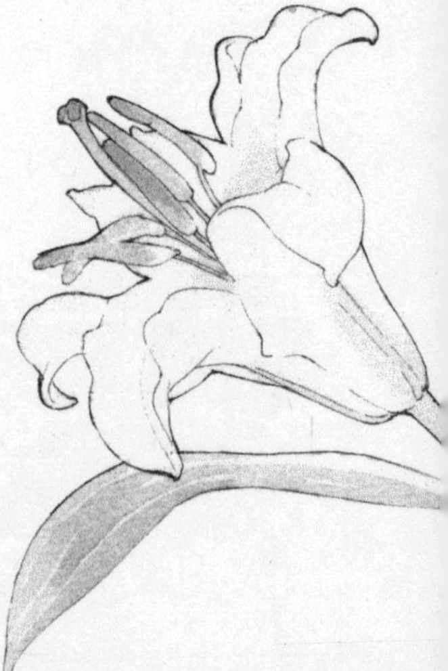

O Maidens in Your Savage Season

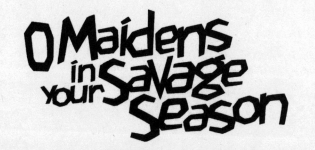

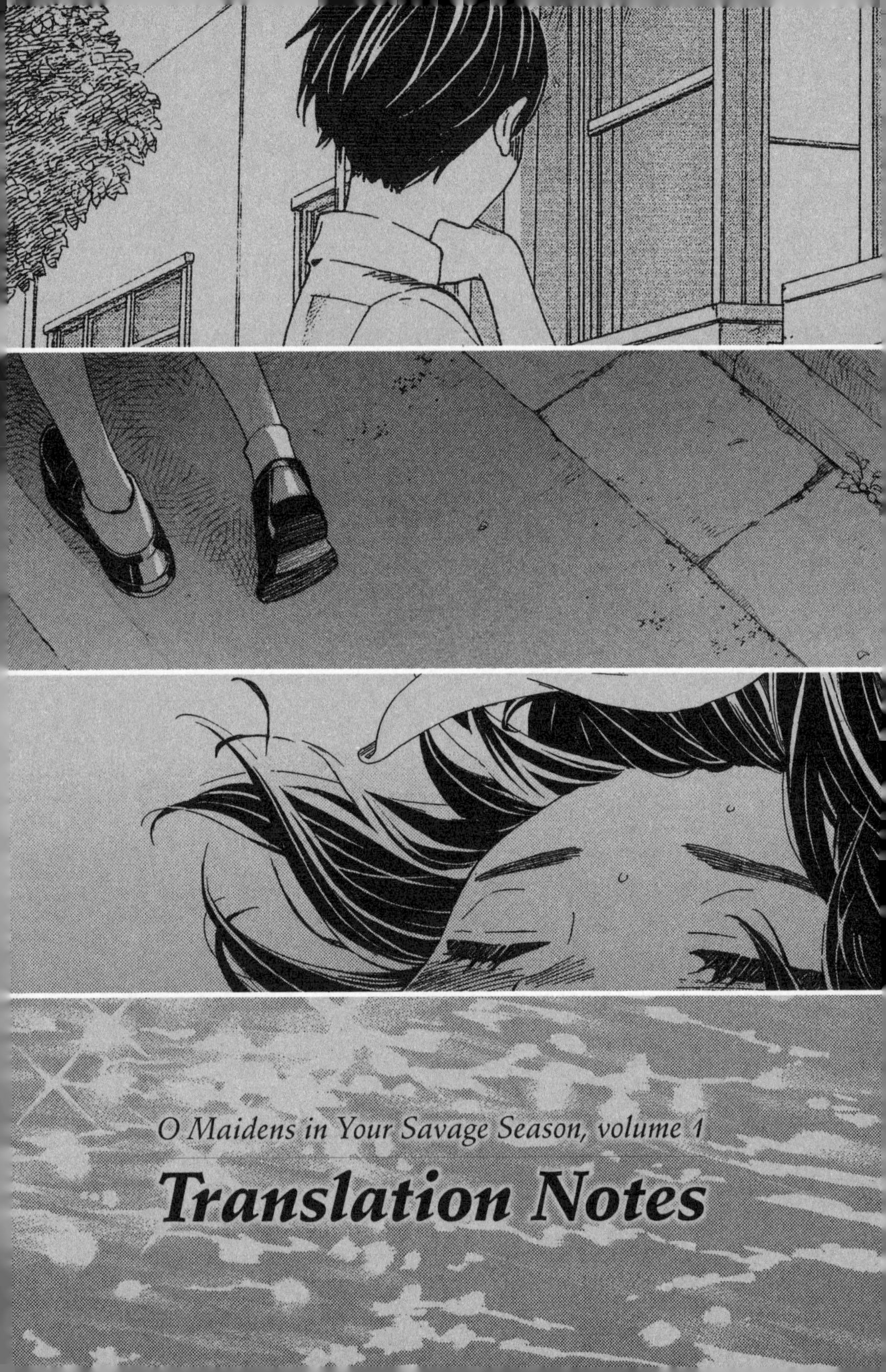

O Maidens in Your Savage Season, volume 1

Translation Notes

page 14

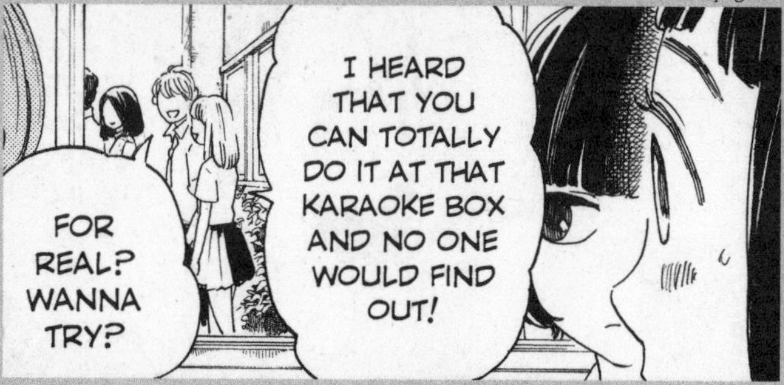
I HEARD THAT YOU CAN TOTALLY DO IT AT THAT KARAOKE BOX AND NO ONE WOULD FIND OUT!
FOR REAL? WANNA TRY?

Karaoke box

In Japan, most Karaoke places are made up of "boxes" or small private rooms. They even have rooms for one customer, and also have rooms for two and more.

page 16

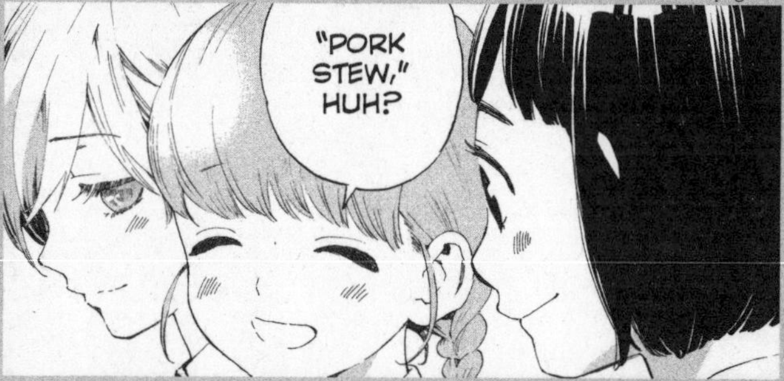
"PORK STEW," HUH?

Tonjiru

A Japanese home-cooked comfort food made with vegetables, pork, and miso. *Ton* means "pork," and *–jiru* means "broth."

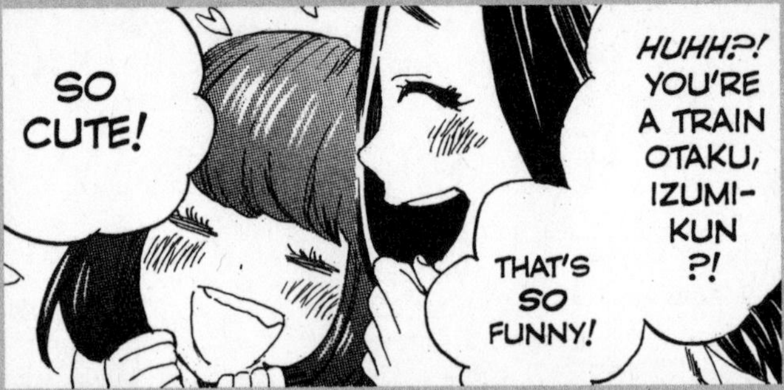
HUHH?! YOU'RE A TRAIN OTAKU, IZUMI-KUN?!
THAT'S SO FUNNY!
SO CUTE!

Otaku

An otaku is an obsessive fan who hoards information and merchandise of their favorite things—there are train otaku, camera otaku, and most famously, anime and manga otaku. The word *otaku* in Japanese is a formal and honorific pronoun that the speaker uses to address "you," reflecting their insider culture.

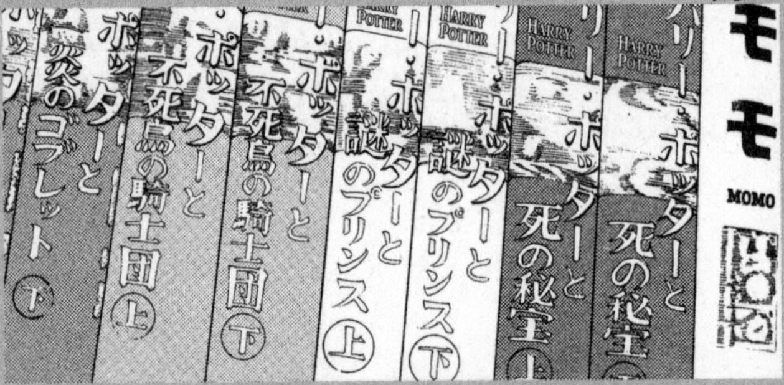
モ
モ
MOMO
HARRY POTTER
ポッターと死の秘宝
HARRY POTTER
ポッターと死の秘宝
HARRY POTTER
ポッターと謎のプリンス(下)
HARRY POTTER
ポッターと謎のプリンス(上)
ポッターと不死鳥の騎士団(下)
ポッターと不死鳥の騎士団(上)
炎のゴブレット(下)

Part 1 and Part 2

In Japan, long novels will be broken up into parts. Most commonly, when a book is broken up into two parts, it is labeled with the kanji character for top (上) and bottom (下). This makes the book easy to travel with, and read during commutes.

page 81

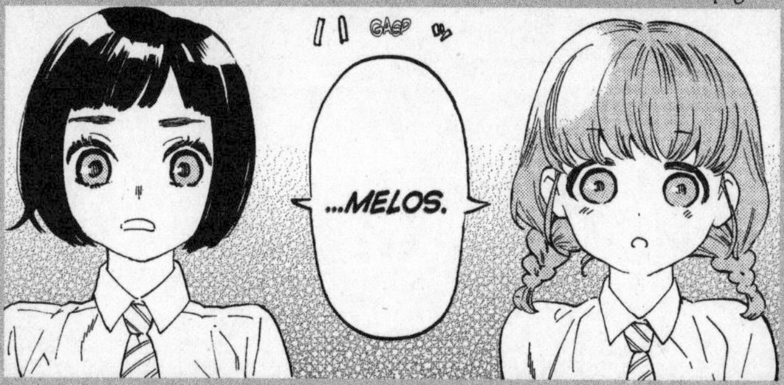
GASP
...MELOS.

Run, Melos

A short story by Osamu Dazai that commonly appears in Japanese textbooks.

page 102

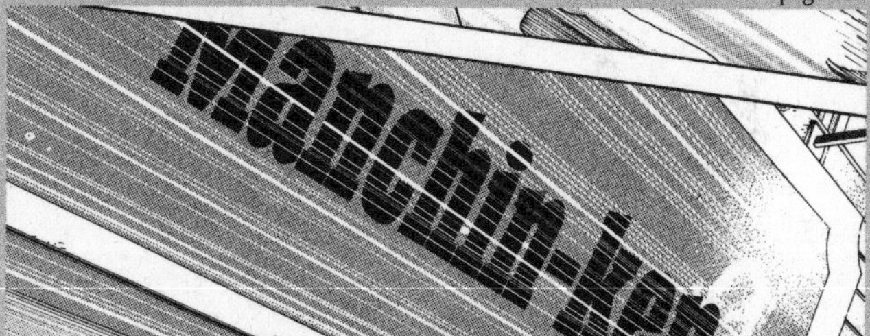
Manchin-ken

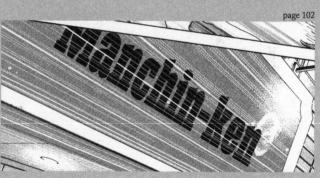

Manchin-ken

Man and *chin* are the first syllables of Japanese words for "vagina" and "penis," respectively.

page 110

Height: **156 cm (Approx. 5'1")**

Blood type: **A**

Activity: **Literature Club**

Favorite book: ***Momo***

Momo

Momo by Michael Ende is a German fantasy book that deals with the concept of time.

page 124

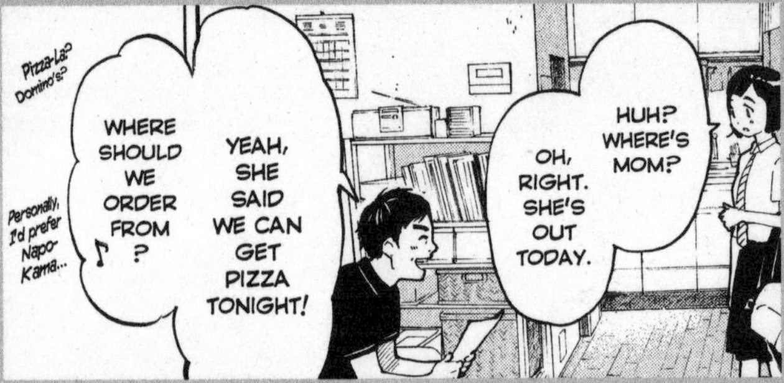
HUH? WHERE'S MOM?
OH, RIGHT. SHE'S OUT TODAY.
YEAH, SHE SAID WE CAN GET PIZZA TONIGHT!
WHERE SHOULD WE ORDER FROM ♪ ?
Pizza-La? Domino's?
Personally, I'd prefer Napo-Kama...

Pizza-La, Napo-Kama

Like Domino's, these are different pizza chains in Japan.

page 138

SO THEN HE GOT HIS CAR!
YEAH, GOING TO A LOVE HOTEL ON FOOT JUST DOESN'T CUT IT.
TANAKA
WOW,

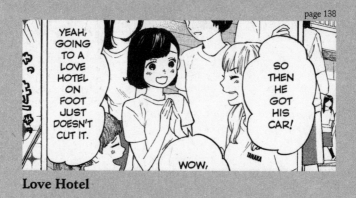

Love Hotel

A hotel that allows short stays and is most commonly used for sex.

page 140

THWAM

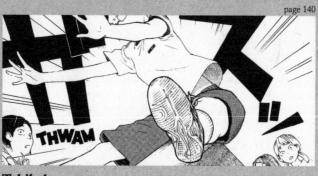

Tobibako

The exercise the students are participating in is called *Tobibako,* or literally "jumping boxes." This vaulting box exercise is common in gym classes in Japan.

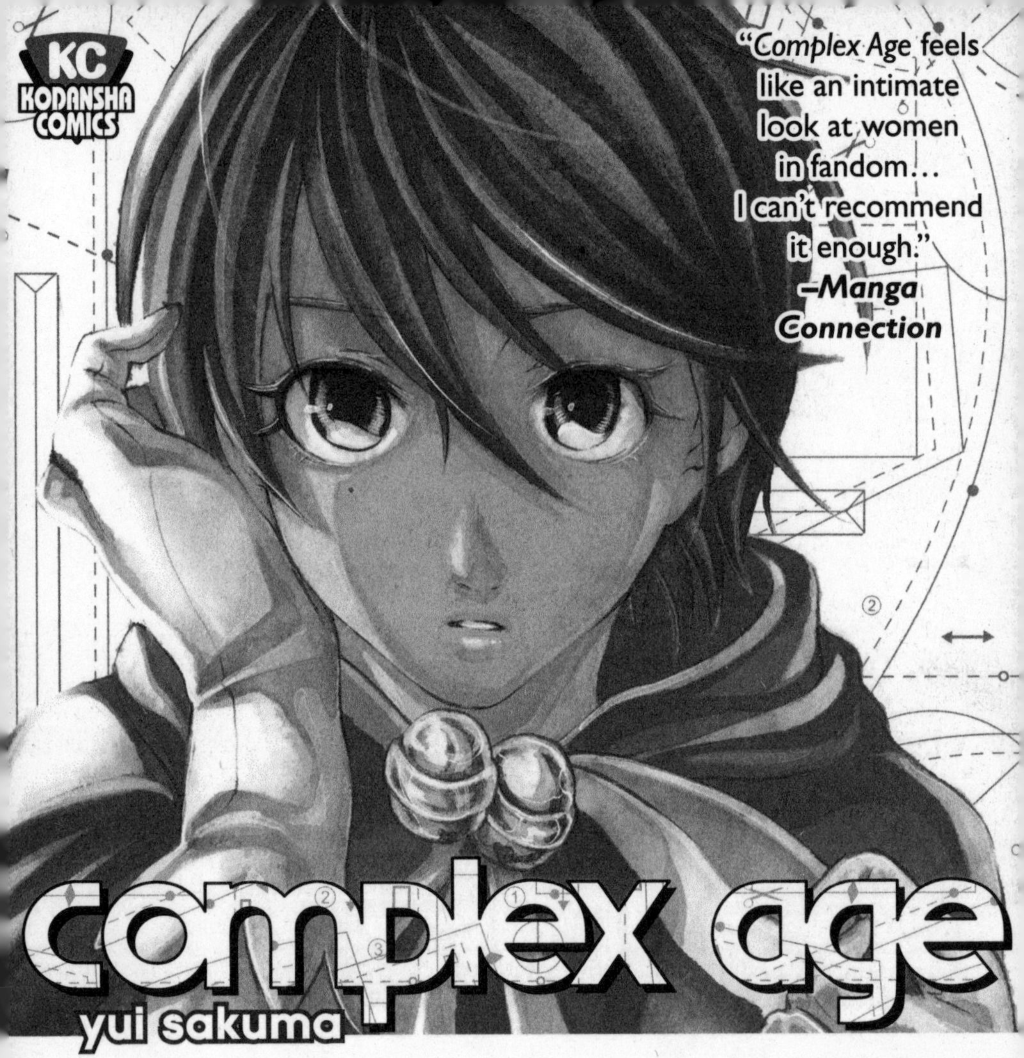
KC KODANSHA COMICS
"*Complex Age* feels like an intimate look at women in fandom… I can't recommend it enough."
–*Manga Connection*
complex age
yui sakuma

26-year-old Nagisa Kataura has a secret. Transforming into her favorite anime and manga characters is her passion in life, and she's earned great respect amongst her fellow cospayers. But to the rest of society, her hobby is a silly fantasy. As demands from both her office job and cosplaying begin to increase, she may one day have to make a tough choice—what's more important to her, cosplay or being "normal"?

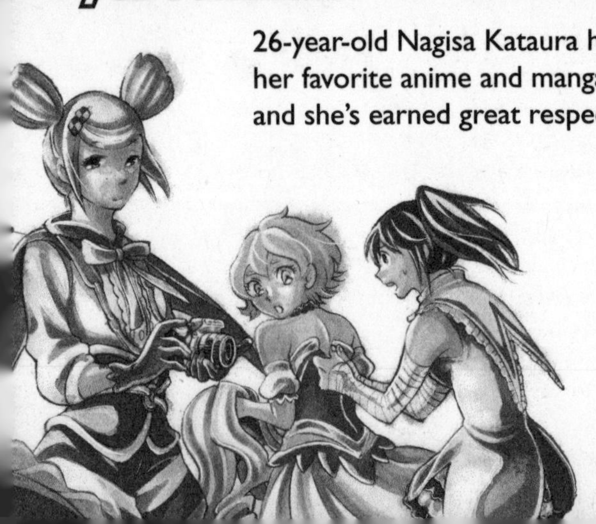

THE STORY STARTS **HERE!**

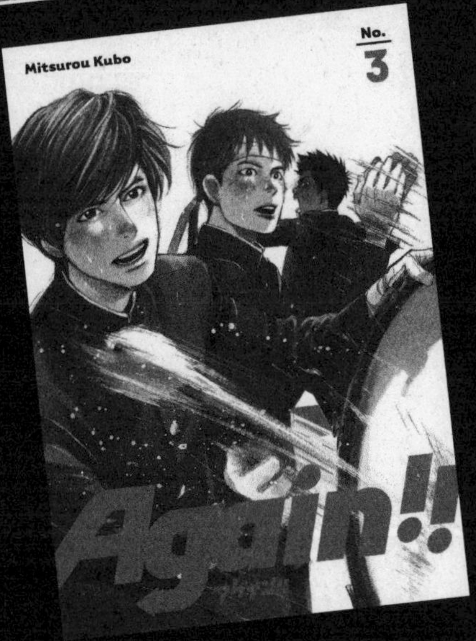
Mitsurou Kubo
No. 3
Again!!

Again!!

アゲイン!!

Kinichiro Imamura isn't a bad guy, really, but on the first day of high school his narrow eyes and bleached blonde hair made him look so shifty that his classmates assumed the worst. Three years later, without any friends or fond memories, he isn't exactly feeling bittersweet about graduation. But after an accidental fall down a flight of stairs, Kinichiro wakes up three years in the past... on the first day of high school! School's starting again—but it's gonna be different this time around!

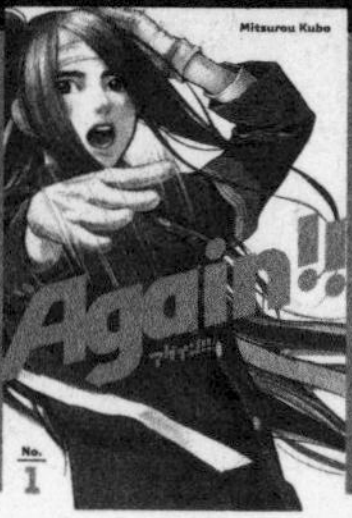
Mitsurou Kubo
Again!!
No. 1

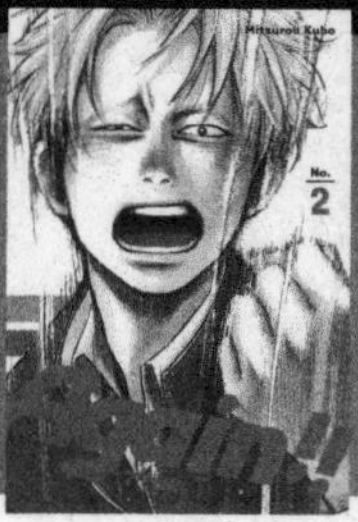
Mitsurou Kubo
No. 2

Vol. 1-3 now available in **PRINT** and **DIGITAL**!
Vol. 4 coming August 2018!

Find out **MORE** by visiting:
kodanshacomics.com/MitsurouKubo

ABOUT **MITSUROU KUBO**

Mitsurou Kubo is a manga artist born in Nagasaki prefecture. Her series *3.3.7 Byoshi!!* (2001-2003), *Tokkyu!!* (2004-2008), and *Again!!* (2011-2014) were published in *Weekly Shonen Magazine*, and *Moteki* (2008-2010) was published in the seinen comics magazine *Evening*. After the publication of *Again!!* concluded, she met Sayo Yamamoto, director of the global smash-hit anime ***Yuri!!! on ICE***. Working with Yamamoto, Kubo contributed the original concept, original character designs, and initial script for ***Yuri!!! on ICE***. *Again!!* is her first manga to be published in English.

KC KODANSHA COMICS

Kodansha COMICS

HAPPINESS

—ハピネス—

By **Shuzo Oshimi**

From the creator of *The Flowers of Evil*

Nothing interesting is happening in Makoto Ozaki's first year of high school. His life is a series of quiet humiliations: low-grade bullies, unreliable friends, and the constant frustration of his adolescent lust. But one night, a pale, thin girl knocks him to the ground in an alley and offers him a choice. Now everything is different. Daylight is searingly bright. Food tastes awful. And worse than anything is the terrible, consuming thirst...

Praise for Shuzo Oshimi's *The Flowers of Evil*

"A shockingly readable story that vividly—one might even say queasily—evokes the fear and confusion of discovering one's own sexuality. Recommended." —The Manga Critic

"A page-turning tale of sordid middle school blackmail." —Otaku USA Magazine

"A stunning new horror manga." —Third Eye Comics

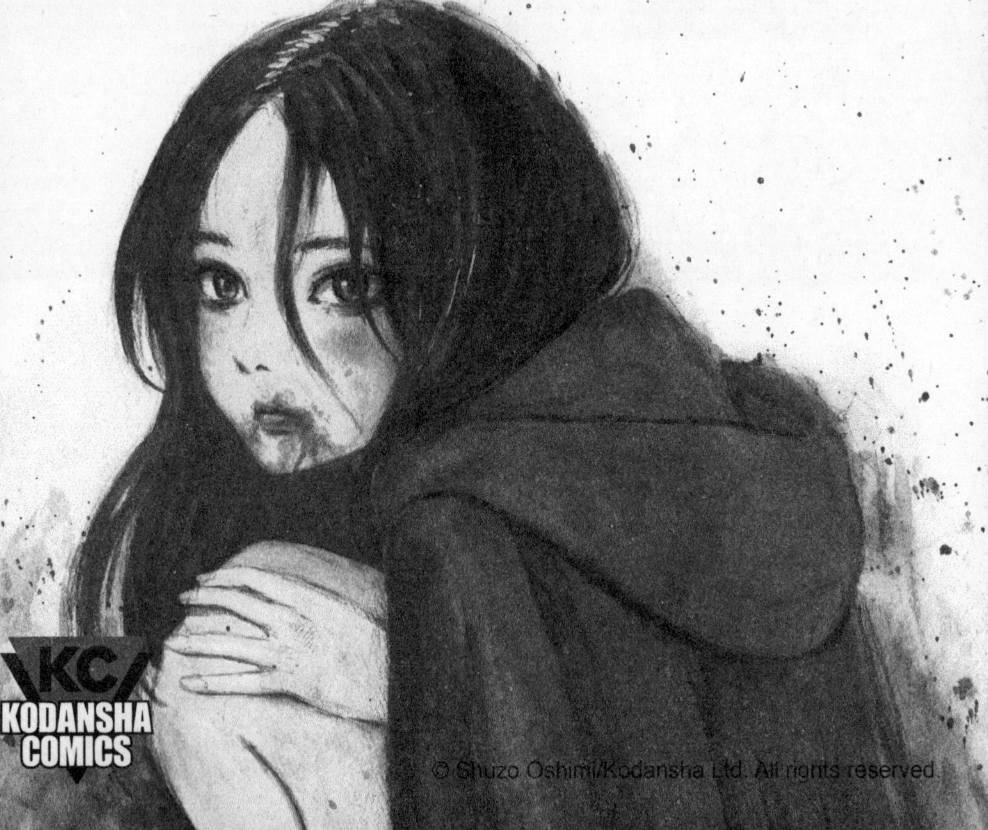

KC KODANSHA COMICS

Japan's most powerful spirit medium delves into the ghost world's greatest mysteries!

Story by Kyo Shirodaira, famed author of mystery fiction and creator of *Spiral*, *Blast of Tempest*, and *The Record of a Fallen Vampire*.

Both touched by spirits called yôkai, Kotoko and Kurô have gained unique superhuman powers. But to gain her powers Kotoko has given up an eye and a leg, and Kurô's personal life is in shambles. So when Kotoko suggests they team up to deal with renegades from the spirit world, Kurô doesn't have many other choices, but Kotoko might just have a few ulterior motives...

IN/SPECTRE

STORY BY KYO SHIRODAIRA
ART BY CHASHIBA KATASE

O Maidens in Your Savage Season volume 1 is a work of fiction.
Names, characters, places, and incidents are the products of
the author's imagination or are used fictitiously.
Any resemblance to actual events, locales, or
persons, living or dead, is entirely coincidental.

A Kodansha Comics Trade Paperback Original

Published in the United States by Kodansha Comics, an imprint of
Kodansha USA Publishing, LLC, New York.

Publication rights for this English edition arranged through
Kodansha Ltd, Tokyo.

First published in Japan in 2017 by Kodansha Ltd, Tokyo,
as *Araburu Kisetsu no Otomedomoyo* volume 1.

ISBN 978-1-63236-818-8

Printed in the United States of America.

www.kodanshacomics.com

9 8 7 6 5 4 3 2 1
Translation: Sawa Matsueda Savage
Lettering: Evan Hayden
Editing: Haruko Hashimoto
Kodansha Comics edition cover design by Phil Balsman